POLITICAL RESPONSIBILITY

NEW DIRECTIONS IN CRITICAL THEORY

NEW DIRECTIONS IN CRITICAL THEORY

Amy Allen, General Editor

New Directions in Critical Theory presents outstanding classic and contemporary texts in the tradition of critical social theory, broadly construed. The series aims to renew and advance the program of critical social theory, with a particular focus on theorizing contemporary struggles around gender, race, sexuality, class, and globalization and their complex interconnections.

For the list of titles in this series, see page 335.

ANTONIO Y. VÁZQUEZ-ARROYO

POLITICAL RESPONSIBILITY

Responding to Predicaments of Power

COLUMBIA UNIVERSITY PRESS

NEW YORK

Columbia University Press
Publishers Since 1893
New York   Chichester, West Sussex
cup.columbia.edu

Library of Congress Cataloging-in-Publication Data
Name: Vázquez Arroyo, Antonio Y., 1976– author.
Title: Political responsibility : responding to predicaments of power
/ Antonio Y. Vázquez-Arroyo.
Description: New York : Columbia University Press, 2016.
| Series: New directions in critical theory
| Includes bibliographical references and index.
Identifiers: LCCN 2015026799 | ISBN 9780231174848 (cloth: alk. paper)
Subjects: LCSH: Political ethics. | Governmental accountability.
| Power (Social sciences)—Moral and ethical aspects.
Classification: LCC JA79. V39 2016 | DDC 172—dc23
LC record available at http://lccn.loc.gov/2015026799

Columbia University Press books are printed on
permanent and durable acid-free paper.
This book is printed on paper with recycled content.
Printed in the United States of America

c 10 9 8 7 6 5 4 3 2 1

COVER DESIGN: Julia Kushnirsky

Para Jennifer, sine qua non

CONTENTS

PREFACE

THIS BOOK argues for a retrieval of a political ethic of responsibility. It challenges the notion that contemporary predicaments
of power need an ethical ground or supplement that is philosophically deduced, either in advance or outside the realm of political life. In this vein, it offers a historically informed exploration and
critique of the current transatlantic "ethical turn" in the humanities
and social sciences and the primacy it grants to ethical responsibility. Absent in these ethical theorizations of responsibility is a conceptualization of the predicaments of power in which responsibility
would gain political edge. Overall, these are ethical theorizations that
privilege a normative ground over the political field of power, and are
symptomatic of the onset of a depoliticized politics that characterize the present in the North Atlantic world.[1] The impact of the ethical
turn is thus contradictory: while having done its share in restoring
the ethical import of responsibility, it has done so to the detriment of
a political conception of responsibility. In the proliferation of rather
solipsistic accounts of responsibility, the intersubjective moment
of commonality that historically underwrites this concept since its
early political incarnations is either abstractly posited, eschewed,
or ultimately disavowed. What one finds instead are *intra*subjective
accounts of responsibility in which relations with others are abstractly
invoked outside the texture of historical and political life. The upshot

of *intra*subjectivity is the desertion of any sense of commonality, of any mediating or shared sphere of action, which is often the domain of political life. One consequence of the turn to *intra*subjectivity is the tacit disavowal of any meaningful sense of collective life, or of how a political situation is constituted, and the virtual eviction of any genuine notion of political responsibility; equally disavowed is a genuinely critical, sober mapping of the contexts impairing or enabling concrete ethical responsibility. Appeals to responsibility that disavow this moment of commonality end up curtailing the possibility of a sense of responsibility that assumes the burdens of acting collectively and is answerable to a genuinely democratic political form and its binding principles. For even a concept like imputation implies something beyond the attribution of an action to an agent: it also connotes having the responsibility to do something, to respond to something.[2] And that something often is an eminently heteronomous and collective predicament.

Accordingly, political responsibility is here understood as the need, on the one hand, to respond to a predicament of power both as an individual and as a member of a collectivity and, on the other, to face the burdens of acting and thinking as a participatory member of a collectivity. From this perspective, one raises important political questions that current accounts of ethical responsibility abjure or distort. One can ask, for instance, how does the idea of responsibility impact or affect the way in which the idea of "the individual" is conceived? Or how do ideas of political personation, collective life, and its political forms, relate to the idea of political responsibility? How does, say, intentionality figure in both individual accounts of ethical responsibility and in the more collective connotations of the term? Can one speak of degrees of responsibility? Or, stated differently: how does one reflect critically on the structural moment of political responsibility? Better still: how do questions of structural responsibility relate to questions about "structural beneficiaries" within political orders? Or how does one adjudicate responsibility to "everyday bystanders"?[3] How do political forms binding and enabling a political order either foster or hinder a sense of political responsibility?

Out of this set of questions, or *within* it, emerges the difficult question of *what* and *who* are the subjects and objects of responsibility: who are the entities that are either deemed responsible or to which an individual or collectivity is responsible? There are two different aspects to this last question, even if both point to the centrality of fidelity in any conception of responsibility: first, the question of *what* is the concrete object or entity toward which one is responsible (say, responsibility toward God, oneself, one's country or collectivity identity, or humanity); second, the question of *who* is the agent and bearer of responsibility. Last, where does political responsibility become actualized and by what means? But the idea of political responsibility also has explanatory power: historically, the question of who is politically responsible requires understanding scopes of action, structures, and contingencies, which are dialectically interrelated in the way a political situation to which a political actor responds is constituted: a political actor that could contribute to radically change, modify, or ratify and further constitute the predicament in question. Therefore, in treatments of these concepts in European and transatlantic political thought one finds the idea of someone being responsible when one has to answer for one's actions or she needs to respond to a particular situation, its imperatives, openings, and constraints. In this case, the concept is already lined up with the idea of freedom. Without a modicum of autonomy and freedom, or meaningful realm of action, there is no responsibility. Similarly, political responsibility involves participation and shared power; without a measure of shared power, there is no genuine political responsibility.

Political Responsibility conceives responsibility as a "problematic," provided this term is understood in terms of Fredric Jameson's recasting of it. What it offers is "not a head-on, direct solution or resolution, but a commentary on the very conditions of existence of the problematic itself," along with a broad sketch of an alternative way of casting the problematic of responsibility politically, a *political* account of political responsibility that critically engages with predicaments of power.[4] Another of Jameson's formulations carefully conveys the stakes of this interpretative principle: "it converts the problem itself into a solution, no longer attempting to solve the dilemma head on, according to its own terms, but rather coming to understand the dilemma itself as the mark of the profound contradictions latent in the very mode of posing the problem."[5] Yet this effort will be carried on by way of crafting a constellation that would map the interstices of this problematic in its conceptual and concrete historical articulations. By thinking about the problematic of political responsibility in this way, this book critically engages with current proponents of a strictly ethical responsibility, or an ethical politics of responsibility, which subordinates the political to the ethical. In so doing, it brings political and theoretical traditions into the same field of vision to serve as both benchmarks and contrasts and thus bring into sharper relief aspects of formulations that otherwise would go unnoticed, or be seen in isolation, as determinations of a particular historical and political constellation.

But thinking responsibility as a problematic is just one dimension of the present inquiry. The formulation of a largely forgotten tradition of political ethic and its corollary ideas of political responsibility is another. It is along these lines that political responsibility is conceptualized as structurally entwined with other concepts and practices both at the level of ideas and in its concrete historical instantiations in predicaments of power. Stated differently, this book sets out to map the current usages and valences of ethical responsibility, situate these within the larger theoretical, historical, and political transformation in which it has emerged as a central concept, and offer an argument for a political recasting of this concept and the problematic it enunciates. Echoing Theodor W. Adorno's well-known formulation about universal history, responsibility needs to be both construed and denied: for to avow its moralizing or solipsistic versions is at best to comply with the status quo and at worst to indulge in a cynical rhetoric of individualism whose main upshot is blaming the victim; to construe, because it is an indispensable component of political life, especially for any participatory account of democratic life anchored in ideas of substantial equality, freedom, and shared power. A critical maxim is thus evoked: to conceptualize political responsibility one *cannot not* think in terms of collective life and ideas of shared political power. The double negative of this maxim is deliberate: it places the question of political responsibility squarely as a question of the advent and sustenance of genuinely democratic, and, by extension, socialist, political orders.

Broadly speaking, this book argues for what Sheldon S. Wolin once called, in connection with Machiavelli, a "political ethic"—or, more precisely, *una poliética*, in Francisco Fernández Buey's felicitous but ultimately untranslatable formulation—that is bound to democratic political forms and formulates the corresponding concept of political responsibility. What is a political ethic (*poliética*) and how does it differ from the ethical politics currently on offer? Paraphrasing Bertolt

Brecht, a political ethic attends to the ethical dimension of political life. Its aspirations are ethical, even if the goal is not to craft an Ethics, but rather to think about the ethical dimension of collective life. By and large, the overarching concerns of a political ethic are best defined as an attempt to re-cognize and theorize the diremption of ethical and political imperatives in political action.[6] The term *political ethic* simultaneously refuses to damp the political element of collective life and to abjure ethical considerations in the realm of the political, while it acknowledges the impossibility of a smooth connection between the two and the intractability of blending the two poles—ethics and politics—in order to intervene in fields of power that demand a *speculative* yet historically concrete rendering of the two, which is precisely what the idea of a political ethic seeks to encompass.[7] It is thus akin to a *public ethic* that deals with questions of collective life and power. It recasts universal commitments in light of the particular political forms that sustain them and understands political ideals—say, equality, freedom, solidarity—as thoroughly mediated by particular predicaments of power in their historical unfolding.[8] Like art, a political ethic is extraethical: there is a politics and ethics of art, but art is ultimately governed by aesthetic criteria; similarly, there is an ethics to political life that respects the specificity of the political as a semiautonomous field, with its imperatives and predicaments.

In this vein, political responsibility is recast as inseparable from the exercise of power to redress a political condition or situation. For political responsibility to be actualized, it requires a meaningful sharing of political power. This emphasis need not disavow questions of intentionality or accountability; rather, it reformulates the terms of these questions in order to fully apprehend the political dimension of responsibility. Responsibility, as the Spanish philosopher Manuel Cruz has accurately suggested, is a "structurally intersubjective" concept.[9] In contrast to moral formulations that heavily emphasize ethical and individualist meanings of responsibility, this book disentangles the question of responsibility from the concern with *abstract* discussions of agency, accountability, and otherness. Instead, political responsibility emphasizes the element of response, recasts the role of answerability, and separates responsibility from notions of guilt, while fleshing out the element of collectivity that its intersubjective and political connotations establish. In contrast to guilt, which is primarily an introverted and solipsistic concept marred by legalistic connotations, responsibility is foremost an intersubjective and dialogical category that, instead of adjudicating culpability, calls for an accountable response. The ambiguity of intentionality in any given political scene, which is frequently due to the mediating role of a vast array of imperatives, from administration and governance to market rationalities, is obvious enough. Yet a political account of responsibility, as opposed to a strictly moral conception, has to critically account for these forms of power and the nature of their imperatives. If, from the perspective of moral responsibility, one can answer to moral law, to a law of conscience, or to an ethical principle, politically one can answer to the state, its laws and imperatives, as in the tradition of reason of state, or one can respond out of fidelity to a political identity and the principles and institutions that promote it. Responsibility, as Joan C. Tronto emphasizes, "has its root meaning in response, and since a response is always a response to something, it is, by nature, even when expressed abstractly, about a relationship," a relationship that, by extension, is always enacted in the context of historically constituted and politically sanctioned situations.[10]

Relatedness, however, cannot be conflated with the hypostatization of abstract intersubjectivity. On the contrary, the intersubjective moment of political responsibility has to reckon with differentiations, spatial and temporal, that only a mediated and necessarily limited sense of responsibility, responsibility *in* situation, can account for. Tronto herself has identified one of the crucial political questions: "who is responsible for caring what, when, where, and how."[11] Responsibility is thus necessarily concrete, and cannot be conceived as infinite, or unlimited. To speak of political responsibility is to raise political questions about allocating responsibility for actions and situations, something that cannot be conflated with individualist notions of blame or blameworthiness. It rather pertains to collective life and how its forms of power are produced and reproduced, structured, restructured, and sanctioned.

In this vein, one can recast the element of answerability: say, from the perspective of a genuine socialism and its democratic political forms, answerability cannot be reduced to answering to the state and its surrogate logics of power, which undermine basic democratic principles of participation, equality, shared power, and accountability. Rather, answerability is conceived as a response that answers to the need to avoid compromising these democratic principles: that is its moment of fidelity. It is thus recast as the need to *respond to* rather than just *answer for* a predicament of power.[12] Emphasis is thereby placed on the responses demanded by virtue of one's inhabiting, as a full participant, a political situation and its attendant scenes of power, the locus where one's responsibility resides—that is, a sense of responsibility bound by a sense of fidelity to one's political identity, but also defined by one's position in the structure of power relations shaping the situation, as well as the benefits that one derives from it, sometimes just by virtue of being a recognized member of the collectivity. To invoke political responsibility today is to pose the need to respond politically to the predicaments of power in the context of the modalities of depoliticized politics characterizing liberal and neoliberal democracies, especially the United States, while pondering the prospect of facing the burdens of acting collectively and exploring the possibilities of critically assuming the obligations involved as a member of a democratic collectivity, one that is attentive to the forms of power it generates as well as to its uses and abuses. Recasting answerability also entails reconceiving "answering for" as "responsibility for" outside of moralism and discourses of lawful subjugation. Rather, political responsibility consists of responsibility for "the care of commonality" and the concomitant practices of "tending" and "intending" that the care of commonality involves. With characteristic political literacy, Sheldon S. Wolin articulated what is politically necessary: "in keeping with the idea of the political with commonality, *res publica*, common possession," the practice of political responsibility requires "'responsibility for' the care of commonality . . . to tend and defend the values and practices of democratic civic life."[13] Not that such a politics, which is necessarily concerned with limits to the exercise of power, only bears the defensive edge Wolin frequently emphasizes. For democracy to be meaningful and sustainable it needs to be similarly offensive: to attack inequalities, patterns of domination, and forms of exploitation embedded in structures of power that ought to be abolished and whose beneficiaries need to be held accountable. This indispensable spirit of attack is not only curbed by the defensive moment invoked by his ideas of caring and tending—any politics worth the name, to be sure, needs a place for both moments—but by the sobering political literacy that only arises out of the political experience of becoming a participatory citizen. Citizenship, the basic category of democratic action in a delimited political space of shared fate between rulers and ruled, requires caring for collective endeavors, acting and deliberating with others, along with the responsibilities that come with the exercise of political power, its lessons, opportunities, and demands. Such care is constitutive of a democratic socialism—central to its political ethic.

It is to Manuel Cruz's credit to have conceptualized the question of responsibility by way of the acute expression *hacerse cargo*—for which there is no exact equivalent in the English language. Possible translations range from felicitous expressions like "assume" or "take responsibility for" to less poetic and overly willful renderings such as "to take up," "take over," "take charge of," or "take on board"—which captures the emphasis on response, as opposed to guilt, and the concept's intersubjective and collective dimensions. Out of the possible English renderings, the verb *assume* or the expression *to take responsibility for* come close to capturing its nuances and thus would be the preferred choices. *Hacerse cargo*, once understood politically and bound to a politically constituted space, demands from a political actor a sense of political literacy and a defined and concrete locus of action. In an important sense there is no such thing as an "apolitical" standpoint, and whoever claims one simply refuses to assume political responsibility in the predicaments of power he inhabits.[14] This is, in short, its core spatial determination.

There is, of course, a temporal determination specific to political responsibility. It is best understood in terms of how the past bears on the present, on a political situation in which one acts and to which one responds as well as the present and future projections that political responsibility entails, the weight of the past and how one is responsible for the historical structures of power bearing one's name and from which one differentially benefits. This, not out of any essentialist sense of belonging, but by virtue of one's benefiting by inhabiting these structures of power as a citizen or becoming their structural beneficiary. Retrieving a sense of historicity is thus constitutive of the citizen's political responsibility. Responding to present-day predicaments of power and acting with others to redress them, while avoiding the reproduction of practices and dynamics of inequality and domination in the present and in foreseeable futures, is what political responsibility for a democratic political life ultimately entails.

Correspondingly, if the collectivity in question is one that in the past had been on the receiving end of asymmetries of power and privilege, political responsibility resides in acting politically to break with the orders of its reproduction, while recasting losses as defeats, rather than dwelling unreflectively on wounded attachments.[15] Unlike guilt, moralism, or liberal pieties of shame that reduce larger dynamics of power into individual conceits that cast a political question in personal terms, or defensively collapse guilt with responsibility, political responsibility entails calibrating one's response, in the midst of emotional and often visceral reactions when one is asked to take responsibility for the actions performed in one's name and for the structures of power that constitute the stage in which one enjoys certain rights, privileges, and status. Again, responding politically to a situation at once presupposes and sustains a degree of political literacy that is attained and cultivated by way of difficult encounters, experiences, and actions. A political ethic of responsibility needs to ponder the obligations—past, present, and future—of human beings in their domain of life and action as members of a political collectivity. Finally, it requires conceptualizing the ethical dimension of collective life from the perspective of the imperatives of political action and the political forms at stake in binding the collectivity in question.

Cast in this way, political responsibility is bound up with democracy, the political form that places responsibility on the many. But the overall substantial commitment of the argument this book sets forth is not to offer yet another invocation of democracy. Instead, the argument seeks to show the limits of ethical conceptions of responsibility to engage with contemporary predicaments of power and how a robust political sense of responsibility is only possible in a democratic socialist order. John Dewey has offered a striking formulation whose force and sobriety remain undiminished and worth reclaiming: "Because it is not easy the democratic road is the hard one to take. It is the road which places the greatest burden of responsibility upon the greatest number of human beings."[16] Yet this powerful insight nowadays is disavowed by liberal-democratic political orders. The disavowal of this enabling burden has gone hand in glove with the fate of substantive democracy and the forms of political literacy it entails in the current age of depoliticized politics.

ACKNOWLEDGMENTS

WRITING IS a solitary endeavor and my need to work in complete isolation only makes it more so. But isolation need not be solipsistic, and I am aware of the many interlocutors that helped me bring this book to fruition, as well as those who offered the necessary enabling conditions, material and otherwise, to complete it. As an undergraduate at the Universidad de Puerto Rico, Río Piedras, I had an excellent education, and was fortunate to have teachers that showed me how every aspect of the intellectual and academic world was open. They embodied the intellectual freedom of studying different traditions of thought and actively encouraged me to learn from both European and non-European intellectual legacies. It is thus a pleasure to express my gratitude to María del Pilar Argüelles, Raúl Cotto-Serrano, Eliseo Cruz Vergara, the late Milton Pabón, and Héctor Martínez. Raúl, Eliseo and Milton deserve special mention as teachers and mentors who in different ways contributed immensely to my education.

At the University of Massachusetts, Amherst, Roberto Alejandro, Barbara Cruikshank, Patricia J. Mills, Nick Xenos, Robert Paul Wolf, and James E. Young taught me many things that enabled me to write this book. Barbara initiated me to a wider world of Theory, and first told me to read Jameson; Pat introduced me to the writings of Adorno and Rose; James encouraged my efforts to think about narrative structures, and introduced me to Auerbach; Wolff taught me Kant's *Critique of Pure Reason* and the rigors involved; and, speaking of rigor, Roberto taught me much about the nuances of interpretation, and his unique combination of intellectual creativity with textual rigor are as exemplary as they are unforgettable. Nick's commitment to historicized history, the role of genres of thought, intellectual independence and wide-ranging knowledge of the history of political thought were pivotal in my formation. He also invited me to present several chapters of this book to his fall 2014 graduate seminar, and both he and his students offered acute commentary that proved crucial in preparing the last version of the book. That Nick is also a close friend is a gift beyond measure.

Despite my reticence, I have benefited from many conversations with colleagues, students and friends, and I would like to express my gratitude to: Ananda Abeysekara, Manuel S. Almeida Rodríguez, Ivan Ascher, Gopal Balakrishnan, Liz Beaumont, Alex Betancourt, Tim Brennan, Brian Britt, Stephen Eric Bronner, Wendy Brown, Susan Buck-Morss, Jerome E. Copulsky, Adam Dahl, Gabriel De La Luz-Rodríguez, Bud Duvall, Monica Espinosa-Arango, Keya Ganguly, Heather Gumble, Mary Hawkesworth, Robert Hullot-Kentor, James D. Ingram, Fredric Jameson, Jyl Josephson, Ron Krebs, Greta Kroeker, Karl Larson, Damon Linker, Silvia L. López, Tim Luke, Nancy Luxon, Brad Mapes-Martins, Karuna Mantena, Robyn Marasco, Andrew Murphy, Scott G. Nelson, Rob Nichols, August H. Nimtz Jr., Andrew Norris, Anne Norton, Carlos Pabón, Quynh Pham, Djordje Popovic, Edgar Rivera Colón, Corey Robin, J. B. Shank, Jakeet Singh, Bailey Socha, Rob Stephens, Dara Strolovitch, Ken Surin, Shatema Threadcraft, Joan C. Tronto, James Tully, Sergio Valverde, Robert Venator-Santiago, Janell Watson, Edward Weisband, Yves Winter, and Marla Zubel. Ananda, Brian and Scott deserve special mention as main interlocutors during my time in Blacksburg; an unlikely trio with whom I had many memorable and often heated discussions whose traces I am sure they would find in these pages. Over the years, other friends have lent indelible support. Sergio and Yves became steadfast friends and interlocutors. Yves's probing intellect always posed the right question and forcefully challenge me to clarify many a point. Sergio is not only an exemplary interlocutor and comrade: our peripatetic walks, which either began or ended at a bar, or both, were as significant as tokens of friendship as they were intellectually memorable. During my time in Minnesota, Joan and Nancy were always eager to engage in impromptu conversations that were stimulating and intellectually productive. For over a decade, Wendy has vastly supported my intellectual endeavors, her work has been a source of inspiration, and she is a precious friend and fierce interlocutor. Wendy also introduced me to Robyn, a loyal friend and coruscating critic. I would like to thank Bob for his intellectual complicity, steadfast friendship, and generosity. Alex and Gabriel have been my main intellectual lifelines: they have read some of my drafts and debated my ideas every step of the way. Their camaraderie is only matched by their intellectual gifts, and their warmth and generosity have sustained me through it all.

I would also like to thank people who more indirectly enabled me complete this project: Sonja Alvarez, Alexis Duprey, Bud Duvall Moira Fradinger, Myrna García Calderón, Regina Kunzel, Stephanie Rosen, Dara Strolovitch, Joan C. Tronto, and Dawn Valverde. My parents, Carmín y Toño, made many sacrifices to give me an education and, early on, taught me about ethics and its proper domains. That my father vividly embodies the political literacy of the ordinary citizen was yet another unforgettable contribution to my education. At Columbia University Press, Wendy Lochner and Amy Allen patiently and diligently supported this project. Two excellent anonymous reviews really helped me to make the best of a rather long and unruly manuscript. One reviewer in particular offered a probing yet generous report that made all the difference. With biblical patience, Christine Dunbar waited for the last version and expertly shepherded it through production. Cecelia Cancellaro bravely tussled with my prose, greatly improving its quality without colonizing it, and I am deeply grateful. The last version of this book benefited immensely from Susan Pensak's expert hand, as she graciously served as my manuscript and production editor. All remaining infelicities are due to my stubbornness.

Jennifer Duprey has been my loving partner, accomplice, and interlocutor. Her sensibility and passion for the world, intelligence and creativity have significantly nourished my own thinking and enriched the life that we have forged together. It is to her, my love, that this book is dedicated.

POLITICAL RESPONSIBILITY

INTRODUCTION

*Dialectic is the unswerving effort to conjoin reason's critical
consciousness of itself and the critical experience of objects.*

—Theodor W. Adorno, *Hegel: Three Studies*

ALFRED COBBAN once offered a memorable judgment about political science that proved to be prescient: "A good deal of what is
called political science, I must confess, seems to me a device,
invented by academic persons, avoiding that dangerous subject politics, without achieving science."[1]

Today, academic political theory is at the very least equally vulnerable to the charge of "avoiding that dangerous subject politics." A
less political cast of mind than that of many a practitioner of political theory in the Anglo-American academy is hard to fathom. Even if
the salience of an academic and hyperprofessionalized cast of mind
has not led to a paucity of intellectual value in the work that has been
produced in recent decades, it has narrowed the field in not insignificant ways. Much of professionalized political and critical theory today
exhibits forms of dehistoricized history, if it draws from history at all.
These academic enterprises largely respond to the internal cogency of
theoretical edifices: even when motivated by a problem in the political world, they are conceived independently of its historical realities. These are efforts that selectively dabble in history and only deal
with the political world in extemporized fashion. This, however, was
not always so. Reflecting on the differences between philosophy and
political theory during the 1930's, Pierre Mesnard confidently wrote
about how, if necessary, Aristotle could get away with ignoring Plato's

Republic, but never the fundamental ideas of the Greek city-state.[2] Today virtually the opposite occurs. With few notable exceptions, most North Atlantic scholars of political theory are *bien pensant* technicians who scrupulously but aseptically study texts. Deftly trained to read every predecessor or contemporary of an author, they are less adroit at grasping the actual historicity of the political realities the author in question responded to or how it bears on the content of her theoretical forms, let alone the internal politics of their own interpretative protocols. And when professing to write about contemporary political problems, they tend to completely ignore the constitutive obduracy of political life by way of distorting idealizations.

Consider, for instance, how as genre of theoretical reflection, North Atlantic "political philosophy" privileges a modality of ethical politics conforming to liberalism, at once proclaiming the autonomy of political philosophy while subsuming political phenomena and its questions into the neutralizing magma of ethical politics, all of which is, in and of itself, the upshot of what Bernard Williams famously characterized as the philosopher's penchant for "the priority of the moral over the political."[3] Here is a formulation from a leading light:

> For though it remains rooted in moral principles, particularly in those serving to define the just exercise of coercive power, political philosophy cannot illuminatingly be described as the application of moral philosophy to the political world. That is because it has to adopt a more reflective stance than is usual in moral philosophy. . . . Herein lies the autonomy of political philosophy, what makes it more than just a part of the supposedly more general discipline of moral philosophy. You have your moral views, I have mine, and each of us is convinced that he is right, standing ready to show the other the error of his ways. But once we confront the problem of how people like us are to live together, we enter the terrain of political philosophy.[4]

That is, in a nutshell, as crisp and candid a description of political philosophy as one is likely to get from a premier practitioner. The domain of political philosophy is thus collective life in a world of different moral points of view.

Notice, however, how questions referring to the mainstay of collective life, or bearing on questions of political form, are not even mentioned. In an all-capitalist universe, the political philosopher does not feel the need to comprehensively conceptualize the forms of power shaping present-day inequalities, or the ideologies sanctioning and/or debarring forms of agency to challenge them. Institutionalized patterns of exclusion and domination on the basis of gendering and racialization embedded in the prevalent political order are thus tacitly normalized. By extension, state power and the conditions for its production and reproduction, or the conditions impairing the realization of the ideals of freedom and equality proclaimed in founding documents, are at best muddled and at worst excluded from the purview of political philosophy. Meanwhile, the class structures and forms of corporate and military power structuring and mediating the political situation that serves as the philosopher's main locus of action, or the fate of citizenship, the increasing corporatization of public discourse, and the whole ensemble of neoliberal practices and rationalities forming the present, are silently brushed aside.[5] Indeed, most of the time the political philosopher's gaze is inclined to consider the ever divisive questions of ethical politics and forging a normative basis for stable conviviality within the confines of depoliticized politics. Forging a liberal ethical politics is the overriding concern. It involves, for instance, judging principles of political legitimacy "by the moral values that lie at their basis."[6]

Another instance of the narrow vision of political theory as an academic field is the privileging of textual commentary over politically engaged theorizing, along with the dehistoricization carried on sometimes in the name of "historical context." Even if exegetical activity has a fine pedigree, exegetical commentary has become a neutralized, strictly academic endeavor. But such neutralization is historically mediated and thus symptomatic of a particular historical situation. And this neutralization of both form and content in the academic article, often clogged with gratuitous scholarly apparatuses, is a far cry from the venerable genre that is the essay. One corollary of this is how sharpness of tone, not to dwell on polemical arguments, is cast as ad hominem attack *tout court* and thus curtly dismissed; likewise, tepidness or lack of political nerve are often swept under the rug as the forms of civility that define scholarly engagement and are therefore exonerated from critical scrutiny. No venom is spared, however, when the tone of an interpretation transgresses the consensus of the tepid that increasingly reigns in this hyperprofessionalized world and is found too jarring, or when a political and ideological context is presented to establish specific mediations and homologies between, say, a thinker's political choices, his historical moment and situation, and the body of theoretical work of which he is the author. Blind peer review is the preferred medium for silencing and chastising in the name of a misplaced sense of scholarly decorum. That such *civility* emerges out of a rather arcane professorial code that is thoroughly mediated by class, gender, and race is probably not the worst entry point for a would-be sociologist to map its habits and customs.

With characteristic wit, E. P. Thompson once described a version of this bias and how rather aseptic ideals of *genuine* communication could silence other forms of argumentation: "Burke abused, Cobbett inveighed, Arnold was capable of malicious insinuation, Carlyle, Ruskin and D. H. Lawrence, in their middle years, listened to no one. This may be regrettable: but I cannot see that the communication of anger, indignation, or even malice, is any less *genuine*."[7] Genuine communication, even in the form of an angry polemic, is central for any reckoning with the political world, especially if one seeks to change how it is structured and ordered. The disavowal of any trace of this form of discourse, so central in the traditions of European, Latin American, and Caribbean political thought, is without doubt the upshot of the professionalization of political science, and by extension political theory, in its academic settings. Undeniably, personal and intellectual temperament largely mediates how one responds to the commotions of one's times. But it does so only to a degree. There is something else at stake. Perhaps the conflation of passion with zealotry is a function of estrangement from political life, of living in times and places in which political life mostly consists of modalities of depoliticized politics, where professionalization and marketization operate in tandem with depoliticization. Be that as it may, nowadays trenchant criticism tends to elicit the specter of arbitrariness and lack of scholarly rigor. Even if there is no malice involved in the chapters that follow, the political impulse animating its sharp tone is part of a larger commitment to a particular form of political theory, *political* "political theory," or perhaps even a critical political theory.[8] In principle, writing and speaking in a more severe style needs no more justification than the equally legitimate tepid prose that has come to define the discipline, let alone polemics or inveighed discourse: from Edmund Burke's *Reflections on the Revolution in France*, through Benjamin Constant's *On Political Reactions* and *On the Spirit of Conquest and Usurpation* to Karl Marx and Friedrich Engels's *The Communist Manifesto, The German Ideology, and The Holy Family*—not to mention Juan Donoso Cortés's speeches or his *Catholicism, Liberalism and Socialism*, or Alexis de Tocqueville's *Recollections*, Friedrich Nietzsche's *On the Genealogy of Morality* and the philosophical hammer that is *The Anti-Christ*—mordant writings have contributed some of the sharpest statements of political theorizing to have taken place across the political spectrum of the postrevolutionary period in Europe. Once accompanied by arguments, sharpness of tone and writing are not only as legitimate as any other scholarly mode but could also be seen as constitutive of political theory as a political activity.

Political Responsibility self-consciously hinges on a *political* approach to critical and political theory, which combines dialectical historicism—and thus places emphasis on the primacy of the situation in the formal architecture of any substantial political theorization—with an argument about the need to carefully distinguish the historicity of philosophical and political concepts, even while prioritizing political contexts. What this book ultimately offers is the priority of a political interpretation of political thought and, by extension, of the problematic of responsibility in it. While some readers may want to skip this discussion, the overall argument of the book becomes more intelligible (and credible) in light of it, as it makes explicit the principles and benchmarks informing it. Obviously, it would be quixotic, not to say at once presumptuous and naive, to pretend to shatter all these conceits with the stroke of one's pen. Better yet, a discussion about interpretative principles is bound to be abstract if not entirely misguided: the critical import of the precepts that follow can ultimately be discerned only in their execution, not on the basis of a rather formalist elucidation, which at worst lends itself to unnecessary posturing and, at best, only gain purchase in their actualization.[9] But the impetus to spell these out comes from a sense that current discussions within North Atlantic political theory have increasingly assumed a somewhat naive reading strategy that is hardly self-reflective about the conceptual axioms, periodizations, and historical accounts it draws upon. If nothing else, elucidating the interpretative approach the book stages dispels the specter of arbitrariness often associated with politically minded inquiries like the present one, which has an explicit commitment to retrieve a form of writing that resists quietist detachment.

WORDS, SEDIMENTS, CONTEXTS

The historical reconstructions and interpretations offered in this book openly prioritize a political interpretation of political theory, which is taken not only as the point of departure but as the ultimate interpretative horizon. This may seem obvious enough, but it is not. The study of political theory, mostly if not exclusively the interpretation—including contextualization—of texts is often carried on by way of literary, historical, or philosophical practices of interpretation that frequently eschew the political, economic, and ideological mediations found in an argument and text. The chapters that follow grant priority to a political interpretation of political theorizing in which the historical context—social and cultural, economic and political—is no mere add-on. Rather, historical context is understood as an indispensable aspect of any interpretation of eminently political works and interventions. Questions about why certain thought forms emerge or reemerge when they do, or what historical determinants generate certain political horizons, or underline, sanction, and mediate them, are central to the approach to interpretation defended in these pages.

A decisive aspect of any interpretation is an examination of both the diachronic moment and the synchronic aspects of a body of work in relation to the predicaments of power that sometimes occasioned its composition or, in other instances, provided the context that made possible the salience of a particular theoretical position. Interpretation is, accordingly, historical and contextual, but not in the commonly received senses of these two terms. It is historical insofar as it avows its own historicity and contextual inasmuch as it operates in discursive, ideological, and political contexts.[10] A discursive context can be, but need not be, philological; in a more contemporary vein, an academic controversy could be what initially prompts reflection on a question. Still, even if controversies along academic or philological lines can undoubtedly provide the immediate point of departure for an inquiry and yield their own unique insights, in the present work the approach to historicization privileges different and arguably politically more meaningful levels of historical context. In this reckoning, political theory ought to be concerned with the contemporary world, the historical forms of power at once enabling and constraining it, and the fortunes of political life and its forms in contemporary predicaments of power. By extension, it needs to be equally concerned with the implications of these processes for a theoretical endeavor seeking to map and apprehend them. But historicizing a text and an authorship also involves historicizing theoretical forms and forms of theoretical reflection, as chapter 1 seeks to do concerning that postmodern phenomenon and symptom called Theory and its mediating role in the advent of the turn to ethics and its depoliticized sense of responsibility.

One can historicize a text in terms of at least three levels of inquiry: the political, or that which pertains to the immediate situation the thinker in question responds to; the social, or that which pertains to larger social forces, ideologies, and discourses that posit questions of racialization, gendering, socialization, and status; and the historical as it pertains to the modes of production in their slower temporal and spatial eventuation and the continuous changes in social destinies in that vast dialectic of continuity and discontinuity that is humanity's history.[11] Herein, these three levels are kept in mind, especially the first and third, with due attention, specific to the particular imperatives and demands of different historical periods and circumstances, paid to the second. The problematic of responsibility, as such, and the thinkers articulating it, will be placed in the contexts of these levels and horizons of history and thus critically pondered. Equally historicized will be the forms and figures of thought—philosophy, historical criticism, Theory—that emerged either in tandem or coeval with the problematic of responsibility, or which served as its condition of possibility.

"Contexts, of course, are personal and social as well as technical and intellectual," writes intellectual historian Anthony Grafton.[12] It could be added that even if each of these can be conceived historically, merely adducing historical context, or the historicity of a particular context, is in and of itself hardly enough, as establishing a relevant context is already an act of interpretation that needs to be argued for. Contexts, therefore, need to be specified; here, as the occasion requires, different contexts will be pondered in relation to the three levels of inquiry that are privileged in the historicizing practice that the book stages. Levels of inquiry that are adduced by closely following the primacy of the situation to which a thinker responds, the concepts she forges, and the historical moment and intellectual matrices that defines it. For one thing is to identify conceptual structures, mapping and describing them along with their mutations, but another interpretative strategy is to identify causal relations between conceptual articulations and the moment of emergence of thought forms. Causality, as such, is, of course, ultimately elusive. But tracing the emergence of thought forms that concatenate within larger processes of historical eventuation, part of broader constellations signaling transmutations, continuities and discontinuities, is not only entirely possible but necessary to adequately grasp the predicaments of power to which one responds. Theoretical texts are thus understood as either tacitly or explicitly responding to a particular situation and/or as symptoms of a particular historical moment. Works thus bear not only their own internal logic, along with immanent sediments from prior articulations, which ought to prevent any facile slicing of them, but also their forms of thought are mediated by the social and political contradictions to which these respond.

Interpreting the history of political thought also entails making a clear distinction between, on the one hand, how concepts are produced, reformulated, and integrated into political controversies and, on the other hand, how the interpreter forges a narrative of this conceptualization and eventuation, its continuities and ruptures. It also requires establishing an equally clear heuristic distinction between political concepts and philosophical concepts, and how neither can be subsumed under an undifferentiated interpretative protocol that casts both as political interventions. Philosophical concepts, however mediated in the work of a politically driven thinker, nevertheless enjoy a relative autonomy, as these hardly move on par with the political concepts that are part of the same constellation within a given political theorization.[13] Even when all concepts acquire their determinations historically, there is less tolerance for equivocation in philosophical concepts, as these bear an internal imperative to cogency and bindingness that, while historically mediated, enjoy a relative autonomy.[14]

Yet, however autonomous, philosophical concepts bear historical sedimentations both from previous philosophical systems—frequently their original locus, as the idea of the "subject" in early modern philosophy—and sometimes, albeit less frequently, from the historical moment of their emergence; in contrast, political concepts—sometimes mediated by philosophical homologues—carry even more political, spatial, and temporal presuppositions. And both have to at once be immanently criticized and historicized. Even if "what the subject feels to be its own autonomous achievement, the achievement of objectification, revels itself in retrospect . . . to be permeated with residues of history," as Adorno observed, the ways these historical residues permeate the objectification of reason has to be carefully historicized.[15] And to understand what such subtle interpretation entails, it is necessary to invoke a constitutive tenet of Pierre Bourdieu's "*Realpolitik* of reason" and its account of "the historicity of reason."[16] Proclaiming the historicity of reason is not to indulge in sociological reductionism. Instead, it is an enabling, critical practice. In Bourdieu's formulation: "By endeavoring to intensify awareness of the limits that thought owes to its social conditions of production and to destroy the illusion of the absence of limits or of freedom from all determinations which leaves thought defenseless against these determinations, it aims to offer the possibility of real freedom with respect to the determinations it reveals."[17] From this perspective, it should be a truism to acknowledge how the "truth content" of a work goes beyond the author's intention. But this insight should be a point of departure, not of arrival. It demands interpretation, and only scrupulous handling of the text and the historicity of its thought forms articulates the truth content of a body of work. Interpreting the immanent logic of these forms, and the situation to which these respond, requires "moving beyond the monadological enclosedness" in which these are often shrouded by prevalent approaches to the historicity of thought.[18]

This seminal insight on the historicity of reason was already lucidly formulated in Adorno's 1960 lecture course "Philosophy and Sociology." Reason may lack the spatial and sociohistorical presuppositions of political concepts, say, freedom or equality, but that hardly means it is devoid of social and historical determinations. And that includes critical reason, which formulates a concept of truth that critically reflects on these determinants in order to transcend them. From the perspective of critical reason, spirit and society are grasped as thoroughly mediated and thus embedded in humanity's natural history.

"Spirit," which Adorno identifies as "the quintessence of human consciousness: at once the universal consciousness of the species, the specific social consciousness and the consciousness of determinate individuals," constitutes "a moment" that is dialectically "intertwined with the life process" of humanity as a species.[19] Spirit, accordingly, is not independent, insofar as it can only exist within a "material life process and its presuppositions refer to it," but at the same time its claim to produce something independent, qua consistent and non-arbitrary, is justified.[20] That is its moment of autonomy and its legitimate claim to bindingness.[21] But once this autonomy as objectification is absolutized, it becomes an ideological untruth, as the unreflective autonomization of objectivity severs it from its moment of dependence. Autonomy then becomes hypostatized, and reason abstract, thus renouncing its critical vocation.

In terms of the problematic of responsibility, the authors and texts under consideration here are interpreted as crafting an idea or concept of responsibility, sometimes entire scenes of responsibility, that even if relatively autonomous from their immediate occasion are responses to particular situations that are mediated by larger if not always universal trends. It is thus important to reconstruct these historically mediated situations in order to map out the traveling and circulation of a concept, like responsibility, the displacements and sedimentations that texts and arguments undergo in those voyages, especially once these ideas find a berth in a very different political situation from the one that prompted the initial articulation, to which these now emerge as a response, and the spatial and temporal presuppositions the concept bears, acquires, and loses as it gains new meanings and determinations.[22] That is precisely what chapters 2, 3, and 4 set out do to with the concept of responsibility. For, in their historical eventuation, political concepts conform horizons and expectations that simultaneously reveal and conceal, express or silence aspects of a political situation.

Naturally, studying the continuities and discontinuities in a political and ethical concept is a complex, multilayered endeavor. Here the focus is on two aspects that are particularly relevant for a critical conceptualization of responsibility *in* history. One can begin by considering an aspect eloquently articulated by Marc Bloch and Carlo Ginzburg. It relates to what Ginzburg calls "the gap between the resilience of words and their shifting meaning" and how to best approach the complex interpretative problems that tracking the transmogrifications of words and concepts elicit.[23] Ginzburg pertinently notes how words do not move on a par with customs, let alone change with them, even when they remain contiguous with the objects, patterns, or processes the words once designated. Second, there is the aspect most cogently raised by Adorno apropos of his critique of idealism and Heidegger: the importance of tracing and confronting conceptual sediments that are historically constituted.[24] Overall, the aim is to understand the changing content of words and concepts—in the case of this study the word and concept *responsibility*—their philosophical and historical sediments, along with the spatial and temporal, social and political presuppositions that have granted political and social content to different formulations.

Accordingly, a relevant concern is that of either echoing the terminology used by the source or author in question or of grafting upon it terms foreign to the author or her milieu. The first track is mostly unproductive, as it could easily miss the changes in meaning that the word undertakes, even if one's inquiry is restricted to a particular author. The second track is not entirely devoid of pitfalls, not least of which is the imposition of a word that was not even in existence when the author in question was writing, but it is the most promising point of departure, one adept at tracing variations, especially once comparisons are undertaken by recourse to a heuristic concept, which is, then, revised and recast in light of what the interpretation affords.[25] Against any superficial analogies or homologies, the interpretative task is constrained by the primacy of the object of inquiry and its historically constituted determinations. It seeks to register variations in the social and historical context of a concept and its temporal and spatial differentiations.[26] From this perspective, one could start with an "anachronistic" concept, with the aim of registering variation, continuity, and innovation, rather than establish abstract analogies on the basis of false or vague terminological equivalences.[27] This interpretative strategy also entails identifying levels of meaning in a body of work and reconstructing as much as possible the different audiences to which it was addressed, as Lucien Jaume has argued in his commanding study of Tocqueville.[28] Equally important is Christopher Hill's analogous suggestion, forged as part of his study of the revolutionary period of seventeenth-century England: "But if we need not be shackled to the words of men and women of the seventeenth century, we must take their ideas seriously, even when they strike us as silly."[29]

These concerns are particularly important for any mapping of responsibility: as reflection on responsibility long precedes the coining of the word. Roger Crisp has offered a rather blunt yet pungent observation that bears on the question of responsibility: "Just because there is no word in Homer that can systematically be translated as 'guilt' does not mean that Homeric characters cannot feel guilty."[30] The same could be argued about responsibility. That, evidently, need not mean that the more individualist modern sense of responsibility, and the institutional apparatus necessary to conceptualize it, which became fully eventuated and crystallized in the modern period, is to be conflated with prior understandings of responsibility, which were less subjective and more objectively codified in terms of the different valences of citizenship, its social textures, political institutions, and customs.[31] Quite the contrary, what it does is to invite a temporally and spatially differentiated historicization of both moments, thus breaking free from one of the conceits of moral philosophy: namely, its "belief in its own unconditionality by making no reference whatsoever to any historical moment," something found in Kantian and non-Kantian idealist conceptions of ethics.[32]

The challenge is, all in all, to avoid the anachronism of collapsing past connotations with present-day ones. Accordingly, one can begin by *anachronistically* posing responsibility as a concept in order to then register its variations and its spatial, political, and sociological presuppositions, while also registering when it actually emerged, alongside the historical conditions of possibility for its emergence and the attendant force field of experiences that was a precondition for a subjective sense of responsibility to crystallize historically. In the end, the more subjective connotations of responsibility betray continuities with older, more objective connotations, amidst the discontinuities between the two. This could be plainly seen in the changing valences of ideas of accountability and imputability in different historical articulations of responsibility as shown in what follows.

Yet there is a second aspect to any historicization of a concept that bears more directly on responsibility as a philosophical concept as opposed to social and political thematizations of it. In this view, the first step is to avoid two commonplace philosophical conceits: that which posits the identity of language with its concepts and objects as something given and the temptation to invent new words, which merely occupy older places without adequately grasping the historical composition of the traditional languages the neologism in question seeks to displace, let alone the historical constraints on the possibility creating a new one. These concerns found acute expression in one of Adorno's early writings, "Theses on the Language of the Philosophers," where he was already critically engaged with Heidegger. There he writes: "Heidegger's language flees history, but without escaping it."[33] The pretension of escaping history creates the expectation that there is a freedom—that is, the freedom of the philosopher—from historical constraints, which is nothing but an illusion. It is as if the thinker's compulsion to bestow reality with a new language is not historically mediated or even a historical upshot.

Adorno therefore considers the need for self-reflection in terms of the history of philosophical thought, its constraints and possibilities. The dialectical critical theorist, accordingly, engages with the historical sedimentations found in the concepts she inherits, the sediments of words, and the historical ruination conforming to these sediments, while avoiding any collapsing of the distance between the words of a thinker and those of the interpreter. Adorno further writes: "Today, the philosopher confronts the decaying of language. His material is the ruins [*Trümmer*] of the words, which bind her to history; her freedom is only the possibility to configure words according to the constraints imposed by the truth contained in them. It cannot be assumed that words are already given in advance or that they can be invented anew."[34] Such truth, as Adorno insisted throughout his intellectual life, is thoroughly historical.[35] And that is why, according to him, the critical philosopher could only proceed dialectically; something that later on he would characterize as a critical practice of immanent transcendence by way of tarrying with the contradictions and sedimentations embedded in words and concepts. Once dialectically understood, philosophical terminology is thoroughly historical.[36] That terminology bears not only the sediments of prior determinations in other systems of thought; philosophical terms also constitute thought's "historical intersections," as Adorno once stated; indeed, as such, "each philosophical term is the hardened scar of an unresolved problem."[37] This sedimentation is primarily conceptual: even if mediated by the objective historical moment of its emergence, philosophical terms are often articulated as part of a larger problematic that bestows them with meaning. In, say, German idealism, the subsequent development of a term responds to its rigorous necessity, and this has a relative autonomy from the prevailing political, social, and economic trends, even if mediated by them.[38] The relative weight that conceptual and historical mediations have on any invocation of, say, necessity, is something to be scrutinized according to the specific difference, the particular determination, of the formulation in question.[39] Ultimately, what is crucial from this dialectical perspective is to discern the content or meaning of a concept in terms of its historicity, qua concept, and the objective realities it seeks to grasp by relating to the intentions of the thinker deploying it and its determination in the overall architecture of a philosophical endeavor.[40] Critique demands not only the study of concepts and the historical sediments these bear from prior philosophical systems but also thinking about identity and nonidentity in the basic relations between concepts and their referents, the objects concepts grasp and seek to comprehend. Always suspended in these mediations, critical theory refuses hypostatization.[41]

One last word about the interpretative approach here undertaken: with the partial exception of Adorno, there is no attempt to offer a sustained reconstruction of an entire authorship. Yet, instead of arbitrarily slicing and dicing texts, this book seeks to scrupulously historicize prevalent notions of responsibility and argue for a political concept of responsibility. In so doing, each chapter emphasizes something different: the historical process mediating the ethical turn that nowadays firmly accompanies this concept (chapter 1), the advent and eventuation of historical and contemporary meanings of responsibility (chapters 2–4), and the articulation of a critical conception of responsibility (chapter 5), whose political valences needs to be recast as part of a larger commitment to a political ethic (chapter 6). Each chapter, accordingly, emphasizes something different, which alters the balance between the conceptual/theoretical and the historical/political, sometimes unevenly—yet what remains in place is that in both cases the interpretation is political. While authorial intent, in the narrowly construed way, is not the overriding concern here, the reasons that motivate a thinker to intervene in a predicament of power are taken seriously. In a way, the intention guiding the specific interpretations offered here has been to craft rigorous interpretations in which theoretical coherence is not sacrificed for historical detail.

Political Responsibility thus avows more historically differentiated accounts of how the restructuring of political space is central in the situations in which predicaments of power emerged and that a thinker confronts. An account of continuity and discontinuity needs to be avowed in order to rigorously challenge hypostatized and undifferentiated stories of ethical responsibility. Only then can one critically avow the mediations of bindingness and contingency in the predicaments of power a political thinker confronts and seeks to address, how he conceptualizes the particular situation that prompts the need to respond, and how the response is theoretically conceived. It is in terms of these contexts that engagement with texts—the actual reading of them—is pursued here. Or, to borrow Michael Hofmann's perfect depiction of the meaning of reading as a critical activity: one reads "to question, to cross-refer and compare, to doubt, to go behind the back of words, to tap for hollowness and cracks and deadness. One reads not with a vise or glue, but with a hammer and chisel, or an awl."[42] Interpretations emerging out of these very precise but subtle touches, real and imaginary at the level of the page, risk fallibility while seeking to unearth historical and conceptual sediments in words along with the conceptual and historical constellations these conform.

THE PRIMACY OF THE SITUATION

A significant corollary of the interpretative principles sketched herein is the concept of "the situation." This term of existentialist provenance, whose most notorious exponents are Simone de Beauvoir and Jean-Paul Sartre, has been recently reworked by Fredric Jameson "as a way of constructing the dynamic of human activity: it is because we organize the data of a given present into a situation to which we are compelled to respond in some way, even if the response is inaction or the passive reception of affect, that we can reconstruct and reinterpret such interactions in terms of acts and praxis."[43] Dialectical critique both registers and constructs scenes to stage these conflicts while conceptualizing the different imperatives that mediate the situations in which these scenes unfold, say, those of contemporary forms of capitalism in order to map out the political totality in question and re-cognize it.

If for Beauvoir and Sartre the situation is conceptualized in relationship to their accounts of freedom, thus progressing from the initial solipsistic accounts of the forties to the more robust political and social theorizations found in later writings, a more contemporary interpretation has to further conceptualize its historical constitution, the mediation of historical sediments in the constitution of political situations, which are, in turn, politically constituted. Analogously, one needs to construe critical mappings of the historical articulations of particular *situations* and, what is more important, the theoretical figurations stemming from them, to think of forms of immanent transcendence, which is one of the dialectic's leitmotifs.[44] Such constructions entail the recognition of how even "pure forms still bear the traces and marks of the content they sought to extinguish," as well as the dialectical mediation between situation and responses and how an author's intentions are quite inseparable from the situation to which he responds, the scenes in which he seeks to intervene and thus act.[45] A situation is both spatial and temporal, and it is nowadays mediated by a vast array of constraints—cultural, economic, political—that mediate subjective responses to any given situation, their antinomies and contradictions.

In *Notebooks for an Ethics* Sartre further writes about how in a political situation there are fissures and openings, occasionally even accidents and unintended consequences, that can be seized upon and capitalized, something he casts as the "indeterminate stability" of "a historical structure."[46] If nothing else, this insight relates to the dialectic of the new and the situation; it relates to how to immanently transcend the situation by way of determinate negation, something that demands a strong sense of political responsibility intimately related to the responsibilities incurred in action in a situation and the consequences of such action. For the sustaining of political orders, or the creation and enactment of new ones, entails a sense of political responsibility whose actual form and content can be pondered in relation to the situation to which a political actor responds. This is a situation that one's intervention, in turn, mediates and grants meaning by re-cognizing it. The situation's temporal and spatial presuppositions and contents, both of which bear on how the logic of the situation enables and constrains modes of political responsibility and of thinking's political responsibility, ought to be equally grasped and re-cognized. The political actor "cannot avoid making decisions or choices; things will not give him any ready-made answers," as Beauvoir once put it; rather, "each new situation" brings with it anew the question of ends and the responsibilities of discerning the necessary means to achieve these without compromising or overwhelming them.[47]

Yet what is perhaps even more relevant here is how Beauvoir's and Sartre's formulations intimate a recasting of the role of contingency and chance, of historical discontinuities, and how their avowal, in and of itself, is hardly sufficient to pose the question of immanent transcendence or, more accurately, the transformation of the situation. This theme is further echoed elsewhere, when Sartre muses on the tricks played by the historical narratives that constitute one's situatedness: "The historical illusion is a double one: on the one hand, retrospective, on the other, prefigurative."[48] What leads to this illusion is a fundamental misunderstanding of a series of mediations, that of the presence of the past and of objective situations and subjective dispositions. Action is therefore always situated, which prompts a sense of realism and sobriety about transcendence.

Even while the language of "illusion" is rather quaint for Theorists, this provides an entry point to recast the role of mediation, as distinct from prefiguration in cognitively mapping one's situation. Roberto Schwarz's comments apropos of literary characters and authors capture another aspect of the mediations of situations, intellectual responses and political actions, understood from the perspective of the primacy of the objective situation in *political* theorizing: "The critical spark does not leap forth from one spot alone, and to stipulate abstract disjunctives is not always more radical and productive than discerning relations. The form of which we are speaking here is entirely *objective*, by which we mean that it foregrounds subjective intentions."[49] These formulations, in short, seek to articulate the historical processes that are constitutive of the situation, their mediation and nonidentity, with the subject that cognizes the situations and construes its representations. Naturally, nonidentity cannot be hypostatized.[50] It is not about positing a changing situation and a stable subject; rather, both the situation and the subject are mutually mediated and thus constituted. Rather than loosening up the concept of the situation, this insight into its historical constitution renders it even more binding: a bindingness that equally holds for the ways the logic of the interpretation is represented in different scenes and predicaments, theoretical and political. Scenes of power respond and contribute to constructing situations, as political predicaments concentrate social relations and historical processes that contribute to the intensification of the logic of the situations in which these predicaments arise and that they, in turn, represent.

Herein the interpretations of authors and themes plead for the need to conceptualize the political situation in which any given body of work emerges as a response, which, of course, it also mediates and thus further constitutes. This complements the collective undertones of the primacy of the situation and the fundamental differences between this approach and other contending views—say, genealogy, deconstruction, or the Cambridge School. The situation is here formulated as a particular moment in a historical process that precedes and outlasts it, but whose lineaments are present and discernible in it. Situations, once again, are irreducible to the historical processes that constitute them, even if historical processes and their enabling constraints significantly structure the logic of particular situations. In how a particular thinker conceptualizes the situation, one can see the desire for its transformation or truncation or both. These situations in which predicaments of power unfold are constituted and mediated by a variety of imperatives, which, even if considered relative, or semiautonomous, *levels* of a *totality,* are traceable to fields of power that are thoroughly mediated by prevalent logics and forms of power in their nonsynchronous synchrony.[51] "The situation" is dialectically conceptualized as a constraint and an enabling condition "whose rigid limits are at one with the very force of the perceptions it enables."[52]

Accordingly, this characterization has the opposite effect of reductionism or automatically reducing political life and its theoretical representations to mere epiphenomena. Once rigorously carried out, it provides an account of the relative autonomy of the different levels at work in the totality that at once constitutes the situation and is further constituted by it and inherently enlarges the scope of interpretation and critique. For the expansion of interpretative and critical possibilities is intrinsic to this form of critique, as is the imperative to articulate the relations and intersections between the different levels that mediate a situation.[53] In Jameson's apt formulation: "The very great merits of the concept of the situation are indeed almost exclusively operative in the field of retrospective and historical interpretation, it allows one to cut across the sterile opposition between determinism and individual will."[54] This is nowhere more necessary than in the dialectical intersections between the individual and the collective that the historical trajectory of the concept of responsibility suggests. Political theories, therefore, can be cast as responses to historically and spatially differentiated political situations in which continuities and discontinuities, breaks and overlaps, silences and avowals can be discerned and apprehended not only as mutually mediated but also in relation to how a body of work relates to (and with) the situations to which it responds, as well as how it responds to the responses of contemporaries. The situation is, at any rate, always collective and inscrutable for political theorizing, regardless of whether or not the thinker in question avows it. "Because there is nothing that can avoid the experience of the situation," to invoke Adorno's formulation, "nothing counts that purports to have escaped it."[55]

At these intersections political theory is best seen as a risk that is forever without a permanently transcendent ground—that is its freedom—but that nevertheless demands critical reflection to discern the actual and the possible from the realm of fantasy in sizing up predicaments of power mediated by obdurate forces, at once contingent and necessary, that are constitutive of political situations in their objective contradictions.[56] Once conceived in this way, political theory cannot afford to bypass careful attention to the sediments of past situations that remain binding in the present and the need for cognitive shifts to more accurately and realistically apprehend them: sediments and innovations, accidents and continuities, closures and fixtures in the interstices of a totality that is always cognitively construed. But to think about the situation in this way hardly reverts to only thinking about it as a tragic predicament (like Weber) or stoic realism; rather, it is a question of navigating the intersection of ethics and political life politically. If reifying labels prove ineluctable, perhaps a more fitting characterization is that of a Hegelian-Marxist *political realism* that refuses to mute the utopian moment while avowing and re-cognizing historical sediments that can either be constraints or enabling conditions or sometimes both.[57] The defining features of this dialectical form of political criticism consist of exploring and dissecting the vectors and movements inherent to the objective situation and the theoretical forms brigaded to grasp and confront it. This is a realism of determinate possibility, not closure; the realist disposition that Beauvoir once described as "the attempt to capture and utilize precisely those forces capable of building the future," along with a sober recognition of the forces impairing it.[58] The goals of critical political thinking consist of mapping situations and following the interventions, risks, and misplacements of political action and ideas; political theory understood as solitary endeavor, as collective predicament.[59]

OVERVIEW

The chapters that follow explore different aspects of the problematic of responsibility, its history and current fate. The abovementioned critical historicism is immediately put to work in reference to the ethical turn in a chapter titled "Historicizing the Ethical Turn," whose emergence it critically maps by bringing into sharper relief its historical and political determinants. It starts with an overview of the basic lineaments of the turn to ethics as conceived by a variety of contemporary critics. This is followed by an examination of the ethical turn by way of an account of its main conceptual and ideological tenets and an exposition and elucidation of its main critics. But the bulk of the chapter seeks to go beyond just mapping the contours of the turn to ethics. It also offers a historically grounded account of the ethical turn's emergence, thus interpreting the historical and political sedimentations found in its conceptual armature and its historical determinants and political conditions of possibility. This chapter, accordingly, ponders the emergence of the turn to ethics and traces its historical origins in relation to the legacies of 1968 in Europe and the traveling of intellectual traditions embedded in this experience to the United States, the emergence of American Theory, and how it converged with the radical depoliticization and conservative backlash of the 1980s and the restructuring of the political field.

After elucidating the turn to ethics, its conceptual and historical lineages, and the intellectual and historical conditions of possibility for its emergence, the chapter that follows, "Responsibility *in* History," zones in on the concept of responsibility as conceived in the history of European and transatlantic political thought. This historicization of responsibility, however, goes beyond commonplace genealogies accorded to this concept. It rather seeks to grasp how the idea of responsibility precedes both the word and the concept. Similarly, this chapter explores the emergence of the problematic of responsibility in terms of a constellation of concepts—duty, accountability, personation, obligation—that have often accompanied not only the concept of responsibility but many of its adverbial and adjectival usages. In these evolving constellations, the concept acquired political determinations that had specific historical and spatial presuppositions—the city, empire, realm, nation—denoting its locus of action and the centrality of limits in these theorizations of political responsibility, which current ethical invocations either truncate or disavow.

If "Responsibility *in* History" zones in on the changing valences and presuppositions of responsibility as a political concept, the chapter that follows—titled "Autonomy, Ethics, *Intra*subjectivity"—concentrates on responsibility as a philosophical concept. In so doing, it maps the autonomization of responsibility and the turn to intrasubjectivity that defines Kantianism and several figures in the post-Kantian milieu, including Thomas Scanlon, a prominent contemporary analytical philosopher. The chapter also sketches the Hegelian articulation of an intersubjective idea of responsibility and interrogates the critical and political import of Nietzsche's highly influential conceptualization of responsibility, which largely constitutes a critique and alternative to the Hegelian legacy. Finally, it engages with the reflections on responsibility found in the influential writings of Bernard Williams, an important heir of Nietzsche within the precincts of analytical philosophy, and closes with some general reflections about the current fate of ideas of political and social responsibility and the need to conceptualize responsibility politically.

The next chapter, titled "Ethical Reductions," focuses on Emmanuel Levinas's theorization of responsibility and its different reinterpretations in the transatlantic ethical scene. It opens with a critical account of Levinas's highly influential formulation of responsibility, which is followed by discussion of the creative appropriation of his thought in the writings of two different thinkers of the liberal left: Judith Butler and Jacques Derrida. The central contention of this chapter is that the phenomenological temptation of formulating a quasi-apodictic ground for a concept of responsibility runs through Levinas's writings, as well as through those of his heirs, as a sediment found in the ways in which phenomenological reductions and pleas for a transcendental ground—however refashioned as "quasi-transcendental"—pervade these bodies of work. The result of these appropriations is a series of antinomies that ensue from an attempt to theorize responsibility as a formal commitment to others anteceding the scenes of power that render such a commitment political, as these bodies of work abstractly posit an intersubjective relation outside of any social relation. These antinomies are then recast, in each individual case, as contradictions stemming from the ethical reductions involved, which either truncate attempts to transcend a liberal-capitalist political form or are insufficient to thematize a political sense of responsibility. In these accounts, responsibility reverts to *intra*subjective personalization and thus becomes depoliticized.

After the critiques formulated in previous chapters, the next chapter, titled "Adorno and the Dialectic of Responsibility," moves from critique to dialectical reconstruction, as it seeks to elucidate the conceptual contours of a critical theory of responsibility. Adorno's work, I argue, formulates a dialectical concept of responsibility that places a narrative of catastrophe—in his particular case the master trope is Auschwitz—at its center in order to frame the question of responsibility in reference to "a new categorical imperative": for humanity to arrange its thoughts and actions "so that Auschwitz will not repeat itself, so that nothing similar will happen." Yet, unlike its Kantian predecessor, Adorno's categorical imperative is anchored in a reworked conception of dialectical thinking that allows for cognitive mappings of the scenes of action that define the openness closure afforded by predicaments of power. It is my contention that based on the conceptual core of Adorno's critical theory, a political ethic of responsibility needs to be formulated to make good on its critical and political promise, a promise that remains truncated within his own writings. The limits of Adorno's conceptualization are thus cast in terms of his well-nigh refusal to theorize questions of collective life and its political forms. The chapter, therefore, criticizes this refusal and argues for the need to conceive his argument about dialectical autonomy politically.

Accordingly, this chapter is followed by the book's last chapter, titled "Political Ethic, Violence, and Defeat," where the most significant lineaments of a political ethic of responsibility are formulated and argues for the need to recast responsibility politically, as the need to respond to predicaments of power. The argument is situated within the tradition of political ethic (*poliética*) found in the writings of Bertolt Brecht, Antonio Gramsci, Niccolò Machiavelli, Max Weber, and Simone Weil, each of whom reckoned with defeat and sought to respond to violent predicaments of power: Machiavelli to the besieged Florentine political scene; Weber in the immediate aftermath of World War I and the German revolution from the top; Brecht to Nazism, interwar capitalist convolutions, and Stalinized communism; Gramsci in the context of defeat and imprisonment in Fascist Italy; and Weil at the onset of Hitler and during the Spanish Civil War. Political literacy and sober realism emerge as important corollaries of the political ethic therein defended. The chapter emphasizes two aspects of political responsibility: responsibility for sustaining a political order, with its internal imperatives, and responsibility for bringing about a new political order and the challenges and demands, including the ineluctable economy of violence, built into it. Overall, this chapter offers an argument about the centrality of the concept of fidelity for a political theory of responsibility that is attentive to the forms of power involved in the violent production of superfluous forms of suffering.

In writing this book I have sought to treat the problematic of responsibility by engaging with scholarship that enables fresh interpretations and avoids the well-worn phrases and well-trodden paths in North Atlantic critical and political theory—something that requires not only rewriting received narratives but also articulating historical contexts and logics hitherto downplayed or ignored. Part of what I do in this book is offer different historical accounts than those that have become sedimented commonplaces in much of North Atlantic thought. Accordingly, some chapters demanded deep scene setting in order to accomplish the goal of re-cognizing the history of the problematic of political responsibility and thus formulate it in a way underexplored up until now. Although I have tried to cast as wide a net as possible, I have sought, above all, thematic coherence and have tried to organize the argument of this book with a critique of the ethical turn as the pivot from which I then conceptualize a *political ethic* of responsibility. And, while trying to avoid the usual roll calls defining writing done for the profession, I have tried to record my intellectual debts throughout the text, even if in some cases no amount of notes can adequately convey it. Similarly, I have provided scholarly evidence, textual and historiographical, for my contentions and interpretations, while only recording those disagreements that I deem intellectually and politically relevant. In doing so, I have sought to make scrupulous use of the existing scholarship in the different fields and intellectual niches my inquiry interlopes, while deliberatively avoiding Byzantine disputes and refraining from unnecessary mudslinging and wrangling. Conversely, my refrain from recording disagreements with figures that enable my inquiry should not be taken as sign of uncritical reliance.[60] Following a similar precept, I have left out any reference to scholars whose works I cannot productively engage.

Obviously, noting how self-conscious many of these choices are hardly endows them with an aura of infallibility or insulates them from criticism. The possible risks and rewards of undertaking an ambitious interdisciplinary inquiry are plain enough. For interdisciplinary endeavors to think critically about political life they need to remain to some degree unencumbered by the disciplinary conventions and protocols of North Atlantic political theory, even if these demand forms of interloping in fields that the scholar in question cannot claim specialty in, much less the intimate knowledge of the lifelong specialist, let alone the linguistic and philological skills that define one. In writing, as in much else, there is always a gap between intention and effect, between what one sets out to do and what one is able to write. Paraphrasing something Wallace Stevens once paraphrased: what ultimately remains is the satisfaction of having really attempted to write a book that irremediably lies beyond.[61]

1

HISTORICIZING THE ETHICAL TURN

If Benjamin said that history hitherto had been written from the standpoint of the victor, and needed to be rewritten from that of the vanquished, we might add that knowledge indeed presents the fatally rectilinear succession of victory and defeat, but should also address itself to those things which were not embraced by this dynamic, which fell by the wayside—what might be called the waste products and blind spots that have escaped the dialectic.

—Theodor W. Adorno, *Minima Moralia*

IN SPITE of the prevalence of ethical tropes in theoretical discussions in North Atlantic scholarly circles, an explicit embrace of the ethical turn in the humanities and social sciences has not been as prominent as that afforded to other so-called turns—including the cultural, linguistic, theological, psychoanalytic, and affective turns—of the past thirty years. Indeed, in contrast with previous turns, the ethical turn displays an almost apologetic reluctance about its self-identity: uneasiness and ambiguity define the attitude of many theoretical proponents of the turn, even if its political practitioners—humanitarians and human and animal rights advocates, among others—are seldom troubled by its righteousness.[1] Proponents of the ethical turn, to be sure, do not move on a par, let alone converge on the content of ethics, ethical politics, and the domains susceptible to moralizing critique; nor are all practitioners of ethical politics equally depoliticized or of similar intellectual caliber.[2] But the different accents of alternative formulations constitute variations of a common theme: the aspiration to find normative principles, however pristine or murky, outside the political realm and its imperatives and deduce a supervenient ethical politics.

Critics have relentlessly denounced this turn's theoretical conceits, political feints, and lack of critical import. Alain Badiou's critique of "'ethical' ideology," for instance, sums up the more salient aspects of the turn to ethics, or what could be cast as its symptoms, in terms of what he calls "its socialized variants: the doctrine of human rights, the victimary conception of man, humanitarian interference, bio-ethics . . . the ethics of differences, cultural relativism, moral exoticism, and so on."[3] Yet he curiously winds up with his own ethical politics of militancy, his "ethics of truth." Something similar is at work in Ella Myers's *Worldly Ethics.* While arguing that the turn to ethics "is less of a common purpose than a struggle over signification," Myers offers sharp criticisms of several of its instantiations in the North Atlantic world.[4] And yet, like Badiou, she forges her alternative within the parameters of an ethical politics. It is as if the grip of ethics, its *englobant* of politics, is such that even an alternative discourse has to be cast as an ethics, albeit of a different kind. What these otherwise acute treatments eschew is a consideration of the historical and political conditions for the turn they decry and the need to formulate ethical considerations beyond the framework of ethics, what Bertolt Brecht once referred to as an ethic whose goal is not Ethics or a political ethic *outside Ethics*, to echo Raymond Geuss's apt formulation.[5]

Invoking Geuss is apposite here, as he has relentlessly criticized "the artificially illuminated circle of 'Ethics'" that extends to current invocations of "normativity," which not only cut across the analytical/continental divide but also figure prominently in hegemonic versions of critical theory (i.e., Habermas & Co.).[6] Today, notions such as "normativity" or the "normative" serve as a sort of analytical sandbox: a placeholder in which the thick web of collective and individual lives, goals, practices, and goods, in their mediations and intersections as part of a historically constituted and politically sanctioned order, is not merely consigned, but actually subsumed, structured, and slanted, if not downright hypostatized, in ways such that a more politically robust elucidation and critique of these practices is severely impaired.[7] And yet, for all the contemporary pervasiveness of this notion, the idea of "normativity" as a "single dominant" category is, in and of itself, an upshot of the larger turn to ethics of the last thirty years.[8] A historicity seemingly unbeknownst to many practitioners who cleverly invoke "normative" principles to adjudicate competing perspectives or "normative deficits" to debar positions, which are then cast as good or bad—an intellectual regression and blind spot in critical theory if there was ever one. In fact, ideas of "normative foundations" have come perilously close to replacing social theory, as such, or any concrete historical analysis that ultimately provides these normative ideas any determination; instead, a "normative monism" leads to a *Supernormativismus* abstractly supervening upon social and political realities.[9]

But it is Fredric Jameson's uncompromising critique of the ascendancy of moral terms to characterize political phenomena that most eloquently epitomizes the terms of denunciation: "In our time, ethics, wherever it makes its reappearance, may be taken as a sign of an intent to mystify, and in particular to replace the more complex and ambivalent judgments of a more properly political and dialectical perspective with the more comfortable simplifications of a binary myth."[10] Or as he subsequently put it apropos of the celebration of the end of history, the sudden reemergence of liberal pleas for "political morality" are symptomatic of a diremption from history proper, which is why he cast this phenomenon not as a *turn* to ethics but as a properly postmodern *return*, an epochal regression that colonizes and thus arrests genuinely political thinking.[11] More recently, Jameson writes about how "the return to ethics as a philosophical subdiscipline and its subsequent colonization of political philosophy is one of the most regressive features and symptoms of the ideological climate of postmodernity" and contemptuously characterizes "the ethical binary" par excellence, good/evil, as "an immense swindle."[12] Regressions sharply registered by Régis Debray across the Atlantic, who, as part of a scathing indictment of the "moral narcissism" of the ethical turn, has written about how "the reappearance of this language of values is never a good omen," especially in a moralist guise (which Debray sardonically calls *moralitaire*) that could be characterized in terms of acquiescence to a normalized present, the present of "ethics after practice."[13] This is worrisome, according to Debray, because it signifies an enfeebling of political life, and its attendant forms of action, at the hands of an ethical politics that excludes any alternative to the prevalent order. "A consistent feature of the moral style," Debray further writes, "is that it 'destroys the verb and inflates the name.'"[14] A nomination that, while hardly shying away from pleading for violence in the name of ethical humanitarianism, nevertheless abjures any sense of political responsibility for the destruction enacted. "Ethical" and "cosmopolitan" wars and "humanitarian interventions" are its expressions.[15]

Closer to the world of Anglo-American academic political theory, other critics have eloquently decried the turn to ethics. Chantal Mouffe, for instance, associates the turn to ethics with "a sort of moralizing liberalism," which turns out to be a somewhat unaware culprit that is "filling the void left by the collapse of any project of real political transformation."[16] In the United States, as Wendy Brown's crisp account of the most recent, postmodern fin de siècle suggests, not only has "moralism" emerged as an antipolitics, it equally betrays political despair among American left liberals: "Despite its righteous insistence on knowing what is True, Valuable, or Important, moralism as a hegemonic form of political expression, a dominant political sensibility, actually marks both analytic impotence and political aimlessness—a misrecognition of the political logics now organizing the world, a concomitant failure to discern any direction for action, and the loss of a clear object of political desire."[17]

All these writers, to be sure, acutely grasp aspects and symptoms of the turn to ethics in the North Atlantic world. What has emerged, according to them, is a vast project of political transformation carried out under ethical guises. Clinching victory in the cold war, the North Atlantic West has inaugurated a new *nomos* of the earth. Domestically, this order is characterized by variations of depoliticized politics that structure the political field in terms of ethical politics, moralism, and moralizations. Internationally, it is defined by ethical formulations of human rights and responsibility to protect, often brigaded to wage war. And yet critics of the turn to ethics have yet to sufficiently record and conceptualize its conceptual, historical, and political conditions of possibility beyond the usual commonplaces about the cold war and neoliberalism. It is one thing to describe a phenomenon, another thing to narrate it, and yet another to explain it. More precisely, critiques of the ethical turn have, for the most part, offered little by way of a careful elucidation of its lineages, theoretical tenets, and political contours, let alone a thorough historicization beyond the perfunctory contextualization that signals 1989–91 as a watershed, a turning point whose particular contours are often only vaguely defined.

A critical account of the theoretical armature and historical advent of this turn requires more conceptual and historical precision than has been offered to date. What exactly is the turn to ethics? How did it eventuate as a transatlantic phenomenon paving the way for a revival of a depoliticized conception of ethical responsibility? Answering these questions requires not only mapping the ethical turn but also historicizing it. What follows is a "metacommentary" on the ethical turn that seeks to historicize it and thus explain its historical and political determinants. It is a critical mapping and historicization of the ethical turn that inverts its priorities and frames and recasts its ethical tenets both historically and politically.[18] Doing so not only requires grasping the actual theoretical and political content of the ethical turn, along with its thought forms, which bear their own immanent logics and presuppositions, but also re-cognizing its moralization of political life as a politically driven feint, as a diversion from a *political* understanding of a world largely defined by liberal-democratic capitalist ascendance and the defeat of the radical left. This metacommentary seeks to grasp the ethical turn's historical objectivity and its intrinsic "politicalness," rather than take its ethical supplementation of political life at face value. In other words, the ethical colonization of political life is an eminently political strategy. When it comes to the turn in question, historical forces have led to political neutralization through ethical politics, not just ethical supplementation, as part of a larger epochal shift in the North Atlantic world. Neutralization and pacification, accordingly, emerge as central political valences of the turn to ethics. All these intertwined processes have emerged at a transatlantic political juncture encompassing the advent of neoliberalism (in England and the U.S.), liberalism and subsequently neoliberalism in France, individualization at the domestic and international levels, and the onset of disaffiliation and depoliticized politics.

MAPPINGS

No intellectual phenomenon that is designated a *turn* consists of an explicitly concerted, let alone always consciously intentional endeavor; which is not to say that it is a thoroughly contingent assemblage of events and practices. Rather, *turns* often constitute historically mediated constellations responding to particular intellectual, political, and economic developments. It is, accordingly, advisable to apprehend the turn to ethics by first considering the theoretical forms it takes and the historical processes that accompany its arrival, which are often present as either sediments or symptoms or both.

Without claiming to be exhaustive, one can zone in on four attributes that constitute the turn to ethics: first, how a particular temporality frames not only its normative content but also the historical narratives on which its proponents tacitly or explicitly rely; second, how the works of its proponents dedifferentiate between the ethical and political realms—fields of action and inquiry that cannot be collapsed; third, which is really a corollary of the second attribute, the ways in which the foregoing dedifferentiations amount to a reduction, or subsumption, of the political within the compass of the ethical—ethic thus displaces politics by colonizing political life; fourth, and last, how intellectual articulations of a new ethics, or of the primacy of ethics in the present, converged with the rise of a humanitarian ideology, accompanied by an analytically and politically distinct narrative of human rights. All in all, the historical eventuation of the ethical turn pivoted on the ascendance of a particular discourse of human rights, the conceptual elisions or deconceptualizations of its theoretical expressions, and the colonization of moral categories over political phenomena. It is thus important to bring these insights into a single field of vision in order to fully grasp the constellation that is the ethical turn and the historical determinants, intellectual and political, enabling its eventuation in the North Atlantic world during the late twentieth and early twenty-first centuries.

THE IDEOLOGY OF HUMAN RIGHTS

Despite genealogies seeking to trace the contemporary advent of human rights to the trials and tribulations that defined the *droit l'homme* during the transatlantic age of revolutions, or from the perspective of the age of catastrophes of the twentieth century, the ascendance of human rights has a relatively recent history. This ideology belongs to the same historical matrix as the ethical turn, as both are the result of a concatenation of events that crystallized in the late seventies and early eighties, gaining further ascendance with the end of the cold war.[19] The most obvious historical determinants of the current salience of human rights include the final blow against the political activism of the sixties; the global defeat of anti-imperialism and the disenchantment with the immediate fate of third world nations; the rise of the figure of the "dissident"; the need for a new narrative of American imperial dominance after the debacle of Vietnam; the discrediting of organized radical politics, especially Marxism, and the demise of Euro-communism; and the rising tide of neoliberalism. That these were the dominant determinants mediating the ascendancy of this discourse can be easily surmised by considering how "the initial breakthrough for human rights" was a weapon in the arsenal of the "anti-totalitarian" front of the seventies in France and thus highly selective in its invocations.[20] Similarly, coeval with the emergence of human rights was neoliberalism, with many parallels in their historical eventuation and undoubted affinities to depoliticized politics, even if their respective political and historical logics cannot be collapsed.[21] This constellation eventually paved the way for the dedifferentiations that characterize the moralization of international politics: in Samuel Moyn's formulation, "today, human rights and humanitarianism are fused enterprises, with the former incorporating the latter and the latter justified in terms of the former."[22] All of this further converged with the ethical concern about genocide and the ensuing imperative of "never again": yet another rhetorical device gaining dominance in the North Atlantic world with the end of the cold war; an imperative that became part and parcel of the dehistoricized consecration of the Holocaust as a negative foundation of North Atlantic ecumene, its "global civil religion."[23]

Amidst all these dedifferentiations emerged a moralized politics that conflates the negative element of "catastrophe prevention" with the more positive task of world ordering; or, stating it differently, world ordering is sanctioned by preemptively debarring an alternative to it in the name of past catastrophes. Hence the elective affinities with cold war liberalism and the counterrevolutionary impetus that drove it forward. Herein the past becomes an ambiguous resource: even if this particular human rights discourse is nourished by an account of the past, it shrewdly severs it from the present; namely, the catastrophe is *past*, while the present, which is no longer catastrophic, is *atoning* for the past catastrophe and thus steadily resolute about preventing forms of political action that may threaten the liberal-democratic-capitalist status quo.[24] Emancipatory projects are thus cast as threat, as harbingering a recurrence of the catastrophe. The present is at once legitimated by a past catastrophe and dirempted from it, cast as discontinuous, as the time *after*. Yet this *after* colonizes the future. It paradoxically looks forward to a future that is nonetheless consonant with the political mainstay and structural imperatives of the present. Accordingly, it cloaks itself with the legitimacy that comes from becoming the custodian of the memory of the recent catastrophe and its portended break from it, while rendering invisible the underlying continuities between past catastrophes and ongoing ones.

In this way the catastrophic nature of the era that had just come to an end is tacitly cast as the logical upshot of the dialectic of revolution and counterrevolution. History has ended. And in this new situation, in which the dialectic of revolution and counterrevolution is brought to a halt, fidelity to human rights anchored in a sort of "transnational individualism," to borrow Étienne Balibar's fitting phrase, prevents any resumption of it.[25] Human rights *after* catastrophe thus debar emancipatory politics and seek to pacify the political field, aiming at a political neutralization that forecloses the conditions for the resurgence of past catastrophes in the future. The convergence of these narratives into a legitimating ideology has the effect of instilling a politically driven ethical imperative that has sought to depoliticize and dehistoricize political conflicts, thus severing them from their historical contexts, which were often politically contradictory and complex, and reducing them to an ethical narrative structured by binaries like good and evil, heroes and villains, saviors and survivors, in a politically driven "antipolitical morality."

This is not to say that human rights needs to be consigned to a rationalization of domination, as merely the moral capital of the North Atlantic West.[26] Quite the contrary, the overall point is how a particular discourse of human rights, in and of itself one political manifestation of a larger theoretical and political inheritance, has elective affinities with the basic tenets of a particular political order and how it is deployed to legitimize it. Conversely, whether or not activists, or advocates and international lawyers, intend to have an apologetic effect, or are even aware of it, is not at issue here. But what demands critical explanation are the historical and structural determinants that serve as conditions of possibility for the effectiveness of these forms of advocacy and how they not only legitimize but also acquiesce to the rise of this new nomos of the earth and furnish it with a new imperial narrative, a normative supplement, for a world order led by U.S. imperial hegemony.[27] That, of course, does not preclude moments of related autonomy for ethical politics; indeed, for the invocation of ethics to be effective, qua ideology, and thus continue to provide the necessary moral capital for what are otherwise imperial ventures, ethical politics needs to preserve a modicum of autonomy vis-à-vis the ends they are meant to serve in the current world order. And on those occasions in which the capitalist order is not at stake, or a powerful or politically sensitive geopolitical ally is not involved (say, Israel), these could be put to work on ethical grounds, even if such moralized deployment often fundamentally distorts and misrecognizes the nature of the conflict in question, as was recently the case in the dominant narrative about Darfur.[28]

In this dominant narrative the cold war is cast as an interval in which liberalism had to carve a centrist, neutral, space between the extreme violence of revolution and counterrevolution. Tacitly built into this account is the rhetorical conflation of these two poles along with the exoneration of liberalism. The cold war, then, is interpreted as an interval, a derailing of normal history—just like the "real existing socialism" that was coeval to it—and its ending represented a return to the norms laid out by Nuremberg (1945–1946), the Geneva Convention (1948), and the Universal Declaration of Human Rights (1948). In a popular narrative that took hold across the Western chancelleries during the nineties, the full implementation of these agreements, after the hiatus of the cold war and the conclusion of its violent cycle of revolution and counterrevolution, marks a return to normalcy. In Robert Meister's trenchant but accurate depiction, the political discourse of human rights that thus emerged constituted "a fin de siècle triumphalism that sees human rights as a global secular religion, prophesized at the end of World War II and proselytized in the 'third wave democratizations' that accompanied the long wind-down of the Cold War."[29] A self-styled restoration that encompasses more than the spread and implementation of these norms: rather, it portends a transmogrification of the ethical valences—responsibility, accountability, justice—that it embraced for the sake of an eminently political project that inherits the problematic of containment associated with counterrevolution during the past century.

What are the main tropes and narrative categories conforming this particular narrative of human rights? How are human rights narrated in this particular discourse-cum-ideology? What is the temporality its theoretical articulations and forms betray? Meister's account of the rise of a liberal ideology of human rights has dissected the temporality underpinning current mainstream invocations and apologies of human rights. He calls this temporality the rhetoric of "after evil," but "before justice," and shows how it reverses the terms of political discourse by positing a catastrophic, evil event as a caesura in historical time. In this late-twentieth-century theodicy, human rights discourse emerges as the only ethical and political response to a past evil, thus preempting any form of emancipatory politics.[30] Emancipatory politics and movements, especially in their socialist guises, are precisely what advocates of this ethical turn blankly associate with the onset of the evil event in the first place. Meister sardonically but aptly characterizes contemporary human rights discourse as "a set of cultural techniques that allow individuals to disavow the collective wishes on which past struggles were based in much the way that missionaries get pagans to renounce their violent pagan gods."[31] Yet there is more at stake in these powerful disavowals than the temporality they involve. For what is at stake is a displacement of any sense of political responsibility for an ethical one, of collective responsibility for individual accountability. Instead of a robust sense of justice, and the forms of political reordering and economic redistribution that it imposes, the liberal human rights discourse casts its shadow backward to a catastrophic moment to which fidelity is owed.

Central to the ethical turn is the decollectivization of political responsibility and the displacement of the collective connotations of this concept, thus eschewing its political and critical import, by an increasingly individualist conception that often conflates responsibility with criminal accountability. In this context, a domestically anchored individualism found its cosmopolitan correlate in a transnational individualism. Concretely, this transmogrification could be discerned by looking at the ways in which any comprehensive account of injustice, structural and institutional, is debarred from these accounts and how the agents that benefit from unjust orders—active defenders, perpetrators, or passive beneficiaries—are disaffiliated from any class or collective political identity; accordingly, their responsibility is solely cast in individual terms. Still, how do beneficiaries of an unjust, often oppressive, order come to be identified with the victims after its passing? Meister goes on to elaborate the complex mechanisms of collective identification and symbolic representation that characterize the tacit, if real, exoneration of old beneficiaries in the new order, where they refashion themselves with renewed zeal. In the temporal *meantime* of "after evil but before justice," Meister writes, "the newly self-aware beneficiary of past sacrifice wants *not* to be identified as a would-be (or would-have-been) perpetrator and thus acknowledges the innocence of all historical victims."[32] Konrad Adenauer's Germany along with the myth of almost universal French resistance in World War II constitute well-known examples of this mechanism at work and the forms of self-imposed amnesia it entailed. One of Adorno's most caustic expressions about Adenauer's Germany at the time clearly captures the spirit of this logic: "In the house of the hangman one should not mention the noose; one might be suspected of harboring resentment."[33]

One can also adduce post-Franco Spain and post-Pinochet Chile as these classic signposts of so-called transitions to democracy betray a similar logic; transitions during which even the architects of the old order are tacitly, if not explicitly, insulated from justice, where denizens are so grateful for the restoration of basic civil liberties (and the tacit erasure of the acquiescence of many to the old order) that any just alternative to the new order is viscerally denounced, often by invoking a dehistoricized, amnesiac fable about the recent past. In these contexts the binary of good and bad victim—good: those victims that acquiesce with the status quo; bad: those who decry it—structures public discourse, while past structural beneficiaries are exonerated in a virtual ocean of universal victimhood. Becoming a militant for the new order, after evil—where the masses exhausted from long-lasting violent repression are grateful for a modicum of freedom and, for the most part, may be trusted not to tamper with, let alone compromise, the capitalist order and its attendant liberal-democratic forms—thus hardly requires addressing the structures of injustice past and their continuities in the present.

Even if the new order unbinds this past beneficiary-turned-militant, this militant conversion seldom demands a confrontation with "the unjust origin of those gains or his fear of those who presently suffer because of them."[34] Just think of the Latin American discourse of human rights, which contrary to legend is not much more robustly political than North Atlantic versions.[35] It rather consists of a modality of depoliticized politics: namely, a defensive ethical politics after the breakdown of leftist emancipatory projects. Human rights offered an ethical politics that effectively scaled back from more robust emancipatory projects and sought to build coalitions on the basis of a negative politics. That such negative politics is hardly negligible deserves emphasizing: eradicating dictatorships and denouncing their violent practices, notoriously torture, are crucial political goals. But it remains a defensive politics without an offensive beyond the parameters bestowed by the transitions. In its name the implementation of political orders that could be trusted not to trample with capitalist regimes of accumulation, its relations of production and reproduction, was undertaken.[36] As such, despite the rejection of cold war topoi by many of its advocates, human rights effectively represented the inheritance of the counterrevolutionary vocation of the cold war, not its transcendence.

Contemporary iterations of human rights discourse, accordingly, rely on a perverted dialectic of the global and the local with a strong depoliticizing effect: "A perverse effect of a globalized 'ethic' of protecting local human rights is to take the global causes of human suffering off the political agenda," just as it disavows the North's responsibility for these forms of suffering and how these are politically constituted; conversely, "the primacy of the global over the local, which was once the basis of a directly political imperialism, is here ostensibly humanized and offset by the primacy of the ethical over the political."[37] In these intersections, as Esther Benbassa has eloquently articulated, suffering, as a trope, remains; but it crystallizes as spectacle, thus "dispensing us of the need to feel the kind of empathy that reminds us of our responsibilities"; rather, it "borders on a form of liberating voyeurism."[38] The political valences of historically constituted and socially sanctioned situations are thus disavowed at the altar of abstract ethical commands to ameliorate suffering.

Replacing the political with the ethical thus entails not only the avowal, however tacit, of depoliticized politics but also the reduction of the ethical to its most solipsistic connotations and the rejection of any political and historical contextualization of extreme violence and the dismissal of any account of "structural violence" or a politics of violence that interrogates the dialectic of conversion at the heart of institutionalized, normalized, and routinized violence.[39] Correspondingly, an *intra*subjective account of responsibility replaces political responsibility; a particular ethics dislodges politics; political life is moralized while ethical life depoliticized; and any robust form of political commitment is either pathologized or demonized.

If this particular discourse of human rights is the most visible political upshot of the ethical turn, there are others, more oblique but no less central, that could be more readily grasped in theoretical forms. These politically infused displacements of the political, its colonization by the ethical, its subsumption, as it were, rely on conceptual elisions, one of which has been cogently dissected by Jacques Rancière.

THE EMPIRE OF ETHICS

At the very outset of his critique, Rancière notes the rather imprecise sense of "ethics" that abounds in discussions of the ethical turn at the hands of both advocates and critics. The turn to ethics is often cast "as a general instance of normativity that enables one to judge the validity of practices and discourses operating in the particular spheres of judgment and action. Understood in this way, the ethical turn would mean that politics or art are increasingly subjected today to moral judgments about the validity of their principles and the consequences of their practices."[40] In this formulation Rancière echoes other critics who have decried the extent to which moral criteria and categories are deployed to judge other fields—say, the political and the aesthetic fields—and thus replace immanently conquered, or hard-won, principles of autonomous critique.[41] But immediately after this assertion Rancière offers a demurrer. As he puts it, "The reign of ethics is not the reign of moral judgments over the operations of art or of political action"; rather, it signifies something else: "the constitution of an *indistinct* sphere where not only is the specificity of political and artistic practices dissolved, but also what was actually the core of the old term morals: the distinction between fact and law, what is and what ought to be. *Ethics amounts to the dissolution of the norm into the fact—the identification of all forms of discourse and practice under the same indistinct point of view.*"[42] Ethics thus constitutes a placeholder that subsumes distinctions and dedifferentiates spatialized logics and practices of power and judgment, while norming and idealizing the present, *what is*, and disavowing any emancipatory alternative to it. The empire of normativity is one recognizable name for Rancière's "indistinct point of view."

What the ethical turn involves, in Rancière's account, is the positing of "the identity between an environment, a way of being and a principle of action," as opposed to an ethical articulation of the forms of subjective orientations that sustain a democratic politics, and its political forms, albeit he does not mention the latter. Still, he writes: "The contemporary ethical turn is the specific conjunction of these two phenomena. On the one hand, the instance of evaluating and choosing judgment finds itself humbled before the power of the law that imposes itself. On the other hand, the radicality of this law that leaves no other choice is nothing but the simple constraint stemming from the order of things. The growing indistinction between fact and law brings about an unprecedented dramaturgy of infinite evil, justice and redemption."[43] This rather inscrutable formulation is eventually unpacked through interpretations of films and other works of art. Suffice it now to indicate what constitutes its central contention: the dedifferentiation of the politically crucial distinction between law and ethics. This collapsing is one among the many other dedifferentiations that have characterized the onset of postmodernity along with the smothering of historicity.[44]

But the dedifferentiation of these fields, the colonization of the political field by the ethical, as it were, has political consequences, as it establishes the monotheistic conceits of the current "law of the earth" and restructures the political field in ways in which any challenge of this ethical code is moralistically excluded. Drawing from Brecht's *St. Joan of the Stockyards*, Rancière writes, "The division of violence, morality, and right has a name. It is called politics."[45] Or, stated differently, the realm of political life is the space in which these divisions are addressed, and through politics different configurations of "violence, morality, and right" are actualized, apprehended, criticized, and rectified. It is within the realm of political life that the mediations between contending moralities and rights occur. A mediation that is further mediated, and in the last instance arbitrated, by the structuring of the political situation in which the conflict unfolds and predicaments of power are inaugurated. Or, as Argentine philosopher León Rozitchner once forcefully argued, the conflict is often between a reigning morality and an alternative ethics, and what is at stake is not moral conduct but collective life.[46] It is precisely this distinction that the ethical turn elides and recasts in moralist, often melodramatic, terms.

Yet, once a new nomos has been inaugurated, the conflict is no longer between ethics and the law or between two ethics. Instead, it is between an all-encompassing ethical order and its enemies. One can interpret what takes place at the onset of a neutralization of the political field, and the emergence of an ethical nomos, as the restaging and depoliticization of political conflict. It is no longer the realist sobriety emblematized by Brecht's political ethic—which recognized that "only violence helps where violence reigns" without consecrating violence—rather, it is a politics of consensus under the guise of humanitarianism that authorizes violence in the name of averting evil, while undermining the conceptual and political distinctions from which it could be challenged. Rather than politics disrupting an ossified consensus of political symbolization, what emerges is an increasingly dedifferentiated sense of collective life in which an ontological trauma, or all-encompassing, unnameable or nonrepresentable evil, or, perhaps, an originary catastrophe, binds us all. Moral categories displace political ones, enmity lines are drawn ethically, not politically, and a reversal of temporality, as Meister also shows, takes place—all of which are central to understanding what the ethical turn has entailed: "First of all, it is a reversal of the flow of time: time turned towards the ends to be realized—progress, emancipation, or the other—is replaced by time turned towards the catastrophe that is behind us. And it is also a leveling of the very forms of that catastrophe."[47] The dedifferentiation and decontextualization of past catastrophes and their narratives, not to speak of their present-day mediations, are plainly at work here.[48] In them, ontological categories, including Evil, Violence, Catastrophe, and (*pace* Rancière) the Other are hypostatized. Rather than a temporally and spatially differentiated map of the political situation, what is posited is an undifferentiated and dehistoricized universal situation from which only a variation of liberalism can save us.

Accordingly, for Rancière the ethical turn signifies the neutralization, if not eradication, of politics in any meaningful way. Nowadays, however, what he calls its *soft* version—"the soft ethics of consensus"—and its accommodation and relative neutralization of radicalism, has been trumped by its *hard* version—"the hard ethics of infinite evil"—which, in its devotion "to the never-ending grieving of the irremediable catastrophe," represents the expunging of political radicalism *tout court*. This neutralization is dominant, while politicization is increasingly residual. Like Meister, Rancière relates this neutralization to a shift in the temporal understanding informing the hegemonic liberal-capitalist discourse.[49] In light of it, he sensibly recommends the abandonment of "any theology of time," which, one might add, is a displacement of one turn for another one (from ethics to theology), as the messianic and miraculous versions of theological feints abstractly posit.

DEDIFFERENTIATIONS, DECONCEPTUALIZATIONS

The most searching examination of the conceptual dedifferentiations in the turn to ethics is found in Gillian Rose's works, as part of her formidable, if a tad idiosyncratic, engagements with an impressive number of thinkers and schools of thought, including the Hegelian-Marxist dialectical legacy. Out of these engagements, Rose forges a trenchant critique of the ethical turn, which prefigures and often surpasses subsequent criticisms. The introduction to *The Broken Middle* powerfully heralds the Hegelian terms of her uncompromising critique of deconceptualization: "The owl of Minerva has spread her wings," reads the opening sentence, which is then followed in the best Hegelian tradition by a plea for *comprehension* and a powerful invocation of *speculative* philosophy's critical import and hope that the watershed emblematized by the end of the cold war would led to a revitalization of critical thought.[50] Obviously, 1989 led precisely to the exact opposite. Rather than a sober conceptual and political reckoning with the new predicaments of power, and the challenges of the contemporary situation in its concrete historical manifestations, what emerged was a refusal to engage in the kind of comprehension that Rose's utopian realism avows. The title of one of her books neatly illustrated this refusal and the mood sustaining it: rather than the reinvigoration of critical thinking galvanized around collective endeavors, mourning became the law.

This melancholic ambience of aberrant mourning, in which loss became a fin de siècle marker of the mood of the North Atlantic left, coalesced with the rise of a despairing antinomian philosophy. In place of "an investigation into the failures of modern regimes of law," Rose writes, a "*new ethics* of the Other" has emerged, one in which, while putatively positing great ethical demands—sometimes even invoking infinity—it exonerates itself from the political dilemmas of law and ethics. She writes: "Non-intentional, *new ethics* expiates for the unexamined but imagined despotism of reason. As a result, the non-representational, non-institutional, non-intentional ethics leaves principled, individual autonomy and its antinomy, general heteronomy, unaddressed and effective. *De facto*, it legitimizes the further erosion of political will."[51] Just like one of Theory's terms of art, *difference* emblematized the critique of "theoretical reason" in the eighties and nineties—and, in its recasting in the jargon of deconstruction, as "différance," it carried a signature deconceptualization—"the Other" became "the hallmark of practical anti-reason" (5).

Rose goes on to unpack the theoretical and political stakes in this new ethics by parsing out the ways in which it occludes the crises that constitute its historical and political determinants. She sees this as a fundamental mistake that displaces reason rather than tarrying with it, and thus leaves the crises in question unattended. "One mistake has been replaced by another in three senses," she writes: "the initial mistake is not properly described; the 'Other' is misrepresented; and the remedy proposed is self-defeating" (5).

Rose illustrates the first mistake by utilizing an architectural analogy: "Le Corbusier has been blamed for the failings of modern architecture," and his aims, which were "humanist and emancipatory" are instead represented as "surveillant and controlling;" a misrepresentation that betrays a failure to consider how "the intervening institutions" have mediated the meanings and intentions of Le Corbusier. A properly critical investigation of these institutions would complicate things by examining "the intended meaning (idea) to built form or material configuration in order to comprehend how the outcome of idea and act is effected by the interference of meanings, that is, by institutions, which were not taken into account in the original idea but which mediate its attempted realization" (6–7). Rose then trenchantly brings her analogy to bear on the ethical reductions of the Other: "*new ethics*, in effect, intends a new transcendence, a purified reason, for it proceeds without taking any account of institutions which are extraneous to its idea, that is, without taking any account of mediation. It intends to affirm 'the Other,' but it ignores the actuality of its intentions. With no social analysis of why political theory has failed, new ethics will be recuperated within the immanence which it intends to transcend" (7). There are two aspects of these passages worth considering: first, the sober realism embedded in the reminder about intentions and actions, inner autonomy, however fictitious, and outer heteronomy, which is very real; second, the awareness of the persistence of new ethics within the obdurate immanence of what is, as opposed to its concrete transcendence, which only a sober reckoning with genuine political theory could begin to encompass. It is along these lines that Rose invites readers to consider "a far more difficult thought," which she formulates as follows: "it is the very opposition between morality and legality—between inner, autonomous 'conscience,' and outer, heteronomous institutions—that depraves us. Simultaneous possession of inner freedom and outer unfreedom means that the border where cognitive activity and normative passivity become cognitive passivity and normative activity is changeable and obscure" (35). The basic mistake of the new ethics is to fundamentally misrecognize the constitutive gap between intention and effect, and how that gap is thoroughly mediated by a political situation, its ordering and structures. And these structures are historically constituted *structuring* structures, mediating this constitutive gap but never closing it.

New ethics is a depoliticizing discourse that nonetheless acquiesces with the imperatives of the status quo by debarring these mediations from critical consideration, both in their conceptual architecture and prescriptions. In place of the triad of *cs*—cognition, critique, comprehension—informing Rose's Hegelian project, what emerged in the North Atlantic intellectual fold were the binaries and dyads that characterized many of the turns that took place with the consolidation of Theory in the United States and the most sophisticated formulations of liberalism of the past decades. Elsewhere, Rose has caustically referred to these binaries as "judged oppositions" that, while claiming playfulness, are, on the contrary, quite ossified. That is, a series of displacements in which the historically constituted gaps between law and right are occluded, while conceptual and institutional mediations are disavowed. These judgments, she forcefully writes, replace "conceptuality with 'discourses,' critique with 'plurality,' conceptuality with 'the Other,' renouncing in general any association with law or with mediation."[52] Or as she frames the question in *Mourning Becomes the Law*, the quest for "an uncontaminated ethics" is part and parcel of a disavowal of equivocation that the ethical turn, no less than other forms of political illiteracy, embodies: "Wisdom works with equivocation."[53] Heirs of Levinas and neo-Kantians—in the quest for pristinely apodictic, ontological, or preontological moments outside of history and predicaments of power or independently of these—disavow this insight, both intellectually and politically. Equally eschewed is the constitutive gap of any historically literate ethic, political or not: that is, the constitutive gap between intention and effect and how the ways that gap becomes ethically and politically meaningful is thoroughly mediated by the imperatives and practices structuring the situations in which encounters with others, practices of freedom and autonomy, are rendered concrete, enacted, and actualized.

In one of her most evocative formulations of the critical vocation of philosophy, Rose deploys another triad—eros, attention, acceptance—and how it is unconventionally recast in light of her critique of the *turns* of Theory and the so-called death of philosophy so prevalent during the nineties: "The much-touted 'end of philosophy,' postmodernism, has sacrificed these connections by defining 'eros' as lack, 'attention' as deconstruction, 'acceptance' as mourning. This restricts instead of enlarging reason, which is maligned as sheer domination."[54] In Rose's rendering, moreover, rather than mending the relation of law and ethics, what the ethical turn effectively achieves is their subsumption in theological or (quasi) ontological categories and discourses, which are ultimately external to the particular problematic itself—that is, posited abstractly and unmediated by the historical nature of the situation that prompted the problematic in question in the first place.

In Rose's account both the proponents of the ethical turn and some of its critics disavow what she terms the triune dimension of political life—universal, particular, singular—while also theoretically foreclosing the possibility for critical mappings of their mutual mediations. The contradictions between law and right, ethics and politics, as well as between different political ethics, are thus *deconceptualized*. But these displacements are, at best, a way of sidestepping the question and, at worst, a way to occlude it. Phrased differently, "We cannot opt out of the difficulty of ethics and law . . . to rediscover 'the passage from the non-ethical to the ethical,' for in so doing we discredit ethics once again by exalting it beyond the way of the world, replacing the broken with the holy middle. If we so do, we collude in the diremptions we intend to sublate."[55] What is at stake in Rose's critique of the ethical turn is a refusal to take ethical considerations out of the historically constituted world, out of its political and profane history.

Rose's critique of the ethical turn entails a re-cognition of the political situations in which ethics and politics emerge and how their

mediations—interdependence, contradiction, or both—and intersections demand a different understanding of the relation between ethics and politics; namely, a *political* ethic adept at comprehending the
sociological texture of collective life and the tragic dimension of political action and political life. Philosophy alongside social and political
thought—all of these thought forms need to be brought to bear to
properly understand the complex intersections between ethics and
politics, ethics and law, soul and city.[56] Only by acknowledging that
there is no pristine standpoint outside the entwinement of authority, domination, and exploitation, in predicaments of power, and how
these conform to structures that we constantly negotiate politically,
can an adequate rendering of the ethical and political dilemmas of collective life be reached.

LEGACIES OF '68

What are the historical determinants—intellectual and political—for
the emergence of this turn to ethics? The main tributaries feeding the
currents of the ethical turn, which increasingly gained recognition
in Europe in the eighties, and notoriety from the nineties on, stream
mostly from France and, to a lesser degree, Germany. The critical juncture for the rise of the ethical turn dates to the revolts of the summer
of 1968—effectively, a planetary concatenation of events—and their
aftermaths in Europe.[57] In the judgment of intellectual historian Julian
Bourg, 1968 is the central crucible: "After 1968 *ethics* gradually became
a preferred term, lens, and framework for grappling with many aspects
of life: from interpersonal relationships (matters of desire, sex, and
gender) to institutions (universities, prisons, and psychiatric hospitals) to politics (violence, law, the state, and human rights)."[58] If, in
terms of participation, the protests in Italy were the only comparable
instance to the massive protests in France, in terms of the cultural
and ideological impact of their ethical legacies on the Anglo-American scene, the French and German revolts stand apart. With very few
exceptions of note, the lineages of the ethical turn run from French
predicaments of power, and the master thinkers who inhabited these
predicaments, all the way to their Anglo-American avatars, all of whom
in one way of another partake in this French legacy.[59]

Whereas from 1968 on, in both Germany and France, the language of ethics became the favored nomenclature to frame and deal with political questions, the differences in the contours of the ethical undertones, as well as the lineages, are striking. The 1968 German scene, for instance, is markedly different from the French and Italian in at least three respects: in Germany, 1968 represented a reckoning with the "Nazi generation" and the political and ethical questions that such a generational confrontation entailed; in doing so, and here is the second contrast, it drew from a coherent and well-established autochthonous body of work, the Frankfurt School, and its actions were explicitly informed by these theoretical traditions (not to dwell on a direct and fairly sophisticated connection with the writings of Marx). Another, equally continuous, tradition those involved in the German scene drew from was the native tradition of romanticism, which nourished thinkers across the ideological spectrum, from Friedrich Schlegel to Walter Benjamin.[60] Green politics is thus a direct descendant of 1968; and so are the Baader-Meinhoff group. What both shared of this common matrix are the ethical overtones of their rhetoric even in the most politically minded expressions of their concerns. In the case of Green politics, an ethically cast ecology has been its leitmotif; in contrast, a staunch ethics of conviction, initially curbed by a sense of responsibility, had been the calling card of the RAF, even if it became increasingly pietistic and brutal as the initial imprisoned generation lost its grip on the movement it triggered.[61] So-called revolutionary action pivoted on a modality of ethical politics of revolt; 1968 in Germany was, first and foremost, an ethical movement that evolved into, and continued to feed, a political one.[62] Green politics and the RAF are the two main poles defining the ethical politics of the legacy of 1968 in Germany.

But what are the intellectual ones? Within the Frankfurt School there were plenty of ethical, romantic, and aesthetic motifs at work, yet conceptualizations of the political field and its autonomous imperatives were sparse at best. In Adorno's reckoning with Auschwitz, there was already a concern with ethical motifs. But while politically driven and alert, Adorno's critical reflections never conceptualized the political realm as an autonomous field of power, let alone political life and its imperatives. Ethical reflection, however, did find expression in his works. Proponents of an ethical Adorno have made much of these motifs. Suffice it for now to state their centrality, even while transmogrified, in Adorno's infamous (and often ill-understood) formulation about poetry after Auschwitz, his invocation of Kantian language to refer to a thoroughly heteronomous new categorical imperative forged to confront conditions of human unfreedom—for humanity "to arrange their thoughts and actions so that Auschwitz will not repeat itself, so that nothing similar will happen"—and the explicit connections he drew between the ethical lessons of Auschwitz and the present.[63] Equally influential on the German scene was Herbert Marcuse's rhetoric of alienation and denunciation, which had moralist (and romantic) undertones, too. So did, earlier on, the communism of Karl Liebknecht and the Spartacist League, much to the scorn and derision of conservative political realists, especially those closer to the right of the political spectrum (say, as in Carl Schmitt's scathing critique in *Political Romanticism*), and the liberal-conservative formulation of responsibility—framed as its antipode—as found in Max Weber's "Politics as a Vocation."

Accordingly, the ethical message of Adorno's political interventions during the sixties exerted significant influence on the ethical cast of the German politics of 1968, albeit not despoiled of a political and critical edge—an edge that would become significantly dulled in the reworking of this ethical impulse in Jürgen Habermas's formulation (via Karl Otto Apel) of discourse ethics and the bland, liberal-democratic politics of his discourse theory of democracy. Indeed, Habermas's discourse ethics provided a final conjoining of two emblematic dates that were already entangled—1945 and 1968—as axial years around which a discourse ethics for a new German republic could be built.[64] But by the eighties these more radical legacies of ethically infused politics increasingly became a distant memory. As with the fate of Adorno's critical theory, which became something to be academically studied as part of the lineage of the Habermasian enterprise, or as a protodeconstructionist current feeding Theory in the Anglo-American scene, the more politically charged edge had fallen from the purview of political and intellectual discussions. Politically, its most lasting imprint has been left by the Habermasian idealizations of the post-1991 international scene, an ethical politics that has normatively consecrated the new humanitarian nomos of the earth.

In France, in contrast, the legacies of 1968 are, by far, less clearly demarcated, as are the events themselves and the memories of their afterlives.[65] This murkiness and relative difficulty in delineating its contours partly stem from a well-known French tendency to mythmaking about the event (*l'événement*).[66] Yet, it also stems, perhaps even more so, from real political complexities, including the polarization of the post–World War II French political scene, one largely structured by the legacies of revolution and counterrevolution and the presence of the French Communist Party, the Parti communiste français (PCF).[67] Here, as elsewhere, an antifascist rhetoric was in place, one that had more political valences due to the experience of Vichy than in, say, Britain or the United States; yet it did not have the stridency and immediacy of that of Germany, where referring to the previous generation as "the Auschwitz generation" was far less metaphorical.[68] Indeed, this overall situation could not be more at variance with that of West Germany. There the Prussian heritage along with other intransigent elites of the ancien régime were soundly defeated along with the Third Reich, no Communist Party was part of the political spectrum, and a staunch orientation to the West had a consensual grip on the political field. But quite the reverse was the situation in France. There the legacies of Vichy and the Resistance were not residual, nor was that of a very recent colonial past, the resolution of which led to a savage and bitterly divisive war whose outcomes were Algerian independence, the abolition of the Fourth Republic, and the advent of the Fifth. All these were significant actors and events that structured the political and ideological field of the sixties. Sedimentations of this post–World War II political field had a bearing on the revolts of May '68 and their immediate aftermath.

Internationally, this mass upheaval has to be situated in a larger context of mass protests spanning two decades that it significantly contributed to and has come to define, even if these larger concatenations, with particular ebbs and flows, are hardly irreducible to it: mass mobilizations, where the Vietnam War (the Tet Offensive took place in January '68) and national liberation movements, especially Algeria, were central themes alongside local particulars defining the immediate situation, and, from the United States to Central America, the Caribbean and the Southern Cone, the inspiration and admonition of the Cuban Revolution. Subsequent political processes, say, the surge of industrial militancy in Italy, the miners' strike in Britain, and the revolutionary situation in Portugal that ended the *Estado Novo* (1974), further conform to this historical constellation.[69] Nationally, the major political conflict structuring the *before* was the anticolonial war of Algeria, whose tumultuous politics conjoined with the more widespread protests against Vietnam, thus bestowing to class politics and leftist ideals of equality an anti-imperialist cast. Meanwhile, a process of modernization and the centralization of state power was under way, accompanied by the increasing ruthlessness of a militarized police force and the proverbial authoritarian-militaristic aura pervading the figure of Charles de Gaulle. The latter bestowed credibility to the charge of a police state emerging in France, something that resonated with analogous claims across the Rhine. It also led to comparisons and parallels with Vichy, which in turn lent force to antifascist rhetoric. By the time the decade was in full swing, Maoism, or at least a radically unhistorical and distorted version of it, had also become an important source of critique within intellectual and militant circles.

It is within these contexts that the insurrectionary core against authority and hierarchy that defined May 1968 and different incarnations in its aftermath ought to be situated. It revived the politics of class struggle and equality, along with a sense of possibility, yet it was not aimed at taking power, something which has divided opinion ever since.[70] For advocates of May '68 that idealize the moment, the extraordinary succession of events in this rather tumultuous month resembles a shooting star: its sudden, exhilarating emergence led to a glowing brightness and then it burnt, leading quickly to an equally sudden demise—a return to normalcy, so to speak. But if the conceit of newness and miraculous imagery that guides interpretations of events as *ex nihilo*—or as starting *ab ovo* in the political fantasy of the "clean slate"—is left aside and "events" are historicized, one realizes that its emergence crystallized over a long period of time.

By the same token, the aftermath of '68 outlasted its suddenness. Indeed, despite the polarization against the PCF by many vocal critics leading up to May '68 and immediately after, as well as the subsequent increasing depoliticization authorized under the mantel of '68 by its ethicist heirs—often one and the same—the immediate aftermath had a direct political impact that nourished more conventional leftist politics: an increase in membership for the communist party, a reunified socialist party, and the 1972 historic agreement on a common program leading to the formation of the Union of the Left, which led to nothing less than the restructuring of the political field in the seventies.[71] But the prospect of a rejuvenated left under the tension-ridden but politically compelling socialist common program met with a concerted effort to discredit it. And it is precisely this *reaction* to the restructuring of the political field that led to the antitotalitarian moment in French politics and thought, which crystallized and further paved the way for an ethical turn in the intellectual realm whose lineage dates back to May '68.

Thus, for all the contemporary and subsequent talk about the revolutionary nature of these upheavals, rather than a renewal of a revolutionary tradition whose last vestiges were found in the Resistance to Vichy (arguably, the last embodiment in recent French history of the counter-revolution that dates back to the dialectic of revolution and counter-revolution unleashed in 1789), there was another side to the aftermath of 1968 that saw a reaction of a different order.[72] The concerted alliance against the left overlapped with the momentous publication in France of Aleksandr Solzhenitsyn's *The Gulag Archipelago*, which without offering any truly new revelations—the Soviet labor camps had been denounced by Ante Ciliga, David Rousset, and Victor Serge and figured in Simone de Beauvoir's *The Mandarins*—became crucial ammunition in the crystallization of the antitotalitarian moment in France that the new philosophers and revisionist historians would make their own. In Régis Debray's caustic formulation, during the 1970s consecration of human rights, with its corollary idealization of "the dissident," became the signature of a moralizing antitotalitarian moment: "Solzhenitsyn and the [Vietnamese] *boat people* unveiled communism's criminogenic nature and inverted the axes of Good and Evil"; with this, the burden of proof changed camps, the villain became the savior; and "with the rediscovery of human rights as the remedy for totalitarianism, the wellbeing of the rich was severed from the woes of the poor. Better: the salvation of the latter hung on the magnanimity of the former, as yesterday's prison guard became the champion of the convicts."[73] Michael Scott Christofferson—the leading historian of this historical moment—neatly captures the role of Solzhenitsyn's *The Gulag Archipelago* in the wars of position against the left: "In ideological debates of the late 1970s, the gulag was less a revelation than a metaphor, the one word that could represent and legitimize the emerging radical repudiation of communism and revolutionary politics."[74]

Claude Lefort, for instance, creatively enlisted Solzhenitsyn's book as part of his original formulation of an "anti-totalitarian" political thought—where he christened the Hungarian revolution of 1956 as "the first anti-totalitarian revolution"—but in other circles it became the rallying metaphor for an intellectually crass, if media-shrewd, circle of so-called new philosophers, who were endorsed by no less an intellectual celebrity than Michel Foucault.[75] Similarly, ex-communists like François Furet, the leading figure of historical revisionism and ideologue of a centrist liberal credo defined by its animus against Communism and Gaullism, and its quest for the normalization of French politics, became part of what henceforth came to be known as the antitotalitarian moment in French thought.[76] Indeed, in what turned out to be the most intellectually vibrant output in contemporary French liberalism, this moment ushered the revival of "political philosophy," which could be traced back to Raymond Aron's and Maurice Merleau-Ponty's then disciple Lefort, but that led to a concerted effort at liberal normalization, politically couched in moralizing terms, in the hands of Marcel Gauchet and Pierre Rosanvallon.[77] The long-neglected tradition of French liberalism, for much of the postwar period eloquently if somewhat quixotically represented by Aron, was thus fetched and reworked in an effort that conjoined a staunch anti-Gaullism and anti-Jacobinism (read: anticommunism!) with a strong moralizing import. It inspired responsibility vis-à-vis a normalized political scene—read: a capitalist liberal-democratic order duly exfoliated of "totalitarian temptations," even if France has never fallen under a totalitarian order—that inspired many transatlantic invocations of political morality and responsibility. Interestingly enough, the massive historical accounts produced by its leading lights, Gauchet and Rosanvallon, have had very little to say about Vichy. In spite of the impeccable liberal credentials of these authorships, the threat of a totalitarianism, which has never taken place on French soil, analytically dislodges the authoritarian, protofascist regime that actually did. Be that as it may, this outlook has yielded a political moralism that, while critical of the pieties of dissidence and human rights of the new philosophers, along with the latter's insistence that the only remaining task was "to write manuals on ethics," partook in the moralizing rhetoric built around *totalitarianism* during the antitotalitarian moment of the seventies.[78]

A number of overlapping, if somewhat contradictory, elements crystallized around the primacy of ethics and the new liberal humanist discourse, at a time in which, according to Daniel Bensaïd, "*Libération* became 'liberalisation' (sic)"; in Perry Anderson's trenchant yet apt expression, "Paris today is the capital of European intellectual reaction."[79] Politically, the unraveling of the leftist union and the subsequent abandonment of socialism by François Mitterrand nailed the coffin of the revolution and, with it, the revolutionary left; intellectually, however, the primacy of ethical discourse has had a longer aftermath around the two axes of responsibility and humanism, which were thoroughly mediated by the antitotalitarian moment and its liberalism. But one thing is intellectual and political history; another the theoretical content of this turn to ethics. Even so, sediments of the former are found in the latter: intellectually and politically, in the words of Bourg, "ethics" emerged as the privileged medium to sort out questions ranging "from interpersonal relationships (especially matters of desire, sex, and gender) to institutions (universities, prisons, and psychiatric hospitals) to politics (violence, law, the state, and human rights)." And this "ethical fascination" certainly sprang from the student revolt of May 1968.[80] Even if there is no a priori teleology leading from 1968 to the turn to ethics or to one particular form of liberalism, the emergence of ethics as a discourse of depoliticization with more than elective affinities to liberalism was not a random occurrence. There were structural reasons for it, both intellectual and political.

By the end of the seventies, the intellectual legacy of 1968 and the increasing disrepute of revolutionary politics had led to an abandonment of the political ethic of Sartre and Beauvoir for the new ethics, from the increasing salience of Levinas to the late Foucault and the defenders of a liberal, humanitarian credo. While irreducible to liberalism, the ethical turn that emerged out of 1968 had an elective affinity to it in its depoliticizing impulses. Accordingly, the slide into its own version of liberal politics was just a short step: Derrida never went beyond left liberalism; Foucault's eventual retreat into Hellenistic practices of the self could be interpreted as a tacit acknowledgment of political exhaustion, even if his anti-Marxism and antisocialism are well-documented; and the communism of desire in *Anti-Oedipus* was radical at the level of theory, metaphor, and trope, while politically rather timid and elusive, even if not entirely acquiescent—yet its antifascism, to be sure, was rather disjointed from the political situation in which this *oeuvre* emerged. For their part, the likes of Luc Ferry and Alain Renault reacted to what they saw as the nihilism of 1968 with an invocation of "a Kantian ethics of individual responsibility," while the liberalism of a Derrida was ethically infused with, even marred by, the abstractions of Kantian imperatives, albeit always to the left of Ferry and Renault.[81] Not to speak of Pascal Bruckner and Michel Onfray, two heirs of '68 whose political whims oscillate between hedonist anarchism and reactionary liberalism, or Alain Finkielkraut, the ever present champion of liberalized human rights. Indeed, it is along the lines of theoretical commitments and the contents of morality that lines of enmity were drawn between the different ethical stands—one representing the spirit of '68, the other denouncing its nihilistic impulses. Remarkably, despite its different theoretical formulations, it is a frequently depoliticizing and disaffiliated (and thus antidemocratic) ethical discourse. A discourse that in due course emerged as the actual content of the libertarian impulses of '68.

If, politically speaking, it was the antitotalitarian moment that became a turning point and watershed for the consolidation of the ethical turn in France, in the world of Theory an antiauthoritarian antinomianism became the signature of the age: Derrida is its emblematic master figure, even if his turn to ethical questions only began in earnest from the late eighties on. By the time that Deleuze and Guattari's *Anti-Oedipus* reached American shores, duly flanked by a preface penned by Foucault, the legacy of the Resistance along with the radical claims of equality and political possibility had gone through the blender of individualism, desire, and sensual subjectivism.[82] At a time when the left was on the defensive across the North Atlantic and European worlds, the turn to ethics and *intra*subjectivity constituted a retreat from the political world, not dissimilar to the retreat found in some of its early intellectual influences—Stoicism, Epicureanism, Lucretius.

Philosophical antinomianism and French liberalism: these two rather different theoretical and intellectual endeavors, sometimes at odd with each other in the realm of ideas, shared not only a common historical matrix and unmistakably French *éclat*, but a deep-seated antipathy to leftist party politics, along with anticommunism and anti-Marxism. *Le Débat* and *Tel Quel* are emblematic of these poles.[83] While *Le Débat* has been described as a veritable *machine de guerre* in its programmatic liberalism and antitotalitarian disposition, as well as in its self-appointed role as harbinger of the "political morality," which it claimed was lacking in the rather irresponsible left, communist and noncommunist, *Tel Quel* was proudly unengaged (*non-engagé*)—surely a political stand, even if one that disavows its politicalness—and was defined by an eclectic spirit that sought to bring into a single field of vision, amidst distances and differences, several strands of structuralism and its heirs.[84] Yet, its self-image notwithstanding, one of the signatures of this eclecticism and call for innovation—the latter a vocation to which it lived up to, as innovative if uneven critical work, ranging from the coruscating to the banal, sometimes in one and the same figure (Julia Kristeva comes to mind), emerged from it—was the effective deconceptualization of theoretical reflection by way of a host of ideas. One example is "intertextuality," which stemmed from an eminently linguistic and literary (modernist) conception of intellectual life. Therein the nondialectical dedifferentiation of philosophy and literature, concepts and narrative categories—Theory's signatures, as it were—emerged in full swing. Politically, an antipode of Marxism, *Tel Quel* contributed to the de-Marxification of French intellectual life and conceitedly took its place amidst intellectual *groupuscules* mimicking the antipolitical logic of ultraleftism. The final fate of this journal is certainly of little importance here. What is important to record is the crucial role it played in the constitution of the moment of Theory that would travel to the United States under the sign of its leading lights. The streams flowing from this particular concept of philosophy constitute the springs of the ethical turn, with Anglo-American Theory its basin, along with the long-standing tradition of American moralist and ethical politics.[85]

The eighties saw the consolidation of these trends on both shores of the North Atlantic. Even if France had no Reagan or Thatcher, with Mitterrand's abandonment of the last vestiges of the common program, a truly transatlantic trend of *disaffiliation* and an ensuing *reindividualization* took place.[86] France thus offered a unique constellation: a delayed neoliberalization, yet the concerted effort toward disaffiliation and reindividualization, which received articulation by and support from new philosophers and liberals alike. And with these came discourses of "responsibilization," making the individual responsible not only for his or her actions in response to a situation, but for the situation itself, or for tasks previously held to be social, and the disavowal of solidarity and any form of welfare safety net that would protect the individual from precarious situations for which he or she is not responsible. Differences of theoretical and cultural orientation aside, these converged in a rabid anticommunism that was constitutive of the antitotalitarian moment against the left in France as well as a rediscovery of Atlanticism: Reaganite or Thatcherite the French were not, but a sort of philo-Americanism existed during the late seventies and eighties as all variants of antitotalitarianism—from Kristeva to Furet—looked excitedly to America.[87] For instance, the intellectuals associated with *Tel Quel* and the revisionist historiography of Furet went on to establish American connections. And so did Foucault, arguably the most formidable intellectual figure to embrace the charade of the new philosophers, a stand stemming from its unyielding anticommunism and antipathy to the left's common program, and, subsequently, Derrida, who in his transatlantic voyages crafted an influential if undercriticized ethical politics. All of which were rooted in a deep-seated anticommunism and all of which converged in the ethical turn, planting the seeds for its American harvest a decade later.

It is not without irony that the most unsettling general insurrection in post–World War II Europe yielded such variations of liberal ethical politics. In spite of the articulation of egalitarianism and antiauthoritarianism, the logic of desire and a French variation of liberal individualism, which made axiomatic an abstract desire for nondomination, is what became of a leftist recasting of the aspirations of 1968. In one possible reckoning, the turn to ethics has not only hijacked the memory of '68 by casting itself as its only legitimate heir, but in it the language of responsibility and humanism has been despoiled of its more political valences and is complicit with processes of reindividualization and the neutralization of the political field. Even so, to speak of "hijacking" can actually be misleading—for, even if it was not the only heir, it is certainly a legitimate one. Meanwhile, a combination of political defeat, a sense of paradigmatic exhaustion, and liberal assault against the left, with its politics of reaction and restoration, along with its antitotalitarian fever, led many a thinker to retreat from the political into the ethical. At this point, during the late seventies and eighties, the ethical turn effectively became a turning away from politics at best and at worst a strategy of pacification and neutralization with the consolidation of the centrist, normalizing antitotalitarian liberal front of the eighties.

"By the end of the late 1970s and early 1980s," as Bourg writes, "ethics was bubbling up everywhere."[88] The defeat of the Union of the Left in the seventies, the antitotalitarian front composed of French liberals in the tradition of Aron and Furet, alongside the new philosophers and the disappointments with Mitterrand's socialist government, make the basic coordinates that led to the crystallization of this turn to ethics as one of the most prominent legacies of '68. An ethical turn that, according to Bourg, was coeval with two other developments: the reassertion of political theory and historical writing as traditionally understood, each with contradictory developments and turns of their own. If ethics, political theory, and history had been brushed aside by the rise and fall of structuralism, they now returned to center stage of French intellectual life. Hence there was an elective affinity between these developments and the reemergence of a triad of ethical thinkers whose politics oscillated within the parameters of the center of the political spectrum: Vladimir Jankélévitch, Paul Ricoeur, and Emmanuel Levinas.

Yet the affinities between the new moralism and traditional moral philosophy were not entirely smooth. In the opening paragraph of his *Le paradoxe de la morale,* Jankélévitch explicitly registers the ethical fervent that pervaded the French intellectual scene at the time—as the first sentence states, "We are assured that moral philosophy is currently honored"—but meets it with suspicion.[89] Such pride of place has hardly led to a proper appreciation of the nature of moral philosophy. Actually, Jankélévitch is trenchant and quite blunt in his assessment: "It is doubtful that the crusaders of this new crusade actually know what they talk about."[90] Still, he goes on to cast moral philosophy as "le premier problème de la philosophie," an assertion in sync with the times, as it also signified the subsumption of other forms of inquiry into it. But Jankélévitch's protestations attest to the conceptual and theoretical looseness of the invocations of ethics and morality in this context, where ethics is frequently conjured as an ill-defined placeholder to anchor the de-Marxification of the French intellectual scene. Even so, it is striking that neither Jankélévitch nor Ricoeur gained much of a footing in the precincts of Theory across the Atlantic. Consider Ricoeur, for instance: a formidable philosophical mind that profoundly meditated on questions of responsibility, offered remarkable contributions to ethics from a hermeneutic and phenomenological sensibility, and is the author of what is arguably the most cogent philosophical account of narrative in the second half of the twentieth century (responsibility, phenomenology, narrative—all putative signposts of Theory!). Yet his commanding body of work, while mostly available in English translation by major university presses, has gained little traction within the context of the ethical turn, even if in not insignificant ways, as a philosopher, Ricoeur is arguably a more substantial figure than Levinas.

So the obvious question is why, out of all the modalities of ethics vying for dominance in the context of the French turn to ethics, Levinas's ethics gained such transatlantic influence and ascendancy. The most obvious answer is that, in contrast to Ricoeur, Levinas developed what effectively amounts to a deconceptualizing and dedifferentiating philosophical project whose ethical reductions have strong affinities with the dedifferentiations of Theory, and the latter's hostility to the conceptual bindingness of older philosophical traditions of critique. That is, at any rate, an intellectual explanation. Politically, the "consecration" of Levinas in the French scene could be placed in the context of the rediscovery of the ethical-religious core of Judaism that was part and parcel of the antitotalitarian mood and the effacement of the revolutionary idea in the early eighties.[91] Or one can equally emphasize the coeval rise of neoliberalism and the defeat of the left in the North Atlantic zone, along with the depoliticization of the latter in increasingly pacified political predicaments.[92] But a closer look at Theory, as a transatlantic phenomenon consecrated in the United States, brings into sharper relief the constellation that made possible the appeal of this subordination of politics to a hypostatization of ethics that Levinas represents. Here the work of Derrida is important. For, in a fundamental way, Levinas traveled to America with Derrida, and both carried Theoretical passports. Derrida's early essay, "Violence and Metaphysics," has been rightly depicted as pioneering the scholarship on Levinas in the North Atlantic world. Even so, one of Levinas's foremost motifs, the theme of responsibility to the Other, remained mostly recessive in Derrida's seminal writings.[93] It only became dominant in the context of Derrida's subsequent turn to ethics.

Notwithstanding the protestations of the master himself, there is an ethical turn in Derrida's work, which coalesces with the turn to ethics and the age of neoliberal ascendancy in the North Atlantic world, especially after the end of the cold war.[94] Philosophically, Derrida's ethical politics became a solution for the ways in which many of the internal antinomies that his channeling of the legacy of German phenomenology—which was thoroughly mediated by his engagement with structuralism and recast in terms of his signature, brilliant, dedifferentiations of philosophy and literature—led when confronted with political questions and predicaments of power.[95] Evidence of these antinomian impasses is found in the debates of the early eighties carried on by Derrida's disciples and the awkward questions raised about the political implications of deconstruction or how it relates to political questions.[96] Politically, Derrida's ethical turn was thoroughly mediated by two external determinants that forced upon him a more explicit engagement with questions of ethics in the terrain tilled by the ethical turn in France. These determinants consisted of the virtually simultaneous eruption of two major scandals that were intimately related to the catastrophic history of World War II: the Heidegger and de Man affairs; both of which constituted less than edifying transatlantic debates that nevertheless deeply affected Derrida's intellectual itinerary.[97] The end of the cold war provided a context in which Derrida finally felt comfortable articulating the ethical politics of deconstruction.[98]

THEORY IN AMERICA

The voyages of these *maîtres a penser* led to a *displacement* of their ideas in a context that initially betrayed and subsequently exacerbated some of the historical and political sediments mediating the armature of their reflections, as these bodies of work became dedifferentiated and subsumed in that piece of Americana that is Theory. For in North Atlantic leftist thought, the ethical turn under consideration occurred under the aegis of what in the humanities scholars refer to as Theory. In the formulation of one of its leading practitioners: "Theory as a genre of works (rather than thinking about thinking) began . . . as a name for a mixture of philosophy, psychoanalysis, linguistics, aesthetics, poetics, and political and social thought."[99] To further dissect and comprehend its depoliticizing impulses, it is important not only to consider the transatlantic voyage of French bodies of work and their christening in the U.S. academy as Theory but also the political situation that gave it a berth on this side of the Atlantic.

In the United States the heyday of Theory converged with a political situation defined by the onset of neoliberalism as a regime of accumulation and the political neutralization of, and the conservative backlash against, the sixties. Its emergence in the New World thus dovetailed with a turn to the right, both intellectually and politically, whose point of transition is perhaps more clearly seen at the intersection between the Carter and Reagan presidencies, when a concerted effort to domestically disavow the sixties and its political legacies coincided with the onset of neoliberalism, patriotic jingoism, and gentrification embodied in Reagan's mantra "morning in America." Theory's arrival also converged and became coeval with a new international situation characterized by the onset of a second cold war, the demise of national liberation movements, and the crisis of internationalist Marxism.[100] By the time that important bearers of the ethical turn secured posts at North American universities, the christening of Theory by academic doyens, mostly visible in strongholds of the humanities like Columbia, Cornell, Johns Hopkins, Yale, and, subsequently, UC Berkeley, UC Irvine, and Duke was already underway. A conference in Baltimore in 1966, titled "The Languages of Criticism and the Sciences of Man," is frequently identified as a crucial episode in the emergence of Theory—in Theory's vernacular, it was an "event" that brought to American comparative literature a hitherto unavailable emphasis on metatheory—even if there is a great deal of disagreement over Theory's other points of inflections and critical vectors.[101]

Politically, the traveling of mostly French bodies of work to the United States and the ensuing consolidation of Theory thus took place as the sixties were disavowed in the political arena and forms of political theory committed to participatory democratic politics came under fire, then coming to be discredited in the intellectual field.[102] The American sixties were framed by the participatory values of equality and anti-elitism, an anti-imperialist disposition, and the fight for civil rights for blacks, Latinos, and women. And, in the United States, elements of shared power and a deep concern with political form crystallized in ways that had no exact equivalent in France. Not incidentally, across the Atlantic, Sheldon S. Wolin offered a trenchant depiction of May '68 and the type of depoliticized revolt it signaled: "The abortive French Revolution of 1968 may be an intimation of the sort of McLuhanesque revolutions in store for advanced societies: brief, vivid spectacles, revolutionary phantasmagoria flashing across the screen, over before it has scarcely begun, yet memorialized by a flood of posters,

books, articles, and television—memorialized but not really experienced, pop revolution for the spectators, instant revolution for the
producers, and an art form for the main actors."[103] Something that
contrasted sharply with Wolin's own formative experience during the
American sixties.[104]

Moreover, in the United States, the absence of a fascist past, or of a
Communist Party, led to a different configuration of the political field,
even if cold war anticommunism, with its unique brand of moralization, was so widespread that it figured prominently in the Port Huron
Statement, the radical manifesto summarizing the political vision of
the Students for a Democratic Society and articulating a robust sense
of political responsibility (a movement that likewise remained at a
pronounced distance from labor struggles), whose most attractive
legacy was the retrieval and recasting of the democratic ideal of participatory politics, a noble and genuinely democratic aspiration.[105] But
this political dimension of the American sixties would eventually be
folded into the idiom of the "counterculture" in many ways an attempt
to either idealize, decry, or depoliticize it. A counterculture in turn
transformed and normalized into forms of revolt defying cultural conventions, mores, and beliefs, but doing so within the parameters of the
liberal-capitalist order. "Repressive desublimation," Herbert Marcuse
famously called it.[106] It is in this context that Theory gained traction in
academic circles, especially in the humanities.

Undoubtedly, the reception of the different bodies of work associated with Theory in the United States included degrees of misrecognition and distortion. But perhaps the most obvious misrecognition,
one widely shared across the political spectrum defining American
Kulturkampf, was of the ethical and political content of these ideas.
For those on the left, the critical ethos of Theory rendered it immediately subversive of hierarchies and exclusion; for those on the right
these subversions were morally reprehensible.[107] But what both positions tacitly shared was the assumption that these ideas were immediately subversive, *tout court*, especially insofar as they were presumably
devoid of any ethical content. Bodies of works that were at best ambivalent, if not downright hostile to Marxism, were taken as a code word
for Marxist radicalism. In these battles the legacies of "The Enlightenment" became straw men: the critiques of "master narratives" of historical progress, an ill-defined but vilified humanism, along with the

universal "subject," were couched in explicitly antinormative stances. But the ethical overtones informing some of the initial articulations of these ideas, which, as already shown, gained ascendance as part of the concerted effort to resist the traditional political forms structuring the Fifth Republic in France, either in response to the antitotalitarian moment of the seventies or largely aligned with its broad contours, were initially cast as politically subversive antiethical stances, even when most of the master thinkers conforming the new canonizations of Theory were central figures in the advent and crystallization of the ethical turn in France. The ethical lineaments of Theory remained mostly recessive across the Atlantic, as sediments that lay dormant during the heyday of "the Theoretical era (c. 1968–87)."[108] But 1987 and the cultural wars that ensued soon after became turning points. From then on, Theory would sport a multifaceted ethical politics, including an ethics of reading, in which the conceit of "ethics first" became paramount.[109] This ethicization of political phenomena and questions of collective life had its share of moralization. More to the point, it had an elective affinity with the larger depoliticization and overall moralization of public discourse already underway in the context of Reaganism.

What were the historical, political, and economic determinants of this moment? These are found in the political logics that crystallized in the "long seventies." The most obvious ideological change was the backlash against the sixties that Nixon's election, with its appeal to a "silent majority," epitomized. Politically, the overall succession of defeats for the left in the transatlantic world contributed to a sense of political exhaustion and a need to break away from political legacies that undermine the political system. The "negative ethics" of tolerance invoked by proponents of pluralism in American political science and discourse gained ascendance in the United States as an ethic of exhaustion seeking to preserve the stability of the political and social order.[110] So did the restoration of American pride and virtue, something advocated by both the law-abiding patriots who were alienated by the radicalism of the sixties and by the *bien pensant* establishment of the Democratic Party, which had been lukewarm, if not hostile, to sixties radicalism and its uncompromising rejection of racial inequalities and the critique of imperialism. America needed to stand tall once again, or so the narrative went, a stance that demanded exorcising the specter of Vietnam and the restoration of national assertiveness and confidence.[111] With Carter's belated embrace of human rights during the historic crucible of the late seventies, human rights became precious "moral capital" providing a much needed healing narrative and a new lease of normative capital for the American imperium.[112] In this crucial historical moment, the domestic negative ethics of tolerance found its international correlate in the negative ethics of human rights.

In a fundamental way, the history of the turn to ethics is inextricably intertwined with the demise of Marxism and the anticommunist political sensibility that crystallized on both North Atlantic shores during the late sixties, which was coeval with the onset of postmodernity as a historical condition, along with neoliberalism and depoliticized politics. In the longer term, the insurrectionary contestation of '68 was channeled by an ethical turn that it nourished and in which its legacies were transmogrified. In due course, revolutionary fidelity yielded to ethical orientations. Yet there are continuities in the transmogrification of political contestation into an ethos of insurrection: for the antinomian spirit of '68 always combined political insurrection with a hedonist, moral, and cultural ethos.[113] Its afterlives, however, have proven which pole has had the upper hand. Although intellectual and political developments scarcely move on a par—different levels of a totality, or a structure, seldom do—a common matrix can still be discerned by the foregoing historical-political constellation. If there is one constant in these voyages of theoretical bodies of work and political discourses, it is the strong depoliticizing drive behind them and the drive to dedifferentiate and disavow any dialectical conceptualization or elucidation of the intersection between ethics and politics, or an historical unfolding of the present condition, in both its continuities and discontinuities. At the theoretical level, an antinomian spirit has led to the dedifferentiation and deconceptualization that characterize postmodernity, with the ethical turn and its colonization of other fields of action as a particular symptom. Politically, the defeat of the revolutionary left and liberal ascendance has marked the political field; it is a context of defeat and reaction that best defines the political situation in which this turn has unfolded.

But alongside political defeat and the neutralization of the left that paved the way for the ethical turn, there are other striking parallels in the ethical turn's intellectual and political loci of emergence and reception: structuralism, in both its American mediations and French moments displayed a sudden rising and no less spectacular demise, which is analogous to that of May '68 itself; French and American reaction to the sixties both pivoted in the embracing of ethical tropes and categories to make sense of political life, something of a common denominator between the heirs of structuralism, the new philosophers, and the Atlanticist insistence on human rights and a (liberal) political morality; anti-Marxism, not to mention anti-Hegelianism, or the stout rejection of any whiff of dialectical categories; the rise of the secular theodicy of human rights and its attendant domestic and international individualisms, as well as disavowals of any robust sense of collectivity (i.e., the fetish of the singular and suspicion of totality in Theory); and the onset of postmodernity, its dedifferentiations and neutralizations. The ethical turn is, accordingly, a symptom of the political neutralizations after the end of history, mediated by, albeit never on a par with, these political, economic, cultural, and intellectual circumstances.

The ethical turn has bestowed upon ethical reflection a colonizing drive that subsumes all fields of action and power, which is particularly evident in the moralizing and neutralizing effects that its colonization of political life has brought about. Resisting the terms of the ethical turn and its corollary sense of responsibility is, accordingly, one step in the direction of recasting the intersections between ethical and political life by crafting an alternative political ethic that not only adequately maps contemporary predicaments of power and is responsive to the situations these configure, but whose locus of fidelity is to democratic political forms and its binding principles. But another step in this direction is to reclaim the concept that has been mostly depleted by the turn to ethics: that of responsibility; a retrieval that has to critically ponder the spatial and sociohistorical presuppositions and sense of limits that have accompanied its historical eventuation before its current depletions.

2

RESPONSIBILITY *IN* HISTORY

We can only think of ourselves as responsible insofar as we are able to influence matters in the areas where we have responsibility.

—Theodor W. Adorno, *History and Freedom*

RESPONSIBILITY IS now a fashionable concept in political theory, philosophy, and critical theory, and, *ceteris paribus*, that is a good reason not to write about it. Large bodies of work exist expounding its various connotations and meanings, ranging from questions of accountability and guilt to the need to respond to alterity. And yet there is something rather elusive about the political connotations of contemporary invocations of responsibility within the context of the turn to ethics in the humanities and social sciences, an elusiveness that at first glance seems largely due to hyperindividualized, abstract, and unhistorical thematizations of responsibility. Indeed, recent discussions of responsibility tend to be innocent to both the history and historicity of this concept, thus concealing the sociopolitical presuppositions that have sedimented in the historical eventuation and actualization of this concept and the practices it connotes or grasps. Equally disowned by prevalent accounts of responsibility are the spatial presuppositions that historically made the idea and practice of responsibility politically meaningful along with its institutional embodiments and political forms. In its multiple historical usages, responsibility has crystallized as an objective practice that can be accepted or declined, assumed or rejected, achieved and disavowed, contracted and acquired, confronted, avoided, sanctioned or rehabilitated, attributed or imputed, behooved or befitted, or something to be had and felt, prescribed or adjudicated.

Likewise, it is frequently found in conjunction with prepositions like *of, in, by, about,* and *over.* Responsibility also operates both as an adjective and adverb, sometimes even as a verb (i.e. responsabilize, or *responding to*). And, depending on which of these connotations is advanced, emphasis is placed on one of the other concepts that further constitutes the constellation of concepts mediating the idea of responsibility and some of its surrogates. For instance, if responsibility is deployed as an adjective—that is, as *responsible*—it connotes a range of things that nonetheless revolve around an axis that, at one end, establishes the idea of fulfilling duties and obligations and, at the other end, posits the question of accountability in terms of attributability or imputability of an act, action, or event. It is within this spectrum that one finds the idea of being responsible as answerable or accountable agent. Answerability and accountability are thus cast in terms of whether or not one lives up to the fulfillment of one's duties or in terms of whether or not actions and their consequences are imputable to a subject. Conversely, its adverbial form, *responsibly,* qualifies the action that is deemed to be responsible as in, for example, acting responsibly in a political or ethical situation.

Historically, the concept and practice of responsibility have been closely related to other concepts, such as obligation and duty, imputability, attributability and accountability. As a concept, responsibility has been unthinkable without notions like capacity and capability. Even if it cannot be rendered as equivalent, let alone identical to any of these other concepts, its conceptual determinations rely on the constellation to which these concepts conform. It is by grasping this constellation that one can apprehend the problematic of responsibility as it has eventuated in history and the historical and social nature of the process through which it acquired its conceptual determinations, along with the spatial and institutional presuppositions, and sense of limits, that make it genuinely political. Although an exhaustive treatment of the permutations, continuities and discontinuities, transmogrifications and displacements in the conceptual history of responsibility goes beyond the scope of the present discussion, it is still possible to map out the key moments in the emergence of responsibility in the history of Western and transatlantic political thought.

In the Western tradition of thought, *responsibility,* as a word, is of relatively recent provenance. Without making a fetish of etymologies, a cursory glance at the history of its usages is instructive. The earliest recorded appearances in Spanish, English, and French date from the seventeenth and eighteenth century on, with an isolated usage recorded in Middle French during the fifteenth century, according to the *OED*, and an appearance in Spanish during the sixteenth century, even if usage was rare before the eighteenth.[1] In the English language its meanings and significations include "capability of fulfilling an obligation"; the quality of reliability or trustworthiness, the ability to be held accountable, or "accountability for something"; the idea of being "in charge" of something or having a duty to someone or something (in Spanish: *estar a cargo, hacerse cargo de algo o alguien*), which also connotes a sense of obligation; the ability to pay a debt or contract, which, revealingly, is an important signification of the term in American English; "the fact of having a duty to do something," which could be another individual, a cause, or a principle; a calling, burden, or task "for which one is responsible," which could be a moral obligation or a political one in conjunction "with a person or thing," and that *thing*, conversely, can be a politically constituted collective identity and its attendant forms or a form of exercising power; a person or entity *to* whom one is accountable or *for* whom one is responsible or *charged with*; and, finally, the capacity, or capability, of a subject to know, recognize, and thus accept the consequences of her actions.[2] The last meaning is tacitly found in Shakespeare's famous line from *The Tempest*, when Prospero claims, "Two of these fellows you / Must know and own. / This thing of darkness I / Acknowledge mine" (5, 1, 277–79). However many corollaries there are to this concept—moral, social, legal, political—which branch out in a variety of directions and fields of power and inquiry, what is clear is the pervasiveness of its external connotations, its projection outward, to what is generalized and common—either toward someone or something: principle, person, obligation, etc.—even in the most individualistically conceived definition.

BEFORE "RESPONSIBILITY"

Notwithstanding the recent origin of this word, theoretical elucidations of the practice of ethical and political responsibility are hardly a modern invention. Reflections on the forms of ethical and political action that this concept has come to convey, as well as about its most prominent surrogates, accountability and answerability, abound in Western thought.[3] Even the most cursory look shows that in Western traditions of ethical and political theory the practice of responsibility is linked with the dilemmas of political action and the ambiguity of accountability. Nascent democratic Athens—whose advent was mediated by Eastern political developments and ideas, from Egypt to Mesopotamia, but whose particular crystallization still constituted a *novum* worthy of the name—was forged against aristocratic power and tyrannical rule and inaugurated the momentous idea of ordinary individuals, famously emblematized by the peasant-citizen, sharing in political rule, thus challenging the politically constituted forms of power at the hands of aristocratic elites and their oligarchic orders.[4] *Isonomia,* at once anchoring and yielding an institutional framework based on a substantive sense of citizenship, became its signature. It signified a sharp break with monarchy and elite rule, thus disrupting the political forms dominant in the ancient world by forging many trends, practices, and ideas into a particular political experience in which citizenship became the central category, even while haunted by the slavery sustaining it.[5]

The idea of responsibility understood as accountability for political actions carried on by citizens became its obvious corollary, a notion that built on older ideas of attributability and tacit imputability already found in the Hebrew Bible.[6] Similarly, there are intimations of something akin to the practice of responsibility in the Homeric poems, but not in the sense of agents autonomously choosing a course of action. Rather, even if the character of the actors is determined by fate, each actor still has to fulfill the obligations of his character and is accountable for any breach in doing what his character demands.[7] Within the Greek tradition the first poetic adumbrations can be found in Greek tragedies, such as Sophocles' *Antigone* and Aeschylus's trilogy *The Oresteia.* The latter stages the question in overtly political terms, namely, from the perspective of the newly inaugurated democratic order and its relationship with the old, as Athene's so-called foundational speech in *The Eumenides* lays out not only a protoconsequentialist political ethic but also suggests the responsibility of citizens for the well-being of the city (681–710). The city was thus questioned on the stage, as the distinguished classicist Luciano Canfora puts it, where, as part of the educational role of Attic theater, questions of ethical and political responsibility in violent predicaments of power were powerfully performed.[8]

But the most sustained discussion of what is now understood as responsibility is found in Aristotle's *Nicomachean Ethics*. Aristotle theorized accountability in relation to his notion of practical wisdom (*phronesis*) where the pursuit of happiness, not duty or obligation, is the central aim. Rather than conceiving ethics based on abstract rules, let alone in subjectivist terms, Aristotle forged an intersubjective moral philosophy that paid particular attention to the life of the individual in a concrete collectivity: the city-state. While one is always in some way a "co-cause" of one's character, Aristotle explicitly emphasized the particulars of the individual and the situation and linked the question of responsibility and purposeful activity with others in situations one partly but never fully constitutes.[9] He thus squarely located his account of responsibility in the predicaments of power mediating—constraining and enabling—collective life. Similarly, it is equally well known that Aristotle painted an image of humans as purposive creatures whose full realization is attainable as members of a collectivity. In this conception, ethics not only presupposes an account of potentiality and act, agent and telos but also of action, situation, and context.[10] Hence, the centrality and interdependence of ends and means in his ethics, an interdependence whose afterlives pervade present-day concerns: that is, how to properly relate means to ends is one of the quintessential questions of a political ethic conceived as an ethics of collective life.[11] This is hardly surprising. For Aristotle's ethics is only fully realized in the context of political life. And that is why prudence is such a central category in his ethical thought, something that demands a sensibility pivoting on a strong sense of limits.[12] In this conception, political and ethical responsibilities are thus cast from the perspective of an acute sense of the limits of human intellect and action.

With the demise of the Hellenic world and the rise of the Roman republic and empire, the practice of responsibility was significantly transformed. The transition from the Greek to the Roman world represented something beyond a change of scale, since Rome emerged as the first territorial empire in Western history. This, momentously, entailed a different conception of citizenship: from an intense, intimate share in power (for those who actually shared it, the citizens) to a less intense conception of political life in which guarantees against power became the overriding meaning of citizenship.[13] Philosophies contemporaneous with the Roman Empire—for example, Stoicism—were incapable of mustering the kind of theorizing that the smaller unit, the Greek city-state, produced. The explanation for this reversal, as Sheldon S. Wolin famously argued, resides in the strong political vibrancy of the city-state, especially Athens: "The decline of the *polis* as the nuclear center of human existence had apparently deprived political thought of its basic unit of analysis, one that it was unable to replace."[14] The contrast between different spaces, that of an imperial order and that of the ancient polis, attested to the relevance of a question that both Plato and Aristotle had posed: "how far could the boundaries of political space be extended, how much dilution by numbers could the notion of citizen-participant withstand, how minor need be the 'public' aspect of decisions before the political association ceased to be political?"[15] These questions pointed beyond the relative homogeneity in the cultural identity of the polis as a political collectivity.[16] Rather, the larger political question involved the fact that the extension of the boundaries of the collective unit represented a shift in the way that citizen participation began to be understood, namely the kind of relationship the citizenry had with its political collectivity. "Where loyalty had earlier come from a sense of common involvement," Wolin perceptively notes, "it was now to be centered in a common reverence with power personified."[17]

This restructuring of political space amounted to a relative autonomization of political power.[18] That depersonalization of political power not only facilitated the defense of private property forms, so eloquently and vehemently defended by Cicero, and the codification of property extracted by means of imperial plundering, it also had the effect of relegating political participation to an ascendant nobility. The result of this was the depletion of citizenship in a political order fostering the conditions for detached and remote forms of depoliticized political identification. In this context the political meaning of citizenship became transmogrified. Citizenship, then, increasingly served a different role: that of an abstract category to encompass cultural, economic, and religious differences—and, most of the time, inequalities—by way of a common status that nevertheless claimed ultimate primacy over other forms of fidelity, fealty, and identification. Henceforth a sense of alienation from the political community brought about a subtle but important shift in the way membership in the collectivity was increasingly understood. In a memorable formulation, Wolin stated, "To compensate for the loss of identity with the community, men looked to legal guarantees against the community."[19] Shared power and its responsibilities rely on proximity and continuous involvement. Only in such continuous closeness is a political actor able to see through the consequences of actions undertaken, sanctioned, or authorized. But the distancing and autonomization of citizenship, its severance from shared rule, enact a different way of conceiving the responsibilities of citizenship for ordinary citizens. It fosters political forms in which a relatively leisured strata is concerned with responsibility in the meaningful sense of shared power. Citizens, in turn, obey rules that protect them, while others govern the political order sanctioning those rules.

With the onset of this order, the idea of being held "responsible" or "liable" became formulated in overwhelmingly legal terms. These formulations found expression mostly in relation to juridical ideas of obligations within the context of Roman law and in terms of individual promises and pledges.[20] The Latin terms *spondeo* and *respondeo*—with their connotations of obligation and promise, appropriate action or reaction, answerability and response—enacted the social dialectic underwriting these ideas.[21] And these reciprocal pledges were presided over by an increasingly vast imperial state. It is thus not incidental that this is the context in which ideas of world ordering gained ascendance in tandem with cosmopolitanism and, eventually, the universalism of a Christianity cloaked by the imperial mantle. All of this constituted historic developments that represented a veritable transition from a visual to an abstract politics and could be considered the first great experience of depoliticization in the Western tradition.[22] Herein, ruling was no longer conceived as a question of shared power, but of legal rule, and the politics of interest trumped the politics of participation. From political life being understood as an association, the onset of an imperial political form increasingly begot a conception of political life as an organization in which citizenship signified a common status, the only common denominator, so to speak, in a rather diverse population that could not even claim autochthony to Rome, much less to the other lands it conquered, looted, and subjugated.

This transformation of the meaning of citizenship is tacitly at work in Cicero's well-known discussion of his two *patriae* in The Laws: the first, the country of origin, the place where one's ancestors rest; the second, and more politically meaningful, the country of citizenship, the one that during Roman times subsumed the other and to which one's ultimate sense of duty is owed (II.5).[23] With the demise of the republic and onset of the empire, this patriotism would become even more abstract as the process of "Romanization" continued to expand and sought to integrate urban patriciates under the one *civic patria* that was Rome. In this context, responsibility was not primarily conceived as a practice, at least not in the Aristotelian sense of the term, but as something closer to an externalized *duty*, as notably articulated by Cicero's treatise *On Duties* (*De Officiis*). But duty here is understood as office, an acceptance of the term that lacks the autonomy and imperative tenor of subsequent connotations, especially within Kantianism. In Giorgio Agamben's exact formulation, to invoke duties signified "what is respectable and appropriate to do according to the circumstances, above all taking account of the agent's social condition."[24] Tacitus's *Agricola* bluntly evidences this contextual dimension and how responsible rule was exercised by a virtuous conqueror, as he soberly foreshadowed some of the themes to which Machiavelli's political ethic would grant powerful theoretical expression (sec. 4, 18–20). Tacitus's, to be sure, was a realist disposition that emerged from sojourns at the outposts of the empire, where the pieties of "a benevolent empire" given expression in Cicero's *On Duties* (II.26–27) were implausible in light of the violence defining these predicaments of power (*Agricola*, sec. 21, 30–32).[25] But it is precisely Cicero's *On Duties* that provides the most formidable theoretical monument of this sense of responsibility. Here the obligations of ruling are laid out alongside the bonds of responsibility that sustain and structure collective life. Candidly, Cicero unveils the *devoirs de situation* that could foster the civic ethic needed to preserve and sustain fealty toward collective life at a time when the aristocratic republican order was disintegrating; equally situational were the multifarious circumstances demanded by the effective exercise of imperial rule.[26]

Written at a moment of acute crisis, *On Duties* is a "manual of civic virtue" that depicts the ideal statesman as a civilian political actor and lays out the necessary virtues that would cement bonds of fidelity and fellowship conducive to the sustainment of a republican order.[27] In *On Duties* Cicero writes about Roman patriotism: "For when with a rational spirit you have surveyed the whole field, there is no social relation among them all more close, none more dear than that which links each one of us to our country—our *res publica*. For this, our native land—our *patria*—weaves together fast and around itself all our loves" (I.57).[28] Political responsibility consisted in fidelity to the patria and its republican political form. The imperial diremption of the two *patriae*, however, created the need for an abstract conception of citizenship in a dual sense: as an abstraction that while providing important legal guarantees is increasingly emptied of any connotation of shared power and as an entity symbolized externally, as above the texture of life that defined the first patria, that of origin; hence, the political significance of Cicero's insistence on codifying the obligations to one's kin vis-à-vis one's fellow citizens as different degrees of fellowship (I.53–57). It is precisely this dislocation, as it were, that led to an acute sense of "context" in Cicero's thought, something that constituted a crucial vector in his account of obligations and how these are to be responsibly enacted (I.31, II.60–61).

After the eclipse of the republic for which Cicero had crafted his political ethic, a narrative of pietas, patriotism, and self-sacrifice emerged, which provided an imperial narrative famously allegorized in Virgil's *Aeneid*: an epic poem retrospectively endowing a much needed legitimating narrative to the new foundation furnished by the Augustan order in the immediate aftermath of the civil wars, which effectively converted partisans into patriots.[29] Patriotism, as Nicholas Xenos has observed, allowed "Augustus to cloak his transformation of Rome's political order in a continuous narrative of the *patria*."[30] Herein, the duties of leadership were closely associated with the founding and preservation of an empire. In this imperial context a strong sense of participation in a community was present in early Christianity, where political thought was at once revived and neutralized.[31] Although the Gospels of the *New Testament* do not envisage anything resembling political questions, strong ethical concerns were formulated. The Sermon on the Mount articulated the precepts of a Christian life, while offering a robust critique of the pernicious effects of the accumulation of wealth that characterized the Roman aristocracy in the age of empire (Matthew 6:24, 11:28, 19:16–30). Fidelity to these principles and the *figure* of Jesus Christ constitute the core of the New Testament's ethics of conviction. Even so, there is a practice of responsibility in this ethic, but it is not conceptualized in terms of Cicero's contextualism or as a protoconsequentialism. Rather, it is expressed in terms of a particular situation demanding a response that in a memorable occasion even invokes "the sword" and thus entails drawing enmity lines (Matthew 10:34–36, 12:46–50). Responsibility was thus recast in ethical terms and in imperatives that were communal in their outward expression, but nonetheless remained restricted to the ethical and theological domain in terms of salvation in Christ Jesus and his message. For, when the Day of Judgment arrives, "He will repay everyone as their deeds deserve" (Romans 2:6), thus conjoining ideas of answerability and imputability.

By the end of the fourth century, the Roman Empire witnessed a significant centralization of power and the effective determination of a hierarchy of status and privilege, with an astonishing concentration of wealth at the top of that hierarchy.[32] At the time, as the Roman Church was beginning to assert itself more forcefully, Christian universalism was increasingly defined by "an atmosphere of relaxed hierarchy" evoking the world of "late Roman society with a gentler face."[33] This is also the historical conjuncture in which a Christianized version of "civic euergetism" structured a transformation in the role of wealthy patrons: from giving to citizens and the city—love of the city—to the vocation and responsibility of giving to the poor—love of the poor—in what constituted yet another step in the eventual consolidation of the church as the locus of civic life in an era of political closure largely due to imperial pacification and depoliticization.[34] If, from the late third century to the fall of the Western empire, the political responsibilities of ruling were the purview of emperors, and the bond tying all cities of the empire to each other was fealty to the emperor by his servants, by the late fourth century this changed significantly.[35] In an age of intense proselytism, bishops bore special responsibilities and acted as "ecclesiastical rulers" answerable to the Last Judgment in a context in which Christianity had become the only meaningful bond between aristocrats and their subordinated dependents.[36] Emblematic of this moment is Ambrose's rewriting of Cicero's *On Duties*.[37] In Ambrose's version, Cicero's emphasis on intense bonds of cohesion is recast in terms of fidelity to the Church. The Church thus emerges as the *res publica*, a displacement at once politicizing the Church and depoliticizing political discourse. The structures of duties—*officium*, with its connotation of action and both its subjective and objective determinants, and originally devoid of the moralism that modern ideas of duty convey—were transformed according to these new specifications.[38]

Responsibilities and duties were accordingly recast in terms of a new configuration of politically meaningful space, as the universal Church reconceived the spatial coordinates of these commitments in terms of its growth and spread while severing these virtues from the space of a political community. The res publica at once enabling and actualizing responsibilities was no longer the city, but the Church. By the fifth century, in places like Gaul, bishops were aristocrats; by the seventh century "a clerical elite" occupied the place and responsibilities once bestowed to the Roman senate, thus transforming the aristocratic-senatorial love of *libertas* and its locus, *Roma aeterna*, into "the solemn façade of Papal Rome."[39] Subsequently, especially in the Aristotelianism of Thomas Aquinas's *Summa Theologica*, an image of humans as purposive creatures, as makers of their own domain and locus of action, continued to lend credence to collective notions of responsiveness and avowed the collective texture of responsibility by depicting a self that is an agent within a community of agents under rubrics of morality and virtue. Still, only within the universal Church could these commitments be actualized; and this in a hierarchical context in which papal authority theoretically coexisted with the independent roles of councils sharing power and responsibilities.

That the categories of political thought were largely transmogrified in the political theology of the universal Church, and political practice was mostly visible in its engagement with the temporal world, need not eclipse the modicum of political life found outside its purview during Late Antiquity and the early Middle Ages. There was another configuration of political space that coexisted with the universal Church and the sense of community it simultaneously fostered and relied upon. Here the Carolingian Empire's attempt to reweld the unity of the West by refurbishing the imperial structure of the fallen Roman Empire is emblematic: Charlemagne presided over an imperial system that sought to recreate a political order in the form of "public" authority presiding over private jurisdictions that involved local public authorities and office holding with political responsibilities as well as sanctioned local rulers, in the forms of lords and bishops, through offices conforming to the supervening grid of public power it sought to establish.[40] Equally illustrative are the transformations generated by its demise and the disappearance of the tenuous public authority it represented. With its collapse, the onset of feudal relations brought with it the "parcellization of sovereignty" that defined this period.[41] Before the onset of absolutism and, with it, the first interstate system, the "political map" of Europe all through the Renaissance was not composed of homogeneous, let alone clearly demarcated, political units: rather, as Perry Anderson writes, "its political map was an inextricably superimposed and tangled one, in which different juridical instances were geographically interwoven and stratified, and plural alliances, asymmetrical suzerainties and anomalous enclaves abounded."[42]

In the Italian peninsula, the early communes that emerged within the interstices of seigniorial structures represented "anomalous" political enclaves.[43] Initially conceived as mostly informal assemblies, these early communes recreated aspects of civic life and constituted a productive precondition for the emergence of the more recognizable political city-states that defined the Renaissance.[44] Creative adaptation within received inherited parameters of elite rule, as part of a defensive response to the demise of public power and the perceived failures of traditional hierarchies, is what ushered the distinctive assemblies that defined the advent of the early communes and their conquest of autonomy. The formalization of these autonomous orders was a steady but nonteleological process in which autonomous city government was increasingly consolidated.[45] In due course, this formalization—which, among other things, encompassed institutionalizing informal assemblies and office rotation—was no longer the defensive response to a power vacuum but represented the actual regularization and routinization of the power these elites had attained.

Institutionally, these communes displayed ingenious creativity and relied on collaboration from below, even if any sense of "communal identity" was a retrospective projection, an invented origin. These were elite bound and ruled and, as such, "shot through" with hierarchies codified along with aristocratic and militaristic values.[46] The formation of the communes pitted traditional aristocratic elites, especially bishops, against the new elites, even if bishops proved adaptable and in some instances continued to exert power in ways that compromised any actual autonomous practice. Stated differently, bishops no longer presided over these autonomous collectivities but became actors within them, acting in complex relationships of competition and alliances with other elites with whom they shared political responsibilities. While hierarchical and violent, these late medieval communes retrieved a stronger sense of self-governance, fostering proximity to the exercise of power, its responsibilities and consequences.

In this context the principal locus of political responsibility was found in the peculiar institution of the *podestá*.[47] This is not to deny, however, the extent to which at the local level—*cappella, contrata, populus, vicinanza*—the political experience gained by a modicum of shared power fostered participation and nurtured a sense of political responsibility. It is also not meant to diminish the transformations brought about by political mobilizations of the *popolo*.[48] But it is hard to overlook the limited significance of these instances of shared power in the political space that was the thirteenth-century city-state, as the experience of shared power and political responsibility was increasingly centralized and thus concentrated in offices like the *podestá* and its sometimes ally and sometimes antipode *capitani del popolo*.[49] Even allowing for the great variation that characterized this office across the different communes, the authority of the podestá frequently included representing the commune in foreign relations, presiding over communal councils and having a voice in the commune's major decisions, enforcing civic order, and, last but not least, the enforcing of justice. Although a salaried officer, not "an independent ruler," this office was often held by wealthy individuals, including lords, who for all their autonomous self-government remained de jure subjected to the late Roman Empire.[50] Indeed, in the late twelfth century the podestá was basically an "imperial vicar," something that began to change with the ascendance of local communal power during the thirteenth century, which is a period also defined by the emergence of the popolo.[51] Of greater significance is that these vicars frequently were not citizens of the city over which they presided. More to the point, these "external lords" sought to preserve or rescue a modicum of civic order by pacifying "factions and feuds" within the cities, yet external lords who not only mediated but also defended and exploited these communities.[52] It is in the city-states of the Renaissance that inherited this autonomy that a robust revival of political life effectively took place. As fitting to a Renaissance sensibility, this period evoked the intense sense of proximity and political life of the cities of antiquity in a unique combination of the forms of participation associated with Athenian democracy and the Roman republic. In the formulation offered by a leading historian, "Right from the start in fact, the notion of *rinascita*, with the whole Renaissance scheme of history, was closely linked in Italy with the revolutions of towns: the revival or survival of *civilitas* or municipal *libertas*."[53] These Renaissance city-states were first and foremost urban units of commercial industriousness, but, like the seigniorial lords ruling the countryside, these cities were violent war-making entities.[54] Yet these republics had limited military capability, as their vulnerability to external incursions and the predatory behavior of neighboring kingdoms and principalities, the encroachments and predations of the papacy, and, later on, the absolutist monarchies of Spain and France amply attest.[55]

These violent city-states provided the spatial configuration for the practices of ethical inquiry that mediated not only Machiavelli's political ethic but that which found subsequent expression in Montaigne and Vico.[56] These humanist inquiries tended to place ethics at the center of social and political life, even if the center of gravity was the individual as an ethical and political actor: inquiries that sought to confront the uncertainties of action in violent predicaments of power by articulating ethical consciousness and political agency in a human-made world. What emerged was either reflection on the ethical dimension of social life—Thomas More in England; Juan Luis Vives in Spain; and Petrarch, Leonardo Bruni, and Lorenzo Valla in Italy—or a reconfiguration of the intersection of ethics and politics most prominently formulated in the writings of Niccolò Machiavelli. Whereas these figures often converged on the rejection of scholasticism and the authority of the Church, what is most significant is the absence of ethics, or ethical treatises, as part of these ethical inquiries. In place of philosophical elucidations of morality, these inquiries constitute reflections about the ethical dimension of existence or individual and collective life. Forms of inquiry that emerged in tandem with the new humanism of the Renaissance reverberated in selective forms of ethical discourse to the present; yet forms of inquiry that are tied to the advent of Cartesian rationality in the seventeenth century, the autonomization of ethics, and the turn to the apodictic in eighteenth-century philosophy ultimately became recessive and remainders, at best, of a different, bygone era.

Similarly, the spatial configuration to which these republican cities conformed, and the forms of republican political responsibility in the context of the self-government they fostered, turned out to be short-lived. Indeed, Machiavelli's *Discourses* could be seen as not only a theoretical monument of this political experience but also an eloquent lapidary statement. At the very historical moment that Machiavelli was composing his political theory and its corollary political ethic, which he famously likened to the voyages of the age that were causing so much awe in Europe for their connection to the classic trope of embarking on "an untrodden path," absolutism was gaining ascendancy in Europe and with it the modern crystallization of monarchical political forms.[57] These momentous historical processes inaugurated a political order that rendered self-government anachronistic, along with any sense of political responsibility associated with participation and shared power. Additionally, a particular diremption of the ethical and the political also occurred within the Renaissance, which had significant implications for the transmogrification of responsibility and its emergence as a concept anchored in the individual. This was partially the result of the breakdown of traditional forms of authority and obligation. It could be seen in philosophical attempts to formulate rational justifications for morality whose context of occurrence can be traced to the onset of political absolutism and the scientific vocation and subsequent revolution.[58] Now the moral domain was sharply divorced from the theological realm. And with such separation came the need to rethink autonomous principles of action for rulers and a concomitant ethics for the ruled.

Within the spatial coordinates brought about by the age of absolutism, yet another transformation of ethical and political life emerged. The word *responsibility* started to appear within the intellectual contexts of two distinctively modern traditions of inquiry: an ethical account of responsibility that took shape within broad Kantian parameters and a political conception of responsibility folded within theorizations of modern constitutionalism in both its monarchical and republican variations. What these have in common is reliance on the individual as the locus of responsibility and action, even if such actions are carried out in the name of reason or the republic.[59] Also in common is the disaffiliation of responsibility from active involvement in collective life: whereas responsibility for humankind tends to despatialize the concept, even while such invocations had important political implications in specific places, responsibility for a republic still had a clear spatial locus, even if its exercise often relied on a ruling elite. The latter still contained a robust connotation, albeit the responsibilities of citizenship became diluted as the sharing of political power was minimized. This diminishment became further exacerbated by the most momentous change of the time: the encounter with the New World and the wave of European imperialism that it inaugurated. This is the historical crucible in which the spatial configurations lending credence to earlier accounts of political responsibility were irreversibly transformed. Citizen, senator, bishop, lord, consul, and podestá—these bearers of political responsibilities were either transformed beyond recognition or rendered anachronistic.

MODERN PERSONATIONS

Carlo Galli has rightly identified the origins of modern politics in a series of *spatial revolutions*: the Copernican revolution and the decentering of the earth; the "discovery of the new world" and its transformation of planetary space, and its ensuing consequences, from changing cosmologies to displacements of trade routes; the crisis of economic spatiality (*spazialità*), from "open fields" to enclosures and the violent spatial transformations that accompanied the "primitive accumulation" of capitalism in Europe; the challenge to Christian conceptions of space by the Lutherans and their conception of interiority, something that greatly contributed to the rise of modern individualism and its rather solipsistic relationship with God, the Other.[60] The Reformation is like a vanishing mediator not only for the advent of the profane modality of politics that eventually governed the onset of republicanism, which contained the most robust sense of political responsibility during the late eighteenth and early nineteenth centuries, but for the emergence of philosophical accounts of modern subjectivity. However solipsistic ideas of salvation or "the priesthood of all believers" often were, they had collective dimensions that modern theorists of power and philosophies of the subject mostly disavowed.

Similarly, in the midst of theological elucidations, questions and problems associated with political thought were worked out. Nowhere was this the case more remarkably than in the retrieval of political responsibility at work in Calvin's account of civil magistrates, their office and duties: for it presaged the account of personation that figures so prominently in Hobbes's civic ethic.[61] In Calvin's account, political office was thoroughly depersonalized, and the figure of the magistrate emerged as an actor who actualizes a law he does not originate. Magistrates and subjects alike owe fidelity to the institution, not its occupant, even if ultimate responsibility was owed to God. Subsequently, in a text that was almost contemporaneous with Hobbes's *Leviathan*, but that belongs to a thinker of a radically different milieu and intellectual temperament, one finds a significant usage of the term *responsible* that tacitly adduces its most important political connotations, even if couched in theological terms. In Pascal's *Provincial Letters* (1656–57), a fictionalized Jesuit priest states: "Do you not know yet that our Society answers [*répond*] for all the books of our Fathers? . . . Thus our whole body is responsible [*responsable*] for the books of each of our fathers."[62] Here ideas of personation and collective identity are evidently at work. And the idea of responsibility is formulated in terms of a corporate body authorizing individual works, with its members owning up and collectively answering for them. Answering and responding thereby emerge as two connotations of responsibility that are related to a collective entity, a collectivity with shared purpose whose members own up to the words and actions bearing its name. The implication of Pascal's Jesuit formulation is clear: every Jesuit, qua member of the order, is responsible for what is collectively authorized by the order and thus bears its name. A sense of responsibility that assumes a diachronic identity, which establishes binding responsibilities across generations of Jesuits for what is publicly authorized and sanctioned in their name.[63] Unlike a political collectivity, spatial coordinates do not bind it, albeit it establishes representations of the place and relations that constitute the identity in question among its members.[64]

Even so, political and philosophical individualizations of responsibility did not develop on a par, as each responded to different imperatives internal to the two very different fields. But, precisely because these are different semiautonomous orders, their coeval actualization is even more striking. Hobbes's *Leviathan* brings philosophical and political individualization, along with abstract and dedifferentiated ideas of space and time, and ideas of *necessary* political obligation, into a single field of vision as part of a coherent conceptualization of personation before the philosophical-subjectivist conception of responsibility constructed within German idealism.[65] One of *Leviathan's* achievements is to show how "Naturall Reason" is able to scientifically deduct binding principles of sovereignty and obedience encompassing the "Right of Soveraigns" and the "Duty of Subjects" by way of the "Science of Naturall Justicĕ" through which "men may learn thereby, both how to govern, and how to obey."[66] Hobbes thus exacerbates the severance of ethics and politics by radically autonomizing political life away from ethical considerations.[67]

Hobbes's political thought thus offers a striking theoretical articulation of the perils the fragmentation of public authority represents by advocating the establishment of a public authority, but without any free legitimized politics. In this scheme the sovereign power has a monopoly on political life and its responsibilities. Individuals are privatized, and there is no deliberation, let alone legitimized contestation, between sovereign and subjects over the public authority the sovereign enacts, its uses and resources, within the "Frontiers of their Kingdomes."[68] It is in chapter 16 of *Leviathan*, titled "Of Persons, Authors, *and Things Personated*," that Hobbes establishes nothing less than the basis of what J. G. A. Pocock has characterized as a "civic morality" of personation.[69] This account prefigured an important aspect of the political and ethical dilemmas subsequently confronted by theorists of political responsibility in the context of the transatlantic age of revolutions: Hobbes formulates a strong sense of the attributability of actions to those who generate the forms of power that make the actions possible and suggests that those who originally generate that power authorize it. But he also poses the important question of the ineluctability of limits in any politically meaningful sense of responsibility qua attributability of the actions of the state to its subjects.[70]

The chapter's opening establishes Hobbes's definition of personhood. By then he is already addressing aspects of the quintessential question of political power, "who, whom" (as Lenin once formulated it) and he stresses the centrality of imputability: "A PERSON, is he, *whose words or actions are considered, either as his own, or as representing the words or actions of an other man, or of any other thing to whom they are attributed, whether Truly or by Fiction*."[71] *Who* personates *whom* and under what authority? Better still, *who* has power over *whom* and is thus ultimately responsible for its exercise? These questions have critical bearing on larger questions of political power and responsibility. Fictional or not, at this point Hobbes is concerned with establishing how a person is an agent to whom actions can be attributed. At the center of this conception of personation is the idea that actions, either a person's or someone else's (as a person can act in the name of someone else and that *someone else* could either be an individual or a collectivity), are imputable to an authorizing agent or entity that is ultimately responsible for the actions undertaken. Drawing on theatrical metaphors, Hobbes makes the point in the following way: "So that a *Person*, is the same that an *Actor* is, both on the Stage and in common Conversation; and to *Personate*, is to *Act*, or *Represent* himselfe , or any other; and he that acteth another is said to beare his Person, or act in his name . . . and is called in diverse occasions, diversely; as a *Representer*, or *Representative*, *a Lieutenant*, a *Vicar*, an *Attorney*, a *Deputy*, a *Prosecutor*, an *Actor*, and the like."[72] All these figures personate the actual source of the actions they carry out, the person or entity that is ultimately responsible for them.

Personating someone is thus to "act in his name." And authority, defined in terms of "the Right of doing any act," is then cast in terms of authorization. But Hobbes then introduces another aspect: authorship. For not only is authority conferred to a person, but "he that "owneth his words and actions, is the AUTHOR."[73] Consequently, Hobbes argues, imputability to actions is broadly conceived in terms of authorization and authorship. What is more, the sovereign actor has the prerogative of drawing from the resources and power generated by the authorizing authorship of a multitude: "And in him consisteth the Essence of the Commonwealth; which (to define it) is *One Person, of whose Acts a great Multitude, by mutuall Covenants one with another, have made themselves everyone the Author, to the end he may use the strength and means of them all, as he shall think expedient, for their Peace and Common Defense."*[74] Hobbes, accordingly, formulates one of the cruxes of a genuinely political sense of responsibility: even if it is someone else who enacts and actualizes forms of power, the members of the collectivity generating that power, and thus authorizing their actualization and enactment, are responsible for the actions carried out by an officer or state acting in their name. While authorization, *pace* Hobbes, is never entirely coextensive with coauthorship, it does enact a sense of accountability and draws a distinction between how actors, authorizers, and authors may be held responsible.[75] In this conception, degrees of responsibility are adduced: responsibility as liability, codified criminally and in terms of positive law for an actor; political responsibility in terms of structural beneficiaries; and responsibility in terms of citizenship. Naturally, access to power largely determines the degrees of responsibility adjudicated to the last category.

Yet, even if Hobbes's theorization opens the possibility of establishing these levels of responsibility, the overriding logic of his account tends to close, if not collapse, the gap between authority and authorization. That this is something attributable to the despotic theoretical temperament that *Leviathan* exhibits goes without saying. Equally attributable to it, even if less noticed, is how Hobbes's civic morality involves thinking of responsibility in hyperventilated terms, a modality of responsibilization *avant la lettre*.[76] In this civic morality, individual subjects are responsibilized for the acts of the sovereign through the identification of authorization and authorship on the basis of which a binding covenant is enacted. Political responsibility is thus made consonant with neutralization and pacification in order to stabilize a political order guaranteeing peace, security, and industry.[77] Rulers rule, while the ruled just assent but nevertheless remain responsible for the actions of their rulers.

This order, however, is based on volition and covenants of words: fragile notions that remained fraught with anxiety throughout the seventeenth century.[78] Hobbes, accordingly, sketched the corollary notion of obligation that ultimately undergirds this idea of responsibility by way of his account of a covenant. No continuous involvement is necessary in the adjudication of responsibility for the author of a binding covenant: "when the Actor maketh a Covenant by Authority, he bindeth thereby the Author, no lesse than if he had made it himselfe; and no lesse subjecteth him to all the consequences of the same."[79] Obviously, as it is widely known, enacting a covenant in Hobbes's *Leviathan* has strict specifications, not to mention clear external limits—the Law of Nature—constraining the extent of the powers surrendered by those entering a covenant, especially as these are secured by the monopoly of violence, its simplification and conversion, which sustains the political order Hobbes figures—"And Covenants, without the Sword, are but Words, and of no strength to secure a man at all."[80] And this is especially so in "an ungrounded political order," one produced by a "self-consciously scientific political theory" replacing older, cultic, approaches that emphasized the need to tend and cultivate political life with the spatial abstractions of modern science.[81]

Still, what is of great significance but largely underappreciated is the centrality of limits to responsibility. Limited responsibility therefore runs in tandem with radical responsabilization. "For no man is obliged by a Covenant, whereof he is not Author; nor consequently by a Covenant made against, or beside the Authority he gave."[82] Forged by the passion for order that is reason, these covenants are completely binding, but limited.[83] Precisely because they are politically binding and supported by politically sanctioned violence, there have to be clear limits to the extent of the responsibilities involved as well as a clear locus of action. Or, as he clearly formulates it: "Every man giving their common Representer, Authority from himselfe in particular; and owning all the actions the Representer doth, in case they give him Authority without stint: Otherwise, when they limit him in what, and how farre he shall represent them, none of them owneth more, than they gave him commission to Act."[84] Hobbes clinches his argument by simultaneously invoking the multitude while neutralizing it. "A Multitude of men are made *One* Person, when they are by one man, or one Person, Represented," Hobbes writes. The unity evoked by oneness is the key term here: "For it is the *Unity* of the Representer, not the *Unity* of the Represented that maketh the Person *One*. . . . And *Unity* cannot otherwise be understood in Multitude."[85] So central is unity, and Hobbes is careful to note how when "the Representative consist of many men" there is a chance of division, which risks an equal split and thus the neutralization of both sides, leaving the actor "mute, and uncapable of action."[86] But in his preferred solution, which bestows unity in the "Representer" who acts, the multitude is then neutralized and bound by a covenant at once enacting and limiting the range and extent of the political responsibility of the authority legitimizing its power.

Personation, accordingly, entails a transfer of the responsibility to act, while tacitly relying on a dual sense of accountability: that of the actor to the broad script provided by the terms of the covenant and that of the author, the ultimate source of authority, and the one in whose name the actor speaks and who ultimately *owns* the actions carried by his authority and in his name. Herein Hobbes's complicated articulation of the intersection between authorization and authorship reemerges once again.[87] Complicated, since at first glance it seems that Hobbes wants to have it both ways: to claim that authorizing is authorship, and thus collapse the gap between the two for the purpose of legitimizing the ensuing order, while also severing the authority and authorization by way of an account of personation in which only the unity of the actor can be an author, even if a multitude authorizes it. What is one to make of this seemingly antinomian argument? One way of parsing out the stakes is to read the passages in question politically; namely, by looking at what it is that Hobbes is trying to do by binding the multitude to the unity of the one, which is the only thing that can make it capable of speech and action; but also by considering how he wants the individuals, not any intermediary or corporate body, to be held responsible for the actions of the sovereign, thus at once insulating the actor from ultimate responsibility, thereby excluding any form of collective agency, while also recognizing limits to sovereign power.[88] Responsibility is thus borne by whoever owns the action, not its agent. Conversely, responsibility is conditional. But the ultimate message of *Leviathan* implies an unmediated relation between the individual and the state that excludes any modicum of shared power; it rather "places all the rights at the representative's disposal and all the burdens at the represented."[89] Similarly, it authorizes the codification of property relations by abstractly making people authors of an allocation that only the sovereign power, qua "Person that Represents" the "Common-wealth," could undertake.[90] This emphasis on the unmediated relation between individuals and the state and on the limits to sovereignty keenly reflects sociological realities of English absolutism; and these are sedimentations that constitute part of the content of Hobbes's theoretical forms.[91] In the architecture of Hobbes's argument, the contrast and displacements of a civic morality of personation, along with its sociological and spatial presuppositions of early modern period absolutism, can be grasped.

The political truncations of Hobbes's conception are real enough. Whereas the capacity for personation is important for a political ethic, its politicalness is depleted in Hobbes's account. Although personation entails the intersubjective ability of politically owning up to the actions of political actors to which one is bound in a covenant, something which is, in and of itself, a central component of a political sense of responsibility, nowhere does Hobbes avow the shared power that genuine authorship and responsibility presupposes and thus requires. What instead emerges are the lineages of a logic of responsibilization that demands shared liability but not shared power. This is, indeed, the nub of Hobbes's argument: whereas personation is emphasized, the continuous sense of shared power and proximity in the exercise of political rule is debarred from his account. For personation to actualize its more robustly political import, authors need to at least have the capacity to meaningfully act in a political order in which shared political power is not secluded to one-time gestures of sanction or approbation, but rather involves its active mobilization and participation. Its depletions notwithstanding, Hobbes's articulation of personation delivers some basic political truths: it portends an economy of political responsibility and obligation that structured subsequent debates about the mystification of authorizations, and the limits of responsibility and accountability, in the republican political forms binding emergent liberal and, later, liberal-democratic orders. But the despotic cast of mind that defines the architecture of Hobbes's theory truncates such articulation and renders it abstract and dehistoricized. It not only remains indifferent to culture and political economy—even while formally reproducing some of the imperatives of the nascent agrarian capitalism underpinning the social formation that is Hobbes's immediate locus of reflection—but his construction has a remarkable *ex nihilo* ring to it. And it is equally indifferent to space and time beyond the smooth spatiality of abstract geometrical reasoning that supervenes his theorization of a *realm*.[92]

These were the main contours of the situation in which the concept of responsibility emerged in seventeenth-century Europe. Sediments of this historical situation, its imperatives and forms, remained in subsequent formulations of responsibility. That this is so can be readily seen in the turn to subjectivity, which became conjoined with the emergence of agrarian capitalism and commercial relations—all of it anchored in individual actors and transactions that created the conditions for an even more overwhelmingly individualized sense of responsibility. Unsurprisingly, with the onslaught on tradition associated with the Enlightenment came a new sense of responsibility in the context of the new social morality proposed by the French philosophes.[93]

But this was a sense of responsibility dirempted from political space and often devoid of any political involvement. The entry for *philosopher* in the 1694 *Dictionnaire de l'Académie française* tells the tale: "Philosopher: one who devotes himself to research-work in connexion [sic] with the various sciences and who devotes himself to research and who seeks from their effects to trace their causes and principles. A name applied to one who lives a quiet and secluded life remote from the stir and troubles of the world. It is occasionally used to denote someone of undisciplined mind who regards himself as above the responsibilities and duties of civil life."[94] Fidelity to a philosophical vocation and its freedom of inquiry became a leitmotif, as the political valences of responsibility were truncated in monarchical orders, with many philosophes indifferent to political life and its forms.

But the transmutations of ideas of the self, with attendant claims of authenticity in the context of this new morality, eventually led to the reclaiming of the idea of the citizen as the bearer of responsibility for a political order that could enact the conditions for its flourishing.[95] It is with the advent of transatlantic revolutions during the late eighteenth and early nineteenth centuries that enlightened ideas of citizenship in republican orders fully recast the Enlightenment's new morality politically. Such recasting and enactment, however, demanded a radical transformation of space. This radical change of scale, and the ensuing transformation of power and political space, can be seen in the rather contemptuous attitude of *The Federalist Papers* to decentralized, local politics. The republicanism advocated in *The Federalist* had specific spatial specifications that bear directly on its plea for a transmogrification of republican tenets to make them consistent with an "extended republic" at once invulnerable to the turmoil and instability that, in their view, led to the demise of its antecessors and suitable for further expansion. This is the historic moment in which principles of New World patriotism and the creation of republics coextensive with nation-states, often of semicontinental size, crystallized.[96]

In this context, a new conception of political responsibility was formulated and actualized. The writings of Simón Bolívar, Benjamin Constant, and James Madison are testaments to how in the settlements following transatlantic revolutions and wars of independence, the democratic moment reactivated by these travails, which required reanimating the idea of ordinary people sharing responsibility for their fate, was transformed, accommodated, and contained by republican constitutions.[97] From then on, political responsibility was circumscribed by an elite of elected officials, and its locus of action was mostly conceived in relation to institutions devised to curtail the possibility of arbitrary power, while the citizen's sense of responsibility was significantly smothered. Simón Bolívar, for instance, spoke about political rights, duties, and responsibilities, in the context of the Latin American wars of independence and the constitutional settlements that followed, in terms of sustaining a new order that involved little political participation on the part of its dutiful citizens.[98] Meanwhile, for Hamilton and Madison, in a "compound republic" the state cannot be "a servile pliancy" to the passions of the moment (no. 51, 71). Rather, its responsibility is toward the people, even when it sometimes leads to clashes with the people. Even if something like "executive power" ultimately depends on the people as a source of legitimacy, it has to be kept above the fray of the democratic passions of the day (no. 10, 63).

That *The Federalist* articulates a republicanism embodying a synthesis of monarchy, aristocracy, and democracy, while emptying out the last of any substantive meaning by radically redefining popular sovereignty, is clear enough. What bears mention in the present discussion, however, is the centrality of responsibility and the distinction of means/ends for these advocates of republicanism, especially in light of their advocacy of an enduring central power. One of Hamilton's formulations constitutes a good starting point for the means/ends question: "A government ought to contain itself every power requisite for the full accomplishment of the objects committed to its care, and to the complete execution of the trusts for which it is responsible; free from every other control but a regard to the public good and to the sense of the people."[99] Hamilton's comment about the need to allocate appropriate powers consonant with the responsibilities imputed to the national government takes place within the context of an intervention that opens up with a rather philosophical elucidation of some of the "maxims of ethics and politics," which offers an explicit engagement with the relationship between "means and ends" that are offered as "primary truths, or first principles, upon which all subsequent reasoning must depend."[100] Here, to be sure, Hamilton is mostly concerned with the extent and range of federal power, not the responsibility of its exercise. But his discussion is relevant for a consideration of the latter. For in elucidating these maxims he suggests that "there cannot be an effect without a cause; that the means ought to be proportioned to the end; that every power ought to be commensurate with its object; that there ought to be no limitation of a power destined to effect a purpose which is itself incapable of limitation."[101] Limitless purposes thus logically require potentially limitless power as a means for their enactment and realization.

The immediate occasion for these remarks was the hotly contested question of taxation. Even so, Hamilton's own appeals to logic and primary axioms suggest a wider, more general applicability of these maxims. "As the duties of superintending the national defense and of securing the public peace against foreign or domestic violence involve a provision for casualties and dangers to which no possible limits can be assigned, the power of making that provision ought to know no other bounds than the exigencies of the nation and the resources of the community."[102] And a national government, as Madison elsewhere emphasizes, holds "not only an authority over the individual citizens, but an indefinite supremacy over all persons and things, so far as they are objects of lawful government" (no. 40).[103] Such momentous power, authorized by "the people" but duly insulated from the masses of ordinary people, demanded an exceedingly powerful yet delicate sense of responsibility on the part of rulers. In the eyes of Harvey C. Mansfield Jr., a champion of Madisonian constitutionalism, every political form ought to be concerned with tyrannical power, including republics.[104] And these have to reckon with the "tyranny of the majority," something particularly ubiquitous in a postrevolutionary political order with long-standing traditions of popular involvement in collective life. The autonomization of the exercise of responsible power, and its concomitant structural insulation, bestows upon this power a delicate sense of responsibility: what Mansfield calls "a new kind of responsibility in executives—constitutional and republican," for the constitution and institutional forms that prevent the tyranny of democracy.

How exactly is responsibility so conceived actually defined? While occasionally presented by Hamilton mostly in terms of the fulfillment of duties assigned (no. 23), it is Madison who forthrightly elucidates this notion. In the context of ruling a large republic, responsibility carries a dual meaning. First, there is responsibility in the exercise of power for the people by agents that exhibit temperance in their use of power. Madison's rendering: "Responsibility, in order to be reasonable, must be limited to objects within the power of the responsible party, and in order to be effectual, must relate to operations of that power, of which a ready and proper judgment can be formed by the constituents" (no. 63).[105] Or in Mansfield's formulation: "'accountable,' 'responsive' to the people, but also on their behalf: responsible politicians in this sense do for the people what they cannot do for themselves but *can* form a judgment about."[106] Responsibility is thus displaced to representatives and ministers who rule in the name of the people. This set the stage for an idea of responsibility whose fidelity is to the institutions sustaining a particular form of life and for a conception of responsibility as the prerogative of an elite.

But there is a second element to Madison's theorization that opens a different vista within the landscape of republicanism. This consists in the tacit avowal of how political responsibility is reinvigorated by the accountability of rulers—in this case "the senate," which is then presented as a "select and stable member of government"—to the people through regularized elections, even if Madison submits that a certain irresponsibility emerges out of the electoral process: "the want, in some important cases, of a due responsibility in the government to the people, arising from that frequency of elections which in other cases produces this responsibility."[107] Elections breed accountability and establish the political equivalent of a community of fate between rulers and ruled, but elections open the possibility for popular passions to have undue influence on government and thus threaten Madison's precious goal of blending "stability with liberty" in an extensive republic whose further expansion the authors of *The Federalist Papers* not only envisioned but encouraged.[108] In this republican order, democratic citizenship is conceived not in terms of equality and shared power, but is recast as equality in consenting to the responsible exercise of power.[109] With the neutralization of popular majorities threatening the new political order by virtue of the dual role of the spatial coordinates of the "compound republic"—its vastness debarred any large majority from coalescing, while it encouraged ideologies of self-reliant improvement on the basis of the expectations and hopes that its "unoccupied space" provided—the stabilization of a republican regime that not merely protected private rights, but encouraged commerce and expansion, was conquered.[110]

That more than just a modicum of depoliticization was purpose-fully built into the American "compound republic" is, therefore, clear enough. Madison famously sought to drown factions in the vastness of the republic, in the "greater sphere of country," to insulate the central power from threats, especially that "rage . . . for an equal division of property."[111] And an expansive republic dilutes the spatial coordinates of political life, thereby impairing the formation of large majorities that might threaten the mainstay of collective life. "Extend the sphere," Madison famously wrote, "and you take in a variety of parties and interests; you make it less probable that a majority of the whole will have a common motive to invade the rights of other citizens; or if such a common motive exists, *it will be more difficult for all who feel it to discover their own strength, and to act in unison with each other.*"[112] One need not go beyond the paper in question to see what the actual meaning of the phrase "the rights of other citizens" is and how the overriding concern is to neutralize threats to the property relations underpinning the social formation, which are cast as necessities "in civilized nations."[113] Of course, much has taken place since Madison penned these words, including the vast transformation of the American polity, the virtual disappearance of the democratic threats from which he sought to insulate the federal government, and the exacerbation of the depoliticization he saw as constitutive of the dynamic stability of the republic. Still, it set the overall coordinates that would pacify political life and made very clear the spatial presuppositions of such neutralization. It runs in tandem with the subsequent individualization of responsibility. Both at once symptomatize and dilute the sphere of political life.[114]

If classical republics had to be small, which was an important element of the antimonarchical core of republicanism—in contrast with the vastness of kingdoms and realms—now republics could dwarf royal realms. In this transatlantic context, representation dislodged participatory conceptions of politics, thus reworking the architecture of Hobbes's theorization while retaining its decidedly antidemocratic bent cloaked in ideas of order and stability. And it is precisely the quest for stability that would become a signature of Constant's political thought, arguably the thinker that reflected most forthrightly on the question of responsibility in the context of "representative" institutions. But a watershed event separates Madison and Constant's ideas of representation and the political responsibilities associated with it: the French Revolution, an event that further altered the spatiality of modern political thought. With characteristic metaphoric intensity, Jules Michelet recorded this change, as he noticed how fidelity to the revolutionary credo and its universalism—liberty, equality, fraternity—fundamentally transformed the stratification of internal political space: the revolution "killed geography," for its eventuation "disregards time and space" by shattering the old regime while smoothing out the political landscape in the name of the revolutionary triad.[115] This reconfiguration of space also had an international dimension, especially during its externalization, the exportation of the 1804 "civil code" across Europe, and the rise of romantic nationalism to resist it.[116] These processes triggered yet another transformation of political space whose implications would reverberate through the concatenations defining the nineteenth-century moment of the transatlantic age of revolutions: from the ascendance and subsequent cordoning of Haiti, the first black independent nation-state in the Western hemisphere, to the republics emerging out of the wars of independence in South America. If Hobbes's theoretical despotism abstracted space for the sake of a variation of absolute power, the French Revolution brought about a dialectic of differentiation and dedifferentiation on the construction of political space that offered a new way of conceiving spatial coordinates for political life in tandem with the necessary neutralization that could eventually render the imperatives of commerce to operate unhindered.[117]

It is in this context that Constant formulated his ideas about political responsibility. In a fundamental way, he conceived it in terms that were largely indifferent to questions of political form: namely, the formal structure of his account could be actualized either as a republic or a constitutional monarchy.[118] For, despite early republican sympathies, Constant's main concern was not the enactment of a republican political form and the forms of responsibility needed to sustain it. Rather, his overriding concern was with stability, the need for a neutral power to stabilize a constitutional settlement that could eliminate arbitrary exercises of political power.[119] It is in terms of these concerns, which he consistently pursued, from his speech in 1798 advocating the eviction of Jacobinism from the French political scene to his speech on the liberty of the ancient and the moderns

at the Athénée Royal in 1819, that he posed the question of responsibility.[120] Constitutional limits and responsible political action
within them: that was the tenor of Constant's reflections on political
responsibility. Or, as he states in his *Principles of Politics* (1815) apropos of "The Responsibility of Ministers":

> It seems to me that responsibility must, above all, secure two aims:
> that of depriving guilty ministers of their power, and that of keep-
> ing alive in the nation—through the watchfulness of its representa-
> tives, the openness of their debates and the exercise of freedom of
> the press applied to the analysis of all ministerial actions—a spirit
> of inquiry, a habitual interest in the maintenance of the constitu-
> tion of the state, a constant participation in public affairs, in a vivid
> sense of political life.
>
> On the question of responsibility . . . what is essential is that the
> conduct of the ministers be readily subjected to scrupulous inves-
> tigation and that, at the same time, they should be allowed ample
> resources for avoiding the consequences of such investigation, if
> their crime, were it proved, is not so odious as to deserve not mercy
> not only from the laws, but also in the eyes of universal conscience
> and equity, which are more indulgent than the written laws.[121]

The first set of assertions is clear enough; the second is everything
but. It actually shows Constant tying himself in knots trying to assert
enough latitude to insulate the exercise of political power from the
arbitrary passions from below while also seeking to live up to the commitment to accountability that defines constitutional limited government. In the version of constitutional monarchy defended in *De la
responsabilité des ministres* (1815), Constant's advocacy of responsibility
only applies to the ministers, not to the monarch. The latter embodies the kind of neutral power whose effectiveness requires complete
insulation from such responsibility. Political responsibility is, accordingly, not entirely devoid of an element of arbitrariness, even if "arbitrary power is, in all circumstances, a serious drawback."[122] Political
responsibility thus leaves a modicum of arbitrariness in place; an arbitrariness that is the responsibility of subordinates to keep in check.
But, absent any genuine sense of democratic accountability, what
is left, predictably, is the typical move among liberals of the period:

euphemistic appeals for "prudence," or some form of aristocratic virtue, as placeholders to fetter arbitrary power.[123]

Constant's reflections can be fruitfully contrasted with Tocqueville's sporadic references to political responsibility. Consistent with the tenor *The Federalist Papers*, Tocqueville writes about the "accountability of public officials," responsibility and freedom, and how in a democracy no centralized power can merely command one to "assume responsibility."[124] Responsibility here connotes, as the French *vous chargerez* conveys, the notion of taking upon oneself a role or the completion of a task.[125] Similarly, he also considers the question of the appropriate means for designated ends, something that relates to the idea of a delimited "sphere of responsibility" and, thus, of power.[126] Comparatively speaking, Tocqueville paid very little attention to political responsibility as such, something curious if not entirely incongruous in light of his conception of democracy: by casting democracy as a social condition, he significantly downplayed institutional questions, the questions that Constant had made his own, along with the duties and political responsibilities of citizenship.[127]

For a robust articulation of any sense of responsibility from below, one has to look at the Giuseppe Mazzini's formulations. Tocqueville's contemporary, and witness of the latter's collusion with the obliteration of the Roman republic, Mazzini's reflections of responsibility were internationalist in scope. In the best spirit of the Enlightenment, he loudly proclaimed duties to mankind while seeking to anchor these duties—to actualize them, as it were, in the political form of a national republic. But what makes Mazzini's account more striking is his sensibility to the social and political presuppositions of any genuine sense of political responsibility. He writes not only that "to-day, your masters, by separating you from the other classes, by prohibiting all association, by imposing a double censorship upon the press, endeavor to conceal from you your duties, together with the needs of Humanity," but he goes on to establish that responsibility entails political literacy and education, which can only be acquired by experiencing freedom: "Be assured that without instruction you cannot know your duties, and that when society does not allow you to be taught, the responsibility for every offense rests not with you, but with it; your responsibility begins on the day when an opportunity of instruction is offered to you and you neglect it; on the day when means are presented to you of transforming a society which condemns you to ignorance, and you do not exert yourselves to use them."[128] There are social and material presuppositions for the exercise of political responsibility, and, by extension, political responsibility needs to be constituted in the political space of a national republic. While Mazzini's overall treatment lacks the systematic rigor of, say, Constant's, it captured a central element for any sense of responsibility beyond that of ministers, a sense of responsibility that avowed the political and social presuppositions for it to be meaningful.[129]

The foregoing accounts constitute different variations of two main themes: how the actualization of the codependence of rights and responsibilities presupposes a modicum of freedom for it to be meaningful and how it also requires a modicum of power, for without a delimited sphere of power there is no responsibility. Revealingly, at the very moment in which modern republics are born the concept of political responsibility is almost exclusively theorized in terms of elites exercising power, not in terms of citizens having a meaningful share in the forms of power they generate and authorize. The spatial configuration of these modern republics as nation-states debarred any notion of ordinary citizens sharing political power and responsibility. Styles of elite rule embedded in these modern republican forms were buttressed by the spatial dimension of the new republics and how the establishment of large, sometimes semicontinental, republics further contributed to the dilution of political participation by distancing ordinary citizens from shared power, even in those republics born out of popular rebellion and revolution and consolidated by a *levée en masse*. A development that set the pattern for subsequent revolutions from above characterizing the consolidation of capitalist states during the late nineteenth century.

By the 1860s the banners of nation building from above had replaced the popular mobilizations nourishing forms of patriotic republicanism from below. The industrial revolution and the emergence of a world market in the Europe of the concert of powers were the defining features of the age. With these developments, an interimperialist rivalry outside the Eurasian landmass set in as the great powers vied against each other in the scramble for Africa and fought over the dismembering Ottoman Empire. The United States, for its part, had already dismembered Mexico and was in the midst of its own internal carnage during the Civil War, soon to be followed by a reconstruction in tandem with the incorporation of western territories at once ensuring the integrity of the nation, as a contiguous landmass from Atlantic to Pacific, while clinching capitalist rule in it. Perry Anderson has vividly described the ideological transformation that characterized this period: "Instead of the banners of Liberty, Equality and Fraternity, the new elites drove conscript masses under the signs of Nationality and Industry."[130] In this context, Mazzini's plea for the duties of mankind, responsibility and freedom, and its commitment to humanity expressed in ideas of equality and liberty, which nevertheless could only find expression through the nation, were a throwback reminder of a more political era and became increasingly out of sync with the *sturm und drang* of industrialized nationalism. Processes of nation building and industrialization paved the way for the consolidation of capitalist nation-states, which increasingly monopolized political space. From this point on, ruling took place by the orchestrated assent of the masses, not by their political mobilization. Only for war were the masses mobilized.

Yet the nineteenth century witnessed three other momentous developments that ought to be registered in any account of the modern eventuation and transmogrification of responsibility. First, imperialist expansion during the second half of the nineteenth century not only bred conceptions of responsibility associated with fidelity to civilizing missions and other imperial ideologies, but changed the spatial presuppositions of the concept in yet another way. Transnational capitalist relations also played a significant role. Cuba, for instance, in the late nineteenth century—precisely after 1882—witnessed a transformation of spatial relations brought about by capitalism as part of that process known in the Caribbean as *absentism*—namely, the exploitation and extraction of agriculture-based wealth from a long distance, and the absence of owners that shared no spatial contiguity, let alone a community of fate with the populations and regions they exploited. Fernando Ortiz offered a succinct formulation of this process: "And so the sugar industry became increasingly foreign and passed into anonymous, corporate, distant, dehumanized and prepotent hands, with a very slippery sense of responsibility."[131] This dilution of responsibility, which had its political correlate at home in the emergence and crystallization of the corporation as a political entity and actor, entailed the autonomization of a managerial class not only from the political order in which the corporation operated but also from its own shareholders, thus posing questions of responsibility increasingly at variance with a more properly political sense of responsibility.[132]

Second, in the context of nineteenth-century political struggles, where workers and ordinary people pressed from below, and ruling elites tacitly compromised by forging revolutions from above, variations of moral and individual responsibility emerged in the context of the "ethology" associated with the philosophical radicalism of John Stuart Mill and Victorian ideas of "character."[133] Stated differently, in Victorian ideas of personal responsibility, or self-responsibility of the person with herself, notions of character found throughout the period became central. These are memorably articulated in George Eliot's *Middlemarch*, where character becomes intertwined with an idea of "duty" that, in opposition to "sublime conceptions of existence," sought to restore individual responsibility while simultaneously opposing accounts like those found in Zola's novels that place emphasis on how moral character is deeply mediated by socially constituted and politically sanctioned situations.[134] Character is a notion that signified a heightened sense of personal responsibility. Cultivating one's character became an eminently individual responsibility, which remained nonetheless socially precious for bourgeois culture, especially as it pertained to sociability with strangers in the context of ever expanding webs of social and economic interactions.

Last, the French Third Republic inaugurated a no less momentous notion of social responsibility that openly contrasts with the individualism at work in ideas of character. Even if already tacitly avowed in Bismarck's so-called inauguration of welfare policies, social responsibility became clearly articulated in the French context. Drawing on a long tradition that posits responsibilities and obligations dating back to the civil code of 1804, whose articles contained many references to obligations and responsibility (say, articles 1383–84, 1386), under the auspices of the Third Republic emerged the idea of the "social state" and with it a "new regime of responsibility" that entailed two main vectors: on the one hand, responsibility as liability for harmful consequences of one's acts in the context of industrial accidents; on the other, responsibility as an obligation to prevent such harms and thus being readily accountable for their occurrences.[135] The consolidation of industrial capitalism had transformed the modes and conditions of human labor power to an extent that laissez-faire conceptions of responsibility as individual liability, and/or imputability, were undermined by increasingly complex patterns of instrumental rationalities and strategies of political neutralization. Accordingly, the advent of the social state and its regime of social solidarity and shared responsibility entailed the inauguration of modalities of regulation that became increasingly cast in terms of the humanization of technology. This represented a crystallization of a fin de siècle sense of solidarity that was underpinned by the attempt to bring individual autonomy in closer relationship to ideas of social obligation. Equally built into the emergent social state were notions of "collective self-determination," which challenged the individualism of earlier notions of responsibility.

But the regulations of the social state, it goes without saying, also contributed to increased exploitation of labor power. Exploitation thus became economically and politically more durable, along with political neutralization, in a dialectical reversal that was characteristic of many of the reformist projects and practices of the age. Even if this robust sense of social responsibility had many afterlives throughout the twentieth century, coeval with it was an equally momentous development that contributed to its eventual erosion. Coterminous with ideas of social responsibility were notions of limited liability in the face of increased risk. This, to the extent that "a philosophy of risk" trumping any sense of social and political responsibilities for accidents at work was born during this period, thus upending ideas of responsibility, qua liability, accountability, and imputability in the workplace.[136] Under the mantle of social solidarity and the provision of insurance, legally, the responsibility of structural beneficiaries was forsworn by an abstract sense of shared fate between employers and employees on the basis of an undifferentiated sense of professional risk.[137] Legally speaking, "professional risk" trumped responsibility, thus absolving from social and political responsibility those who are direct and structural beneficiaries.[138] The upshot: the depoliticization of the main site of struggle in which capital had confronted its enemy throughout the nineteenth century, as workers provided the social base that rendered the critique of capital politically meaningful. Undoubtedly, in an important way, insurance and limited liability signified an improvement from nineteenth-century individualization of responsibilities—frequently folded into laissez-faire ideologies of individual freedom and freedom of contract—that increased vulnerabilities and diminished responsibility, even if the vulnerabilities in question had direct structural beneficiaries and were systematically constituted and politically sanctioned. And yet, under the guises of insurance, professional risk, and limited liability, the political and social vulnerability of workers became depoliticized, and the political responsibilities of beneficiaries within capitalist nation-states disavowed.

IRRESPONSIBLE MASSES?

Eventually, capitalist orders came under the pressures of a socialist and communist credo that sought to anchor a sense of responsibility outside the constitutional bounds of the nation-state, portending an international sense of responsibility whose end was to seize power in the name of emancipated humanity. With the idea of the proletariat, Marx not only attempted to reclaim the idea of a politically active demos to wrest power from the bourgeoisie and inaugurate a more egalitarian order, an order actualizing real humanism, but also sought to trenchantly anchor it in an internationalist cast and orientation, an internationalism that recognized the ineluctability of political space as the locus of responsible action.[139] Yet internationalist socialism, for all its eloquence, is not what dented liberal civilization and precipitated its collapse. Rather, interimperial competition abroad found a homology at home, as forms of national chauvinism gained actual political traction within nationalist discourses for the first time and various atavisms, social Darwinism, along with idealizations of violence and war, gripped the imaginations of ruling elites. By now, mottos about the duty and responsibilities of mankind like Mazzini's rang hollow. In the late nineteenth century, many embattled elites saw with great apprehension the rise of mass politics and sought to countervail popular challenges to their rule from below with the conservative and sometimes counterrevolutionary mobilization of the "composite lower-middle class, both urban and rural" often fueling jingoist nationalism.[140] All this became part of the political and historical constellation of the run-up to the European Great War and its implosion of the spatial coordinates that defined international and domestic politics in the second half of the nineteenth century.[141] With the outbreak of the Great War, all kinds of rabid nationalism, including fascism, with its biologization of community, its irredentism, resentment, and revanchist compensation, would cast the actual practice of responsibility as unconditional fidelity to the preservation of the integrity of the nation and the imperatives for its defense.[142]

Communist internationalism was the historical antipode of imperialism, even if it betrays a despatialization of its own. The emergence of a historical novum, the USSR, a communist state of semicontinental size, heralded the advent of a pure political order whose identity bore the aspiration of spatial limitlessness. Perry Anderson has offered a penetrating formulation of the latter: "In 1917, workers and soldiers led by the Bolshevik Party carried out a socialist revolution in Russia. The regime that emerged from this upheaval was the first and only state in history to include no national or territorial reference in its name—it would simply be the Union of Soviet Socialist Republics, without designated place or people."[143] A political order whose identity was purely political and thus bereft of ethnic or national determinations. Sure enough, this designation—USSR—embodied the best traditions of socialist internationalism. But it indirectly attested to the collapse of a spatial political ordering and the difficulty of forging an alternative sense of bounded political space, beyond the coordinates of the leading capitalist-imperial powers. But communism's global projections could no more dispense of internal differentiations than capitalism's. The appeal to republican forms, defined by a commitment to socialism that nonetheless formed a federative entity, eloquently voiced such differentiations and the enabling borders these tacitly presuppose. Yet, all differences notwithstanding, in both communist and capitalist camps spatial disorientation eventually led to a dilution of the political life of ordinary people and a diminished sense of political responsibilities; in the case of the USSR, not least because of the consequences of civil war and counterrevolution, aided by expeditions to drown the revolution: American, British, Canadian, Finnish, French, Greek, Japanese, Romanian, Serb, Turkish. By the middle of the twentieth century, political rule effectively became centralized and hierarchical under the guise of organizational imperatives—bureaucratic, modernizing, managerial—presiding over both blocs and their otherwise divergent war economies. Though governed by different rationalities, the business corporation and the bureaucratic state converged in further diminishing and depleting any meaningful sense of political responsibility within a politically bounded space. Political responsibility became secluded to elites only accountable either to the party or the shareholder, not to a shared collective life or the general well-being of the collectivity. Moreover, with the onset of the cold war both communist internationalism and its capitalist counterpart converged on imperial forms of rule that further extricated any community of fate between these empires and those it effectively ruled.

Writing at the onset of this period of high politicization, Georg Simmel articulated a view that ran parallel to Weber's depiction of the heroic politician and its sense of responsibility. In it, however, both the main contours of the turn-of-the-century preoccupation (and obsession) with the fate of individual responsibility and the advent of the masses of ordinary people as political actors are more keenly articulated. What Weber's discussion of Caesarism and the politician tacitly assumed, Simmel rendered explicit: the collective, which, following the conventions of the social sciences of the time, Simmel dubs *the mass*, "lacks consciousness of responsibility."[144] This formulation is found within the context of a discussion of "mass crimes" and how "moral inhibitions are easily suspended" when individuals act with others: "This suspension alone explains mass crimes, of which, afterwards, the individual participant declares himself innocent. He does so with good subjective conscience, and not even without some objective justification: the overpowering predominance of feeling destroyed the psychological forces that customarily sustain the consistency and stability of the person, and hence, his responsibility."[145] In this view, individual responsibility is undermined, if not entirely obliterated, when individuals act together in concert. Amidst generalized irresponsibility, mass crimes ensue. In this reckoning, the sovereign individual with a personal sense of responsibility is besieged in an age of mass politics and collective action.

Naturally, these were commonplaces about collective action by the masses in Simmel's political and intellectual milieu: its artistic and intellectual landmarks range from Émile Zola's *Germinal* (1885) to Sigmund Freud's *Mass Psychology and the Analysis of the I* (1921), Fritz Lang's *Metropolis* (1927) and *Fury* (1936), along with Hermann Broch's *The Sleepwalkers* (1931–32), with José Ortega y Gasset's *La rebelión de las masas* as the most cogent political theoretical achievement in this genre.[146] What is significant about Simmel's account is how he zoned in on the question of responsibility and explicitly formulated what other theorizations tacitly stated; namely, how in an era of high politicization critics of the masses as political actors rejected any collective sense of responsibility, let alone conceived the possibility of politics emerging as an ethics of collective life. The crowds lacked individuality, which in elite responses to mass political organization functioned as the other pole of an entrenched binary (or, in less theoretically charged terms, a dyad) that foregrounded lettered responses in late nineteenth and early twentieth-century Europe. In Stefan Jonsson's perceptive formulation, "By affirming that members of a crowd lacked individuality—reason, identity, character, culture—crowd psychology usually served to dispute the lower classes' ability to function as responsible political agents."[147]

But not only a rejection of the possibility of responsible collective action, of political responsibility on the part of ordinary people engaged in collective action with others, is at stake here. The corollary of this rejection is an articulation of how collective action impairs individual responsibility within the framework of increasingly politicized nation-states. Even when there is a delegation of responsibility, such delegation turned out to be nugatory, as the ultimate upshot is not so much delegation to a leader but the shattering of the individual and its capacity for individual responsibility. Even as Simmel avowed how sometimes an individual shares "a co-responsibility for all collective action," the overall tenor is clear enough: in collective action, there is a "delegation of duties and responsibilities" both horizontal and vertical: "the group interest (true or ostensible) entitles, or even obliges, the individual to commit acts for which, *as* an individual, he does not care to be responsible."[148] Ultimately, individuals seek a higher power in order to be "relieved of responsibility."[149]

WITHERING RESPONSIBILITY

In the context of the transatlantic revolutions of the late eighteenth and early nineteenth century, the meaning of responsibility was primarily political, as newly inaugurated constitutionally bound republics operated under rubrics of popular consent and sovereignty. These

republics presupposed citizens responsible for authorizing and enacting these principles; by extension, these republics sought to produce
such citizens by instilling a strong sense of fidelity toward republican
political forms. Coeval with this political conception, philosophical
articulations of responsibility crystallized in terms of freedom and
necessity, determinations and the will. It is only in its subsequent historical eventuation, as the concept gained its main determinations
from the nineteenth century on, that responsibility came to be closely
associated with legal obligation and culpability, or accountability, and
thereby cast in terms of law and sanctions, and individual imputability
came to be closely associated with liability. Therefore, while initially
conceived in terms of the well-being of the social formation or collectivity where a would-be responsible agent is spatially and temporally
situated, by the turn of the nineteenth century the idea of responsibility was increasingly temporalized and rendered spatially abstract. It
increasingly meant an appeal to larger, more abstract entities including God, universal reason, or humanity.

Conversely, a veritable multiplication of its meanings began to
crystallize at this juncture. Ideas of social and religious responsibility
coexisted side by side with the idea of political responsibility, which
became associated increasingly with citizens and their representatives
in the ever expanding electorates of the late nineteenth and twentieth
centuries. But even if a proliferation of contents—social, religious,
political, individual—hardly altered the formal contours of the idea of
responsibility, its scope and spatial presuppositions were significantly
impacted by this expansion of meanings. Formally, responsibility still
entailed assuming a task vis-à-vis an object that imposes imperatives
to which the subject needs to respond, and the responses are guided
by fidelity to certain ideas, principles, or political forms. A corollary
of this dissemination of connotations was the idea that a responsible
actor, a bearer of a strong sense of responsibility, should be capable
and able to foresee the potential and likely effects of her actions and
behaviors. Not only that, a responsible actor should factor her political praxis either by preemptively curbing these effects or calibrating
her actions in light of them. Consequentialism thus became an important corollary in the historical and theoretical eventuation of the idea
of responsibility. And so did attention to historical and political contexts, or to the situation that thoroughly mediates the actualization

or enactment of ethical and political responsibility, which is what renders it mute or actual, abstract or concrete. Even so, the locus of action for the exercise of political responsibility increasingly became unstable, not to say muddled. This muddling eventually led to an overt disavowal with the onset of neoliberalism in the North Atlantic world during last two decades of the twentieth century.

In contemporary invocations of neoliberal responsibility these formal attributes are essentially reproduced. Although frequently cast as the undoing of liberal democratic ideas of autonomy, what neoliberal responsibility actually encompasses is the displacement of the locus of autonomy and responsibility into the economic domain, along with the valorization of human capital and its imperatives of marketization, self-entrepreneurship, and branding, not its depletion.[150] What Friedrich von Hayek called "the burden of choice" still abides, as does the commitment to autonomous individualization and individual responsibility.[151] But, with the springs of political action that conquered a modicum of political autonomy against the background of the postwar economic boom gone, the modicum of autonomy hypostatized in liberal democratic theory is displaced and transformed. With the deepening of neoliberal consolidation, its reproduction has entailed the expansion of its governing rationalities to a domain hitherto governed by traditional political considerations. Fidelity to the rule of law, a cornerstone of liberal-democratic ideas of justice, is thereby undermined by fidelity to the rules of the market economy and the imperatives of corporatized ideas of freedom.[152] Autonomy, always compromised and diminished within liberal-democratic capitalist states, is further depoliticized and recast to neoliberal specifications. With it, political responsibility is even more comprehensively disavowed and ultimately extricated by neoliberal strategies of responsibilization.

Responsibility is, accordingly, no longer moral or political, but recast in terms of human capitalization and thus further despatialized as the responsible self- investor and provider is embedded in a world economy, an economy that supervenes the interstate system upon which its coordination fragilely depends. Thus processes of social and political "disaffiliation," long under underway, are exacerbated in an age in which neoliberal responsibility praises individual self-reliance while in practice making social and economic independence increasingly porous by dismantling the social and political fabric that would sustain it.[153] The political depleting of citizenship in spaces devoid of affiliation, fraternity, and civility fosters a misplaced sense of fidelity in which it is impossible to cultivate the sense of political responsibility needed to sustain a genuinely democratic political life. Fear, powerlessness, and aggression all coalesce in the depoliticized yet ethically responsible citizen. But if there is one lesson that the foregoing historical account of the practice of political responsibility delivers, it is that it could only be actualized in a meaningful way in a context of shared political space where a politically constituted community of fate is forged, a context in which what is political, general, and thus common is not diluted in ways that render already difficult practices of shared power and self-rule nugatory.

3

AUTONOMY, ETHICS, *INTRA*SUBJECTIVITY

An ethics of conviction is an ethics that seek refuge in the pure will,
that is, it recognizes the interiority of the moral subject as its only
authority. In contrast to that, the ethics of responsibility take as
their starting point an existing reality, though in certain
conditions this may be a mental reality, as perceived by
the subject to which it is then counterpoised.

—Theodor W. Adorno, *Problems of Moral Philosophy*

NE UPSHOT of the contemporary ethical turn is the proliferation of solipsistic philosophical accounts of responsibility. If discussions of political and ethical responsibility historically emphasized social and intersubjective relations, the dominant philosophical formulations of responsibility privilege autonomy and *intra*subjectivity, even when abstract invocations of *inter*subjectivity are adduced. Modalities of solipsism that engage in Platonic soul-crafting and dwell on the inner life of the subject, her mental reality, over consideration of the predicaments of power she inhabits, or how these are historically constituted, politically sanctioned, and socially reproduced situations that thoroughly mediate that subjectivity. But these modalities of solipsism suggest something else: a pronounced dedifferentiation of theoretically conceived Ethics and historically constituted moral practices, which constitute yet another example of the dedifferentiations that characterize the onset of postmodernity in the North Atlantic world. Philosophical ethics is thus marshaled as part of the quest for ethical politics, which consist of binding principles—pristine or not—outside the political realm, and its distinctive practices and imperatives, or antecedent to it. Similarly, dehistoricized and abstract ethical imperatives, or normative principles, supervene upon moral-practical questions or bind the realm of the politically possible on the basis of an apodictically valid ethical politics. Two dedifferentiations are at work here: first, that between ethics qua theoretical reflection and moral practices qua ethical activity, which are the practices and values forged by individuals as they traverse concrete, historical situations or collective predicaments; second, the dedifferentiation between the realms of ethical activity and political action.[1]

The theoretical structure and historicity of this phenomenon can be fully grasped by zoning in on the axial moment in the history of European modern philosophy that mediates ethicist conceits. Kant's critical philosophy, the idea of philosophy as a science, constitutes such moment. Kant's transcendental philosophy abstracts from all given objects in order to grasp cognition itself, as well as the apodictic conditions of possibility for practical activity. Thought is thus autonomized in hitherto unprecedented ways. Indeed, autonomy is the crucial category in the form and content of the critical philosophy Kant inaugurated, which reconceived questions of obligations and duties. If, historically, ethics was the domain of knowledge that made practical-moral questions its object—its domain of inquiry—within the context of Kant's critical philosophy, ethics became further autonomized from the historical conditions and concrete situations that are inexorably constitutive of the practical-moral problems ethics generally reflects upon. There is, of course, something deeply paradoxical about this autonomization of ethics as moral philosophy: the more dirempted ethics becomes from ethical activity, the more it seeks to determine, even colonize it. It is as if the autonomization of the ethical self has led to a severance of ethical activity from political action that nevertheless conflates ethical activity with ethics and colonizes political action by way of philosophical conceits about the primacy of ethics over politics.

KANTIAN *INTRA*SUBJECTIVITY

How exactly does Kantian philosophy conceptualize responsibility? It is well known that Kant's account of duty and the responsibilities of the subject hinges on his conceptions of freedom and knowledge. In the *Critique of Pure Reason* (1781, 1787) he offered a formalist solution to the concerns of traditional epistemology by giving a theoretical account of the conditions of possibility of knowledge. Indeed, the whole enterprise of critical reason relied on the sharp separation of form and content: this separation allowed Kant to rework the philo-sophical problem of how consciousness relates to its objects by rigor-ously establishing the power of critical philosophy to make universal and necessary claims about possible experience—i.e., the a priori exis-tence of pure concepts, intuitions, and categories, as well as synthetic judgments—while proclaiming the impossibility of knowing "things in themselves." Subsequent works, like *Groundwork of the Metaphysic of Morals* (1785) and *Critique of Practical Reason* (1788), attended to the practical dimension of pure cognition and its actualization. Kant's project thus involved consciousness of not only the limits of what can be known but of how everything that exists is not produced by consciousness. It is in that sense that the idea of "transcendental" in his formulation of critical reason is best understood: namely, the formal categories of consciousness transcend experience, and thus have validity independent of it, but such validity remains predicated upon the relation of these categories to possible experience and how even ideas of practical reason are ultimately mediated by the objects of experience. Or, as he famously expressed it, "our knowledge begins *with* experience," yet it never "arises *out of* experience."[2]

For Kant, morality ties autonomy and duty to the rational laws emerging out of universalizable maxims of moral behavior. Kant laid out a sense of duty in which the form of a moral law is more important than its content and is also indifferent to the locus of action in which it occurs. Unlike previous moral philosophies—including those in the tradition of eighteenth-century British moralists, for whom vir-tue and vice are always measured in response to others rather than being defined by solipsistic acts—the solipsism of Kantian formalist duty is striking.[3] If the argument of the *Critique of Pure Reason* is taken as a point of departure, the precondition of the autonomous moral self that rigorously follows the precepts of the categorical impera-tive resides in the interstices of the antinomy of freedom and neces-sity.[4] In the universe laid out by the *Critique of Pure Reason*, only as a noumenal self can one be free, and thus held responsible for acting out of duty and not out of inclination—this is where the autonomy of the self resides. And, for this autonomy and its corollary duties to be actualized, a radical diremption of the realms of pure and practical reason was required. But it is precisely this diremption, which sal-vaged autonomy, that created a gulf, making its actualization almost impossible.[5] A severance not easily extricated. It rests on a distinction crucial for his epistemology.

In the *Critique of Pure Reason* Kant presents a rigorous distinction between two senses of the self. On the one hand, the phenomenal self—the one that an "I" closely identifies with its experience—is the empirical storage of the manifold experiences that it apprehends. On the other, there is the "I's" truer self, which is *noumenal*. The empirical self is regulated by the laws governing other physical bodies and hence incapable of being autonomous and free. If the empirical self seems to be the storage of experience, the noumenal self is the self that is rational, the one in which all the formal rational qualities reside. Though solipsistic, the self is split: the noumenal self makes the moral rules that the phenomenal self follows. These two selves, the noumenal and the phenomenal, and their two distinct realms, correlate with another crucial distinction built into the architecture of Kant's argument. Concepts, herein cast as binding rules, are acquired through factual experience, but their transcendental status is deduced by means of establishing their "objective validity."[6] In a way, the burden of the argument in *Critique of Pure Reason* is to close the gap between the two selves and establish a unity of apperception in which the ultimately unknowable noumenal self provides the categories for understanding that organize and make sense of the manifold experience collected through the phenomenal self. And, ever since its publication, commentators on the *Critique of Pure Reason* have pondered the exact relation between the two selves.[7] But this elusive intersection bears on more than matters of epistemology. It has consequences for Kantian moral theory: duty is the province of noumena, but inclination is part of the phenomenal self. Even so, duty prevails over inclination, and for the empirical self—that is, that self which is experiencing inclinations—to behave ethically it has to be subjected to the imperative of duty, whose formal contours have a content and an impact on it, despite Kant's disavowal of the content of this formalism. Perhaps the most important aspect of the centrality of duty is the sharp demarcation between acting *out* of duty, which is moral, and acting *according* to duty, which in the strictness of Kantian ethics is not.

The relationship between selves is clearly asymmetrical, since for the noumenal self the content of the empirical self, mediated by the texture of everyday life, its memories and predicaments, is morally irrelevant.

And the form of the categorical imperative has a content that is indifferent to that of one's empirical self. Consequently, the end result of Kantianism is dehistoricized formalism that asserts the autonomy of the rational subject as a precondition of freedom and moral responsibility; here responsibility pivots on the idea of ascribed actions to the autonomous subject. Herein autonomy displaces heteronomy as a source of morality; *intra*subjectivity supplants *inter*subjectivity. All of this reflects Kant's concern with establishing the binding authority of principles and practices deployed ordinarily in everyday life, while bulking the binding legitimacy of the concepts of freedom and agency that these moral considerations presuppose.[8] For instance, in the *Groundwork for the Metaphysics of Morals* this is formulated as part of the idea of duty and the moral law that are the necessary corollaries to his quest for "the *supreme principle of morality*," a quest that is cast as necessarily binding for all rational agents; meanwhile, in *The Metaphysics of Morals*, ethics not only deals with formal conditions but "goes beyond this and provides *matter* (an object of free choice), an end of pure reason which it represents as an end that is also objectively necessary, that is, an end that, as far as human beings are concerned, it is a duty to have."[9]

Necessity is, accordingly, an intrinsic component of his ethics of imperatives. It entails following rules, which, in turn, are the form of the norm, or imperative. Being bound to and by rules is constitutive of normativity in Kant's critical philosophy: the ideal of necessity (*Notwendigkeit*) that underwrites his critical epistemology demands an obligation to act in accordance with a rule, the same sense of necessity supporting his morality of duty. Autonomy thus resides in being bound by rules that one gives to oneself and is responsible for, a sense of bindingness that is already at work in Kant's theory of mental activity. As Robert B. Brandom has shown, Kantian judgments are not only "minimal units of *responsibility*," which are already at work in the synthesizing act that the unity of apperception carries on, but these units already express *commitments*, thus enacting epistemological responsibilities antecedent to the formulations found in Kant's practical philosophy.[10] These epistemological variations of responsibility—integrative, critical, ampliative—already render the Kantian self "responsible for *doing* something" and take place outside of history.[11] Herein responsibility emerges as a fundamentally *intra*subjective category.[12] But if this idea of responsibility is historicized and brought to bear outside of that noumenal "realm of ends," and considered embedded in political situations constituted by binding historical processes characterized by continuities and discontinuities, this imperative of necessity fares unevenly, to put it mildly.

Once cast in historically constituted scenes of action, the intersections between acting out of duty and according to it are significantly muddled.[13] Here, in the realm of ethical activity, the mediations of law, institutions, and political forms are ineludible. Indeed, Kantian responsibility equivocally oscillates between moral obligation and legal constraint, both of which are necessarily binding, albeit on different grounds.[14] Even duty may be internal and external: "The very *concept of duty* is already the concept of *necessitation* (constraint) of free choice through the law. This constraint may be an *external constraint* or a *self-constraint*"; yet duty is thus "not merely a self-constraint . . . but also a self-constraint in accordance with a principle of inner freedom, and so through the . . . representation of one's duty in accordance with its formal law."[15] The objective obstacle against which responsible autonomy is measured is not unknowable noumena, but inclinations. It is in the interstices of these antinomian constraints, and the eminently *intra*subjective dialectic of internalization and externalization defining them, that Kantian ideas of responsibility are formulated. The grounds of responsibility are ultimately found in the "normativeness of the conceptual" and the forms of action it inaugurates.[16] Hence we are responsible for the acts that follow from our sense of fidelity to behaving in accordance with the rules of the categorical imperative. Within Kant's ethics, despite the immersion of the individual in a web of institutionalized and intersubjective relations, responsibility necessarily remains an individual moral endeavor autonomous from these conditions. Kant's is the most cogent philosophical articulation of the modern idea of individualized intrasubjective responsibility.

After Kant, questions of *intra*subjective responsibility were replaced by ideas of freedom-in-necessity.[17] Even so, the many facets of the problem of subjectivity—cognition, self-knowledge, autonomy, and phenomenological experience—that triggered and mediated these philosophical discussions, were inherited from Kantian philosophy. In Robert B. Pippin's lucid rendering, what is at stake are "the conditions under which one could be said 'to actually *lead* a life,' wherein one's deeds and practices are and are experienced as one's own"; namely, subjectivity is the extent to which freedom and responsibility are possible: the former defined as "being able somehow to own up to, justify, and stand behind one's deeds (*reclaim* them as my own), and that involves (so it is argued) understanding what it is to be responsive to norms, reasons."[18] If in Kant such understanding involves owning up to actions that are the outcome of obedience to self-legislating, rational laws, an obedience that is grounded in acting correctly in accordance with duty, Hegelian accounts of responsibilities and duties incorporate as central the historical dilemmas of institutionality and predicaments of power that mediate action and the dialectic of independence and dependence that is constitutive of freedom. For Hegel, action, like the self, is historical, and what binds the two are complex webs of institutions that mediate the texture of collective life. In this conception, to borrow Terry Eagleton's lucid formulation, "institutions are how others are constitutive of the self even when they are unknown to us."[19] Intersubjective relations are thereby thoroughly mediated by social and historical relations.

HEGEL; OR, DETERMINATE RESPONSIBILITY

That owning up to one's actions and their consequences is a constitutive tenet of a rational concept of responsibility is uncontroversial enough from an ethical or political perspective. But how to precisely conceive this idea became one of the challenges that post-Kantian Germany philosophy had to face, as it had also to reckon with new social and political dimensions, the modern imperatives of institutionality and power mediating them, and the collective dimension of many actions. In this context, Kant's unresolved philosophical questions and problems were inherited and recast in a context thoroughly mediated by these political and social questions. One prominent heir was Hegel. Brandom has offered a discerning formulation of his inheritance of the Kantian problematic:

> The problem is to understand how the *authority* to undertake a determinate responsibility that for Kant is required for an exercise of freedom is actually supplied with a correlative determinate *responsibility*, so that one is intelligible as genuinely *committing* oneself to something, constraining oneself. This coordinate structure of authority

and responsibility ("independence" and "dependence" in the normative sense Hegel gives to these terms) is what Hegel's *social* model of *reciprocal recognition* is supposed to make sense of. He thinks . . . that all authority and responsibility are ultimately *social* phenomena. They are the products of the *attitudes*, on the one hand, of those who *undertake* responsibility and *exercise* authority, and on the other, of those who *hold* others responsible and *acknowledge* their authority.[20]

This socially and historically determinate sense of responsibility embodies a dialectic of authority and responsibility that does not revert to individualized responsibilization. Rather, it emphasizes the social and political content, and the sociohistorical presuppositions, of responsibility. It is embedded in the texture of collective life, its determinations and limits. As such, it reclaims intersubjectivity as central to the idea and practice of responsibility.

In this way, Hegel grants the Kantian problematic an Aristotelian dimension by emphasizing the social nature of responsibility and how determinations and institutional mediations are crucial for freedom and for both ethical and political accountability. For Hegel, accordingly, institutions provide a crucial mediation for the actualization of freedom and responsibility. This leads him to conceive freedom in terms of different degrees of realization and determination, depending on the texture of institutional and other imperatives mediating one's scene of action. Unlike Kant, Hegel proceeded historically in order to retrace the different moments of self-constitution that authorized collectively over time, as well as the emergence of binding norms for which one is responsible; hence the centrality of memory as recollection in Hegel's account of *Geist*'s unfolding in history and its consciousness of freedom as recounted in *The Phenomenology of Spirit* (1804). Indeed, in this vein Hegel rearticulated the role of necessity in ethical life by casting freedom in determination and in his insight that the realization of freedom relies on historical and institutional determinations.

For all its notorious abstraction, Hegel's philosophy takes as its point of departure actuality, the existence of situated concrete historical agents *in* history, thus portending a realism in which the dialectic of rationality and actuality is at work. Hegel's philosophy speculatively formulates the identity and nonidentity of rationality and actuality in the widely misunderstood formulation of the identity and nonidentity of the real and the rational.[21] This realism is important for his account of ethical life, an account of the historical world that addresses the collective nature of ethics and the forms of interdependence that defined the lives of individuals in the historical, social, and political world. It is the world of freedom actualized in relations of reciprocity whose concrete actualization is the purpose of ethical life, its *end*. Certainly, there is more than a tinge of Aristotle in Hegel's account of ends, even if his notion is irreducible to a belated Aristotelianism. Rather, it is as part of conceptualizing this externalization of action that he reworks and speculatively renders the intersections between intentionality, responsibility, and purpose.

Hegel thus complicates and sublates the Kantian account of duty and offers an account of duty that externalizes it as activity.[22] In it, the individual re-cognizes her or his relationship to the law comprehensively; namely, she or he is conceived as responsible for the law, whose corollaries, not preconditions, are, then, responsibility to and before the law. Ethical life is thus conceived as collective. And it is along these lines that Hegel's dialectic debars moralizing and abstract critique. Instead, it registers contradictions in the situation, which is thus soberly confronted as contradictory and as mediated by the different institutional imperatives in the actualization of freedom. It also offers a novel account of the interdependence of means and ends in the externalization and actualization of political and ethical responsibilities.[23]

Central to this account of ethical responsibility is a dialectical formulation of the idea of will, which is the driving principle of Hegel's account of ethical life. Indeed, Hegel's *Philosophy of Right* traces the conceptual unfolding and concretization of the will, whose development he situates in conjunction with three analytically distinct stages: abstract right, morality, and ethical life. The last is the realm of the realization of freedom as the end of ethical life, *end* here understood as purpose. Thus the central insight at work in Hegel's political thought is the notion of freedom as a result whose determinations are actualized in the context of "ethical life," in the world that spirit (*Geist*) has immanently created for itself as a second nature (§§ 4, 151; cf. § 272).[24] This is an eminently historical world whose conceptualization and comprehension is always a form of self-knowledge.[25] A core idea of the *Philosophy of Right* is precisely how "recognition" and "right," notions that are central for his account of civil society and the state, "come into effect through the mediation of the arbitrary will," an activity that is "the more precise definition of what is primarily meant by the universal idea of freedom," an ideal whose actualization is thoroughly mediated (§ 206; cf. §§ 104, 121).[26] The *Philosophy of Right* takes the reader through the path of these mediations in the sphere of the family, civil society (where a collective sense of responsibility initially crystallizes), and the state.

It is in this dialectical journey that Hegel introduces the discussion of purpose and responsibility, which had occupied him at least since the Jena *System of Ethical Life* (1802–1803), within the context of Morality, the realm of the individual.[27] Rightly so, Hegel relegates questions of guilt and criminal liability to the realm of Abstract Right, and discusses responsibility within the context of Morality's higher but still abstract actualization of freedom (§§ 104–5). Therein, he lays out the formal aspects of his conceptualization of responsibility, even if these only become fully actualized as part of ethical life. As in the Jena version, responsibility is linked with intentionality or, to be more precise, with purpose (§§ 115–18). At this stage, by way of the externalization of its activity, the subject is the corollary of the legalism that defined the discussion of abstract right. It thus conceptualizes and comprehends the relationship between actions and intentions as partial, one defined by motives and intentions, but not by consequences. This, to be sure, constitutes a more superior conceptualization of responsibility than the solipsism of abstract right, but one still riven by antinomies. Responsibility, for long-term aftereffects, or structural effects that go beyond the immediate purpose, is severed from the agent: "The will thus has the right *to accept responsibility* only for the first set of consequences, since they alone were part of its purpose" (§ 118).[28] The *moment* of truth in this formulation, of course, resides in the awareness this conceptualization of responsibility betrays of the gaps between intention, action, and effect; namely, the distinction between necessary and contingent consequences, even if at this moment these are abstracted from concrete social relations. Only as part of ethical life can a comprehension and conceptualization of the circumstances mediating the consequences of actions, the necessity of contingencies, and the mediations of the actualization of freedom as a historical process, be comprehended as part of a dialectical conceptualization of responsibility encompassing both internal and external determinations.

The culmination of this conception of responsibility is found in the idea of citizenship as a productive activity whose actions are the basis for freedom and responsibility and where the gap between intention and effect would be more comprehensively staged without disavowing the centrality of consequences for an ethics of activity.[29] Responsibility, moreover, relies on a realist reckoning with actuality that resists abstract autonomizations and equally abstract *Sollen*. Hegel's is an account of responsibility that avows the structuring role of imperatives that constrain choices and the possibility of action, which always happens *in* history and *within* a historically constituted situation. Ends, means, and circumstances are all contained in the situation, as apprehended by the subject, and in the action itself. Here are, *in toto*, the different moments of the dialectical externalization of responsibility. Its ultimate locus of action for the actualization of freedom is collective political life. "According to Hegel," in Max Horkheimer's formulation, "rationality consists concretely in the unity of objective and subjective freedom: that is, in the unity of the general will and the individuals who carry out its ends,"[30] provided this *unity* is *speculatively* conceived. Formally, Hegel's was a move in the direction of mediations that allowed for a critical mapping of the ways in which freedom and necessity intersect politically; political freedom requires equality and political literacy. Hegel's *Sittlichkeit* thus develops Kantian themes of autonomy and freedom and seeks to render them concrete, as part of a historically situated social process.[31] However, in a world of dualisms, of dirempted reason and market rationality, this conception of freedom became increasingly difficult, not to say aporetic. Even so, out of the post-Kantian tradition, Hegel remains the best expositor of dirempted reason and its contradictions and an indispensable point of reference for attempts to retrieve the dialectical legacy and conceptualize responsibility qua ethical activity outside Ethics, beyond methodological individualism and other liberal conceits. Indeed, it was by reflecting on Hegel's *Philosophy of Right* that the young Marx was able to conjure an obvious corollary of Hegel's ideas of sovereignty and responsibility: "the subject" as the "self-incarnation of sovereignty," the "becoming a subject" of the revolutionary citizen.[32]

Unsurprisingly, Hegel's dialectical formulations of ethical life, let alone anything like a Hegelian-Marxist political ethic, have had little ascendance in North Atlantic scholarly circles. The dominant strategy has been to formulate versions of ethical politics, which seek to preemptively anchor, and curb, political commitments in ethical principles. In its analytical guises, the afterlives of the Kantian legacy largely consist of efforts to set up in advance an imperative, however heteronomous, without consideration of how the space of action, its locus, is constructed by a regulatory matrix, and what forms of response it enacts and forecloses. And when abstractions are left behind—and history is let in—the entrance of historical determinations and contingencies has a loosening effect: once historicized, these seemingly chiseled moral principles quietly unravel, which is perhaps why their proponents so zealously seek to autonomize them. Yet, before examining contemporary autonomizations of moral responsibility within analytical philosophy, it is worth considering Nietzsche's significant contribution to *intra*subjective ideas of responsibility.

THE NIETZSCHEAN MOMENT

Interpreting Nietzsche's highly influential conceptualization of responsibility presents unique challenges. Even though he is one of the figures that most fiercely dreaded the emancipatory political processes that took place during the nineteenth century, his political thought is consistently whitewashed in contemporary interpretations both within the walls of academic critical and political theory and in the Anglo-American wing of Nietzsche *Studien*. But Nietzsche's conceptualization of responsibility from the perspective of the "party of life" cannot be unreflectively imported to contemporary discussions of responsibility committed to different political values. Hardly a politically aloof figure, this is a thinker that with great acuity registered the underlying crisis of liberal-capitalist civilization, which reached its apogee and crystallization in the second half of the nineteenth century, and his body of work is deeply mediated by a heightened consciousness of historical processes: historical processes that he was not only aware of, but to which he vehemently responded by forging a politically infused recasting of aristocratic radicalism that openly avowed the codification of hierarchies for the sake of a future *große Politik*.[33]

And yet little if any of this could be surmised by looking at current aseptic interpretations of Nietzsche.[34] These interpretations *read* Nietzsche, as the jargon of Theory would have it, as a thinker bent on overcoming modern forms of domination, either committed to a generalized overcoming of the leveling tendencies of mass society for the sake of a new individual freedom and responsibility beyond the pieties of the day (his and today's, that is) or as an ambiguous aesthete mostly committed to a cultural overcoming that, while allergic to liberalism, socialism, and Christianity, miraculously remains politically indeterminate.[35] Likewise, a well-nigh infinite malleability disavowing conceptual and historical determinants is present in these metaphorical and allegorical *readings*. It is in connection with the prevalence of politically aseptic interpretations of Nietzsche, and his allure in contemporary theoretical discussions, that Malcolm Bull has polemically asked, "Where is the Anti-Nietzsche?"[36] An invocation that brings into view the paradox of embracing a body of work forged at the high pitch of politicization during the nineteenth century in the name of reinvigorating democracy in contexts largely defined by modalities of depoliticized politics—embraces that are either historically naive, at best, or perverse, at worst.

Consider the following interpretations of Nietzsche's critique and conceptualization of responsibility: for Robert Pippin, Nietzsche is best understood as "one of the last great 'French Moralists'" whose critique of responsibility as accountability urges readers "to give up another remnant of the Christian system," which consists in "our belief in the ontologically distinct subject as agent, separable from, supervising, willing into existence, and individually responsible for her particular actions"—an interpretation that leads Pippin to ask: "should not Nietzsche be aware that, by eliminating as nonsensical the idea that appears to be a necessary condition for the deed to be a deed—a subject's individual causal responsibility for the deed's occurring—he has eliminated any *way* of properly understanding the notion of *responsibility*, or that he has eliminated even a place for criticism of an agent?" In contrast, and preempting this sort of questioning, Bonnie Honig has identified two senses of responsibility at work in Nietzsche's critique: first, the critique of responsibility as accountability for actions, which pivots on the idea of guilt, and, second, a "recovery" of responsibility that entails overcoming "the need to make sense of misfortune by linking it to blameworthy agents, to move beyond the self-destructive agency of moral responsibility," thus "severing the resentful ties that bind the subject to his past but also the tie that binds the subject to his fellows": an account that reverberates in Vanessa Lemm's interpretation of Nietzsche's "agonistic politics of responsibility," which consists of "a continuous resistance to the institutionalization of freedom," since "neither what one has by virtue of an instituted right nor what one is given by virtue of a mutual agreement, but always only what one fights for, what one conquers"—responsibility thus recovered "reflects a power that results from the overcoming of the need to dominate others" as well as "the privilege of those who give and promise to the other and who see in this gift and giving the greatest extension of their power." Meanwhile, less sanguinely but no less aseptically, David Owen glosses Nietzsche's account of responsibility in reference to Machiavelli and Emerson and writes that "Nietzsche allows for degrees of ethical virtù" and his "figure of the sovereign individual dramatizes an attitude, a will to self-responsibility (in Emerson's language: self-reliance), which is manifest in the perpetual striving to increase, to expand, one's powers of self-government such that one can bear, incorporate and, even, love one's fate—one's exposure to chance and necessity," while "committed to a processual (i.e., non-teleological) perfectionism." If Owen offe/s a Nietzsche where Machiavelli meets Emerson, Christian Emden strikes a Weberian note when he argues that "Nietzsche's ethic of responsibility seeks to address that, virtually in every case, the world of ethical action is simply gray," as a thinker that scorned "the moralization of the political" and posed a "double-bind of autonomy and responsibility" that defines his free spirits—which are also the heralds of "autonomous individuals" able to coolly "avoid the effects of demagogy and political fanaticism"—and whose "political realization" is to be sought in "Nietzsche's idea of Europe." Meanwhile, for Robert Gooding-Williams, self-overcoming emerges as the conditions of possibility for assuming political responsibility: "In the wake of the demise of peoples, the creator's responsibility for transforming humanity into a people *must fall to individuals*. . . . This responsibility is a *political* responsibility." Finally, Paul Franco has suggested that after the death of god "we must become our benevolent gods and take responsibility for all the things that we have hitherto left to chance"—by the time of Nietzsche's *Zarathustra* what is at stake is "the transition from the apolitical free spirit to the responsibility to rule" that demands "self-cultivation."[37]

Unquestionably, these are serious interpretations that capture important aspects of Nietzsche's reflections on responsibility. But, in their prudishness, each interpretation distorts one fundamental aspect of Nietzsche's theorization, and certainly not an expendable one: namely, how his overcoming of responsibility as accountability, and his emphasis on a different sense of responsibility, are conceived as a political response to the threat of equality that affirms a form of sovereignty predicated on hierarchy, war, and an order of rank. All of which is part and parcel of the quasi-transcendental argument about valuation that he formulates to defend and ultimately hypostatize inequality.[38] In the effort to conceptualize Nietzsche's avowal of a different kind of responsibility, not only are his own historically informed pronouncements evaded, silenced, or perfunctorily adduced, but other figures, either prior or posterior—Machiavelli, Weber, Sartre—are brigaded to elucidate the political import of Nietzsche's recovery of responsibility without dealing with the explicit and implicit political content as it is expressed in his writings: his deliberate responses to historical political situations and predicaments and how *ruling* and *ruled* are built into this account.

This is not to say that Nietzsche's views are negligible and are irremediably shackled to his formulations. Nietzsche's account of responsibility amounts to a body of work of immense intelligence and polemical intensity, which conjures illuminating insights on the intersections among responsibility, critique, memory, and the future.[39] Thus the critical import of Nietzsche's critique of responsibility as accountability has been amply noted, either in terms of the ways in which it paves the way for late modern critiques of liberal subjectivity, of an accountable yet powerless subject who resentfully reacts rather than acts, and moralizes, or in terms of the ways it challenges the idea of the docile political subject, one who is "calculable" and whose regularized behavior is predictable.[40] What is often brushed aside, however, is the rather solipsistic and ultimately *intra*subjective nature of

Nietzsche's recasting of responsibility, along with the politically reactionary nature of his disavowals of collective action and his avowal of an aristocratic "party of life."[41] All of this is predicated on a political ecology of value in which domination and exploitation figure as necessary for genuine valuation.[42] Peter Dews has offered an accurate formulation when he writes: "Nietzsche knows as well as Walter Benjamin that 'there is no document of civilization that is not at the same time a document of barbarism.' It is just that he thinks the pact is well worth it."[43] It is this *key* valuation that constitutes the generative matrix of his political thought.

Politically, Nietzsche was responding to the advent of mass politics and revolution in post-Napoleonic Europe, a context that saw the Paris Commune—a traumatic experience for both him and Marx: for Marx because of the repression of workers, for Nietzsche because of the supposed burning of the Louvre by the Communards—the emancipation of slavery across the Atlantic, women's suffrage, anarchism, and socialism. And all this he contemptuously derided in his published works and private letters.[44] With historical and philological acuity, Domenico Losurdo has painstakingly shown how many of the concepts and categories of Nietzsche's political thought—order of rank, pathos of distance, party of life, war, rabble, annihilation, aristocracy—need to be understood in relation to philosophical, intellectual, cultural, and political contexts. This carefully teases out the level of embeddedness of Nietzsche's ideas in the political and intellectual discussions of his times.[45] A critical reckoning that leaves room for an accurate discernment of that which Losurdo calls the "theoretical excess" (*eccedenza teorica*) that emerges by carefully interpreting Nietzsche's thought. Such a critique demands breaking free from what he sardonically calls the "hermeneutics of innocence" in mainstream Nietzsche scholarship:

> Carrying out a political and historical reading of the philosopher, and situating him in a larger tradition of critics of the revolution, which, passing through its most favorable moment in the antidemocratic reaction in the late nineteenth century, finally results in Nazism, by no means settles accounts with Nietzsche and ignores the problem of theoretical excess. A singular ideological process occurred a propos the reading of Nietzsche. The triumphant West has repressed (*rimosso*) the dark pages of its history. And so terrible statements like

the "annihilation of the unsuccessful" or the "annihilation of deca-
dent races" are placed in immediate relationship with the horror of
the Third Reich. To liberate the philosopher from the shadow cast
over him by the aforementioned dismissal, the hermeneut of innocence has not been able to do better than appealing, in turn, to a further repression (*rimozione*), one that ignores or passes in silence over
the most disturbing claims of the philosopher or miraculously trans-
forms them into a set of improbable metaphors. The demonstration
of the unreliability of the hermeneutics of innocence, however, does
not mean the end of the discussion. Far from being in contradiction
with it, comprehension of the theoretical excess of Nietzsche presupposes both the historical contextualization and political reading of
his thought.[46]

There is a touch of anachronism in Losurdo's contention about the
immediate connection of nineteenth-century exterminatory violence and Nazism, but the overall historical judgment holds, as does
his larger interpretative point.[47] Or, as he later states, in conjunction
with his interpretation of the dogmatic and nondogmatic moments
in Nietzsche's aristocratic radicalism, a differentiated account adept
at discerning the contradictions found in this body of work, including the moments with a potential emancipatory import: "Underlining
the character *totus politicus* and consistently reactionary of Nietzsche's
thought hardly means indulging in reductionism and losing sight of
the theoretical excess."[48] As such, this *eccedenza* needs to be scrupulously pondered and recast without disavowing the obdurate sedimentations from the situation in which it emerged and the contents
Nietzsche accorded it. For Nietzsche's "grand politics" portended fantasies of "breaking in two" the history of humanity that invited radical rupture. But his was a plea for rupture that was hardly politically
indeterminate. Rather, the content of this formal hypostatization of
rupture is profoundly counterrevolutionary, as is his account of the
responsibility of "free spirits," whose fidelity is geared as it is for a form
of politics of hierarchy. Any "theoretical excess," as it were, needs to be
critically reconstructed without whitewashing his political thought.

    The intuitive appeal of Nietzsche's critique of ethics and retrieval
of responsibility has something to do with the bidirectionality of
Nietzsche's critique: while opposing the coldness of Kantian duty, he

is equally contemptuous of Hegelian ideas of ethical life. A double-edged critique that, nevertheless, has tended to conceal the ways in which Nietzsche hypostatizes an *intra*subjective solipsism as part of his retrieval of responsibility. In Nietzsche's thought, responsibility is largely a surrogate for the creative destruction that he avows: the creation of new values by wiping out the sedimentation of the old in radical acts of solipsistic defiance. Responsibility thus figures largely in his mature philosophy, from the so-called middle period on, where a radical ethos of critique meets a politics of memory and both are folded into a longing for a hierarchical politics of mastery in the sphere of culture that, nevertheless, is firmly supported by an order of rank hostile to any form of egalitarianism (liberal, socialism, anarchist, democratic, let alone Christian).[49]

In Nietzsche's writings there are at least two senses of responsibility: the critique of it as accountability and a radical retrieval of responsibility as central to the critical ethos of the philosopher of the future, the philosophy of the "dangerous perhaps," that acts and responds to a predicament of power largely defined by leveling historical forces. Nietzsche's is a new philosopher whose spiritual fortitude is the provenance of the few, but who soberly and fiercely confronts nihilism and acts in the face of it by means of the creation of new values.[50] These are themes that in the early twentieth century would certainly resound in Max Weber's plea for a political hero in "Politics as a Vocation." But, in contrast to Weber, what Nietzsche longs for in *On the Genealogy of Morality* is a *tabula rasa,* a clean slate, "to make room for new things," that entails the sort of forgetfulness "memory" impairs. Its correlate: the "memory of the will," which defines the responsible individual, his ability to make promises, and his presumed capacity to foresee the consequences of his acts.[51] Here we see the radical critique of responsibility as accountability and the fetters it imposes on the will. The critique of responsibility thus yields a critique of memory, which in Nietzsche's one-sided view is the antipode of forgetting.[52] But something akin to this memory of the will defines "the new philosopher," whom Nietzsche conjured in *Beyond Good and Evil,* albeit in recast form; this figure, "the man of the most comprehensive responsibility," is a lawgiver for whom the past is "a means, an instrument, a hammer" for the enactment of new values and whose responsibility resides in creating these new values and an ensuing "order of rank."[53] The new philosopher has to discern what is life-affirming and life-denying and have a fidelity to the former. That a memory of a usable past is presupposed by this reactionary ethos goes without saying. The past is not there just to be abolished *tout court*; it is there to show instances of life-affirming hierarchies, orders of rank that serve as a model and yardstick to criticize, say, the egalitarianism of Christianity and the French Revolution.[54]

Even so, this is a far less straightforward account than most interpreters make it out to be. Roberto Alejandro has perceptively shown how "in the first essay [of *On the Genealogy of Morality*], free will is invented by the slaves, but in the second essay, free will, along with self-mastery, is one of the defining features of the sovereign individual."[55] Moreover, in his characterization of the origins of free will and of responsibility as accountability, Nietzsche conflates any sense of equality with sameness, and his retrieval of responsibility aims to go beyond the forms of guilt that have defined and ultimately subdued powerful communities by way of the moralization of duty.[56] While the "the origins of *responsibility*" reside in the processes of "*making* man to a certain degree necessary, uniform, a peer amongst peers, orderly and consequently predictable," it bears an *unpredictable* aspect that is discernable once looked at retrospectively:

Let us place ourselves . . . at the end of this immense process where the tree actually bears fruit, where society and its morality of custom finally reveal what they were simply *the means to*: we then find the sovereign individual as the ripest fruit on its tree, like only to itself, having freed itself from the morality of custom, an autonomous, supra-ethical individual (because "autonomous" and "ethical" are mutually exclusive), in short, we find a man with his own, independent, enduring will, *whose prerogative it is to promise*—and in him a proud consciousness quivering in every muscle of *what* he has finally achieved and incorporated, an actual awareness of power and freedom, a feeling that man in general has reached completion. This man who is now free, who actually *has* the *prerogative* to promise, this master of the *free* will, this sovereign—how could he remain ignorant of his superiority over everybody who does not have the prerogative to promise or answer to himself, how much trust, fear, and respect he arouses—he *merits* all three—and how could he, with his self-mastery, not realize that he has necessarily been given mastery over

circumstances, over nature and over all creatures with a less enduring and reliable will? . . . The proud knowledge of the extraordinary
privilege of *responsibility*, the consciousness of this rare freedom and
power over himself and his destiny, has penetrated him to his lowest
depths and become an instinct, his dominant instinct.[57]

Mastering "circumstances" and "all creatures with a less enduring and
reliable will" is thus not ancillary to Nietzsche's retrieval of responsibility; a recovery that explicitly disavows any collective connotation
of responsibility and rather anchors it in an elite capable of self-
overcoming. As such, it requires mastery, something only accessible
through an unspecified but decidedly hierarchical political order, an
order that serves as a political condition of possibility for the kind of
cultural creation he defends, which he hopes to keep undefiled by the
rabble, the masses.

   Two contrasting passages shed further light on the political import
of Nietzsche's critique and retrieval of responsibility: first, a statement
twice repeated in *Beyond Good and Evil*: "every great philosophy has
hitherto been . . . a confession on the part of its author and a kind
of involuntary and unconscious memoir"; second, an assertion in *On
the Genealogy of Morality*: "there is no such substratum; there is no
'being' behind the deed, its effect and what becomes of it; 'the doer'
is invented as an afterthought,—the doing is everything."[58] Here it is
worth parsing out what is implied in these passages: on the one hand,
how the avowals and disavowals, conceits and rhetorical maneuver-
ing on the part of an author are as important to understand an oeuvre
as is its manifest content; on the other hand, however, he posits the
diremption of "doer" from "deed" in ways that resonate with modern
philosophical concerns about agency. It is because of the latter that
Nietzsche is interpreted as a critic of sovereign agency. In the context
of the section in question (*On the Genealogy of Morality*: essay 1, section 13), the critique of an objective and transcendental substratum of
meaning is put forward as part of a larger displacement of responsibility. This displacement is in sync with Nietzsche's ontology of innocence and the moral indifference of nature, and is equally homologous
to his debunking of the transcendental structures of meaning associated with German idealism. Conversely, these passages at once link
ideas, concepts, and doctrines to the subjective, even psychological,

dispositions of the type of individual that would formulate them, but also chasten any sense of sovereignty of the doer over the deed, thus undermining the connection that would ascribe responsibility for an action in the context of a collective ethical life.[59] Attribution, and, by extension, accountability, are thus severely weakened, but not effaced. These are both affirmed and denied.

Something like a dialectic of imputation is at work here, one frequently construed as the cornerstone of Nietzsche's critique of accountability as docile calculability or as a critical affirmation of the constitutive gap between agent and action in human predicaments. Yet, for all their attractiveness, these constructions are, at best, the theoretical excess of Nietzsche's thought, not its actual content. For the weakening of attribution and imputation is part and parcel of a radically aristocratic quest for unfettered creation, a retrieval of a *new* futurist sense of responsibility, a recasting of responsibility that paradoxically assumes a burden without any strong sense of attribution. This is an eminently *intra*subjective idea of responsibility that nevertheless pivots on an ecology of values from which it is insulated and thus unaccountable, even if its actions reverberate in the forms of domination and exploitation that are its condition of possibility. That such ecology of values cannot but find institutional expression in profoundly hierarchical cultural and political orders goes without saying—and *assuming* this new form of *intra*subjective responsibility is predicated on the disavowal of responsibility qua *imputation* and *accountability* vis-à-vis the predicaments of power it both sustains and inaugurates.

Evidently, not every act has an agent immediately behind it, nor is every form of violence traceable to an intention or will. That is the moment of truth in Nietzsche's critique. Even so, violent predicaments of power and suffering are not always directly constituted and sanctioned by the classes and groups benefiting from how particular situations are structured. And sometimes those presiding over the social order in question do not intend such predicaments. But, by virtue of their role in their social reproduction, such predicaments can be attributed to the orders these actors preside over and sanction. Therein lies their responsibility qua political actors. Assuming responsibility beyond an imputable will demands forms of attribution and accountability, along with ascertaining degrees of responsibility. And that is precisely what Nietzsche's account sets out to exclude. In contrast, his retrieval of a new responsibility largely consists of a quest for a life-affirming culture and its institutional conditions of possibility, which include an order of rank whose attainment is paved by ennobling suffering, violence, and war. Its explicit *locus* and *end* is the cultivation of this new order and the process to achieve it; implicit is the ecology of values it presupposes and the hierarchical *Macht* politics required to sanction and sustain it. Achieving these orders requires undermining older notions of responsibility, including severing the constitutive mediation between doer and deed, and the forms of imputation and accountability these avow, for the sake of the self-responsibility that defines the unfettered overcoming of oneself.

That the foregoing are not arbitrary deductions of the political valences, or import, of Nietzsche's account of responsibility, but rather textually anchored, can be ascertained by considering a remarkable formulation found in *Twilight of the Idols* titled "My conception of Freedom." Here Nietzsche asserts that the value of a thing often resides in what it takes to attain it, the process itself rather than the outcome. Still, what is ultimately at stake in Nietzsche's account is the possibility of a concept of freedom that carries the forms of struggle associated with war at its center in an inhospitable world, as a world constituted by ideas of equality, freedom and fraternity, communism and abolitionism, fetters the instincts for hierarchical orders of rank and their constitutive forms of domination.[60] War is a "training in freedom," but freedom not understood in the chimerical sense of the party of movement, let alone in the Kantian and Hegelian accounts—one ethereal in its rationality, while the other is frustratingly anchored in collective institutions. Rather, for Nietzsche freedom rests on the solipsistic determinations of "self-responsibility" involving struggle.[61] Struggle is thus hypostatized in a no less reified idea of overcoming whose tragic dimension is secluded in the new aristocracy of free spirits.

Nietzsche casts this constant overcoming, which has ethical implications for the free spirit, in a more explicitly political vein:

> The nations which were worth something, which *became* worth something, never became so under liberal institutions: it was *great danger* which made of them something deserving reverence, danger which first teaches us to know ourselves, our virtues, our shield and spear,

our *spirit*. . . . Those great forcing-houses for strong human beings, for the strongest kind there has ever been, the aristocratic communities of the pattern of Rome and Venice, understood freedom in precisely the sense which I understand the word "freedom."[62]

In *The Antichrist* (1888) the political contours of the concept of responsibility embedded in his aristocratic radicalism become even more overt and bluntly expressed:

> The order of castes, *order of rank*, only formulates the supreme law of life itself; the separation of the three types is necessary for the preservation of society, for making possible higher and higher types—inequality of rights is the condition for the existence of rights at all. A right is a privilege. The privilege of each is determined by the nature of his being. Let us not underestimate the privilege of the *mediocre*. Life becomes harder and harder as it approaches the *heights*—the coldness increases, the responsibility increases. A high culture is a pyramid: it can only stand on a broad base, its very first prerequisite is a strongly and soundly consolidated mediocrity.[63]

Nietzsche's contempt for equality largely stems from an aristocratic cast of mind that avowed struggle and war and rebukes liberal neutralizations not for revolutionary purposes but for counterrevolutionary ones. Other nineteenth- and early-twentieth-century European figures shared a similar aristocratic cast of mind: Tocqueville, Weber, and Ortega y Gasset readily come to mind. But, unlike any of the aforementioned thinkers, Nietzsche was uncompromising with the democratic forces of the masses as political actors, and toward the end of his productive life, during his period of "reconciliation," he insisted on actualizing this cast of mind into the "party of life:" That new party of life, which would tackle the greatest of all tasks, the attempt to raise humanity higher, including the restless destruction of everything that was degenerating and parasitical, would again make possible that excess of life on earth from which the Dionysian state would have to awaken again. "I promise a tragic age; the highest art in saying Yes to life, tragedy, which will be reborn when humanity has weathered the consciousness of the hardest but most necessary *wars without suffering from it*."[64] In the face of it, this is a rather inscrutable formulation. But, once interpreted in light of his severance of responsibility from a collectively shared predicament of power, a shared fate between rulers and ruled, this lack of suffering could be possible in the context of wars that, while presided over by the party of life, have consequences that are not assumed by it: namely, wars whose initiators and instigators are accountable to no one and only responsible to themselves, wars that are the means and ends of their self-overcoming. The party of life is insulated from imputability and severed from any community of fate between its members and the casualties incurred in its violent endeavors.

This is, at any rate, what a nonarbitrary interpretation of the meaning of Nietzsche's invocation of a "party of life," and its tenets of destructive creation in the context of his diremption of doer and deed, might yield, but an interpretation that, however tenuous, is truer to the textual evidence than the starchy euphemisms of many a hermeneut of innocence. Clearly, in light of Nietzsche's objections and disavowals, this party of life is hardly a mass party, even if his account of the "ascetic priest" in *On the Genealogy of Morality* raises questions about the prospects of analogous elites at the service of *life*.[65] It is no plain metaphor either. Rather, it foreshadows an eminently *intra*subjective sense of self-responsibility embedded in the will to power. It is in the conjuring of the party of life where his recovery of responsibility is most clearly politically cast. In the summer of 1885 Nietzsche was very forthcoming about the political content of his transmogrification of responsibility:

Inexorable, hesitating, terrible as fate, the great task and question is approaching: how shall the earth as a whole be governed? And *for what* shall "man" as a whole—no longer just one people, one race—be raised and bred? The legislative moralities are the main means of fashioning out of men whatever a creative and profound will desires, assuming that such an artistic will of the highest rank holds power and asserts its creative will over long periods of time, in the shape of laws, religion, and customs.

"Such men of great creativity," Nietzsche laments, were missing during his own time. Their advent, which may well be unlikely in the foreseeable future, was fettered by "morality"—that "morality of the herd animal" which eschews unhappiness, tragedy, and hard living for the sake of "security, harmlessness, comfort, easy living" and thus forges a misplaced sense of responsibility on the basis of "'equal rights' and 'sympathy with all that suffers'" for which Nietzsche had nothing but contempt. Nietzsche even went on to toy with the idea of "the *new* Columbus" able to "discover the world of antiquity," an idea and figuration that are emblematic of his account of self-responsibility. But this Columbus would rediscover a new old world. Or, as he writes:

> However, anyone who has thought carefully about where and how the human plant has hitherto sprung up most vigorously must suppose that it was under the *reverse* conditions: that the danger of man's situation has to grow huge, his powers of invention and dissimulation to fight their way up through protracted pressure and coercion, his will to live become intensified into an unconditional will to power and overpower, and that danger, harshness, violence, danger in the alleyway and in the heart, inequality of heart, secrecy, stoicisim, the arts of temptation, devilry of all kinds, in short the antithesis of everything desirable for the herd, are needed if the human type is to be heightened. A morality of such reverse intentions, which wants to breed men to be high not comfortable and mediocre, a morality whose intention is to breed a ruling class—the future *masters of the earth*—must, if it is to be taught, must introduce itself starting from the existing moral law and sheltering under its words and forms.[66]

That these statements are uttered in the age of the Berlin conference, as European powers engaged in their scramble for Africa, which offered plentiful opportunities for European mastery of the world, albeit not in the terms Nietzsche advocated, is seldom acknowledged. Better still, equally unacknowledged are how rhetorical strategies that precisely involved "starting from the existing moral law and sheltering under its words and forms" had, by the late nineteenth century, become a trademark of the counterrevolutionary right in its subversion and resignification of values, something of which this avid observer of the political processes unfolding of his present would not have been unaware.[67] Similarly, Nietzsche's unabated and unwavering contempt for liberalism, democracy, and socialism rests on a largely imagined and thus idealized aristocratic past that is invoked not out of restorative impulses but rather as a way to prefigure a world to come. And Nietzsche's vaunted recovery of responsibility is part of this vision. Herein, *intra*subjective responsibility is conceptualized as a response to a situation that needs to be redressed by a return to an earlier moment, a reversal that is nonetheless projected to a future, and reckoning with that future demands discipline, fortitude, and fidelity to the party of life in order to face unscathed the suffering and violence that seeking it involves, something that only a free, self-responsible spirit can truly stomach.[68]

Nietzsche's account thus deflates any sense of responsibility for existing suffering and dismisses it as nothing more than a chimera of the weak, thus debarring any consideration of political responsibility for superfluous forms of suffering, both those traceable to an agent and its structural variations, at the heart of which there may not be an imputable will, but certainly many a beneficiary of an order that is nevertheless politically sanctioned. But, in Nietzsche's estimation, "the revolt of the man who *suffers*, against God, society, nature, forebears, educations, etc., imagines responsibilities and forms of will that do not exist."[69] Even if philistine and delusional, the revolts seeking to redress superfluous forms of suffering were not ineffective. And Nietzsche knew it and thus galvanized his considerable intellectual powers to debunk the ideas of responsibility sustaining these mass mobilizations. The self-overcoming, which he associated with the new sense of responsibility of the party of life, demands emancipation from the fetters exacted by older ideas of responsibility.

ANALYTICAL AFTERMATHS

Within analytical philosophy, responsibility is overwhelmingly cast in terms of individual accountability for actions and/or answerability to moral duties or principles.[70] Unfortunately, much in these discussions is either so deadening, or marred by stunting commonplaces that symptomatize anodyne platitudes about the afflictions supposedly besieging present-day liberal democracies, as to make one cringe. If at all, the political dimension of responsibility is only perfunctorily avowed.[71] But not every account in the analytical tradition reverts to these fatuities. Consider, for instance, Thomas M. Scanlon's *What We Owe to Each Other*. While Scanlon explicitly avows the Kantian lineage of his project, he forcefully avers the heteronomous nature of his version of contractualism, an avowal that grants the work an admirable sense of theoretical sobriety, and this without dwelling on how the book's title already portends his concern with the collective dimension of ethical life.[72] These concerns are elegantly exhibited in his treatment of the question of "moral responsibility" in a series of formulations that rival, and in some respects surpass, many of the formulations found within continental philosophy. For instance, although he anchors responsibility in individualist terms and his account bears an ethereal relationship to culture and market imperatives so characteristic of analytical moral philosophy, Scanlon takes seriously the existence of "background conditions" as mediating factors in determining responsibility.[73] Similarly, in his *Moral Dimensions*, he allows for variation in the ways that one's ethical commitments and responses are mediated by different imperatives and stakes, depending on the scene of action in which one acts, for example, the extent to which the "permissibility of an action" does not rest solely on intentionality but also on how the situation is structured.[74] In considering these, and in pointing out one's ability to do otherwise as a central component of responsibility, his account allows for more politically robust conceptions of responsibility. For one either responds or not to a predicament of powers and, by extension, one is responsible for such a response or lack thereof.

In this vein Scanlon presents a dualist account of responsibility: he distinguishes "responsibility as attributability" from "substantive responsibility."[75] Such a distinction resides in what he calls "the value of choice," and Scanlon ultimately distinguishes blame from responsibility on the basis of it. He thus summarizes the distinction: "When we ask if a person is responsible in the first of these senses [responsibility as attributability] what we are asking is whether that person is properly subject to praise or blame for having acted in that way. To say that someone is responsible in the second sense [substantive responsibility] for a certain outcome is, in the cases I have been concentrating on, to say that the person cannot complain of the burdens and obligations that result."[76] The "cases" that Scanlon's formulation alludes to range from an injury at an excavation site, to establishing agreements with others or criminal punishment. But it is his rendering of the case of the "willing addict" that illustrates the stakes in the distinction. As a *willing* addict, a person is responsible for his actions in a substantive sense, but not so in the case of an *unwilling* addict, who is responsible for his acts as these are attributable to him, but is not responsible in the second, substantive sense. The actions are attributable in both cases, but Scanlon regards the unwilling addict as not free and thus not responsible in the substantive sense that involves punishment. Even if, at times, he seems to collapse responsibility with guilt, his dualist conception of responsibility militates against such collapsing.[77] And, while his examples are stereotypically prosaic, the political import of his theorization of responsibility goes beyond them. Indeed, his distinctions echo Arendt's famous differentiation of responsibility and guilt in the Third Reich: "There are many who share responsibility without any visible proof of guilt."[78] That is, ordinary Germans who supported the regime may be held responsible in the first sense identified by Scanlon, but not in the second.

By separating these two senses of responsibility, and including the forces mediating the predicaments of power one inhabits, one can undercut the solipsistic bent of this moral theorization of responsibility. Similarly, unlike treatments of responsibility that present it as a commandment antecedent to action, or even as preontological as in Levinas and his disciples, Scanlon's dualist perspective has the sobering effect of considering the socially constituted conditions impairing substantive responsibility. It also considers the mediations that at once enable and constrain one's choices and one's ability to assume responsibility for actions.[79] Yet fully accounting for these mediations militates against an individualist sense of responsibility, as it opens up the possibility of spatially and temporally mapping the predicaments of power in which one acts and the mediating imperatives of, say, processes of racialization, which mediate and further constitute the situations in which would-be responsible agents act.

Indeed, the thorny question of racialization is a theme that Scanlon takes on, even if he does so in a partial way. It actually shows both the promise and the limits of his account. In a discussion of the first "Cosby controversy," which, at the time, constituted the most recent instance of how, under the guise of "personal responsibility," the ever alluring practice of bashing the poor rears its ugly head, Scanlon shows how his dualist concept of responsibility offers a nuanced formulation of individual responsibility. For Scanlon, ever the liberal, it is a question about striking a centrist position: "It is possible that many poor blacks are properly criticized for behaving in self-destructive ways and *also* that the government should, as a matter of justice, do more to improve their condition—in particular that it should do more to ensure that people are not placed in conditions that generate this kind of self-destructive behavior."[80] Scanlon's conclusion is predictably ambivalent, and it is tempting to sneer at him for it, not to mention the tropes at work in his formulations. Better still, he hardly acknowledges the ways in which systematic, modern, and postmodern forms of power, including but not reducible to capitalism, constitute not just the predicaments of power in which agents act but also forms of political subjectivity consonant with it. Even so, his theorization of responsibility opens up a way to conceptualize some of the constitutive elements of any genuine sense of political responsibility: a clear distinction between responsibility and guilt, substantive responsibility and blame, the need to recast accountability, and the mediation of historical formations and discourses of power in one's scenes of action.

But arguably the most influential account of responsability within the parameters of analytical philosophy is found in Bernard Williams's *Shame and Necessity*.[81] In contrast to the aseptic and individualist conceits of philosophical ethics, Williams famously offered a rendering of what he considered the four constitutive elements of responsibility: cause, intention, state, and response.[82] These "universal materials" are for him the defining elements of any concept of responsibility, however different any given configuration of them may be: namely, any concept of responsibility is a constellation composed of these pole stars, and what varies is the relative weight that is placed on each element in different situations. Different emphases yield different formulations. But Williams's account places considerable emphasis on the elements of the configuration adjudicating accountability. Blameworthiness is thus emphasized. And while the need to respond is still theorized, it mostly plays a subordinate role to the question of accountability, of guilt and blameworthiness. Stated differently, the ethical response is framed in terms of an action imputable to an agent, namely, an identifiable action that antecedes any sense of response. Accordingly: "The first of these elements, cause, is primary. . . . Without this, there is no concept of responsibility."[83]

The need to elicit a response is thus cast in terms of answerability, as an answer to a wrong that an agent caused, even if she did not intend to do so. Intentionality is rightly described as ambivalent in this context, and the need for a response is thereby avowed. Yet, even as the connotation of response is theorized, for Williams its role is such that rather than playing off the intersubjective dimension of responsibility, what emerges is an account still confined to individual responsibility in a situation brought about by her. Besides, the centrality of response is not cast in terms of responding to a situation, its contradictions, fissures, and imperatives; rather, the sense of response is projected inwards and reduced to "what is expected, demanded, or required of the agent, or what is imposed on him."[84] Williams's examples, from Homer to Sophocles, attest to this preference. But Williams qualifies his argument in two important ways: first, from the perspective of modern-day legal discourse, where people are held accountable and "criminally liable not only for outcomes they did not intend . . . but in some cases for outcomes they did not even cause"; second, in what amounts to a corollary of the previous qualification, he acknowledges that in "any complex society" the allocation of causality is often problematic and difficult.[85] But Williams's perfunctory invocation of complexity reveals the inadequacies of his theorization of responsibility when considered from the perspective of scenes of power constituted by historically entrenched patterns of domination: "There are, of course, particularly in any complex society, endless problems that arise about this point, such as the allocation of causality between several agents who have between them brought about some effect. There are issues, too, about collective responsibility. But these are difficulties in applying the primitive idea I am discussing."[86] By placing so much emphasis on causality and individual answerability, Williams comes close to surrendering to the conceit of enmeshing responsibility with guilt. Although sorely lacking in the literary cadence and grace of Williams's prose, Scanlon's dualist perspective precisely allows for such distinctions.

Ultimately, Williams is fundamentally committed to an urbane individualism and only vaguely concerned with sociological realities and contexts, and his vaunted invocations of *history* and *realism* are equally innocent of history as an obdurate process of continuities and discontinuities, and to the historical realities of capitalist accumulation and imperialism, racialization and gendering, constituting contemporary predicaments of power in both their temporal and spatial specificities.[87] In the caustic formulation of an otherwise very sympathetic critic, "he felt as naturally comfortable in paddling about in the tepid and slimy puddle created by Locke, J. S. Mill, and Isaiah Berlin as he did in most other places."[88] Indeed, for all the talk about historical sense, and his acute sensibility to the thought forms found in

Thucydides and Greek tragedy, Williams was mostly unable to come to terms with the actual political meaning of the "primacy of the situation," its impossible but ineluctable predicaments, and the necessary "economy of sympathy" constitutive of a genuinely political ethic of collective life. Like most analytical moral philosophers, his account remained uncritical about the liberal-democratic capitalist states structuring the spatial and sociological realities it took for granted.

What, then, is the political import of this formulation? Williams's formulation is better suited for personal responsibility, for responsibility understood as an ethos, as a virtue of character, which is a necessary but insufficient condition of political action. It is thus instructive that while Williams refers to "any complex society" he nowhere satisfactorily theorizes such complexity or how it produces a specific subject, an agent and a *habitus* that is culturally mediated, even if it presents itself as not.[89] Williams's analytical dissection of the "universal materials" of responsibility is best reformulated in terms of Hegel's elucidation of the different aspects of the problematic of responsibility. This reformulation consists of articulating the dialectical mediation and interdependence of Williams's materials: these can be reworked by conceptualizing responsibility as "being committed to, responsible for, and authoritative about" collectively shared ethical and political ends and the means needed to attain them.[90] But accounts like Williams's abstractly posit the individualization and autonomization of responsibility. The concrete sense of space and limits that characterize political conceptions of responsibility are disowned, or fundamentally slanted, as is any collective significance of the idea of ethical responsibility.

POLITICAL, NOT MORAL

The aforementioned individualist conceit has saturated both philosophical conceptions of responsibility within North Atlantic analytical philosophy and discussions of "personal responsibility" in the United States, most recently in the political context of disaffiliation that vividly crystallized during the eighties and nineties. Neoconservative and neoliberal iterations of this idea range from James Q. Wilson and George L. Kelling's "broken windows" theory to William J. Bennett's *The Book of Virtues* (1993) and the "Personal Responsibility and Work

Opportunity Act" of 1996.[91] In these accounts the collective and political dimension of responsibility is mostly disavowed. For even if always ultimately anchored on an individual disposition, overall responsibility can only be conceptualized in relation to the situation in which the agent of responsibility is situated and to which he responds as a member of a larger collective. As Manuel Cruz has forcefully argued, the need to avow an intersubjective account of responsibility is sine qua non of a political and genuinely critical conception of responsibility:

> Beyond question, conservative sectors are using the notion of individual responsibility with the thinly disguised aim of draining all content from the notion of collective responsibility—a notion which makes them uncomfortable, as it means a costly commitment to the most disadvantaged sectors of society. These sectors prefer not to speak of society's responsibility to the unemployed, the sick, refugees, and, in general, all those who are marginalized; rather, they propose making it the individual responsibility of the unemployed to obtain a job, of the sick to take their medicine, of the active workforce to provide for their own pensions, and so on.[92]

But to speak of social and political responsibility entails re-cognizing how vulnerability is historically mediated, systematically constituted, and politically sanctioned. For natural and historical modalities of vulnerability are thoroughly mediated by imperatives of power.[93] And *political* responsibility, as historically embedded in the domain of collective action, needs to transcend the *intra*subjective model of action and not only avow *inter*subjectivity but also incorporate reflection on external imperatives, limits, and constraints. More important, whereas responsibility as a philosophical concept has tended toward individuation, it cannot be treated as an exclusively individual attribute. Rather, just like the content of one's behavior, one's responsibility is largely impersonal and thoroughly mediated by the situation, its institutions, and the social and historical processes one is responding to. Intentionality and individual responsibility is not only constituted in reference to external, impersonal institutions but also in relation to the historically constituted, material situation, along with its immanent principles and imperatives, in which the subject is embedded. What Vincent Descombes has written apropos of the concept of intention equally holds for that of responsibility:

"The concept of intention seems to call for us to locate the intentional subject (in his head) but it quickly becomes apparent that that is not its place. It is rather that the subject, in order to acquire a mind, must be situated within a milieu that would have been described in classical French as 'moral' or in German as 'spiritual' [*geistig*]. This moral milieu is formed by institutions as providers of meaning that individual subjects can make their own."[94] Indeed, if one casts the invocation of "moral" and "spiritual" along more materialist lines, these formulations stand, *mutatis mutandis*, for the social dialectic of intra- and intersubjectivity at the core of a properly dialectical concept of responsibility. The subject of responsibility is, by extension, also a socio-cultural object in historically constituted and politically sanctioned predicaments of power. It is a materialist subject—in the dual sense of that word: subject qua agent, subject qua object—with its own natural history, along with the sediments that emerged out of the way in which subjective habitus and practices are objectively mediated.[95]

One of the challenges, accordingly, consists of forging a concept and practice of political responsibility able to respond to and rein in—to the extent that it may be realistically possible—the forms of power structuring and mediating political life. Another challenge is to recast answerability politically. For answerability can be interpreted in a variety of ways: one can answer to the moral law, the civil law, the rules of order and the imperatives of the market, and to a transcendental ethical other; or, less solipsistic and more politically, one can answer to the law of the state or else respond out of fidelity to a political identity and the principles and institutions that promote it. Political responsibility, to be sure, cannot be just answerability. The emphasis needs to be placed on the response by virtue of inhabiting scenes of power, where one's responsibility resides precisely by virtue of the political form at stake and on one's position in the situation to which one responds within a structure of power. Ideas and practices of commitment and responsibility *for* and *to* predicaments of power, along with relations of authority, thus constitute enabling conditions based on limits and constraints, which are constitutive of a political ethic of responsibility; or, stated differently, these are determinations that form the concept of political responsibility that is constitutive of a political ethic, an ethics of the collective life. These enabling conditions are the external determinants that mediate the concrete articulation of "causality" and "intention," but also "state" and "response." For "state" is hereby considered as the locus in which political action in a demarcated and, by extension, limited predicament of power becomes possible, predicaments of power that are the occasion concretely demanding a response.

Yet for these notions to gain political import, for these to have political traction and teeth, as it were, they have to be conceptualized as always-already eventuating *in situation*, as operative in historically structured and politically sanctioned predicaments of power. At the very least, political responsibility requires assuming one's actions, reflecting on their nature and consequences, and giving an account of them. Political responsibility thus entails a reflective response to the actions done in one's name as part of a political order in which historical practices and processes of, say, racialization or capitalist relations, often render individuals either as structural beneficiaries, subordinated or dominated denizens, or bystanders, all of which is irreducible to assuming responsibility, let alone attributing causes for individual responsibility. Furthermore, the dilution of intentionality and agency in contemporary predicaments of power needs to be incorporated into any conception of responsibility that seeks concreteness, something that can only be encompassed by mapping the ways that imperatives of power mediate the present. Such cognitive mappings cannot be offered as later additions, but need their role to be adequately theorized. Equally ineluctable are accounts of the constitutive gap between intention and act and the concrete configuration of a political situation in which action eventuates and becomes concrete. For one always already acts in situations whose historicity thoroughly mediates both the *internal* moment of intentionality and its *externalization*, the moment of actualization. Conversely, these mappings and accounts demand an acute sense of what constitutes the limits, spatial and temporal differentiations, and economic and political imperatives impinging on both moments of intentionality.[96]

That is, at any rate, one mode of conceptualizing responsibility politically. It is a way for political responsibility, which by virtue of its historical specificity is always limited, to become politically viable and concrete. A sense of political responsibility that is central for a robust sense of political life. And that entails fidelity to its binding political forms, in which intentions, causes, and responses are determinations that are always temporally and spatially located in historically mediated and politically constituted situations.

4

ETHICAL REDUCTIONS

The almost insoluble task is to let neither the power of others,
nor our own powerlessness, stupefy us.

—Theodor W. Adorno, *Minima Moralia*

IF THE problems inherited from the Kantian tradition, including the critique leveled by Nietzsche, contributed to *intra*subjective ideas of responsibility, it is Emmanuel Levinas's work that has mediated the prevalence of the concept in efforts to overcome the "autonomous subject" and thus presumably formulate *inter*subjective theories of responsibility that give primacy to the Other. Indeed, Levinas is the sage in most transatlantic theorizations of ethical responsibility as "responsibility to the Other." He is credited with formulating the overcoming "of the very horizon of egology," an overcoming that paves the way to "re-conceptualize responsibility as a being 'for the other,'" something that effectively challenges "the primacy of egology and the predominance of the will" that define previous ethical accounts of responsibility, including Nietzsche's.[1] An overcoming that consists in excising the "communitarian moorings" that have sanctioned so much pain and suffering, something that demands inheriting his "decidedly nonegological" account of the ethical relation, an account suitable "for an ethics in dispersion" that is responsive to the claims of alterity.[2] Upending the claims of the self to be identical with itself—and, as Derrida once remarked, self and same were already quasi-folded in the French word *même*—Levinas rewrites theological discussions of the Other in terms of an ethics as first philosophy pivoting on the idea of infinite responsibility to the Other.[3]

Whereas the persistent structure of Levinas's ethics defies succinct summary, and a thorough reconstruction of its origins and transmutations is beyond the scope of the present discussion, some basic historical and conceptual elucidations are necessary. This is important not only as a way to situate his contemporary heirs within an intellectual matrix, but to offer a more discerning account of the historicity of his thought, a historicity that is fundamentally misrecognized by uncritical reliance on his autobiographical pronouncements.[4] On the basis of these retrospective pronouncements, Levinas is piously characterized as a Lithuanian Jew, or Holocaust philosopher, outside the dominant logic of Western modernity and its logos, or as a sage from the age of catastrophe whose thought bears the forms and contents of ethical possibility in its aftermath. By following Levinas's own self-descriptions, critics tend to overstate the centrality of Nazi horror in the architecture of Levinas's philosophy, most of which was conceived prior to any awareness of these horrors, even if developed as a response to the French postwar predicament. Sylvie Courtine-Denamy's one-liner succinctly conveys this view: "A la démesure des crimes de la Shoah, correspond chez Levinas une responsabilité démesure."[5] But, as Samuel Moyn has convincingly shown, such *démesure* is hardly commensurate with the experience of the Shoah, but has a different ideological matrix: "Levinas always remained a pre-Holocaust philosopher insofar as his thought continued to be governed by interwar premises" and the ethical tenor of his writing was forged in the context of a broader turn to ethics in French letters as part of how the postwar political field was structured with the onset of the cold war.[6] Likewise, it is important to offer a more searching account of the conceptual architecture of his thought and the sediments it bears from the intellectual traditions he has inherited and the political situations to which it responded. Understanding the intellectual traditions he drew from is of particular importance in apprehending the ethical and political significance of certain formulations that nowadays have acquired axiomatic status: say, the timelessness of Levinas's quasi-solipsistic, preontological account of responsibility.

LEVINAS IN CONTEXT

By the early twentieth century, the spatial coordinates defining the European *Belle Epoque* had imploded. During this time, Europeans witnessed capitalist convolutions, along with the ensuing crises and transformations, and an intensification of interimperialist rivalries. These processes concatenated into an unprecedented brutality signifying a profound crisis in the interstices of liberal civilization, as this civilization plunged into interimperialist warfare and carnage, revolution and counterrevolution. These crises marked the onset of the European civil war and within it the detonation of a process defined by the crumbling of late nineteenth-century imperial nation-states and their eventual denouement in the Great War. Ideologically, this gave way to a biological-racial nationalism that fueled variations of fascism and radicalized the forms of chauvinism already at work in the leading capitalist nation-states in and outside Europe. One important outcome of these processes was the ultimate destruction of the fragile late-nineteenth-century attempt "to spatialize politics in a stable way," a destruction that further contributed to the deep sense of spatial disorientation so acutely registered in European letters.[7] This erosion of spatiality was coeval with the "empires of time" setting the agenda in the world of science.[8] One corollary outcome of this convergence was how, both politically and intellectually, space became increasingly temporalized.

Philosophically, this temporalization symbolized a momentous episode that significantly obfuscated the spatial presuppositions constitutive of political responsibility. This spatial disorientation is readily grasped in the temporalizing of abstract space in the leading schools of early twentieth-century European philosophy. Both neo-Kantianism and phenomenology shared a drive to further despatialize philosophical reflection. In the case of neo-Kantianism, centrality was accorded to a philosophy of introspection concerned with "a priori objective validity," something that would be recast and radicalized in Husserl's "phenomenological reductions" and the temporalization of space that became the signature of his phenomenology, which would then become further radicalized in the internalization (and ontologization) of history as historicity in Heidegger.[9] Even Heidegger's invocation of facticity purportedly went beyond historical processes and their enabling constraints. It rather conveyed "the being of 'our' 'own' *Dasein*" duly cast in overwhelmingly temporal terms.[10] Theorizing places in ways that temporalize space, as sites for the concealment and deconcealment of Being, or the "Being of beings," ultimately displaced the conceptualization of spaces of actual historical eventuation.

It is in the philosophical problematic inaugurated by these thinkers that one first glimpses the lineages of the conceptualization of responsibility that found fuller expression in the writings of Levinas and are reproduced in the thought forms of his transatlantic heirs.[11] These temporalizations, despatializations, and reductions thus constitute the historical sediments that crystallized in the thought forms that eventually became constitutive of the unhistorical and despatialized idea bearing Levinas's signature: "responsibility to the Other." The architecture of Levinas's philosophical reflections was thus forged as part of intellectual debates within European thought during the interwar period. More specifically, these reflections constitute the harvest of long-standing engagements with the phenomenological tradition of Husserl, the philosophy of Heidegger, Judaism and Jewish philosophers, especially Franz Rosenzweig, along with the great Protestant theologian Karl Barth.[12] These engagements largely predate his turn to ethics—which is best exemplified in his notorious claim about ethics as first philosophy—and which only crystallized in the context of the broader turn to ethics characterizing French letters with the onset of the cold war.

Levinas's phenomenology of the other was formulated way before it became the signature of his ethics. Barth is of particular importance in this genealogy. The theological motifs suffusing many of Levinas's philosophical formulations of the Other—say, the asymmetrical, unmediated, and nonreciprocal relation to the Other—have him as a main source. But the philosophical problematic to which Levinas's ethics, and its turning away from history to the realm of the preontological, corresponds is already at work in Husserl's phenomenology, especially in the ways in which Husserl's idea of the "phenomenological reduction" posits the disavowal of historical mediations, and political and economic imperatives, as part of his quasi-transcendental philosophy.[13] Whereas Husserl's idea of the "phenomenological reduction" is deployed throughout his corpus at different levels, undergoing several reformulations, there is a persistent structure to it: it brackets out not only the historical self—the "I" as a concrete historical reality, as an upshot of different institutional, natural-historical and social mediations—but history, as such, in its attempt to grasp the historicity of consciousness, understood as the consciousness of historical experience.[14] Husserl's bracketing of history as part of his reductions still invokes an abstract historicity from an "egological" perspective. Heidegger, in contrast, went on to sidestep the problematic of the subject by recourse to an idea of *Dasein* that continued to bracket out history, while abstractly recasting it as historicity and remaining committed to phenomenology as a method of wresting the historically concrete out of actual history for the sake of a more originary historicity prior to history or, most of all, a fundamental ontology.[15] In *Being and Time* history is ontologized in the pseudoconcreteness of a historicity without history.[16] Levinas went on to further radicalize Heidegger's displacement of egology, while retaining the formal contours of phenomenological argumentation by positing a reduction to the realm of preontology on the basis of which he eventually made the notorious claim on behalf of ethics as first philosophy.[17] And traces of both phenomenology and "his foray into theology" ultimately became sedimentations that mediated the political and critical import of the theological philosophy he forged in the interwar period and the ethics he formulated on the basis of it.[18]

How exactly does Levinas undergo the recasting of the philosophy of the Other into an ethics? While the Holocaust left an indelible mark in Levinas's thought, it is not as a response to it that his philosophy forces the ethical *englobant* of politics that is his signature.[19] Rather, Levinas's own the turn to ethics unfolded in the context of the cold war, through his response to Sartre's *Anti-Semite and the Jew*, Sartre's quarrel with Camus, along with Levinas's own version of the moralist rejection of utopia, and his radicalization of Judaism and the dedifferentiations ensuing from it.[20] Levinas's ethical turn was largely a politically infused philosophical response to the political crucibles of a specific historical situation.

Accordingly, the early cold war is the relevant context to probe the historical determinants mediating the development of Levinas's mature philosophy. This is a context in which antiutopian sensibilities were radically articulated as part of an overall suspicion of collective agencies and the intensification of political life that defined the interwar period, thus leading to the hypostatization of individual existence.

In the wider European context, bifurcation of individual existence and collective life took shape as a sharp diremption of morality from politics and history, part of an eminently political attempt to discredit the forms of collective agency and action that could harbinger revolutionary prospects in postwar Europe. That containment of such revolutionary prospects—communists and other radicals were central in the antifascist Resistance in France, Italy, Yugoslavia, and Greece—was central to American strategic vision for Europe and world capitalism is well documented.[21] In French intellectual circles, however, these concerns found expression cloaked in the language of antiutopia, or antipolitical existentialism, a rehearsal of Kierkegaard's polemic against Hegel and Hegelianism—Sartre and Merleau-Ponty, along with Albert Camus and Gabriel Marcel, were central figures. Herein, ethics first emerged as an alternative to politics qua collective agency and historical endeavor. Fleeing history and debarring collective agencies and action as a situated modality of shared praxis, with its own autonomous internal imperatives and principles, thus became a historical determinant that further sedimented the theological and phenomenological tenets informing Levinas's ethical thought. Kierkegaardian and Barthian motifs, along with the illusion of immediacy running in tandem with sediments of the argumentative structure of the phenomenological idea of "reduction," coalesce around an eminently political form of ethical partisanship that sought to discredit any revolutionary challenge to the emerging political order: America's Europe. In these efforts the ethical became inoculated from history, the individual from the collective, ethics from politics. Better yet, in the context of the anti-Marxism of a cohort of French intellectuals—who in the name of an antiutopian, antipolitical, and existentialist ethics decried forms of collective agency associated with the Hegelian-Marxist legacy—modalities of ethical politics conforming to the parameters of the defensive politics of militant North Atlanticism crystallized. And Levinas's turn to ethics responded to this situation. His response found primary expression in terms of his recasting of Judaism as a universal ethics. In Moyn's formulation, "Levinas's presentation of Judaism as a safeguard against the wistful and treacherous desire for a revolutionary alternative to the burden of responsibility not only followed his creative interpretation of the Jewish tradition but also form a transconfessional imperative during the Cold War of thinking 'after utopia.'"[22]

A recasting that entails not only the internalization of the Other and its reconstitution as ethically binding and thus present in the very constitution of the self—an internalization that amounted to the dedifferentiation of the divine encounter and human ethics, something that Rosenzweig has carefully conceived as distinct—human ethics is derivative of the divine encounter, "neither identical nor analogous to it"—but also posited the need to demarcate ethics from politics as part of a moralizing stance that ultimately amounted to a defensive ethical politics.[23] Just as it would be the case with the ethical politics defining the ethical turn of the late seventies, Levinas's flight from history and political life was thoroughly historical and political.

In this vein, Levinas writes about how politics "is opposed to morality, as philosophy to naiveté."[24] And responsibility squarely belongs to ethics, not to politics. It is embedded in ethics as first philosophy, thus prior to political life. Indeed, all the formulations Levinas offers of the idea of ethical responsibility are to be understood as strictly moral, therefore dirempted from the realm of political life. Responsibility, which in this account is spatially indeterminate, is conceived as at once illimitable and stark. This seems to be as far from what Simone de Beauvoir once called "the ethics of ambiguity" as one can go; yet it is equally distant from any historical concreteness, or awareness, of the obduracy of humanity's natural history, sedimentations and ossifications, let alone the spatial determinations, constituting predicaments of power.[25] On the contrary, the obduracy and starkness of the imperative of responsibility that Levinas conjures up is derived precisely from its abstract nature, and how it is bereft of particular, historically constituted, determinations. The upshot: a strategy of compensation in the form of a commandment whose emphases on starkness, illimitability, and compulsory bindingness seek to compensate for powerlessness. Or, to invoke Peter Dews's observation: "by detaching the ethical command so completely from any empirical human interest, or from any development discernable within history, he surely risks producing the opposite effect from the one he intends."[26] It risks futility qua ethics, even if, by effectively debarring forms of political agency, it is politically productive in a negative way. Even if such sternness is justified in the name of a historical experience, or axial event—say, Nazism for Levinas—its severe formalism bears sediments and traces of the modalities of history it seeks to extinguish, both political and philosophical histories, not least in the compulsions of its formal imperatives and the hypostatization of chastened subjectivity.[27]

Ironically, Levinasian heteronomy is more removed from actuality than Kant's vaunted autonomy. While autonomy is scrupulously separated from empirical inclination in the Kantian system, Kant's philosophy of history at least offers the supplement for its historical actualization, its collective eventuation in history. On this score, the Kantian *Sollen* is actually more palatable than Levinas's. Undoubtedly, his account of the subject is hardly the ethereal, disembodied entity of Kantian *noumena*, nor is it akin to that conception of subjectivity that he famously reproached Heidegger with conjuring. Critics have pointed out how, in contrast to these disembodiments, Levinas deploys many a powerful adjective to thematize the constitution of subjectivity, its corporeality and creatureliness—fatigue, malaise, nausea, pain, passivity, sensibility, suffering—and his account of *the Other* is equally peppered by allusions to thirst, hunger, clothing, and shelter.[28] But there is something dampened, vacuous, and abstract about these invocations. Their deadness brings to mind one of Brecht's quips from his *Dialogues of Refugees*: "Germans have a weak aptitude for materialism. When they stumble upon it, they immediately make it into an idea, and a materialist becomes someone who believes ideas come from material conditions, not the other way around, and here is where the matter ends."[29] This is, mutatis mutandi, the case with Levinas's invocation of these adjectives, an adjectivization that merely amounts to *abstract* invocations of embodiment. The irony is that this critic of cold Enlightenment rationalism conjures an unencumbered image of a naked self, a self barely partaking in what one associates with humanity (say, culture) that few if any rationalist defenders of the Enlightenment ever dreamed of.[30]

Yet Levinas's invocation of embodiment is too often uncritically accepted. Terry Eagleton has explained its intuitive appeal, even while acknowledging its severity: "The harshness of the Kantian moral law remains firmly in place; but its brutal lack of realism is tempered by a phenomenological vocabulary (openness, otherness, bodiliness and so on) more hospitable to a late modern sensibility or postmodern age. Sensibility becomes the medium of obligation."[31] This holds. Still: if sensibility constitutes an unmediated mediation in ethics, and that is a big *if*—as sensibility is thoroughly mediated by humanity's natural history—does it not become hypostatized and thus depleted of any critical import in these formulations? More to the point: how binding is this hypostatized obligation when the abnegated subject actually encounters others and such sensibility is treated as culturally mediated? Indeed, such sensibility is prereflective and precritical, and in this precise sense Levinas remained a precritical philosopher, which raises the question of the possibility of brigading him within the context of critical theory, a philosophical tradition for which critical reason is the sine qua non. For if there is something that emerges from the twenty-five years of critical philosophy, and that remains an obligatory point of departure for genuinely critical theory, it is Hegel's insight about process and mediation as intrinsic to the experience of consciousness.[32] These are, at any rate, some of the hard-earned lessons of critical philosophy.[33] Sidestepping without tarrying with them by way of neologisms is a regression, a relapse into a precritical disposition and its antinomies. All the same, Levinas's wager is that such a self is constituted in reference to an originary otherness, which recasts the dyad self-other; a relational constitution that debunks hypostatized ideas of the "I" and its conceits about autonomy, but which is ultimately an asymmetrical nonrelation of abnegation. Again, what emerges in lieu of the "I" is a thoroughly heteronomous idea of responsibility pivoting on a formalism in which the Other compulsively upbraids it. This is a chastising that is no less obliging than the sometimes despotic sense of necessity found in Kant. In a way, it is even more despotic. Because it consists of an obligation without economy or regulation, there is no sense of limits to it, nor any reckoning with the primacy of the situation in which it is actualized, let alone its mediations or the forms of responsibility such economy demands. It is cast as immediate in at least two senses: it is preconceptual, and thus tacitly assumed as immediate, and it is outside any social and cultural, much less institutional, mediation.

HYPOSTATIZING THE OTHER

Contemporary accounts of philosophical ethics indebted to Levinas brook none of the spatial determinations characteristic of more robustly political ideas of responsibility.[34] The different connotations of political space and limits that figure as enabling conditions of the practices of responsibility are largely decried in theoretical and philosophical articulations of ethical responsibility. Among the casualties of these dismissals are not only conceptualizations of responsibility in terms of conceptual activity, as in Kant, but also robustly political ideas of answerability to predicaments of power or accountability for them. In this way, these posit the primacy of ethics over politics, or at least ethics supervening over political life, and, by extension, moral conceptions of responsibility over political ones. The modes of reflection that nowadays prevail in continental and theoretical approaches to the question of responsibility can be accurately described as late modern, or postmodern, versions of *prima philosophia* advocating for modalities of ethical politics at odds with hegemonic ones. But, like every other version of ethical politics, these attempt to anchor ethical responsibility in advance of the scenes of power in which encounters with others occur. While these philosophies often profess fidelity to the Other, the texture of collective life mediating and structuring the spaces for these encounters is mostly abstractly posited, or partially thematized, but never conceptualized with their particular historical, economic, and political determinations. Rather than political responsibility, what emerges is a hypostatized positing of ethical responsibility to the Other that then, it is argued, is supposed to supervene on political life.

How exactly this is so can be grasped by considering Maurice Blanchot's *The Writing of the Disaster* (1980). Symptomatically, this book was published at a time in which the late twentieth-century turn to ethics in the French scene was reaching a peak. In Blanchot's extravagant account of responsibility one encounters an inheritance of Levinas and an anticipation of most of the themes that would reverberate in North Atlantic appropriations:

Responsibility: a banal word, a notion moralistically assigned to us as a (political) duty. We ought to try to understand the word as it has been opened up and renewed by Levinas so that it has come to signify (beyond the realm of meaning) the responsibility of an other philosophy (which, however, remains in many respects eternal philosophy). Responsible: this word generally qualifies—in a prosaic, bourgeois manner—a mature, lucid, conscientious man, who acts with circumspection, who takes into account all elements of a given situation,

calculates and decides. The word "responsible" qualifies a success-
ful man of action. But now responsibility—my responsibility for the
other, for everyone, without reciprocity—is displaced. . . . *My* responsibility for the other presupposes an overturning such that it can only
be marked by a change in the status of "me," a change in time and
perhaps in language. Responsibility, which withdraws me from my
order—perhaps from all orders and from order itself—responsibility,
which separates me from myself (from the "me" that is mastery and
power, from the free, speaking subject) and reveals the other *in place*
of me, requires that I answer for absence, for passivity. It requires, that
is to say, that I answer for the impossibility of being responsible—to
which it has already consigned me by holding me accountable and also
discounting me altogether. . . . For if I can speak of responsibility only
by separating it from all forms of present-consciousness (from will, resolution, concern; from light, from reflective action; but perhaps from
the involuntary as well: from all that is indifferent to my consent, from
the gratuitous, the non-activating . . .), if responsibility is rooted where
there is no foundation, where no root can lodge itself, and if thus it
tears clean through all bases and cannot be assumed by any individual
being, how then, how otherwise than as response to the impossible . . .
will we sustain the enigma of what is announced in the term "responsibility," the term which the language of ordinary morality uses in the
most facile way possible by putting it into the service of order?[35]

One is hard-pressed to surmise a more hyperbolic and depoliticized
sense of responsibility than this. Blanchot gives expression to some
of the conceits found in appropriations of Levinas across the Atlantic:
the rejection of political responsibility; rather simplistic reduction
of accountability to the tenets of "bourgeois morality"; faint-hearted
echoes of Nietzsche in disavowals of knowledge or calculation of
means/ends; the preontological temptation, or perhaps conceit, that
seeks to anchor an ethics of imperatives in advance of the scenes actualizing the commitment in the context of predicaments of power; fleeing history and swimming upstream to the river of the dyad conscious-
ness/unconsciousness; an ethereal response outside any order, which
entails the temporalization of responsibility and a corollary despatialization; and so on. In a Levinasian key he also writes: "My responsibility is anterior to my birth just as it is exterior to my consent, to my

liberty."[36] Responsibility is immediate, as there is no mediating scene, let alone constitutive situation, or any sort of differentiating process structuring its allocation: "Immediacy not only rules out all mediation; it is the infiniteness of a presence such that it can no longer be spoken of, for the relation itself, be it ethical or ontological, has burned up all at once in a night bereft of darkness."[37]

All of this amounts to a rejection of robust forms of collective and political agency, as well as of the cognitive mappings that political literacy in navigating predicaments of power demands; equally absent is a sense of enabling boundaries or limits. Instead, Blanchot's formulation pivots on the simplification and reduction of responsibility, as an ethical and political category, to a caricature of bourgeois morality. That these displacements and disavowals are reductions, displacements, and transformations of what the concept of responsibility has historically connoted is clear enough. Less readily accepted, however, is how politically disabling these formulations of responsibility are, and how symptomatic of a turn away from politics largely triggered by antipathy to radical leftist politics. For the idea of infinite responsibility to the Other, a responsibility frequently cast as a limitless and "preontological" imperative, or an ethical injunction and commandment anteceding the scenes of actions that could render it concrete, is at best a labile stance of left-liberals and at worst a neutralization of forms of collective agency threatening the mainstay of depoliticized politics. It is out of this particular constellation that the elective affinity between Theory, one of the legacies of the structuralist moment in French philosophy, and Levinasian ethics can be discerned. If Levinas's ethics is one response to a philosophical and historical problematic, his emergence as a signpost in the works of otherwise very different figures like Judith Butler and Jacques Derrida is the final result of a set of intellectual and political historical processes and concatenations. The main historical and political determinants have been addressed; what follows is a more immanent critique of two influential heirs.[38]

IMPOSSIBLE RESPONSIBILITY

In *Adieu to Emmanuel Levinas* Derrida exemplarily casts the intersection between ethics and politics in Levinasian terms.[39] Yet, however much an influence, his discussion of responsibility is irreducible to it. In Derrida's work the problem of responsibility is part of an attempt to elucidate the intersection between ethics and politics that is also enmeshed with Nietzschean concerns about the fate of responsibility once conceived beyond calculability and recast as a radical response. In *Politics of Friendship*, for instance, Derrida expands on his formulation of responsibility and the intersubjective moment built into the grammar of this concept. Intersubjectivity is thus cast from the perspective of what he calls the "question of response" along Nietzschean lines: "a brief grammar of the response—or rather, of 'responding'—will afford a preliminary insight" into the question of the intersection between "responding" and "responsibility"; he thus juxtaposes and unpacks the interdependence of a series of connotations associated with answerability: "'to answering for,' 'to respond to,' 'to answer before.'"[40] Throughout these reflections on responsibility one finds a set of recurrent themes: the primacy of ethics over politics, the (im)possibility of the decision, and the unconditional responsibility to the "Other," which is proclaimed in terms of well-nigh infinite generosity and hospitality. That last, especially once cast in terms of a radical openness to the Other, sometimes takes the form of a commandment or imperative as an unmediated and thus abstract *Sollen*. Derrida, on the one hand, rehearses the Kantian themes of antinomies and imperatives, along with a quasi-transcendental mode of argumentation that by way of the legacy of phenomenology and its method resets the quintessential Kantian question of "conditions of possibility" into "conditions of impossibility"; on the other hand, it poses the question of responsibility in terms of the need to have an unconditioned acceptance and openness to the "Other."[41]

But to fully grasp the significance of these themes, a brief look at one of Derrida's more compelling enactments of his thought is necessary. In his remarkable essay, "Psyche: Invention of the Other," he offers a succinct yet powerful formulation of the intersection between deconstruction, invention, and the Other, which bears on his theorization of responsibility. Derrida prefaces his essay with a provocative assertion: "deconstruction loses nothing by admitting that it is impossible"—and his elucidation of this *admission* runs like this: "For a deconstructive operation, *possibility* is rather the danger, the danger of becoming an available set of rule-governed procedures, methods, accessible approaches. The interest of deconstruction, of such force and desire as it may have, is a certain experience of the impossible: that is, as I shall insist in my conclusion, of the other—the experience of the other as the invention of the impossible, in other words, as the only possible invention."[42] Possibility is thus deconstructed as impossibility, and the impossible is thus formulated as that which is presently impossible *within* the given parameters of thought, but whose possibility would implode these parameters. Derrida's figurations of possibility and impossibility are folded in a modernist conceit that praises singularity and innovation as ends in themselves: these posit the new and that anxiety about the persistence of the old, thus effecting a call for unmediated, virtually *ex nihilo*, invention.[43] Invention, accordingly, evokes what Fredric Jameson in another context refers to as a "break," a break from what precedes the invention in question in order to aver the connotations of singularity found in this concept and the futurist disposition that is a central animating impulse, which it, in turn, seeks to enable.[44] While not unblemished by modernist conceits, Derrida's recasting of the impossible leads to brilliant local insights about the aporetic status of the concept "invention." Aporias that, accordingly, conjure the futurity of "to come," "the other," "the new," "production," and the "public." "Deconstruction is inventive or it is nothing at all," Derrida writes, but not just any invention counts.[45]

Derrida's essay is, among other things, a sustained reflection on the same problem that the dialectical legacy since Hegel has tarried with, and often refers to as the dialectic of the actual and the possible, and how its complexity can be rendered speculatively, thus rendering the space, the middle, between identity and lack of identity, and so on. But Derrida's concern is not with the landmarks of dialectical thinking: "determinate negation," "mediation," or the triad of the universal, the particular, and the singular. Rather, the emphasis is on the last element of the triad, but isolated from the rest: invention of the singular. Deconstruction mines the transgressive moment that lies at the intersection between invention and production. It is not regimented by the "statutory limits" imposed on it by those that license it, or commissioned it, Derrida asserts. Rather, it challenges them. Hence its transgressive quality: "An invention that refused to be dictated, ordered, programmed by these conventions would be out of place, out of order, impertinent, transgressive" (10, 21). The challenge is to avoid subsuming the singularity of the new in terms of the old or the different in terms of the same. A daunting task given the situated nature of any invention in a milieu, in a scene, if you wish, that mediates its constitution or serves as a precondition for it. As such, an invention is "susceptible to repetition, exploitation, reinscription," and so Derrida's deconstructive move is to offer "a reinvention of invention": "So it would be necessary to say that the only possible invention is the invention of the impossible" (6, 42, 44).

But the last formulation is too quickly reached, as other formulations avow a dimension of invention whose implications Derrida's essay sidesteps: the role of mediation, which is another way of saying that the singular cannot not be thought without the universal and the particular—especially once cast politically, from the perspective of responsibility. One formulation that betrays the role of these mediations is when Derrida deducts the public dimension entangled in the concept invention: "The status of invention in general, like that of a particular invention, presupposes the *public* recognition of an origin, more precisely of an originality. The latter has to be assignable to *a human subject*, individual or collective, who is responsible for the *discovery* or the *production* of something new that is henceforth *available* to everyone" (28). Stated differently, there is a *recognizer* who fulfills this public role of re-cognizing the invention as such and thus attributing it to someone. A recognizer who has the power to do so is authorized by someone and operates in a concrete *scene* in which the invention occurs and is acknowledged as such. Yet Derrida hardly pursues this aspect of invention, which from a different perspective could be interpreted as raising the quintessential political question. Aside from a rather glib comment about the "modern politics of invention"— "The modern politics of invention tends to integrate the aleatory into its programmatic calculations"—Derrida consistently disavows the theoretical significance of this admission, even if at other points of the essay he abstractly invokes a "we" in relation to the invention of the other (37). How does Derrida manage to sidestep these eminently political questions? Why does he stop at the point in which it becomes crucial to historicize and politicize the question of invention? Two potential determinants can be presented: a modernist conceit with the new, which has political import, but is entirely unsuited to think about political transitions and change, and a phenomenological conceit that seeks to transcendentally address questions prior to the actual, historically constituted scenes in which these eventuate.

The foregoing questions figure prominently in Derrida's more political texts, texts in which he explicitly casts the intersection of ethics and politics as a fundamental question for deconstruction: *Specters of Marx*, *Politics of Friendship*, and *Rouges*. These works exhibit Derrida's usual shrewd and coruscating readings of canonical figures, while broaching political questions of democracy, justice, inheritance, mourning, and responsibility. In dealing with these questions, Derrida undoes the different binaries that pervade these questions and linguistically reframes the terms of the discussions, but the political import of these interpretative moves appears largely indeterminate and elusive. Such elusiveness is part of a philosophical temperament in which performing an ethos of critique takes center stage and eludes the mainstay of political theory, the concerns with power, authority, collective life, its identity and forms, and the state, just to mention a few. Some of Derrida's formulations mine the rhetorical figures of language to exert a critical effect, to unsettle sedimented modes of discourse and patterns of thought. What is missing, however, is an account of the central category of the dialectic, from Hegel to Adorno: mediation, a category that some of his formulations presuppose, but that he disavows.[46] This absence bears on the political import of his account of responsibility.

In *The Gift of Death* Derrida offers a formulation of responsibility that illustrates the handicap of recanting mediation. Derrida presents an argument against responsibility being "motivated, conditioned, made possible by a history." In contrast, he alternatively formulates the relationship between responsibility and history in the following way: "History can be neither a decidable object nor a totality capable of being mastered, precisely because it is tied to *responsibility*, to *faith*, and to the *gift*. To *responsibility* in the experience of absolute decisions made outside of knowledge or given norms, made therefore through the very ordeal of the undecidable."[47] Derrida thus wants to challenge conceptions of history as informing responsibility, as offering a set of guidelines and calculations to what responsible action is; say, what Nietzsche called "the memory of the will." There is, of course, a moment of truth in Derrida's account, as decisions sometimes take place outside the bounds of received knowledge, and sometimes acting out of a decision entails transgressing such parameters. Even so, no ethically meaningful action, however murky the moment of decision is, and uncertain its outcome ultimately may be, is outside history.

In his celebrated essay "Faith and Knowledge" Derrida once again tarries with history and responsibility, but this time in relation to his idea of a "messianicity without messianism," the coming of the other, "the advent of justice." In terms that echo Walter Benjamin's thesis on the concept of history, Derrida juxtaposes "the ordinary course of history" (Benjamin's "historicism") with interrupting, or "tearing history itself apart" (Benjamin's messiah), and responsibility figures largely in relation to the latter as an act of volition, "doing it by deciding," that correlates the decision of the other in me, which for him "does not exonerate me of responsibility."[48] This responsibility, he has claimed elsewhere, is infinite, and without which there could be no "moral and political problems."[49] Even so, one may wonder: how can the infinite enter the finitude of historical time? But the question may be misguided. The answer is simple: it is outside of it, transcendentally primal, preontological, as it is for Levinas. In a passage from *Otherwise Than Being or Beyond Essence* that Derrida cites approvingly, Levinas states: "Responsibility for the Other is not an accident that happens to a subject, but precedes essence in it, has not awaited freedom in which a commitment to the Other would have been made."[50] Responsibility is thereby conceived as preontologically binding and thus insulated from any reckoning with the social and political world.

While Derrida's recasting of responsibility as a response contains a moment of truth, as it were, it becomes less compelling when it is conceived as an effective turning away from politics in order to ground the ethical obligation in advance of any concrete encounter with others. But the ahistorical tenor of his reflections is not entirely reducible to a distilled Barthian motif—even if the Levinasian disavowal of institutions he inherits is shot through with Barthian and Kierkegaardian conceits—or to Levinasian sediments that remain in his thought forms. Rather, it is a philosophical tenet that deconstruction has inherited from Derrida's own long-standing encounter with Edmund Husserl.[51] Something exacerbated by Derrida's engagement with the structuralist moment in French philosophy after his return to the École Normale Supérieure in 1964.[52] Early on, Derrida's critique of structuralism and of Western binaries—speech/writing, presence/

absence, mind/body, subject/object—took its primary cue from Husserl's distinction between the empirical and the transcendental. In the context of his critique of the historicism of his day, Husserl identified a relativist tendency of historicism. Such relativism, according to Husserl, could be curbed by transcendentally establishing the basis of apodictic knowledge, by establishing the priority of phenomenological to empirical inquiry. Traces of this antihistoricism plague Derrida's framing of the question of responsibility, its infinite obligation, and its "impossibility."

From Husserl's phenomenology Derrida inherited and productively reclaimed a transcendental "scheme" that rehearses the transcendental turn of Kant's critical philosophy—Derrida has claimed to be at heart a Kantian, "an ultra-Kantian" that is, nevertheless, "more than a Kantian," which is consistent with the role of the quasi-transcendental in deconstruction—but rather than asking about the conditions of possibility for knowledge, it asks about conditions of impossibility.[53] The transcendental thus gives way to the quasi-transcendental. But even if Husserl's pseudoconcrete "phenomenological reduction" is thoroughly deconstructed, its theoretical structure of argumentation continues to frame the way Derrida approached theoretical questions. In so doing, Derrida distanced himself from the post-Heideggerian hermeneutic claim that interpretation takes place *within* a historical horizon of meaning, however open such a horizon remained, a position famously formulated in Hans-Georg Gadamer's *Truth and Method*.

Out of his engagement with Husserl's phenomenology, Derrida establishes the transcendental status of difference, but also its instability, which he would thematize as différance: "neither a word, nor a concept," but one of deconstruction's terms of art that at once involves "spacing" and "temporalizing," both of which conjure "the possible that is presently impossible"; it precedes and thematizes "the opposition between passivity and activity" and constitutes a constitutive "primordial nonpresence."[54] Derrida writes: "Thus we no longer know whether what was always presented as a derived and modified re-presentation of simple presentation, as 'supplement,' 'sign,' 'writing,' or 'trace,' 'is' not, in a necessarily but newly, ahistorical sense, "older" than presence and the system of truth, older than 'history.'"[55] Even so, Derrida would claim a (quasi-)transcendental primacy, if not priority, to these notions as a "primordial" "scene, a theater stage" that is deconstruction's version of the "transcendental reduction."[56] Or as Peter Dews has felicitously put it, after deconstructing Husserl's transcendental reduction, Derrida travels *upstream* to the shifting grounds of différance in transcendental consciousness, while other critics of Husserl, say, Adorno, traveled *downstream* to "an account of subjectivity as emerging from but entwined with the natural and historical world."[57] And therein lies the crucial difference between deconstruction and critical theory.

Returning to the question of responsibility in a way that correlates with Derrida's disavowal of history, one could then ask: what does it mean, politically, to theorize responsibility in ways that render this ethical commitment political when such theorization is anchored on a decision that dispenses with the elements by which one can discern the ordering of cultural, social and institutional arrangements that mediate one's subjectivity? In *The Politics of Friendship* Derrida's notion of responsibility is once again elaborated in relation to a (ultimately disavowed) dialectic of avowal and disavowal of knowledge in the decision that sheds light on this question,

> To give in the name of, to give to the name of, the other is what frees responsibility from knowledge—that is, what brings responsibility unto itself, if there ever is such a thing. For, yet again, one *must* certainly *know, one must know it*: knowledge is necessary if one is to assume responsibility, but the decisive or deciding moment of responsibility supposes a leap by which an act takes off, ceasing in that instance to follow the consequence of what is—that is, of that which can be determined by science and consciousness—and thereby *frees itself* (this is what is called freedom), by the act of its act, of what is therefore heterogeneous to it, that is knowledge. *In sum, a decision is unconscious*—insane as that may seem, it involves the unconscious and nevertheless remains responsible.[58]

In this formulation Derrida displays commendable sensibility to what Arendt notoriously called the "natality" of action, those moments of creation that are not determined by what already exists that break with the continuum of history.[59] The radical gesture of this passage captures something that Gayatri Spivak has insisted defines deconstruction as a critical ethos: the experience of impossibility, of the incalculable—

here signaled in the disavowal of knowledge—with an awareness that "legal and political decisions must be made, empirically scrupulous but philosophically errant."[60] But the critical and political import of these gestures remains elusive, if not foreshortend, when the imperatives of power that mediate these decisions are not conceptualized.

Still: why is the "philosophically errant" moment of impossibility so crucial? Why does it matter so much? And why hypostatize lack of certainty and the possibility of equivocation? The latter runs the risk of reifying in thought the limiting historical conditions of the present. Here the distance between deconstruction and dialectical critical theory is clearly seen. In contrast to deconstruction, critical thinking is foremost an immanent task that needs to avoid these reifications, and not just to acknowledge the complexities of action, but critically re-cognize the predicaments of power where these political decisions intervene. But to carry on such re-cognition requires a concept of mediation that is not a part of deconstruction. Although sometimes presupposed, dialectical thinking is disavowed in Derrida's inheritance from Marx, as are the collective forms of agency that historically characterized Marxist legacies. Derrida, however, claims a radical politics for these "philosophically errant" gestures: "Deconstruction has never had any sense or interest, in my view at least, except as a radicalization, which is to say also *in the tradition* of a certain Marxism, in a certain *spirit of Marxism*."[61] And it is in terms of this inheritance from Marxism that Derrida further thematizes deconstruction's idea of responsibility. "The responsibility, once again, would be that of an heir," he writes. Even so, this inheritance is as ineluctable as it is universal: "Whether they wish it or know it or not, all men and women, all over the earth, are today to a certain extent the heirs of Marx and Marxism."[62] This is, to say the least, a strange claim from the philosopher of différance. It is particularly intriguing when one considers the coupling of this universal heritage with a strong sense of responsibility, since it comes in the form of a stern imperative that one is unable to disown and that brooks no geographical limits or exceptions. "And whether we like it or not," Derrida's severe tone reminds the reader, "whatever consciousness we have of it, we cannot not be heirs. There is not inheritance without a call for responsibility. An inheritance is always the reaffirmation of a debt, but a critical, selective, and filtering reaffirmation, which is why we distinguished several spirits."[63] And therein lies the centrality of responsibility in this process of inheritance: one needs to responsibly distinguish, out of the universally received spirits, which ones are to be inherited.[64]

This inheritance entails annihilating those ugly spirits (Stalinism?) of Marxism and retrieving what is critical for a "democracy to come," deconstruction's ultimate political gesture. But here the process of selection ultimately empties out the critical import of Marxism. The universalization of this legacy takes away what made it specific, rendering it critically diminished. Other than a list of plagues afflicting the then newly proclaimed world order, which are never politically theorized, one is hard-pressed to find any genuinely critical reckoning with this order. Derrida's "antidecalogue," as even a sympathetic critic as José María Ripalda has noted, lacks the specific mediations that are constitutive of any concrete civility that could actualize its tenets politically.[65] In this radicalized Marxism, there is no analysis of power, capital, and the mediations between the cultural, the economic, the aesthetic, and the political that in turn mediate the *scenes* where encounters with others take place, where responsibility is enacted.

In contrast, in Derrida's formulations, responsible action consists of absolute decisions, which more often than not come in the form of imperatives outside any political, economic, or cultural mediation. Ultimately, these are solipsistic decisions whose impossibility never seems to hinder their imperative necessity, regardless of the scene of power where they act. These are rather decided entirely outside it.[66] Responsibility thus disavows knowledge, even basic knowledge of subject positions, or the place of the addresser and the addressee in the social formation where the responsible act eventuates and unfolds. No wonder Derrida sees an intimate relationship between responsibility and faith: "Responsibility and faith go together, however paradoxical that might seem to some, and both should, in the same movement, exceed mastery and knowledge."[67] Responsibility is despatialized and thus abstractly universalized and severed of any politically meaningful context that betrays an elective affinity with the variations of ethical politics defining the present.

That many a judgment goes amiss, or pseudoproblem hypostatized, in Derrida's ethical politics of responsibility is precisely seen in what is probably the single most dismal sentence found in his published writings: "How would you ever justify the fact that you sacrifice all the cats in the world to the cat that you feed at home every morning for years, whereas other cats die of hunger at every instant?"[68] This passage probably betrays thinking that never got a second thought. Still, this utterly abstract universalization of limitless responsibility is perfectly consistent with the overall tenor of Derrida's account of ethical responsibility. For both ethical and political responsibility entail limits and a dose of realism. *Pace* Derrida, one's ethical and political responsibilities are necessarily limited to the locus of action available in the scenes of power that shape the political and ethical situation one inhabits. Or, as Eagleton has lucidly put it, "Universality means being responsible for anyone, not *per impossible*, for everyone at the same time. To assume that it does, even while insisting on its impossibility, betrays a certain hubris of the infinite, however apologetic and self-castigating in tone."[69] Politically, this hubris lends itself to sanctioning neoimperial ethical doctrines, like current invocations of "responsibility to protect," that brook no sense of equality, accountability, or community of fate between those in need of protection and those perfunctorily responsible for providing it and thus, at best, revert to a tutelary relationship or, at worst, become the ethical supplement to the current world order.[70] Overall, anonymous relations with others within a political collectivity in which one is recognized as participant are necessarily political and mediated by institutions.[71] For these anonymous relations to be minimally democratic, a community of fate between rulers and ruled has to be in place. Such community is expandable in ethical relations—which are necessarily proximate in ways that political ones are not—but concrete limits are constitutive of both. Though Derrida's ruminations on responsibility could be allusive, they hardly amount to a sense of political responsibility, or purpose, much less transcend what seems to be a radical Nietzschean-cum-Levinasian solipsism that is only abstractly concerned with others. These gestures, moreover, do not threaten the liberal-capitalist order, let alone respond to present-day predicaments of power where capital is increasingly unfettered and when centralized forms of state power are increasingly unaccountable.

PRECARIOUS RESPONSIBILITY

Judith Butler's inheritance of Levinas's ethics exemplifies the quest to preontologically ground a commitment to responsibility that is prereflective, prior to the historically and politically concrete—that is, to historically situated encounters between selves, others, and objects. Accounts like Butler's balk at epistemological approaches to the scenes of power on the basis of their presumed inability to account for the constitutions of the self that inhabit such scenes. In *Giving an Account of Oneself,* she eloquently states this objection: "The possibility of this epistemological encounter presumes that the self and its object world have already been constituted, but such an encounter fails to inquire into the mechanisms of that constitution. Levinas's concept of the pre-ontological is designed to address this problem."[72] Out of her engagement with Levinas, Butler explores and seeks to comprehend the constitution of the "I" prior to the encounter with others in order to preontologically ground a concept of responsibility based on answerability to the *Other.* That this engagement has led to some of Butler's finest writing in the last two decades is beyond dispute. It has led to a rich elucidation of the imperatives found in narratives of the self, their limits, and the ethical import of the chastened sense of subjectivity that ensues.

Yet, for all its eloquence, important questions pertaining to the constitution of the encounter, which are the mainstay of political theory, remain unaddressed. What is left out of this account are the foremost epistemological-political aspects, such as the constitution of the scene of the encounter itself, or how such a scene mediates the constitution of the "I," and the ensuing responses to it. The "I" is neither prior to these encounters nor just a product of them. An "I" is arguably a bundle of mediations: some are explicitly dialogic and intersubjective and others are not, but the constitution of the "I" is unthinkable without them. Moreover, strictly speaking, the intersubjective moment of any "I" requires communication with others, which is always in place within historically constituted situation, and is equally constituted by the mediation of historical relations that are not necessarily intersubjective but always social.[73] A critical conception of responsibility needs to attend to these mediations, to cognize them and the imperatives that they inaugurate, more than it needs to try to elucidate an indefinable ontological moment that is always thoroughly mediated. But Butler's *Giving an Account of Oneself* is mostly silent about this epistemological task. And this silence renders the political import of its reflections rather elusive.[74] For instance, while insisting on casting the act of narration that forms the subject, however opaquely and incompletely, the giving of an account, as an "act," Butler truncates the political import of such an "act" by the terms in which she casts it. Such narrative acts—as Butler rightly suggests, these narratives do not merely relay information but are constitutive acts of subjectivity—carry transformative possibilities at the level of the constitution of the self, which she connects with Socratic *parrhesia*.[75] However, Butler does not relate these to the mainstay of the political life of the city but, rather, reverts to the Platonic project of soul-craft. She quotes Foucault's one-sided interpretation of *The Apology* approvingly: "the target of this new parrhesia is not to persuade the Assembly, but to convince someone that he must take care of himself and of others; and this means that he must *change his life*."[76] Notice how in one stroke this rendering brushes aside much of what Socrates does say about the city, as well as his fealty to its democratic political form and its attendant practices. But what is even more revealing about this formulation is the extent to which it betrays a preference for Socrates as a moral thinker rather than as a political theorist, as one who foreshadows a subordination of political life to ethical imperatives conceived independent of it, if not a retreat from the political *tout court.* Practices of the self tacitly but effectively oust any consideration of political rule by the selves, by the many.

A more concrete attempt to render this type of preontological commitment to the Other political is found in Butler's *Precarious Life*. There she offers a shrewd effort to theorize ethical responsibility on the basis of "grief" and "mourning," to theorize the possibility of "community on the basis of vulnerability and loss" in order to be responsive to claims of justice and solidarity with others, especially in the aftermath of 11 September 2001. In this text she gives an alternative response to an experience of loss that quickly became a legitimizing event for a new phase of U.S. imperial ventures. In Butler's account, grief is a valuable conduit to theorize "fundamental dependency and ethical responsibility."[77] At a general level, her intent is commendable: to avoid facile exonerations, stigmatizations, and self-righteousness so as to counter a hegemonic response that is based on aggressive militarism and imperialist zeal. In such a predicament, to think "what, politically, might be made of grief besides a cry for war" is an imperative question.[78] Yet, somewhat anticlimactically, Butler seeks to address this question ontologically; namely, her preferred strategy of counteracting contemporary versions of *raison d'état* is calling for an insurrection "at the level of ontology."[79] This ontological insurrection carries at its core the recognition of one's vulnerability, "a common human vulnerability, one that emerges with life itself," as constitutive of the human condition.[80] Vulnerability is thus elevated to the plane of ontology: it is recognized, acknowledged, but not *re-cognized*. Stated differently, what emerges from this acknowledgment of human vulnerability is a rather foreshortened ontology whose critical and political import remains vague.[81] It is a strictly ontological perspective, which ultimately leaves unattended the role of power, and its structural imperatives, in the human experience of vulnerability.[82] Accordingly, this is a formulation that comes perilously close to reifying powerlessness, since it ultimately disavows any sociopolitical analysis of vulnerability, or of the configurations of power that are complicit with it and mediate the various degrees of vulnerability political subjects experience in scenes of power constituted by structural inequalities of class, gender, and status. Some are more vulnerable than others, even if we all share the frailty of embodied existence. But discerning *degrees* of vulnerability cannot not be a historically grounded and politically infused cognitive mapping—a mapping that, while reacting to the somatic dimension of subjectivity, apprehends it epistemologically in its sociopolitical mediations.

In *Giving an Account of Oneself* Butler once again voices this reifying tendency in her plea for a chastened conception of subjectivity that would make room for "an ethics of the unwilled"; that, in turn, stems from a Levinasian "primary exposure to the Other," an exposure that serves as a reminder "of a common vulnerability, a common physicality and risk." That physicality of the self, which is presubjective, one "from which we cannot slip away," enables an experience of vulnerability that grounds a sense of responsibility prior to any choice, but serves as a condition of possibility for it.[83] Although Butler quickly adds that "common" in Levinas does not mean "symmetrical," an exploration of this distinction dictates re-cognizing and reconceptualizing the materialist bent of her argument and bringing it to bear on the overall theoretical forms that frame her reflections. Yet that demands a more historically grounded critical theory, along with a consideration of the spatial dimension of responsibility, one that in Butler's formulations is consistently subjugated to temporal considerations.

"One finds oneself fallen. One is exhausted but does not know why. Something is larger than one's own deliberate plan, one's own project, one's own knowing and choosing."[84] The experience of loss may very well instill such feelings, but these do not occur in a vacuum, especially when the losses under consideration are political. Besides, if there is one point that Theory has driven home, it is that the "one" in this construction is likely to be located in different "subject positions" in any given scene of power. Namely, asymmetrical relations of race, class, and status oftentimes mediate the ways an individual experiences loss, and these are historically entrenched in political and cultural contexts. This is especially so in the United States, an antidemocratic society that presumes to be democratic, but is characterized by entrenched inequalities of power and status. Yet, while writing in this context, Butler does not meet it head-on. She rather insists on "fundamental vulnerability" by means of her endorsement of Levinas's contention, as distinctively elucidated in his *Otherwise Than Being or Beyond Essence*, about the absence of a "self prior to its persecution by the Other," a "persecution that establishes the Other at the heart of the self, and establishes that 'heart' as an ethical relation of responsibility."[85] Who, then, is the audience here? Again, for "persecution" to possess any critical import, it needs to be thoroughly mediated, recast from the perspective of the scenes of power in which the encounter with others, and with any third involved, takes place, along with one's position in it. Persecution and loss are no different from death, when it comes to thinking politically about their meaning and elucidations. And here the mediations of the "we" that Butler invokes come to haunt her account, for the invocation of a sense of responsibility, say, a republic of mourning—no less than the "republic of suffering" that was conjured in the aftermath of the American Civil War—relies on a series of institutional and collective mediations for it to have any political import.[86]

But none of this can be discerned from a rebellious act at the level of ontology. Actually, examining critically the historical and structural variables that hinder one's capacity to act politically in the face of loss is primarily an epistemological task. In lieu of the current fate of democracy in the United States, the immediate context of many of these theorizations, more productive questions would consist in interrogating, say, What are the political and ethical implications of compromising one's political identity by actions carried on in one's name? What are the demands that ensue from this compromise, in light of the forms of power a collectivity generates, and what are its uses and abuses? How is a democratic identity, and one's fidelity to it and the political forms and processes that actualize it, transmogrified by actions that betray it rather than promote it? What is lost in such compromises? Paradoxically, interrogation along these lines requires a culture of commonality that both contemporary forms of power have rendered either politically anachronistic or suspect. Invocations of a "we" like Butler's always presuppose a binding political identity—a collectivity that is responsive to the language of solidarity, common purpose, and shared power.[87] Stated differently, Butler's account consistently fails to acknowledge what it presupposes throughout: an account of the political identity and forms binding the collectivity, a democratic "we," which she constantly invokes.[88] It also fails to conceptualize how the forms of power crystallized in the late modern state sabotage it. This failure, however, is not merely a simple omission. Rather, it is built in the conception of theory that tries to negotiate political tensions in ontological terms. Levinasian formulations like these run the risk of mistaking historical limitations for ontological ones.

In subsequent writings, Butler has at once complicated, modified, and expanded some of the arguments advanced in these two texts, even if her arguments betray a persistent structure that remains unchanged. In *Frames of War*, for example, she has sought to register historical and political differentiations as part of her elevation of a shared condition of vulnerability and precariousness to the level of ontology. By means of a distinction between "precariousness" and "precarity," Butler seeks to bring to the fore something that was only perfunctorily adduced in earlier formulations, and which had little ascendance in the overall architecture of her theory and ethical vision: historically and politically constituted forms of vulnerability and precariousness and the different modalities of framing that could either reveal or occlude particular variations of precariousness.[89] Herein, precarity appears as mediated precariousness, even if it is never formulated as such, as the concept "mediation" is foreign to Butler's philosophical orientation and the theoretical armature of her writings. Conversely, as the title of her book explicitly portends, Butler has gone on to offer sustained reflection on how frames and framing operate, something that raises important critical, epistemological questions. Unquestionably, these are important developments, and are hardly perfunctory. Even so, these epistemological inquiries continue to be one-sidedly anchored in a set of ontological commitments stemming from her original formulation of ethics first and ultimately subordinated to it.

That this is so is nowhere clearer than in *Parting Ways*, her courageous reckoning with Jewish legacies as part of her eloquent critique of Zionism, which constitutes her most politically bold theoretical statement to date. There she summarizes her efforts as an attempt to formulate "an ethics of dispersion" from the perspective "of a certain ethical relation, decidedly non-egological," which makes good on the ethical and political import of Levinas's ethics.[90] Consider the following passages, "The responsibility that I assume, or, rather, that claims me in this instant, is the result of the precariousness I see, the violence that I may cause, the fear of that violence. As a result, the fear must check the violence, but this does not happen all at once. In fact, the unlimited responsibility that I bear toward the other is precisely the result of an ongoing struggle between the fear induced in me by the commandment and the violence my existence does to the Other. If I fear for the Other, it is because I know the Other can be destroyed by beings like myself."[91] These passages constitute a brilliant unpacking of Levinasian ideas of unlimited responsibility, and betray an anxiety about the self and the need to consistently upbraid it. Yet for these injunctions to carry any concrete political or ethical import, they need to be historicized. The universal abjection these formulations convey is so abstract that, at best, it becomes indeterminate and meaningless, or, at worst, elevates a logic of equivalence that reinscribes identity in the name of difference, the Other, to the preontological scene. Such elevation would bracket out much of what makes responsibility meaningful—limits, differentiations, the constitution of social and political space, perpetrators, victims, bystanders, or structural beneficiaries— especially in a colonial situation inaugurated by a settler-colonial state, Israel, with its structuring imperatives.

Once historicized, however, it becomes clear that for these injunctions to gain any traction, and avoid the righteous frivolity of "neither/ norism," they need to bear on those in structural positions of power or structural beneficiaries of a politically sanctioned condition. In light of Butler's ethical sense and political commitments, one immediately surmises that this "I" could hardly be a Palestinian living in Gaza, let alone any colonized, dominated, or actually persecuted subject. Rather, the "I" is most likely a citizen of the Jewish state, or an American or European Zionist, or any fellow non-Zionist Jew or fellow North Atlantic denizen that identifies with the Shoah as a form of civil religion. This is not to say that a colonized subject has no responsibilities in the colonial predicaments she inhabits. But to introduce a differentiated sense of responsibility, the necessary distinctions and determinations that constitute a situation structured to achieve and clinch her dispossession have to be mapped. And such mapping is irredeemably impaired by the hypostatization of an upbraided "I" and its Other.

Even if Butler's appeal to a particular tradition of Jewish ethics can be explained by identifying her audience, one question lingers: why this particular ethic, and why the need to think of ethics first? What exactly is at stake in the attempt to ontologically ground an ethical obligation? Why posit such an abstract obligation as an anchor for ethical politics? Why cast it in terms of ethical reductions, which also constitute the reduction of politics to ethics, and why the insistence on ethical politics antecedent to predicaments of power that muddle it and render pseudo-ontological commitments mute? Do these reductions amount to much else besides a philosophical conceit, one that is thoroughly mediated by liberal anxieties and the promise of anchoring politics on something beyond itself? Or is it an upshot of the depoliticized politics of contemporary liberal-capitalism and the forms of ethical politics sustaining it? Simply put, in the case of Butler, this may well be a philosophical conceit. Butler inherited from Levinas a conceit about ethics as first philosophy that despite its vaunted concern with the Other and the nonidentical, consists of its own version of *prima philosophia*. Butler is, to be sure, hardly concerned with traditional questions of epistemology and is thus not positing an epistemological absolute first, nor is she concerned with the plausibility of the Husserlian phenomenological reduction. Yet, out of the asymmetrical primacy of the Other, Butler posits precariousness as a shared condition that occupies the place of the "originary" insofar as it is cast preontologically, which is another way of asserting immediacy and thus disavowing mediations. Following the architecture of Levinas's ethical reduction, Butler offers a quasi-transcendental version of the "absolute first," or a primordial scene, which ostensibly challenges the illusion of immediacy, as her concern with "normative violence" could be construed as lending a voice to the Other, the nonidentical. But this quasi-transcendental structure of phenomenological argumentation still posits a foundational moment. The illusion of the absolute first thus persists: in place of constitutive subjectivity, difference and a relational dyad—self-other—is formulated, as an ethical reduction dislodges the phenomenological reduction without altering its structure of argumentation.

But the positing of a relationship, even if construed as thoroughly mediated, is bound to flounder. First, it conflates a concept of relation with one of substance or reflection. The former claims an immediacy that is thwarted by the latter. What emerges out of critical reflection is the idea of mediation, which, if genuinely conceived, undoes any claim of the ontological, let alone preontological, first. Second, and more obviously than in a concept of substance, the two moments in a relation are thoroughly mediated not only by the two poles informing the dyad—which only suggests an internal conceptual mediation—but also by the scene in which the mediation occurs, which despite its autonomization in thought is thoroughly mediated by historically constituted and politically sanctioned situations. Relations thus involve mediations, residues, and sediments. And the most obvious mediation is that of consciousness itself.

If there is one lesson to be derived from critical reason, it is that consciousness is no less a condition of possibility of the relation between self and other, subject and object, than of subjectivity, or even otherness, which can only be critically grasped not as a primal moment but as situated in our concrete webs of relations with others, which are both actualized and undone in history, and constituted through the texture of cultural and social relations and their political sanctioning, rejection, or codification, as the socially and culturally embedded creatures humans are. Otherness is, in a nutshell, painstakingly mediated. Even conceiving the relation to the Other, its primacy in the constitution of the self as preontological is already an operation mediated by a consciousness. The relation self-other cannot be comprehended without the consciousness from which it is abstracted as part of the process of autonomization inherent to critical reflection. In lieu of a unity of consciousness, in these accounts one finds a no less mediated relation, and yet a relation that while emerging from consciousness is nevertheless hypostatized as severed from it. Better still, the unity of consciousness that abstracts the dyad self-other as constitutive of the self, as preontological, is itself fractured and never at one with itself, as it is already thoroughly mediated by concrete historical processes. Just as there is no empirical self without the concept, and no concept without an empirical self, there is no relation to the Other outside encounters with real others. Accordingly, there is neither *constituens* nor *constitutum*, neither purely ontological nor preontological, neither pure subjectivity nor pure objectivity; rather, these are all dialectically constituted and thus thoroughly mediated.

Yet "mediation is mediated," as Adorno once observed.[92] And so are the two moments that constitute the initial dyad—self-other, subject-object—and, as such, mediation cannot be hypostatized.[93] This is a fundamental insight that Adorno's immanent critique of Hegel's philosophy yields. Whereas the very essence of the concept is to be immediately mediated, the idea of mediation is also mediated by the immediate. And the mediation of the immediate is a reflective determination (*Reflexionsbestimmung*), meaningful only in relation to the immediate, even if this objective immediacy is blocked from consciousness: reflection has no access to the immediate—that is the block—but it re-cognizes this limit and refuses to subsume it under mediation.[94] Nonidentity extricates not only the hypostatization of immediacy; it equally refuses any hypostatization of mediation, even if such refusal is thought through immediately mediated concepts.[95] Accordingly, at the level of the subject there is the mediation of the concept, itself mediated, and the mediation of the nonconceptually immediate, but at the level of the totality one can speak of another sense of mediation: that of the objective social processes mediating the cognitive process itself in both its subjective and objective mediations. More to the point, once these relations are re-cognized as entirely mediated, the necessary next step is to consider and interpret the historical processes structuring the situation from which the "self-other scene" has been autonomized. Once the binary is thus speculatively re-cognized, as mediating and mediated by a historical condition, one can critically discern the "experiential content" and historical sediments in rather abstract formulations and concretely pose the question of its political and critical import.[96]

As the foregoing intimates, the inherent problems of the kind of substitution Butler tacitly introduces were already foreshadowed in Adorno's critical engagements with Kant and Hegel, Husserl and Heidegger. Here is one formulation of Adorno's critique: "The qualification of the absolutely first in subjective immanence founders because immanence can never completely disentangle the moment of nonidentity within itself, and because subjectivity, the organ of reflection, clashes with [*widerstreitet*] the idea of an absolutely first as pure immediacy."[97] Here the key word is *reflection,* and how any account of I, or Other, is always already mediated by that "clash," so to speak. It is by tarrying with that clash and thus conceiving subjectivity at once as *constituens* and *constitutum*—as thus subject and object in both social and epistemological terms—that Adorno goes beyond even the most radical antifoundationalism in dialectically conceiving knowledge and accounting for the enabling limits of mediation. Succinctly put: even post-Kantian antifoundationalism—from Heidegger to Habermas—continues to posit a "unity of consciousness," even if constitutive subjectivity is supposedly debunked. Thus, the critical task has been largely conceived in terms of overcoming metaphysics. In sharp contrast, Adorno's critique reopens the question of metaphysics through his materialist negative dialectics. This yields a more discerning account of the historically constituted and socially sanctioned doing and undoing of subjects beyond distended ontological or psychoanalytic conceits. Rather than unities of consciousness dirempted from history, what this dialectical perspective invites is to think of the mediations involved to avoid both hypostatizing categories of reflection or historical symptoms, as phenomenological abstractions or reductions tend to do.

Outside epistemological considerations, there is, politically speaking, something deeply abstract about positing ethical obligation prior to the scenes of action in which it becomes actualized. Insofar as it is quasi-transcendental, and thus "prior to" engagement in the actual historically constituted world, the foregoing ethical obligations are utterly dirempted from the texture of political and ethical life and have little bearing on how one actually relates with others. By extension, meaningful mediations, distinctions, and differentiations, central for making good on any idea of ethical and political responsibility, are entirely bracketed out. But the question of spatial and political differentiations, or degrees of vulnerability, is one thing; how to conceptualize degrees of responsibility is another. Properly conceptualizing the nature of the imperatives shaping predicaments of power, both historically and politically, is something that the antinomian spirit underlying these inheritances of Levinas is not able to do. Instead, antinomianism is in and of itself a symptom or a particular response that flees political life in the hope of a more effective intervention. But leaving obdurate structures unattended, or tacitly taking these for granted, does not make them go away. Rather, it leads to a tacit acquiescence to them.

For absolution from these criticisms, a more sympathetic reader may ask: so what? Even if, say, Butler's theoretical commitments do not move on a par with her political commitments, these have not preempted Butler from engaging in activism or articulating a compelling ethical-political stance in the present. Indeed, to the left of Derrida, Butler is a more politically minded activist whose politics go beyond the platitudes of Derrida's interventions. That holds, as far as it goes. But theoretical limits find a corollary in her political stance. This is readily seen vis-à-vis the questions of nonviolence and Palestine.[98] In this essay she offers moving reflections on Edward Said and his political legacy by way of a beautiful poem by Mahmoud Darwich. This essay not only exemplifies Butler at her critical best, it also offers an astute account of the logic of dispossession built into Zionism as a settler-colonial project. Even so, despite the momentary avowal of a political ethic and the historical, political, and social mediations structuring Zionism's relationship with its others, which also include non-Zionist Jews, Butler's otherwise compelling political commentary is abruptly shortened by a feeble plea for a futurist exilic politics. Similarly, she neglects to consider the important question of how this concrete political scene she reconstructs demands something beyond her ethical politics, as the ethical obligation is severed from the political situation mediating and constituting any action within it. It is a political scene demanding political responses irreducible to the ethical scene of obligation the book abstractly invokes and ultimately hypostatizes.[99] If only an immanent appeal to democratic principles—their nonidentity in Palestine, so to speak—allows us to unveil the logic of the exclusion, dispossession, and domination of Palestinians in Palestine, why the appeal to Levinasian ethical politics in the first place?

The answer to the last question probably lies in her philosophical vocation and identification with Judaism. One can readily surmise that in *Parting Ways* Butler's audience is fellow Jews, whom she hopes to interpellate by recourse to Jewish ethical resources, which were most forcefully expressed during the heyday of "Jewish modernity."[100] Butler movingly writes as someone who "wishes to affirm a Judaism that is not identified with state violence, and that is identified with a broad-based struggle for social justice" and thereby reclaim "Jewish traditions that oppose state violence, that affirm multi-cultural co-habitation, and defend principles of equality," which she rightly casts as a "vital" yet mostly "forgotten or sidelined" ethical tradition.[101] "I am trying," Butler further writes, "to delineate a political ethics that belongs to the diaspora, where Jews are scattered among non-Jews, and to derive a set of principles from that geographic condition and transpose them into the geopolitical reality of Israel/Palestine."[102] In the midst of the Zionism pervading American Jewry, Butler's aim is gutsy and commands respect. Still, one cannot take it uncritically, and the passage invites several questions. One: can one speak here of a political ethic when the aim in question is indifferent to the specificity of each political situation it invokes? Second: even if one grants that "cohabitation" or *convivencia* are indifferent to political forms (and in this case they are not), can one freely extrapolate historically specific principles and practices that were mediated by political forms and import these into a colonial situation largely defined by the conflict between two ethnic nationalisms? This, in a historical moment in which the sociological springs of diasporic traditions are virtually extinguished. And this without dwelling on one of the peculiarities of this settler-colonial situation: while this is colonialism without a metropolis, Israel has benefited by the imperial powers lording over the region ever since the early twentieth century—first Britain, then the U.S.[103] Last: how *political* is a political ethic that brackets out consideration of the spatial presuppositions of any meaningful cohabitation that can only be politically implemented and sanctioned, and immanently discerned, by considering the political logic of the situation itself beyond the conceits of ethical politics.

Be that as it may, out of this inheritance of Jewish ethical traditions, she formulates an ethical politics of nonviolence, which rejects both state violence and violent resistance to it. Politically, she pits Jewish ethical politics against Israel's *raison d'état* and the ethical politics of the American imperium and its avatars. As part of her retrieval of alternative Jewish traditions, Butler works overtime on Arendt and Benjamin. But Butler's expansive readings notwithstanding, there is little by way of Jewish ethics in Arendt or Benjamin. In the case of Arendt, to read her through an ethical prism is to abjure or distort much of what makes her a genuinely political thinker: among other things, her compelling account of degrees and levels of political responsibility. Indeed, once ethics is cast as antecedent to politics, as an ethical scene prior to it, the kinds of questions that Arendt posed are cast aside. Unlike Arendt's political conception of responsibility, Butler frames her reading of Arendt, along with the even less assimilable Said, in a perspective of ethical responsibility resulting from preontological precariousness, something that distorts the inner logic of these bodies of work. Something similar is at work in her reading of Benjamin. Butler offers an expansive interpretation of the role of responsibility in his thinking by juxtaposing the "Theologico-Political Fragment" to his notoriously inscrutable "Critique of Violence." The upshot: a quasi-Levinasian Benjamin enlisted for a tamed messianism that holds out "for a way of thinking and acting politically that does not presume that self-defense or self-destruction are the only two alternatives."[104] This reading is accomplished through careful but selective slicing of Benjamin's text. She focuses on Benjamin's discussion of the commandment "Thou shall not kill" and in the responsibility of either wrestling with it "in solitude," or ignoring the commandment's "nondespotic powers" (83). She then clinches the emerging reading: "As a form of ethical address, the commandment is that which each individual must wrestle without the model of any other. One ethical response to the commandment is to refuse . . . it, but even then one must take responsibility for refusing it. Responsibility is something one takes in relation to the commandment, but it is not dictated by the commandment. Indeed, it is clearly distinguished from duty and, indeed, obedience. If there is wrestling, then there is some semblance of freedom" (84). But a closer look at Benjamin's rather cursory glossing on this question suggests that far from having "resonance with Levinas's position" it actually subverts it (87).

One need not go any further than the passage itself to see how different this account is from Levinas's. The wrestling or tarrying with the commandment happens in history and the commandment could be refused and the ethical actor needs to take responsibility for such refusal, which also has implications for the consequences of this refusal. And that is part of any politically robust sense of responsibility, a thematization of responsibility that offers a more promising path to think about the political valences of responsibility beyond the reductions and conceits of Levinas's ethics. Even so, Butler implausibly claims some resemblance to Levinas and rounds up Benjamin's formulations by conscripting his critique of violence to an "anarchistic" disposition: "Benjamin's point is to show at least three interrelated points: (1) that responsibility has to be understood as a solitary, if anarchistic, form of wrestling with an ethical demand, (2) that coerced or forced obedience murders the soul and undermines the capacity of the person to come to terms with the ethical demand placed upon her, and (3) that the framework of legal accountability can neither address nor rectify the full conditions of human suffering" (87). These "points" can certainly be found in Benjamin's text, but they carry different connotations and are never hypostatized. But what about what this enumeration leaves out? Benjamin's formulations occur in the context of his account of "divine violence" and his articulation of "revolutionary violence" and the political ethic required to articulate its economy:

> For the question "May I kill?" meets its irreducible answer in the commandment "Thou shall not kill." This commandment precedes the deed, just as God was "preventing" the deed. But just as it may not be fear of punishment that enforces obedience, the injunction becomes inapplicable, incommensurable, once the deed is accomplished. No judgment of the deed can be derived from the commandment. And so neither the divine judgment nor the ground for this judgment can be known in advance. Those who base a condemnation of all violent killing of one person by another on the commandment are therefore mistaken. It exists not as a criterion of judgment, but as a guideline for the actions of persons or communities [*Person oder Gemeinschaft*] who have to wrestle with it in solitude and, in exceptional cases, to take on themselves the responsibility of ignoring it.[105]

Several things are worth noting. First, as Butler acknowledges, the commandment is noncompulsive, which creates a vast gulf between this formulation of responsibility and the hyperventilated bindingness of Levinas's responsibility to the Other. Here the encounter with the commandment is not only nondespotic but is also historically situated and need not be reduced to the individual, but could be collective. Second, both individual and communities are avowed, so solitude is best interpreted as suggesting a condition devoid of any transcendental anchorage or guarantee and not a solipsistic encounter with the commandment. The commandment is, in sum, thoroughly mediated. And these mediations are intimately related to the situation, its imperatives and conditions, which is what can render judgment on the specific action or deed in question, a judgment irreducible to the commandment.

Benjamin's formulation offers the possibility of a different reckoning with the commandment in the context of violence beyond the reductive terms that Butler rightly wants to challenge, but cuts in a different direction than the one she envisions: it opens the possibility to contextualize the absoluteness of the command and to grasp its historical determinants and determinations. This last point was something lucidly pursued by the late León Rozitchner, an Argentine Jewish philosopher also critical of Israel, who offered an interpretation of the commandment that distinguished between an absolute-absolute and an absolute-relative: *absolute*, insofar as the principle is constitutive of an irreducible self qua unity of consciousness; *relative*, insofar as it recognizes the relative nature of this self in a world beyond itself, a world in which the self relates to others, but one that also sustains it, mediates and constitutes it, and in which any "I" is relative to her own historical situation.[106] This dialectic of the relative and the absolute is conceived as constitutive of any historically situated relationship between self and other. At once irreducible and relative, the self, as an absolute singularity, turns into absolute what is relative to his situation and tarries with it in historically constituted and politically sanctioned ethical and political predicaments. Accordingly, in contrast to the absolute-absolute that Levinas formulates, which is severed from any historical determination and yet cast as supervening on political life, the absolute-relative is historically determinate and differentiated.[107]

Out of this phenomenological differentiation emerges the difference between *violencia* and *contra-violencia*: a distinction easily translated into English as violence and counterviolence provided that the latter is disassociated from any logic of preemption.[108] To deny this

crucial distinction is to homogenize violence and indulge in an absolute-absolute interpretation of the commandment "Thou shall not
kill" that is thoroughly unhistorical and conflates the violence of those
who rebel against an oppressive order—their "counterviolence"—with
that of those who preside over that order, rule them, or subject whole
classes and groups to a routinized violent predicament in which the
dominant group is either a major structural beneficiary or represents
the interests of those who are. As Rozitchner perceptively observes,
there is no violence in general or killing in the abstract; violence and
death are always concrete and situated in space and time, admitting
both qualitative and quantitative distinctions.[109] Violence is, accordingly, always specific: objective or subjective, structural or individual,
revolutionary or restorative. Counterviolence is thus asymmetrical to
the constitutive violence structuring the predicament in question. It is
downright false, if not frivolous, to conflate violence and counterviolence in asymmetrically constituted situations, situations of extreme
violence in which the violence seeking to subjugate another with the
aim of exploiting and/or dominating that other and ultimately placing her at the service of a dominating or ruling group, class, or entity,
sometimes killing and torturing her, cannot be equated with the counterviolence of those defending themselves in such predicament, those
who fight not to be dominated and debased, tortured or annihilated.[110]

Yet this distinction, and the conversion it presupposes, can never
be hypostatized; instead, what it demands is a sober reckoning with
the historical realities and forces at work in any given predicament of
power. But doing so requires abandoning the philosophical conceit of
the preontological and descending downstream to history, the inevitable constitutive mediation of consciousness. Once thus conceived,
one can formulate a political ethic whose economy of violence frames
"counterviolence" in terms of the absolute-relative bound by the commandment of preserving life and the possibility of a political order
enabling conditions of equality, freedom, and shared power, while fully
re-cognizing the tragedy of the predicament in question and assuming
responsibility for the lives lost. Preserving life is thus a binding imperative that is the precondition of any effective emancipatory political
ethic, even if it is an absolute-relative insofar as death may arrive, but
not because it is sought as end or means. Rather, the point of departure of a political ethic is the preservation of life and its dignity, while

acknowledging how a predicament might impose death and the need to take responsibility for it. A political ethic is, accordingly, about limits, especially in light of the tragedy of confronting extreme violence and the dangers involved. Only by recourse to limits articulated by an economy of counterviolence can these be curbed, especially as one confronts forms of extreme violence.[111] This is, at any rate, more consonant with the spirit of reckoning with the commandment in solitude as a member of a political collectivity, something demanding distinctions and mediations that the architecture of Levinas's own politically infused ethics militantly preempts by fleeing history and not tarrying with the thorny dilemmas of authority, law, and ethics, along with the structures constituting differentiated patterns of domination and exploitation. Only then can the dialectic of fidelity to a commandment or principle assuming concrete ethical and political responsibilities be construed.

ETHICAL POLITICS

Politically more courageous than her fellow ethicists, Butler's political and ethical commitments bracket out any sustained theoretical and historical reckoning with the historical processes and the structural dynamics—that is, with the objective historical and political conditions—that can render her inheritance (and thus recasting) of ethical legacies effective. Reckonings that, in turn, could soberly call into question the formulations of the relationship between ethics and politics that she posits. Although Butler has bravely taken up the thorniest political questions and unflinchingly reflected upon them, and thus has risked the most politically and theoretically by descending down the rivers of historical processes, their imperatives and contingencies, continuities and discontinuities, history as a process is not allowed in her theoretical armature; rather than letting it bear and thus challenge her philosophical commitments and signposts, history is invoked and drawn upon as part of the politically concrete scenes and predicaments of power with which she engages after an ethical injunction framing her politics is formulated and invoked. But the historicity of such injunction is not reflected upon. Contrary to an initial perception, there is no genuine primacy of the situation here, as Butler's theoretical commitments are ultimately insulated from the situation she invokes. Politically constituted and sanctioned historical imperatives are not let in, nor are these allowed to interrogate the soundness of her Levinasian tenets.

What about Derrida's version of ethical politics? What are the political upshots of Derrida's ethical politics and its heretical deconstruction of responsibility? It is clear that despite perfunctory gestures to the political, the ethical has the upper hand in Derrida's ethical politics of responsibility. Moreover, unlike Butler, there is something fundamentally labile about his variation of defensive ethical politics, especially once contrasted with the theoretical radicalism of deconstruction. Eagleton has once again offered a pithy formulation that captures the contrast between the radical tenor of deconstruction and the liberalism of its master thinker: "There is a bathetic contrast in the writings of both Levinas and Derrida between the arresting avant-garde pitch of their theory and the tediously familiar brand of multiculturalism which it seems to involve in practice."[112] Even if, apropos of Levinas, Eagleton's judgment goes astray—as there is a sodden, even distended, quality to his theological upending of the self and the ensuing inflation of the Other—regarding Derrida it holds. If anything, it is understated. Bluntly put, there is something noticeably platitudinous about Derrida's ethical politics: an unruly, often iconoclastic, philosophical radicalism consistently yielded a defensive *bien pensant* politics. From his early evasive liberalism on the Algerian question, which became something of an axial and thus politically defining moment, to the 2003 rapprochement with Habermas as part of the North Atlantic version of "Her Majesty's Loyal Opposition"—with panegyrics to Mandela, interventions in academic politics, and his Free Mumia moment somewhere in between—these political interventions oscillated through the coordinates of the liberal center, albeit mostly located to the left of the centrist bandwidth without threatening it.[113] Anticlimactically, virtuoso theoretical performances conjuring the possibility of something genuinely singular and new, and thus unfettered by the old, yield a version of the defensive politics characteristic of North Atlantic left-liberalism. For all the rhetorical boldness of his theoretical moves, puns, and feints, there is a strong inflection of what Barthes famously called the neither/nor criticism when it comes to politics. For, if nothing else, the neither/nor strategy is a "mechanism of double exclusion," which under the ruse of resisting one dichotomy, and the rhetorical blackmail it purportedly stages, tacitly adheres to its own pristine position above the fray of the structuring the terms of the binary enact.[114] A position Barthes acerbically, but correctly, characterizes as "the fine morality of the Middle Party" that rewrites the initial binary into its own new dichotomization.[115] Or stated in more Hegelian terms: the initial pair conforming the dichotomy is cast as located in *the way of the world* and thus to be resisted, but resisting the terms staged in the initial dyad, and the derision to which their consignment to the way of the world entails, especially once compared to the rather pristine standpoint of the critic, introduces a new dichotomy: that of a deconstructive version of the virtue of one's fine morality and the way of the world. In other words, for all the dedifferentiations that deconstruction authorized—not least the entwining of the philosophical, literary, and rhetorical—and the binaries it undid, tacitly it introduces a new binary between conventional politics and itself, with Derrida cast in the role of the ethical "beautiful soul" who for a long time could not find a place within the rich leftist bandwidth of the post-1968 French political spectrum.[116]

Clearly, at his most forceful, Derrida's overwhelmingly defensive politics have the effect of denouncing selected localized injustices. But to connect the preemption of injustice, or the condemnation of this or that injustice, to an allegation that the injustices in question are profoundly structured and embedded in institutionalized and patterned social arrangements, sanctioned by relations of rule and domination, that should be abolished is simply never in the cards. Just consider how for all the pathos of Derrida's eventual invocations of Algeria— invocations oftentimes lionized by critics—politically Derrida's actual position vis-à-vis French Algeria amounted to little more than a chastened version of Camus's "good colonialist."[117] Likewise, his denunciation of the ten plagues in *Specters of Marx* fails to critically relate them to a broader critique of the structural injustice of the liberal-capitalist mainstay defining the North Atlantic orders, which Derrida as an indefatigable traveler so often traversed, and that, incidentally, constituted the transatlantic space for deconstruction's ascendance. Theoretical hesitation under deconstructive wraps often reverted to political vacillation when the political stance in question demanded something more than a defensive politics quietly acquiescing to the neutralizations constitutive of the often fierce depoliticized politics of the transatlantic north. For all the talk about a democracy to come, one searches in vain for any sustained reflection on citizenship as a politically meaningful category. This is arguably a function of Derrida's unhinged deconstruction of fraternity amidst his dislodging of the other two moments of the revolutionary triad—freedom and equality.[118] The overwhelmingly defensive cast of his politics thus sits comfortably with his futurist disposition, a disposition that is conveniently unencumbered by "the difficulty of sharing power and governing ourselves in common."[119] Derrida's ethical politics consists of a modality of liberalism, a defensive politics that preemptively neutralizes forms of agency that can mount a threat to the mainstay of the present while portending an unmediated future. This politics "to come" is so radically underdetermined from the present, and aloof from any commitment to the collective agencies that can break from what is, that it simultaneously remains miraculous and still recognizably liberal.

5

ADORNO AND THE DIALECTIC
OF RESPONSIBILITY

*Resistance is whatever does not allow its law to be prescribed by
the given facts; to that extent, it transcends the objects, but in
the closest possible contact with them.*

—Theodor W. Adorno, *Lectures on Negative Dialectic*

"**K**AFKA'S POPULARITY**,**" Adorno observed, is due to "that comfort in the uncomfortable which has made of him an information bureau of the human condition, be it eternal or modern, and which knowingly dispenses with the scandal on which his work is built." He goes on to say that Kafka's work "is assimilated into an established trend of thought while little attention is paid to those aspects of his work which resist such assimilation, and which, precisely for this reason, require interpretation."[1] Ironically, Adorno's work has arguably suffered an even harsher fate.[2] Even if his work is often praised, especially his aesthetic theory and the ethical import of his critique of German Idealism and identitarian thinking, his popularity often resides more in assimilations of his thought to contemporary philosophical or theoretical trends than in careful engagements with his complex body of work and with those aspects requiring, even demanding, interpretation. In these assimilations, the *scandal* of his critical theory, its roots in the dialectical legacy of Hegelian Marxism, is dispensed with, or quietly played down, with largely perfunctory gestures acknowledging its obdurate presence.

Nowhere is this more clearly at work than in the "ethical Adorno" that pervades many an interpretation of his thought, or what a scholar has characterized as the different "ethical turns" that have defined the Anglo-American reception of Adorno's thought.[3] Descriptions of the ethical impulse informing Adorno's work vary, to be sure, even if neglect of the scandal is a common thread: Adorno is said to be the proponent of an "ethical modernism," an ethical stance that should be seen as a nonthreatening contribution to the predominant analytical approach to ethics, or brigaded as the bearer of an ethical message that is seen as a forerunner or precursor of deconstruction or as a thinker of neo-Nietzschean "generosity" that seeks to radicalize the ethos of liberal democracy.[4] Efforts such as J. M. Bernstein's, for instance, lead to a very un-Adornian position, one that does little justice to the political and dialectical impulses animating Adorno's philosophical reflections.[5] But once compared with other interpretations, Bernstein's account is fidelity itself. Consider, for instance, Martin Seel's rather inane assertion that "it may be time to free Adorno's philosophy from the dogma and trauma of negativity, from its sometimes-obsessive fixation with Hegel. . . . It may also be time to lay bare the ethical coordinates that mark every line of his social and political diagnoses. Adorno finally belongs with Nietzsche and Heidegger." [6] In this *reading*, what the critic does not like is unceremoniously dispatched in the name of "freeing" Adorno from "restrictive readings," parallels with Nietzsche and Heidegger are duly if superficially contrived, and Adorno is enlisted as a contemplative ethical philosopher of the Other. Or consider Hent de Vries's celebrated work, *Minimal Theologies*, where, from the very outset, Adorno's negative dialectics is translated into proto-deconstructionist terms. By way of "a careful interpretation," de Vries cuts Adorno down to size and forces him to echo Levinasian motifs. Once passed through the Levinasian blender, Adorno's critical theory is characterized as "premised on a similar oscillation between formalization and abstraction, on the one hand, and materialization qua singularization, on the other"; and both Adorno and Levinas are presented as placing "determinants (the ethical, the political, the cultural, the juridical, etc.) under erasure."[7] And, just like that, Adorno becomes a deconstructionist *avant la lettre*, closer to the Heideggerian legacy he detested than to that of Hegel, which he scrupulously worked through and considered central to his own philosophical project.

But, notwithstanding these efforts, the political and ethical import of Adorno's original inheritance of the dialectical legacy cannot be taken in isolation from Hegelian Marxism. While inflected with strong and important Nietzschean and modernist motifs, Adorno's critical theory derives its sharpest edge from his inheritance of this legacy. After all, his *Magnus Opus* was *Negative Dialectics*, and its most important axial concepts are politically and socially infused, as evidenced by his central themes—including "totality," "constellations," "reification," "mediation," "exchange-process," "the total social process," "the culture industry," "the objective theory of society," "autonomy," and "emancipation," among others. These notions profoundly mediate the political and ethical import of his negative dialectics, which goes well beyond the conceits of the ethical turn.[8] Mediating every word Adorno wrote was a profound articulation of the dialectical legacy, a politically infused commitment to social critique, and a no less important commitment to conceptual rigor and bindingness.[9]

That this is so is readily evident in Adorno's "morality of thinking" as he expounds it in *Minima Moralia*, a conceptual formulation that is utterly infused with dialectical and political concerns.[10] What is more, Adorno's critical theory resists hypostatizing theoretical knowledge. Rather, thinking proceeds from a politically infused sociological and cognitive perspective.[11] And these are constitutive moments of his dialectical critical theory that are not only inseparable from the ethical motifs of his work, but without which Adorno's critical theory is bound to be truncated. Accordingly, an elucidation of the place of political responsibility in Adorno's writings, of the ways in which his reflections radically restage the intersections and antinomies between freedom and responsibility in predicaments of power largely defined by capitalist domination and analogous modalities of instrumental reason and depoliticized politics, needs to reckon with the aforementioned "antinomies," not in order to mend or hypostatize them as aporias, let alone reconcile or, worse yet, displace them by neologisms. Rather, an effort has to be made to dialectically render these antinomies as contradictions arising from a historically constituted situation. For a defining attribute of Adorno's thinking is its *distanced nearness* to history. Yet history conceptualized as an objective process, a conceptually bound narrative account of the mediations of human interaction with nature, not as in Heidegger's hypostatized "historicity," is the central objective experience of negative dialectics, for which Adorno's critical theory is its subjective expression. As such, it is important to not only expound its centrality in the theoretical armature of his writings, but to understand it as a mediating objective reality that is fundamental for a comprehension of Adorno's reworking of the dialectical legacy and the historical and political situation to which his critical theory is a response.

Although there is little doubt about the continuities in Adorno's thought—from his 1931 essay "The Actuality of Philosophy" to his posthumous *Aesthetic Theory*—his thinking was thoroughly mediated by historical experience, inflected by it to its very core; and as it is fitting for a dialectical thinker, many discontinuities and changes of emphasis and inflections took place in response to changing situations.[12] Of course, the formative importance of Germany's Weimar Republic, along with the intellectual and artistic milieu defining it, is relatively well-known in the English-speaking world, and so is the formative role of the years that Adorno and his cohort of émigrés spent in the United States, first in New York and then in California.[13] Suffice it for now to mention an obvious historical point that ironically is seldom accorded the theoretical attention it deserves: with the arrival of critical theory on American shores, an important moment of mediation and transmission took place, one in which ideas not only traveled, or were productively misplaced, but one that also provided Adorno with an objective reality from which his reworking of the dialectical legacy cannot be dirempted. Indeed, during this period of exile ideas underwent a moment of transmission and mediation that left a permanent imprint in Adorno's critical theory and its thought forms.

Nowhere is this perhaps more obvious than in how experiences of catastrophe and exile are central for the crystallization of a critical theory that, in turn, would become fully formulated through another mediation: Adorno's return to Germany. Adorno's conceptualization of negative dialectics not only responded to philosophical questions immanent to Hegelian Marxism but also constituted a response to objective historical experiences and is thoroughly mediated by them. Carefully exploring how experiences of exile and catastrophe are constitutive mediations in Adorno's critical theory yields a more nuanced understanding of Adorno's theoretical forms and his political responses to the German scene. These historical experiences are part of the content of Adorno's minimalist humanism, which is best characterized as "an enormous minimalism."[14] This enormous minimalism dialectically conveys historicity and history in its minimalist forms, as these betray a force field of social relations and mediations that is rendered visible by way of its economy.[15] This minimal humanism is forged by exile, which emerges as a central concept for the constellation of categories and concepts, ideas and motifs that constitute Adorno's critical theory.[16]

Autonomy, emancipation, and distanced nearness—these are some of the axial concepts constitutive of Adorno's critical constellation during his American exile, concepts directly bearing on his conception of responsible thinking. Upon his return to Germany, these concepts gained a different set of political valences, not least in relation to how the catastrophe, Auschwitz, had an entirely different resonance in a German context than it did on the Pacific coast. Furthermore, the onset of the cold war led to a different international situation where Adorno's account of the catastrophe yielded to a richer insight into the reality of torture as a catastrophe that pervades and historicizes Auschwitz.[17] All this became central for his postexilic conceptualization of the possibility of ethical and political life after Auschwitz and all this was mediated by his response to the situation conformed by Adenauer's Germany, the cold war, and the subsequent radicalism of the sixties. By the time Adorno returned to Germany, a peculiar modality of liberal democracy—what Jan-Werner Müller has acutely referred to as "militant" or "constrained" democracy—had crystallized in the Federal Republic. It had become a liberal-democratic order largely defined by insulation of both ruling elites and markets from direct encroachments by the masses, a mild aversion to popular sovereignty, staunch anticommunism, and prohibitions and exclusions sanctioned by constitutional courts.[18] Just like his American exile, returning to this new Germany was in and of itself an instance of "transferring the untransferrable," albeit in a fundamentally different way.[19]

"AFTER AUSCHWITZ"

Traces of Adorno's experience of exile are found in the emphasis on nonidentity in his negative dialectics, which takes as its point of departure for reflection the concreteness of objective existence, its historical sediments, and politically constituted forms of suffering. This commitment to abolishing suffering is famously laid out in a passage from *Negative Dialectics* where he stated that "to lend a voice to suffering is the condition of all truth."[20] The basic contours of this statement can be discerned in Adorno's more explicit treatments of the question of suffering. For instance, in his 1962–63 lectures on philosophical terminology Adorno spoke about the need to "translate pain into the concept," namely, the need for conceptual thinking to attempt to grasp, in distanced nearness, the pain and suffering of subjective experience as mediated by objective realities.[21] Even if one cannot reproduce the suffering of the other at its most intimate, nor can it be subsumed in an autarkic concept or universal imperative, one can conceive it and, more important, conceive of the ways in which it can be ameliorated. And, as part of his formulations of concepts and categories, Adorno writes about physical suffering in more forthcoming terms when he writes that "all pain and all negativity" constitute "the moving forces of dialectical thinking."[22] Emancipated social relations demand redressing suffering—"The *telos* . . . would be to negate the physical suffering of even the least of its members, and to negate the internal reflexive forms of that suffering."[23] The critical vocation of leading a voice to suffering also demands the need to understand its history, its political and ethical conditions of possibility, and the imperatives that structure its advent.[24] It is a political-ethical commitment.

The concrete universal that serves as Adorno's point of departure, that instance of a material and historical process forcing imperatives upon critical thinking, is that of catastrophe in the twentieth century. This is best grasped as part of Adorno's consideration of metaphysics as mediated by history and "the question whether one can *live* after Auschwitz," which became the immediate point of departure for his more mature reflections on ethics and responsibility.[25] Auschwitz became the overwhelming concrete experience that signified the catastrophe of genocide in the twentieth century. But rather than using a particular Jewish term like *Shoah,* or a religiously charged one, such as *Holocaust,* or even a more general concept, say, genocide, Adorno always referred to this catastrophe by the concrete location of one of its most infamous killing centers, Auschwitz. Auschwitz, which for Adorno embodied the collapse of Western civilization, thus became a constant point of reference in his reflections. But it was not just an anomaly in an otherwise straight path of progress. According to Adorno, Auschwitz could be historicized without losing sight of its particularity, something that is consistent with the materialist moment of his formulation of critical theory.[26]

Even so, and this is no less important, the centrality of Auschwitz does not lead to its elevation to a transhistorical moment of revelation. For while it symbolizes a caesura—hence, the centrality of "After" [*Nach*] in Adorno's formulation, which is his way of offering the figuration of such rupture—critical thinking about Auschwitz requires an avowal of historical mediations. Particularly important is to grasp the *before*, that which precedes it and provides conditions for its intelligibility, but equally important is the *after*. As a catastrophe, Auschwitz is mediated by general historical trends. It thus punctuates a *particular* instantiation within these historical processes that is not reducible to a mere *particularity* of them. Hence both its identity and nonidentity with the total social process that mediates both the continuities and discontinuities it undoubtedly represents. Nor does "After Auschwitz" entail a negative benchmark that renders ongoing catastrophes invisible, or the normalization of a time after evil yet before justice, to use Robert Meister's acute formulation of the ethicist responses prevalent in contemporary liberal ideology and discourse.[27] On the contrary, as Adorno more than once indicated, the caesura that Auschwitz figures is in relation to how the world was experienced and apprehended. It need not lead to an ethical suspension, nor to a bland ethics of negative freedom, much less to the liberalism of fear. Rather, it imposes a new imperative that is materially conceived and mediated through and through and that refuses to acquiesce to the neutralizing ethical pieties of current invocations of "After Auschwitz" at the service of domination, including imperialist domination by way of humanitarian ideology.

Out of the many formulations Adorno offered, a comment during one of his lectures is apposite here: "I do not know whether the principle that no poem can be written after Auschwitz can be sustained. But the idea that we can say of the world as a whole in all seriousness that it has a meaning now that we have experienced Auschwitz, and witnessed a world in which that was possible and threatens to repeat itself in another guise or a similar one—I remind you of Vietnam—to assert such an idea would seem to me to be a piece of cynical frivolity that is simply indefensible to what we might call the pre-philosophical mind."[28] "We" is a particular we in these formulations, however universal the lessons of the catastrophe are. Asserting its particular nature does not mean a disavowal of the universality involved. On the contrary, it asserts the simple insight that the instantiation of a universal always has a particular point of departure that its universality cannot extricate. Adorno's "we" points out the way in which the caesura in question is particular to the European mind, but the critical import of his negative dialectics prevents any hypostatization of Auschwitz, either in his hands or in others. While Auschwitz is characterized as an evil, this catastrophe is something that pertains to humanity at large—just like, say, torture in Vietnam—but for which a particular collectivity was primarily responsible.[29] In this case, the German Federal Republic: both the successor state of the Third Reich and protectorate of the United States, the country waging war in Vietnam.

Adorno thus grappled with the question of Auschwitz mostly in terms of the crucial question of cognitive representation, which is where the political import of Adorno's critical theory, and that of much of Western Marxism and its heirs—Fredric Jameson, Gillian Rose, and Slavoj Žižek come to mind—truly resides. Among the topics he reflected on are the impossibility of metaphysics as traditionally understood, art, education, as well as the significance of Auschwitz in the way memory, collective identity, individual autonomy, and democracy are understood in its aftermath. For instance, in "Education After Auschwitz" he states the seemingly rather modest, though essential aim of a reconceived education after the catastrophe. "Since the possibility of changing the objective—namely societal and political—conditions is extremely limited today, attempts to work against the repetition of Auschwitz are necessarily restricted to the subjective dimension."[30] This statement attests to a moment of resignation that resonates with the common charge brought against Adorno of always finding refuge in a realm outside politics, say, the aesthetic, or, more damaging still, introducing a Kantian hold-out for the individual, which brings dialectical mediation to a halt and disavows the collective dimensions constitutive of ethical and political life.

But this awareness never amounted to acquiescence.[31] What Adorno is alluding to in the foregoing passage is precisely the refusal to acquiesce, even when the prospects for change look dim in the current situation. In light of such political closure, he emphasizes the centrality of education and autonomy without hypostatizing either; what Adorno also refers to, in this essay and elsewhere, as an education for autonomy, for critique, that seeks to break with the indifference toward the stored human suffering permeating present-day forms of power.[32] In any case, the sense of powerlessness that one might identify in some of his formulations responds to an awareness of the role of institutional and market imperatives in constraining, even depleting, individual autonomy in a liberal-capitalist society and the increasingly absent forms of effective political contestation in Western Europe, which was also a time of political defeat and the closure of alternatives within the German Federal Republic. Yet a critical concept of autonomy is still possible, and Auschwitz constitutes its historical-material cornerstone. "All political instruction finally should be centered upon the idea that Auschwitz should never happen again." In a similar vein, Adorno proceeds to criticize the doctrine of "reason of state," as he rightly sees in that political logic "the horror . . . potentially already posited."[33]

Commentators and critics have found it tempting to interpret these as an iteration of the "never again" of the ethical turn. That is, however, anachronistic. Instead, what emerges from Adorno's formulations is a critical conception of autonomy that seeks to *educate* individuals to have a critical attitude toward power and the leveling tendencies of commodification and instrumental rationality.[34] And this cultivation of critique Adorno revealingly yet laconically linked to genuine democracy, not to be confused with the depoliticized militant democracy bequeathed by the victorious Anglo-American Allies and shrewdly steered by Adenauer and his successors.[35] For Adorno, the aesthetic provided a realm where the somatic aspect of re-cognizing suffering could be apprehended, and with it the possibility of concentrated attention on its levels of constitution, and on the layers of historical sedimentation, found in its concrete manifestations.[36] Auschwitz thus yields one of Adorno's most well-known formulations, the need for a new categorical imperative: "a new categorical imperative imposed by Hitler upon unfree mankind: to arrange their thoughts and actions so Auschwitz will not repeat itself, so that nothing similar will happen."[37]

"After Auschwitz, our feelings resist any claim of the positivity of existence as sanctimonious, as wronging the victims; they balk at squeezing any kind of sense, however bleached, out of the victims' fate."[38] But rather than the impossibility, or lack of ethical and political import of representing Auschwitz, this passage suggests a critique of the frivolous redemption of Auschwitz in crude instrumentalizations, not an ethical dictum against representation as such.[39] Auschwitz, precisely because of the imperative it imposes, needs to be comprehended from the perspective of negative dialectics. Indeed, destruction is associated with the principle of identity. And from the perspective of the materialist moment of his negative dialectics, it is necessary to represent this catastrophe in ways that draw attention to contemporary forms of superfluous suffering, exploitation, and domination.

Responsibility after Auschwitz thus demands responding politically to the different instances of human suffering that are historically constituted and politically sanctioned, not an undifferentiated imperative—again, negative dialectics consistently debunks any such hypostatization. Accordingly, Adorno's claim in *Negative Dialectics* about lending a voice to suffering as the condition of all truth cannot be read literally, as an undifferentiated dictum, but rather in light of the constellation of mediations and differentiations that *Negative Dialectics* comprehensively stages. Once interpreted that way, it is evident that Adorno's critical theory avows the imperative for critical cognition to apprehend the historically superfluous forms of suffering that are at once socially and politically produced and sustained. Intrinsic to the primacy of the object, which is the signature of Adorno's formulation of dialectical thinking, is to record historically constituted catastrophic and tragic suffering— including that which conforms to humanity's natural history—in its particular instantiations, not as *particularities* of a general trend.[40] Thinking can either acquiesce, tacitly or explicitly, to it, or sharply re-cognize it and thus denounce it.[41] It is on the basis of the primacy of the object that the "transition to materialism" in Adorno's critical theory is predicated.[42]

Even the eminently subjective idea of the will is mediated by this dialectical conception of material objectivity and the mediation of historical processes. In a set of arresting formulations, Adorno discusses the ineluctability of a dialectical concept of the will and its heteronomous nature. Heteronomy understood as the determinate opposite of autonomy, as mediated by it. He establishes such constitutive heteronomy of the will by adducing the presence of physical impulses (*Körperimpulse*) in the will, as part of its constitution and actualization—impulses that the will ultimately "tames" and "potentially negates." Therein lies its dialectical character. Following this argument, Adorno goes on to present a striking formulation that bears on his idea of immanent transcendence and his dialectical rendering of tradition: "It is the force that enables consciousness to leave its own domain and so to change what merely exists; its recoil is resistance."[43] But the possibility of good will hardly offers moral certitude, which at best is a mirage and at worst immoral. Even so, it is a real possibility whose constitutive heteronomy needs to be avowed.

Adorno's is a dialectical recasting of the will that, while echoing Hegel's arresting immanent critique of Kantian formalism, takes its constitutive heteronomy in a different direction. As is well known, in his *Philosophy of Right* Hegel's critique demonstrates the *abstract* nature of Kantian duty and proceeds immanently to show how Kant's formalism, in and of itself, cannot encompass anything historically particular or concrete (§§133–34). After that he goes a step further to question Kant's formalist claim to bindingness: "From this point of view, no immanent doctrine of duties is possible; of course, material may be brought in from outside and particular duties may be arrived at accordingly, but if the definition of duty is taken to be the absence of contradiction, formal correspondence with itself—which is nothing but the establishment of abstract indeterminacy—then no transition is possible to the specification of particular duties nor, if some such particular content for acting comes into consideration, is there any criterion in that principle for deciding whether it is or is not a duty" (§135).[44] While Adorno shares elements of Hegel's critique, including the impossibility of an apodictic doctrine of autonomy and duty, he is not primarily concerned with the absence of criteria for normative judgments, let alone sublating the critique of Kantian autonomy in a robust conception of ethical life, although he would gesture in that direction.[45] Rather, Adorno's concern is about a *minima humana*, one that cares about living rightly.

These concerns are further specified when Adorno challenges the Nazi hypostatization of the irrational moment of the will and then writes: "The self-evident good will becomes obdurate in its illusion, *a historic sediment of the power* which the will ought to resist." "Die

Selbstverständlichkeit guten Willens verstockt sich im Trugbild, ge-schichtliches Sediment der Macht, welcher der Wille zu widerstehen hätte."[46] The will, once dialectically understood, forces us to dispense with the illusion of "moral certainty" and its platitudes. In a passage that echoes the critique of moralism from the perspective of a politi-cal ethic, something akin to that found in Brecht and Lao Tse, he fur-ther writes:

> There is no moral certainty. Its mere assumption would be immoral, would falsely relieve the individual of anything that might be called morality [*Sittlichkeit*]. The more mercilessly an objective-antagonistic society will comport itself in any situation [*jegliche Situation*], the less can any single moral decision be warranted as the right one. Whatever the subject or the group may undertake against the totality they are part of is infected [*angesteckt*] by the evil of that totality, and no less so is the one who does nothing. This is how original sin has been secular-ized. The individual subject who thinks he is morally certain fails and is bound to become complicit because, being clamped to the social order, he is hardly able to do anything about the conditions but appeal to the moral *ingenuim*: crying for their change. . . . All conceivable definitions of the moral aspect down to the most formal, the unity of self-conscious-ness *as* reason, were squeezed out of that "matter" with which moral philosophy did not want to dirty its hands. . . . Without recourse to the material, no ought could be issued from reason; yet, once compelled to acknowledge its material in the abstract, as a condition of its own pos-sibility, reason must not cut off its reflection on the specific material.[47]

Adorno accordingly reclaimed an aspect Hegel's idea of ethical life, but recast it in a materialist vein by showing how heteronomy is already interiorized in the idea of autonomy. Namely, ethics cannot be solely founded on reflection and reason, even if it ought to be rational in its means and ends, or on the somatic aspect of the will as residing in a body that is historically and socially mediated, but has to rest on the dialectical mediation that mutually constitutes its actualization, devoid of a first principle or of the illusion of an abstract reconcilia-tion between the two.[48] This constitutive heteronomy of the will is a far cry from the hypostatization of the relationality of the subject found in Levinas and his heirs.

THE DIALECTIC OF RESPONSIBILITY

How does this materialist account of the dialectic of the will, along with its political-ethical imperative about the need to respond to suffering after Auschwitz, relate to the concept of responsibility? Whereas responsibility, as a concept, figures sparingly in Adorno's published works, responsibility as a practice pervades his reworking and inheritance of the dialectical legacy, as the foregoing discussion has sought to expound. Yet in his lectures, especially his 1963 lectures on the problems of moral philosophy, responsibility is at last explicitly reflected upon. In what must seem like an unexpected shift, at least for proponents of an ethicist Adorno, it is Weber who offers a point of departure for his reflections. Therein Adorno conjoined two efforts hitherto separated in his writings: the concern with the "good life," as expounded in *Minima Moralia* in terms of subjective experience, and the central political ethical problem of the relationship between freedom and law, which figures prominently in the model on freedom in *Negative Dialectics*.[49] In these lectures, responsibility emerges as a fundamentally heteronomous concept, an avowal of the moment of heteronomy that is constitutive of autonomy once dialectically understood.

But Adorno's conceptualization is not just a consequence of the centrality of the object in his negative dialectics, albeit the primacy of the object figures prominently in it.[50] It is also a corollary to his account of natural history, as expounded with Horkheimer in *Dialectic of Enlightenment*, where the dialectical nature of sacrifice is memorably conceptualized by way of Adorno's reading of Homer's *Odyssey*: self-preservation, whose violence only the violence of reason can arrest, is constitutive of the catastrophic nature of human history, of our natural history. Consequently, responsibility emerges here as a central category that is intrinsic not only to cognition but also for political action, where an ethics of conviction is bound to be abstract. This is how Adorno draws the contrast between the two: "An ethics of conviction is an ethics that seek refuge in the pure will, that is, it recognizes the interiority of the moral subject as its only authority. In contrast to that, the ethics of responsibility take as their starting point an existing reality, though in certain conditions this may be a mental reality, as perceived by the subject to which it is then counterposed."[51]

A concrete instantiation of the conflict between the two—which in Weber leads to an antinomy that could nonetheless be dialectically reformulated—is staged by way of Henrik Ibsen's *The Wild Duck*, in connection with which Adorno verbally conjures a scene of responsibility whose stakes he thus articulates:

> what Ibsen defends against Kant and against the ethics of conviction—and here he is absolutely Hegel's heir—is the ethics of responsibility. What is meant by this is an ethics in which at every step you take—at every step you imagine yourself to be satisfying a demand for what is good and right—you simultaneously reflect on the effect of your action, and whether the goal envisaged will be achieved. In other words, you are not just acting of pure conviction, but you include the end, the intention and even the resulting shape of the world as positive factors in your considerations.[52]

By conceptualizing Ibsen's staging of this question, Adorno accurately situates the question of the ethics of responsibility as part of the problematic inherited by Hegel. The Weberian problematic is subtly, yet vigorously, recast in Hegelian terms that go beyond the Kantian lineages mediating his conceptualization of autonomy and freedom in *Negative Dialectics*. For Adorno, genuine individual freedom is dialectically dependent on the freedom of the whole, and his negative dialectics reframes what is ultimately an echo of Hegel's account of the dialectical mediation between individual and collectivity.

Nevertheless, the end result of Adorno's formulation of this relationship remains antinomian. For the language of "collective life," in Adorno's view, has been hijacked by nationalism and fascism.[53] "Consequently," as Gerhard Schweppenhäuser accurately points out, for Adorno "the way forward consists either of a *political ethics* as the basis of a normatively just, collective praxis, or, so long as this route is blocked, of the ethics of noncooperation."[54] The latter, the ethics of noncooperation, acknowledges the impossibility of a genuine, meaningful sense of responsibility in situations of unfreedom. Hence the inadequacy of the question of responsibility as framed by the primacy of accountability that Adorno associates with "criminology:" "Are you responsible or not responsible," a question that rings hollow once understood in solipsistic terms in a situation of unfreedom.[55]

"Freedom in the sense of moral responsibility can only exist in a free society," Adorno unequivocally suggested.[56] Responsibility, then, is only meaningful in a free society whose corollary is the absence of unfreedom and a sense of shared power: "We can only think of ourselves as responsible insofar as we are able to influence matters in the areas where we have responsibility. . . . Responsibility, then, is the touchstone by which freedom can be measured in reality, by which freedom can be imputed, as the lawyers put it. But if responsibility truly is the critical zone of freedom, we can say that today there is a complete mismatch between responsibility and influence" (203–4). Herein, responsibility is bounded. Its limits largely reflect the differentiations of power within a social and political order. It is circumscribed to fields or areas where "we have responsibility," something that has to be carefully pondered and critically mapped. Adorno, then, makes explicit the Hegelian connotations of this conception of responsibility as thoroughly mediated by subjective dispositions and historical objectivity. Or as he states it, "This is that, while freedom appears to us as a subjective quality, as if the judgment about whether freedom exists is one that falls exclusively to the subjective mind, this insight enables us to see *how dependent* freedom is on *objective* realities and to gauge the extent to which we are capable of influencing the real world with its *overpowered, structured institutions* by what we do as *formally* free subjective agents" (204, emphasis added).

Thus a properly dialectical account of freedom is as crucial for his political ethic as it is for a philosophy of history. Adorno reflected on this question from the perspective of his critical materialism and the pondered refusal of abstractions that could easily revert to reification or hypostatization. In relation to these concerns, Adorno argued:

> This is the problem of a philosophy of history of freedom—and, for that matter, of all such profoundly historical concepts; and the challenge facing such a philosophy of history must be to preserve identity, the permanent component, of such concepts throughout the changes they undergo, and not to contrast these changes abstractly with something permanent. But by saying this, I really express nothing more than the principle that governs dialectical thinking in general. In the final analysis, we must say that we should not think of freedom as a merely abstract idea. . . . Instead, we can only speak

meaningfully of freedom because there are concrete possibilities of freedom, because freedom can be achieved in reality.

(180–81, cf. 207)

Freedom is "something social," and unfreedom is a form of "super-fluous domination," however entrenched and sedimented as second nature the latter may be, both of which are concepts thoroughly medi-ated by the concrete situations in which these emerge—indeed, free-dom is a *problem* to be dialectically elucidated (183, 201). Content and form are thus dialectically rendered. Or, as Adorno formulated it in conjunction with the question of responsibility: "For to think about mankind in terms of the contents of people's lives would essentially be a question of responsibility, responsibility towards empirical exis-tence, self-preservation and the fulfillment of the species to which we belong for good or ill."[57] Even so, it is in collective, public matters where moral problems pertaining to the species at large arise. If this collective connotation is disavowed, what remains is the abstract pos-iting of the question of freedom and determinism along the antino-mian lines exposed in bourgeois morality, where "freedom as respon-sibility" is placed "in the service of repression."[58] Adorno thus states what he considers the overriding concerns in ways that resonate and complement his account of moral life "after Auschwitz:" "No man should be tortured; there should be no concentration camps—while all this continues in Asia and Africa and is repressed merely because, as ever, the humanity of civilization is inhumane towards the people it shamelessly brands as uncivilized."[59]

The conclusion to Adorno's "Freedom Model" in *Negative Dialec-tics* succinctly encompasses what is at stake in this critique of formal freedom and responsibility, as well as registers Adorno's sense of an ethics of political responsibility at a time of political closure: "In the socialized society no individual is capable of the morality that is a social demand, but would only be a reality in a free society. Social morality would only still exist once it at last puts an end to the bad infinity of nefarious exchange. But the individual is left with no more than the morality for which Kantian ethics—which accords affection, not respect, to animals—can muster only disdain: to try to live so that one may believe himself to have been a good animal."[60] Echoes of Brecht's staging of the dialectic of objective and subjective ethics

reverberate in these formulations. Paraphrasing one of Brecht's assertions in *Me-Ti, the Book of Changes*, it is unethical to speak of ethics
in a situation that is structured to deplete it of substance, for only
in a different social and political order could the demands of moral
obligation and legal constraints animating the best formulations of a
Kantian sense of responsibility be actualized in the context of a collective sense of ethical life.[61] But this is precisely what Adorno ultimately
disavowed, even if the actualization of the political ethic of responsibility that emerges in his reflections demands it. Rather, he ultimately
rests on noble ideas of decency and integrity that come close to pit-
ting powerless virtue against the way of the world. In Adorno's own
formulation, "life itself is so deformed and distorted that no one is
able to live the good life in it or to fulfill his destiny as a human being.
Indeed, I would almost go so far to say that, given the way the world is
organized, even the simplest demand for integrity and decency necessarily leads almost everyone to protest."[62] That is Adorno's wager, but
the tepidness of the formulation tells the tale about the chances for it
to bear fruit.

This wager, however, is instructive. Out of an immanent critique of
it, some of the basic contours of a robust political ethic of responsibility more evidently emerge, even if it, ultimately, calls for a different
stance. Adorno's "good animal" here could be contrasted with Brecht's
stance toward the very same dialectical dilemma of political ethics,
albeit one penned in the 1930s—these are St. Joan's words, after real-
izing how her good acts ended up having pernicious consequences in
lieu of how the situation in which she acted was structured:

> Oh inconsequential goodness! Oh negligible virtue!
> I changed nothing!
> Soon to vanish fruitless from this world
> I say to you:
> Take care that when you leave the world
> You have not merely been good, but are leaving
> A better world[63]

Here, in a nutshell, are the contrasts between Adorno's political ethic
of noncooperation in an epoch of political closure and the need to preserve freedom in the interstices of one's natural history, with Brecht's

militant political ethic, one in which the tragic dimension of political life, and the sobriety of reckoning with it, refuses to be satisfied with just being good. It, rather, demands a political ethic of responsibility that should be grafted on our natural history. It is not enough to be a good animal, but a good animal that responsibly tried to make a better world, even if only by actively refusing to compromise with *what is*, let alone acquiesce with it, by delineating lines of flight to immanently transcend it, by an uncompromising realism that critically tarries with the obdurate imperatives of political life but nevertheless imagines otherwise. All of which has to inhabit the dialectical contradictions defining ethical life and the predicaments of power conforming the situation in which one acts and to which one responds. All in all, a political ethic of responsibility with a sense of fidelity to Adorno's dialectical forms, not to his pronouncements or particular contents.

VANISHING THE POLITICAL

The contradictions and impasses in the formulation of a political ethic, the subjective and the objective moments of ethical life in an unjust order, are keenly staged in Adorno's *Problems of Moral Philosophy*. After taking note that Kant's philosophy of history was, precisely, an attempt to do so, one that ultimately does not work but which betrays the fundamental problem and responded to the right intuition, Adorno, surprisingly, turns to Brecht to further elucidate this question. By reference to Brecht's literary figurations, he construes scenes in which the speculative mediation of the object and the subject that is constitutive of a political ethic is enacted, as well as its limits. In Adorno's interpretation, in two of Brecht's plays, *St. Joan of the Stockyards* and *The Good Person of Szechwan*, one finds a subtle account of "the parting of the ways between the personal or subjective morality and objective morality" and the diremption of the two in capitalist and bureaucratic orders.[64] In the first play Joan follows a Kantian sense of duty, which here Adorno associates with the ethic of conviction, that leads to her downfall, and "what we see is that thanks to this she becomes the agent of the very worst and most dangerous interests, and that what Johanna [sic] does turns into the very opposite of what she wants"; in the second play the main character, also female, and who also wants to "do good," ends up discovering "that in a society that is felt to be deeply questionable she can only succeed in doing good by making herself evil."[65] Yet, rather than articulate this problem in proximity to political life, with its own internal imperatives, which requires going beyond a moral conceptualization, Adorno arrests the movement of this discussion and turns to a qualified defense of Kantian formalism.

This defense, however, is consistent with Adorno's one-sided characterization of Hegel's idea of "ethical life." Apropos of Hegel, he writes that "what the ethics of responsibility amounts to is that existing reality—that which Hegel calls the way of the worlds [*der Weltlauf*], which he defends against the vanity of protesting interiority—is always in the right over against the human subject."[66] This is so obviously wrong that it scarcely merits comment. But this formulation cannot be conflated with the totality of Adorno's reflections about politics. Although never theorizing the political as such, his critical theory of responsibility exhibits a keen understanding of one of its constitutive dimensions: the primacy of the situation and the crucial role of theoretical re-cognition. Both constitute essential elements of any conceptualization that goes beyond the antinomy between the subjective and the objective that seems to emerge out of his misrecognition of the collective contents of ethical life and the ensuing curtailing of a substantive political ethic.[67] This truncation of his political ethic leaves Adorno vulnerable to the charge that he is arresting the movement of dialectical mediation and, by extension, leaving reflection in a state of "judged oppositions," in this case, that between subjective and objective ethics, an opposition that while dialectically formulated ultimately arrests the dialectical moment of thinking that can lead to a conceptualization of ethical life and the political forms and institutions actualizing it.[68] Nonetheless, this hardly leads Adorno to a neo-Kantian fossilization of the antinomian nature of this opposition. It emerges out of Adorno's response to his historical situation, one scarcely removed twenty years from the Nazi past. Adorno's partial disavowal of the political ethic, a necessary corollary of the primacy of ethical life over individualist morality within the dialectical legacy, is historical through and through.

How and why this particular antinomy is best recast as a historically mediated contradiction in the architecture of Adorno's critical theory is best grasped in one of his very last essays, "Marginalia to Theory and Praxis," in which he confronted the dialectic of theory and praxis in close proximity to the predicaments of power mediating the West German political situation of the late sixties. What this text, and the different conceptual movements and mediations staged in it, reveals is Adorno's real struggle with these mediations, which, in turn, suggests that these contradictions are symptoms of a historical impasse. Furthermore, by way of his articulation of the dialectic of theory and practice, he reflects upon one of the central questions of any political ethic, the intersection between means/ends in political life, with unexpected results. Early on in the text, Adorno revisits the question of the relationship between subjective and objective, but this time he casts it in more recognizable philosophical terms by way of juxtaposing Kant and Hegel: namely, as the perennial dialectic of the universal and the particular, the individual and the community. While Kant's enlightened morality is individualist, namely, a moral philosophy for which "the individual" is "the substrate of correct—that is, for Kant, radically reasonable—action," Hegel's conception of ethical life completely reframes the question. "Hegel in effect dissolves the concept of the moral by extending it to the political. Since then no unpolitical reflection upon praxis can be valid anymore."[69] Even while tacitly recognizing how the Hegelian formulation entails a speculative recasting of the intersection between ethics and politics—one that in Hegelian, Hegelian-Marxist, and Marxist thought has sometimes been conceived as a political ethic, as opposed to an ethical politics—Adorno levels a familiar charge against Hegel (one that elsewhere he has formulated with great power and acuity): in Hegel "the political extension of the concept of praxis introduces the repression of the particular by the universal."[70] Thus, once again, Adorno articulates a Kantian holdout that cuts off a fuller articulation of ethical life and its forms and how a properly dialectical mediation between individual and collective need not entail the repression of the particular.

Implicit here is Adorno's contention that in Hegel the particular is ultimately reduced to a particularity of the universal.[71] However, in these formulations Adorno comes extremely close to hypostatizing the individual qua particular and thus truncating the movement of negative dialectics. "Humanness," Adorno acerbically argues, "which does not exist without individuation, is being virtually re-canted by the latter's [Hegel's] snotty-nosed [*schnöselige*] casual dismissal. But once the action of the individual, and therefore of all individuals, is made contemptible, then collective action is likewise paralyzed."[72] Here Adorno overshoots his target. His own account of the dialectical mediation of objective and subjective ethics attests the need for collective agencies beyond his abstract denunciation of Hegel, which in the *Phenomenology of Spirit* is far from rendering the individual standpoint contemptible *tout court*. All the same, this seems like a damning verdict on Hegel, not least in its barely concealed contempt for what Adorno takes to be Hegel's cavalier dismissal of the individual. But, as Adorno notes in the sentence that immediately follows it, the critique of both moments hardly leads to any transhistorical condemnation of the ineluctability of a political ethic that could be actualized only in conditions of freedom and equality. Ultimately, it suggests a historical impasse, the limits of a particular historical moment: that is, a historically mediated contradiction, one that if cast as merely an antinomy conceals its historicity and historically determined nature. Its sediments. Or, as he formulates the historical contradiction,

> Spontaneity appears to be trivial at the outset in the face of the factual supremacy of the objective conditions. Kant's moral philosophy and Hegel's philosophy of right represent two dialectical stages of the bourgeois self-consciousness of praxis. Polarized according to the dichotomy of the particular and the universal that tears apart this consciousness, both philosophies are false. Each justifies itself against the other so long as a possible higher form of praxis does not reveal itself in reality; its revelation requires theoretical reflection. It is beyond doubt and controversy that a reasoned analysis of the situation is the precondition for political praxis at least.[73]

Thus, by historicizing the opposition, the antinomy is re-cognized as a contradiction and the possibility of undoing it is related to the question of praxis. Ultimately, only in reference to the concrete political situation is a different staging of this contradiction possible and, by extension, the possibility emerges of enacting new scenes of political responsibility, scenes that can only become meaningful by carefully pondering the situation, its possibilities and closures.

In a moment of defeat, and epochal neutralization, the locus for responsible action immediately consists of rigorous reflection upon this condition, its sources as well as its fissures, especially in an age of defeat and closure characterized by modalities of domination: bureaucratization in the East and capitalist standardization and reification in the West.[74] A measured grasp of the situation was for Adorno indispensable for a political praxis aiming at its eventual transformation, and this often involves nothing less than fulfilling the vocation of critical theory in the realm of representation, as theory emerging out of concrete contacts with the objective historical situation and, by extension, transcending it in thought as a precondition for actualizing its historical transcendence. And, in a situation of political neutralization and epochal closure, it is imperative to resist idealizations or embellishments of *what is* and refuse to relent on critical thinking. By the same token, it was politically illiterate to dismiss the modicum of democracy that, in Adorno's case, West Germany's Federal Republic represented in terms of recent German history. Hence the overwhelmingly defensive politics that defined Adorno's intellectual and political praxis in the sixties, yet a carefully calibrated, and thus temporary, defensive politics that refused to acquiesce to the predicament of power.

One of Fredric Jameson's formulations can be invoked here to shed light on this question:

Of the antinomies, perhaps we can conclude . . . that their ceaseless alternation between Identity and Difference is to be attributed to a blocked mechanism, whereby in our own episteme these categories fail to develop, fail to transform themselves by way of their own interaction, as they seemed able to do in other moments of the past (and not only in the Hegelian dialectic). If so, the blockage can only have something to do with the absence of any sense of an immediate future and of imaginable change . . . for us time consists of an eternal present and, much further away, an inevitable catastrophe, these two moments showing up distinctly on the registering apparatus without overlapping or transitional stages.[75]

What Jameson calls the "blockage" is historical, as is the impasse between subjective and objective ethics, theory and praxis, that Adorno faced. There is not even a vanishing mediation between the two opposing moments, which could then be experienced as antinomian, or aporetic, or hypostatized as one or the other. Yet, once cast as antinomies, the historicity of the opposition is disavowed, a theoretical formulation that acquiesces with the stifling of historicity that has fallen upon the North Atlantic West, the perpetual present of postmodernity.[76]

How high are the stakes when thinking about the importance of historicizing the situation, including thinking historically about the relative powerlessness of theory and praxis in the face of larger, objective, historical trends, is adduced in Adorno's scathing rendering of what he considers to be the deformation of spontaneity at the hands of actionism [*Aktionismus*]. These formulations simultaneously betray Adorno's frustration with the actionism of the student movement and his commitment to a historically mediated, and thus contextual, reckoning with the situation, as he makes no bones about the impoverishment of theory once it is entirely severed from a political praxis, and vice versa. Theory certainly owes fidelity to praxis in order to live up to its critical vocation, but that actually entails resisting the imperatives to unreflective praxis. Here is Adorno's rendering:

> The transition to a praxis without theory is motivated by the objective impotence of theory and exponentially increases that impotence through the isolation and fetishization of the subjective element of historical movement, spontaneity. The deformation of spontaneity should be seen as a reaction to the administered world. But by frantically closing its eyes to the totality and by behaving as though it stems immediately from people, spontaneity falls in line with the objective tendency of progressive dehumanization: even in its practices. Spontaneity, which would be animated by the neediness of the object, should attach itself to the vulnerable places of rigidified reality, where the ruptures caused by the pressures of rigidification appear externally; it should not thrash about indiscriminately, abstractly, without any consideration of the contents of what is often attacked merely for the sake of publicity.[77]

Several themes can be teased out of this set of formulations, but for the purposes of the present discussion exploring three suffices. First, notice the uncharitable and ultimately inaccurate depiction of the German situation that the last clause of the last formulation conveys, one of several that say a lot about Adorno's own political temperament, the fallibility of his political judgment. Second, and what is most important at this point: irrespective of the unsoundness of some of his local judgments, these formulations state and perform the form of re-cognition that his critical theory defends. This is clearly grasped by how, in a fine dialectical reversal of the received terms of discussion, actionism, which is presumably more objective than the purportedly ethereal contemplation of critical theory, turns out to be subjectivist, while critical theory emerges as closer to the objectivity of the historical situation. And these are not mere conceptual pirouettes. On the contrary, these formulations articulate what lies at the core of Adorno's argument, the objective and subjective mediation of both theory and practice and how critical theory as negative dialectics provides the most adequate conceptual armature to forge a realist political ethic. Indeed, it is in light of his own critical theory that one can not only critically undermine and debunk Adorno's own conceits but also denounce the lack of realism of actionism and its moralizing impulses. Third, witness the ways in which he grasps the totality, and by extension its determinations, through concentrated thinking, alert and thus attentive to objective needs and the vulnerable places of the totality as grasped in the actual situation—*attention* and *concentration* that further seek to be responsive to suffering, by thinking as best he could of finding ways to lend a voice to suffering, as well as to the conditions of its amelioration. Yet vulnerability is articulated politically; for what is at stake here is not a hypostatized vulnerability of the subject, but the objective points of vulnerability of the structure of power as such. Insofar as Adorno seeks to articulate both forms of vulnerability—that of the system and that of socially mediated and historically constituted vulnerable individuals and groups—he is able to articulate some of the broad contours of a political ethic, or at least part of its conceptual, critical, and cognitive armature.

Re-cognizing the situation, its structure and coordinates, is crucial for genuine political action. Adorno unequivocally writes: "An analysis of the situation is not tantamount to conformity to that situation. In reflecting upon the situation, analysis emphasizes the aspects that might be able to lead beyond the given constraints of the situation."[78] This imperative to map the situation as accurately as possible is intrinsic to a realist disposition that unexpectedly emerges in a thinker so often chided for political aloofness. A mapping that is constitutive of his version of an economy of violence: whereas Adorno avows violence in the context of waging war against counterrevolutionary fascism for the sake of an alternative order, he contended that violence had lost validity in the West German context of the late sixties.[79] The contours of this realist disposition can be further grasped in his discussion of the dialectic of means and ends and how this has become distorted in a world so dominated by the imperatives of instrumental reason.[80] Equally troublesome to him is the autonomization of means: the nightmarish spectacle of "actionism," a political practice in which means are severed from ends.[81] In this way, Adorno's critique does not disavow the dialectic of means/ends. Instead, what he places under severe criticism is the extreme autonomization of means that comes out of the attempt to fulfill ends without concentrated reflection, a form of unreflective practice in which means overwhelm ends or supplant them altogether. But Adorno treads carefully and avoids abstract pacifism, with its inevitable contradictions, as he refuses to idealize violence. Only a reckoning with the situation and its imperatives, its openings and closures, can decide the recourse to violence.[82]

It is in this vein that conceptualizing the relationship between ends/ means along the lines of his dialectical critical theory becomes constitutive of the practice of political responsibility in the new German predicament after World War II. How does Adorno recast this dialectic? He does so by reintroducing ends to the realm of rationality, along the lines of the philosophical anthropology sketched in *Dialectic of Enlightenment*. According to the minimalist humanism formulated in these exilic philosophical fragments, rationality is intimately conjoined with self-preservation. By extension, Adorno argues, rationality cannot relinquish the preservation of humanity or "simply be split off from" it.[83] From this perspective, humanity's preservation is an ineluctable controlling *end* that is historical, through and through, and not an abstract invocation of historicity. Drenched in history, it is an argument that risks fallibility but avoids hypostatization. It also firmly grounds Adorno's critique of the instrumental as part of the effort to objectify an emancipated rational society.[84] The commitment to humanity emerges as an end to which rational means need to respond, a concrete universal utterly mediated by particular situations and their constitutive predicaments of power. And the dialectic between the two avows the primacy of the situation and how the relationship between theory and praxis conforms to how the latter is structured. Clearly, there are no guarantees; nor can self-preservation by reified.[85] If left unchecked, self-preservation can lead to the establishment of "society itself as a vast joint-stock company for the exploitation of nature."[86] Still, certain political questions are ultimately put aside in Adorno's account: for instance, that of how to politically actualize, or make good on emancipated self-preservation, its political-ethical corollaries, sociological basis, and political contents. Without addressing these questions, his realist recasting of violence, means and ends, remains limited. Overall, the limits of Adorno's political ethic largely stem from his neglect to theorize political forms, to dialectically conceptualize the political level of the totality his conceptual constellation re-cognizes. But this is not a hypostatized antinomian stance; rather, it amounts to a contradiction. Symptomatically, the discussion ends with a rather tenuous invocation of Hegelian "ethical life," even when Adorno ultimately refused to conceptualize ethical life and other realms of collective power where any form of political action takes place.[87]

Elsewhere, Adorno cogently articulated his understanding of critical theory as a form of practice, even if he never conceived of it as a substitute for genuine political praxis. Critical theory is a form of praxis in the realm of representation; there it has a pedagogical function it fulfills by cultivating forms of education and political literacy vigilant of the forms of power mediating, if not enacting, practices of domination and exploitation. His guiding conviction is the relentlessness of dialectical critique. An activity that demanded from him critical distance at a moment of political closure:

> Thinking is not the intellectual reproduction of what already exists anyway. As long as it doesn't break off, *thinking has a secure hold on possibility*. Its insatiable aspect, its aversion to being quickly and easily satisfied, refuses the foolish wisdom of resignation. The utopian moment in thinking is stronger the less it—this too a form of relapse—objectifies itself into a utopia and hence sabotages its realization. Open thinking points beyond itself. For its part a comportment, a form of praxis, it is more akin to transformative praxis than a comportment that is compliant for the sake of praxis.[88]

Emancipated democracy, beyond the horizon of capitalism, at once demands such distance and rejects it. For an emancipated and genuine conception of autonomy the dialectical relationship of theory and praxis needs to be preserved in their *distanced nearness*. But for Adorno's critical theory of responsibility to become a political ethic of responsibility, it needs to conceptualize the initial situation it objectively encounters—the situation that at once constitutes the point of departure for subjective action and a historical consequence. This must occur alongside Adorno's accurate observation of how the moment of conviction is immanent to an ethics of responsibility, an ethics that to become concrete has to encompass reflection on how the preceding shape of the world mediates and constrains the situation in which one finds oneself and how one's actions alter it as well. All in all, this points to a cognitive process for which his critical theory is fundamental.

Adorno's critical theory never amounted to a sustained reflection on political life, let alone political forms. Even so, the foregoing discussion makes clear how one-sided the presentation of Adorno as a thinker who offers "Beckett and Schoenberg as the solution to world starvation and threatened nuclear destruction" actually is.[89] Rather, for Adorno, the aesthetic provided a realm where the somatic aspect of re-cognizing suffering could be apprehended.[90] Adorno has thus bequeathed a conceptually bound account of the dialectical legacy that is a formidable point of departure for the re-cognition of contemporary predicaments of power. The challenge is thus one of dialectically conceptualizing both subjective re-cognition *and* political forms that would allow for a truly emancipated humanity—political forms and critical orientations defined by a sense of critical fidelity. At the level of the subject, the stakes of this immanent transcendence are memorably formulated in *Minima Moralia*, "Dialectical thought is an attempt to break through the coercion of logic by its own means," an attempt devoid of guarantees—for "it is at every moment in danger of itself acquiring a coercive character: the ruse of reason would like to hold sway over the dialectic too"—of arresting the compulsions of instrumental reason's coercion by way of the bindingness of critical reason.[91] The primacy of the object entails moving away from this grip, a step that would dialectically recast and render concrete Karl Kraus's aphorism "Origin is the goal."[92] In this genuinely new origin a broader politics, which always encompasses a defensive moment but also an offensive politics, could be actualized.

Adorno's defensive politics never reverted to a platitudinous ethical politics but represent a truncation of the political ethic presupposed by his reflections. But out of Adorno's critical theory it is possible to formulate a dialectical concept of responsibility that allows for cognitive mappings of the scenes of action that constitute contemporary predicaments of power. Stated differently, on the basis of the conceptual architecture of his negative dialectic, a political concept of responsibility needs to be formulated to make good on its critical and political promise, something that ultimately entails conceptualizing the political field of power as such, with its own internal problematic and imperatives. In the end, this entails pursuing an intellectual itinerary on the basis of the thought form he bequeaths, which Adorno himself never pursued. The limits of Adorno's conceptualization consisted of his well-nigh absolute refusal to theorize questions of political form and thus recast dialectical autonomy politically. The challenge Adorno bequeaths us is to conceptualize what political forms, which in their autonomous logic can only be actualized by a nontruncated dialectic of subjective political responsibility and objective institutionalization bound by a fidelity to an emancipated social order, can enable his commitment to redress the production and reproduction of superfluous sufferings, domination, and exploitation.[93] Therefore, to cast negative dialectics politically, the political field, its imperatives and forms, have to be conceptualized. And for this conceptualization of the political field and of political life, Adorno's concept of the situation as well as his dialectical account of "spontaneity as an activity," mediated yet never predetermined, are promising points of departure for a dialectical model—for a constellation of political life, as it were—and for a conceptualization of the dialectic of objective and subjective ethics as part of a political ethic and its ensuing forms of political responsibility.[94] If critical theory is the subjective side of negative dialectics, its objective moment cannot not be politically theorized, as a nonidentical object of critical theory. Recasting Adorno's critical theory politically thus demands making good on its promise of emancipation by soberly re-cognizing contemporary predicaments of power and whether or not lines of flight may be discerned in their interstices. Only then new possibilities for how to adequately redress the present arise, a genuinely political ethic emerges, and new scenes of political responsibility can be enacted. In these quests there is perhaps no better companion than the *wound* that is Adorno's negative dialectic, one that remains unhealed in the false dwellings of contemporary posthistorical liberal-capitalist orders.[95]

6

POLITICAL ETHIC, VIOLENCE, AND DEFEAT

The fidelity exacted by society is a means to unfreedom, but
only through fidelity can freedom achieve insubordination
to society's command.

—Theodor W. Adorno, *Minima Moralia*

I N THE United States a first impression would imply that the ethical
turn has crystallized around a particular discourse of catastrophe
that emerged in the last decade of the twentieth century. With a fin
de siècle mindset, various cultural and literary historians argued for the
centrality of catastrophe, as a historical experience, concept, or narrative trope, in understanding the era that had just come to an end. In
the early 1990s, cultural critic Cathy Caruth already referred to it as
"our own catastrophic era."[1] About a decade later, the editors of a col-
lection of essays on mourning and loss echoed a similar sentiment: "At
the dawn of the twenty-first century, mourning remains."[2] Alongside
loss and mourning, responsibility also became a prevalent theme in reference to the century coming to an end, its seemingly unprecedented
violence, and the question of how properly to mourn it and respond
responsibly to its afterlives. Yet politically this moment was defined by
epochal closure and political neutralization, for which mourning and
loss became symptomatic expressions. The mournful gaze of left-liberal
critics mostly found articulation in theoretical forms that tacitly acqui-
esced with the political neutralizations defining the decade. More to the
point, these mournful politics not only misrecognized the recent past
by conferring it "a wholeness that never did exist" but frequently converged with the rejection of forms of collective agency, and the enmity
lines these symbolize, while hypostatizing suffering and loss in terms

of a "renewed privatization" of experience that reproduced "the reduction to the present" so characteristic of contemporary capitalism's dislodging of political historicity and the forms of depoliticized politics sustaining it and promoted by it.[3]

Undeniably, out of this elevation of mourning, powerful theorizations emerged, but they were ultimately bereft of an adequate mapping of contemporary predicaments of power. Theoretical heavy lifting resulted in a rather faint political minimalism. Thus the ensuing affective, psychoanalytic, and ethical *turns* all converged in mostly depoliticizing political gestures and disaffiliated conceptions of collective life that were given antinomian expression in ethical discourses of responsibility whose disavowal of the robustly collective connotations of the practice of responsibility mirrored the political disaffiliation so characteristic of depoliticized politics.[4] But, however hypostatized, the centrality of loss in these discussions unwittingly betrays something else. For these could be interpreted as distorted expressions of the sense of defeat that the onset of a new world order and the stabilization of the neoliberal regime of accumulation in the North Atlantic world brought with it. But, to fully register this historical dimension and its sediments, loss needs to be recast politically.

LOSS AS DEFEAT

The turn of the century predicament was described as one of loss: the loss of the idea of reason as a privileged standpoint; the loss of an alternative system to capitalism, namely, the loss of the socialist dream; the loss of humanity in wars and genocides and from atomic weapons; for American liberals, the loss of innocence from the sixties on; and, more recently, the loss of human life, along with a sense of security and invulnerability in the aftermath of 9/11 and the wars it triggered.[5] Of course, many of these are not really losses. Psychically, as Sigmund Freud notoriously argued, one can actually lose what one never had and thus mourn something that has never existed. But losses, real or imagined, frequently lead to a condition of grief, especially the loss of human life at the hands of catastrophes such as terrorism (statist and nonstatist) and genocide. Or, as the editors of *Loss* put it, given how the past century "resounds with catastrophic losses of bodies, spaces, and ideals, psychic and material practices of loss and its remains are productive for history and for politics."[6] Yet, while this invocation of politics and history is promising, in the volume in question these are labile, mostly perfunctory gestures toward the historical and the political. Indeed, what is striking in most reflections on loss is that the recognition of loss has not led to a careful reckoning with its historicity; neither has it led to a nuanced understanding of the political configurations in which losses became such, nor to a theorization of the possibility and desirability of substantive political action in their aftermath. Oftentimes, the language of loss has been transplanted from the psychoanalytic connotations, better suited for individuals, to the collective, with little sustained reflection on the ways the challenges and demands of the collective are occluded by the solipsistic connotations built into individual categories. Politically, asymmetrical relations of race, class, gender, and status mediate the ways an individual experiences loss, and these are historically entrenched in political, cultural, and economic contexts. But none of these mediations can be discerned on the basis of psychoanalytic accounts of loss and mourning, however much else these accounts may contribute and enlighten. Critically examining the historical and structural variables that hinder one's capacity to act politically in the face of loss is primarily a critical-epistemological task with different obligations than those defining individual losses.

Overall, political losses are the outcome of struggles for power, which sometimes lead to predicaments of suffering and deprivation. In some cases these are the product of struggles about the identity of a collectivity—whether it is bound by a democracy, oligarchy, or military dictatorship—or of technological and economic developments that have led to the loss of democratic values and aspirations.[7] Accordingly, rather than speaking of loss, which in its psychoanalytical connotations tends to turn the political subject inward, in a political context one may prefer to speak of defeat or at least cast loss from this perspective. Although not every loss is the outcome of defeat, political losses are oftentimes entangled with the defeat of a specific project or vision. In terms of political losses defining the nineties, one can count political visions of genuine democracy and socialism. In contrast to psychoanalytic loss, loss as defeat suggests a projection outward that demands a reconsideration of the historical and political trajectories, as well as the travails, of one's commitments in the spirit of soberly confronting one's fate for the sake of a realignment of forces, of a redrawing of the lines of enmity, so to speak, in the hope of securing a future for one's animating ideals. Defeats thus unfold as part of political history outside of which the complexities and political valences of loss and *losing* cannot be made sense of. All this demands a projection outward and critical reckoning with historical predicaments of power. It also suggests a reassessment that is anchored in a reflective yet persistent commitment to action in a predicament of power where one may have already lost, a situation in which responsive action avoids reifying enmity without erasing its demarcating lines or removing their role in the constitution of one's political identity and ensuing political forms. Political life unavoidably entails drawing enmity lines, even if these vary and fluctuate. And these fluctuations are largely conditioned by the collectivity's political form and the political identity it enables and fixes.[8]

Yet the oscillations in the intensification of political enmity mostly stem from the structuring of the political field as a space of contestation in which intensification is not just a function of radicalism, but of the relative power and balance of forces of the collective agencies in play. Conflicts and forms of enmity must be assessed not by recourse to moralizing categories, or other extra-political supplements, but by reference to the internal criteria of the political, as an autonomous field of action and judgment with its own codes and references, principles and rules. One of Wolin's most sobering formulations captures yet another dimension of the question of enmity and its relevance in reckoning with loss as defeat: "power struggles produce losses, and, as a consequence, things of value go out of the world." One needs to add to this that defeat is therefore central to power struggles, as is victory.[9] Sometimes even democratic orders are serendipitously won in defeat, as the late León Rozitchener once observed apropos of Argentina's transition to democracy in 1983, an origin that leaves sediments in the new order that emerges out of it and that explains the pacified and rather labile form of democracy *won* in defeat.[10] Still, the terms of engagement in power struggles, victories, and defeats and the forms and contents of political orders change over time, sometimes suddenly, even when many a continuity and sediment of past struggles remain. And this leaves openings for yet unforeseen possibilities.

There is, to be sure, a venerable tradition of sharp political and politically minded theorizing from the perspective of defeat. From Thucydides to Machiavelli, from Tocqueville and Marx to Weber and Schmitt, Gramsci and Weil, Benjamin and Adorno, the experience of loss as defeat has imposed a different burden on theoretical reflection, a projection outward, to and for the world, leading to a set of sobering questions that better apprehend the fate of their animating ideas by means of historically grounded reflections.[11] Better yet, acknowledging defeat need not lead to bowing in front of the victorious. In Ana María Amar Sánchez's almost untranslatable formulation, "los derrotados no se dan por vencidos."[12] Namely, the defeated hardly surrender in the face of defeat; rather than bowing to the victorious, the defeated have decided to persist and prevail, intractably clinging to their sense of fidelity to political convictions and political-ethical principles. From this perspective, loss is thus closely connected with failure and defeat (even if both these connotations have yet to be established in U.S. political discourse, mediated as it is by the American conceit of *winners* and *losers*). Losses, in this sense, could sometimes be the outcome of unwitting acts, but that need not always be the case. For defeat, the possibility of loss and failure is precisely what is risked in political actions and interventions: defeat is, then, always a possibility and often the outcome of conscious—but no less tragic—decisions to stake out a political claim at a critical juncture, which could lead to a tragic and/or dramatic finale.[13] Responding to loss and defeat can lead to either acquiescence to *what is* or an unyielding resistance to an accommodating consensus, the two poles around which most responses to loss are situated. At these two poles one finds questions of utopia, political sobriety and literacy, and political responsibility all entangled with defeat and memory, as well as with the memory of defeat.

It is at this juncture that the stakes in avoiding the conflation of individual processes of mourning losses with political losses and defeat become clearer and more sharply delineated. Remembrance, the memory of injustice and the political, demands something quite different from, if not the absolute opposite of, moving on in the psychological sense of the expression. For instance, individuals living through dictatorship and misery have to cope with the predicaments of losses (psychic and real) that these experiences inaugurate, and it would be foolish, not to say moralistic, to disavow individual needs in dealing with loss and the forgetting that sheer survival often entails. And yet this hardly needs to be extrapolated at the collective level, even if a political actor is sometimes afflicted by both loss and defeat. Herein resides the crucial difference between loss and defeat, which current invocations of loss tend to dedifferentiate: one mourns the loss of loved ones, but the correlate of defeat is the disappointment of a setback, failure, and dissatisfaction, not mournful loss. Overcoming political setbacks, however, precisely demands mourning the personal losses involved, which is a necessary if insufficient condition to preempt a moralist response to defeat or a politically truncated mournful stance.

Politically speaking, defeat involves neither perpetual melancholia nor mourning understood as *moving on*, but the acknowledgment that in its aftermath one needs to resist it and its corollaries as the sole alternatives, which for all political purposes lead to acquiescence to an unjust present in which mourning, resignation, and forgetting are presented as the only feasible alternatives, thus cast as the politically and ethically responsible thing to do. Rather than acquiescence, an alternative way of reckoning with these predicaments is to understand defeat not as the ultimate failure of one's project, but as the situational outcome of a particular struggle. These outcomes demand reflection, resistance, and a sense of hopeful stillness—the last is best conceived as sober anticipation—for a future reckoning with the victor, the imperatives and forms of what the victor has sought to inaugurate and/or perpetuate, and what their overcoming demands.[14] Or, to cast it in terms closer to Gramsci, a staunch theorist of a political ethic: as a political actor, one can experience defeat after an attempt at a "war of maneuver," but that experience need not lead to estrangement from the political field; instead, what it calls for is continuous *wars of position* that soberly confront these predicaments and set the stage for future *wars of maneuver*.[15] Or, in the less militant but no less compelling formulation offered by María Zambrano, a sober reckoning with defeat entails grasping the larger continuum of history, rather than hanging on to the immediacy of the moment of defeat, no matter how much it hurts, envisaging and anticipating a future in which the present moment will be redressed.[16] That a prisoner of Mussolini and an exile from Franco conjured these thoughts in their darkest hour is in and of itself exemplary of political literacy and fidelity, a political literacy that, from the perspective of a political ethic, represents fidelity to ethical and political values, to oneself and to one's collectivity or the principles binding one's political vision. Their dignity accentuates the lack of political imagination and nerve so characteristic of those at the receiving end of less arduous defeats in far less dangerous political predicaments, say, those defining the depoliticized politics characteristic of the North Atlantic world.

There are, of course, temptations associated with the perspective of the defeated. One is to find silver linings in the present, to find redeeming qualities and thus facilitate compliance to it; another, closely related, is to retreat to an ethics of conviction in which, rather than being a provisional, if crucial, stage in the political field, resistance becomes its permanent feature. The latter's tendency to slip into moralism or into what the French call *gauchisme* is plain enough. Or, better still, to retreat to an ethics of conviction that abandons the political field and tacitly abdicates any sense of fidelity to political forms that embody one's values and aspirations and thus renders a setback into a permanent defeat. Indeed, there is the temptation of self-satisfied consolation and the misrecognition of the scenes of power either by a backward gaze that leads to melancholy and resentment or by unreflective and disoriented hopefulness. Think of the fate of left liberalism in the United States, for instance. Adolph Reed Jr. has offered a trenchant but accurate characterization of this left as one that "careens from this oppressed group on crisis moment to that one, from one magically or morally pristine constituency or source of political agency . . . to another;" a left that not only "lacks focus and stability" but also betrays a "dilettantish politics [that] is partly the heritage of a generation of defeat and marginalization, of decades without any possibility of challenging power and influencing policy."[17]

How to effectively curb these temptations and the erratic political strategies these lead to? An avowal of political literacy and sober realism might serve as an entry point to a future realignment of the political field and to structuring it in ways more congenial to one's political values and aspirations for collective life. Doing so entails, among other things, surrendering the temptations of moralism and confronting defeat soberly and squarely, while learning from intelligent versions of the positions of one's opponents. This need not mean a suspension of political-ethical judgment on their actions and principles, but rather an attempt to dissect the structural field and grasp what led to their victory and our defeat. At least two positive outcomes can emerge from such a reckoning: first, learning whatever can be learned about the strategies and tactics of the victorious party and emulating what is consistent with one's own political-ethical principles and values; second, which is a corrective to the first, becoming alert to the extent to which one's actions and practices may sustain rather than challenge current predicaments of power and, even worse, reproduce practices and principles that one abhors in one's political enemy.[18]

To critically re-cognize loss as defeat calls for a historically infused understanding of the political form that binds the collectivity in question. Recognition needs to become re-cognition. The latter term, as Wolin has theorized it, suggests a "cognitive shift" that enables one to apprehend the forms and discourses of power that are operative in one's scene of action. As such, this shift demands "a radical revision in the culturally produced representations" of oneself and others from the perspective of the ideals and values that are fostered by one's binding political identity.[19] If the political identity in question is genuine democracy, re-cognition also implies acknowledging the need for both a culture of commonality and a fidelity to the ideals—equality, shared power, self-governance, and freedom—that are constitutive of this political identity and that need to be sustained by collective agency and constituted political forms. A political identity is constituted by values that set the parameters for collective life and its institutions—its political forms—along with a conception of political action and agency that demands fidelity to it. Fidelity to, say, a democratic-socialist identity, and its corollary political forms, requires steadfast resistance of the impulse to understand responsibility as loyalty to the state and its imperatives. It, rather, stresses both a commitment to the aforementioned principles, which serve as controlling ends, and a strong sense of accountability that privileges participatory values of equality and shared power, while defending the forms of collective agencies and institutions that could reproduce and enable them.[20] The latter can hardly be overemphasized, for it entails dispelling myths of abstract inclusiveness and avowing democratic enmity lines, lest one cease to strive for its substantive sense. Re-cognition along these lines invites a sense of political sobriety and literacy that encompasses, among other things, the eradication of categories and euphemisms impairing a clear mapping of the structural imperatives that mediate the predicaments of power one navigates. It is therefore crucial to recast political loss both historically and politically.

Finally, loss, or defeat, cannot lead to the abandonment of critical thinking. On the contrary, the experience of loss in, say, the aftermath of catastrophes demands its re-cognition in the concrete historical junctures in which that loss has taken place, as well as re-cognition of its effects. The passing of utopia, or its defeat, as Susan Buck-Morss has lucidly argued, should not conflate "the loss of the dream with the loss of the dream's realization."[21] More so than the former, the latter has to be re-cognized as thoroughly political. Political loss and defeat, therefore, can be critically re-cognized and their political import reclaimed. When, for instance, the loss in question consists in the loss of power and the capacity to participate politically in meaningful ways, one's reflection on the conditions leading to these losses has to be accompanied by a political response. Doing so entails re-cognizing the configurations of power in which one's political identity is anchored. If genuine democracy is the political identity and form at stake, re-cognizing loss involves demanding responsive forms of action that are uncompromising about the preservation of democracy in a meaningful sense—gestures that also require an avowal of "the paradoxes of 'empowerment'" from which no collectivity can escape.[22]

In her magnum opus *The Broken Middle*, Gillian Rose puts it well when she renders what is at stake in critical efforts as a question of risking what we "know, misknow, and yet grow"; that is, to re-cognize "learning, growth and knowledge as fallible and precarious but riskable."[23] In contrast to passivity, doing so involves the "constant risk of positing and failing and positing again 'activity beyond activity,' to cover the ethical nature of the description, and to distinguish it from the Levinasian 'passivity beyond passivity,' the idea of ethics as the ego-less substitution of one for 'the other.'"[24] This account is crucial to formulating a political ethic of responsibility, one that avoids abstract openness to "the other" and seeks the centrality of political action for its concrete realization. That is, to think of this question politically involves reclaiming the category of "democratic citizen"— one who not only acts collectively but also thinks about both his or her predicament from the perspective of a collective identity and how that identity is either enacted or compromised by the actions done in his or her name—for a political horizon beyond liberal-democratic capitalism. In lieu of the current depoliticized fate of democracy, the more productive questions consist in interrogating the political and ethical implications of compromising one's political form by actions carried out in one's name. What demands ensue from this compromise in light of the forms of power a collectivity generates—and its uses and abuses? How are democratic political forms, and one's fidelity to a socialist vision, transmogrified by actions that betray it rather than promote it? What is lost or betrayed, or inverted, in such compromises? But this interrogation requires a culture of commonality, a "we," which contemporary theoretical discourse has rendered suspect. In invocations of a "we," however, a binding political identity is always presupposed: namely, a collectivity that is responsive to the language of solidarity, common purpose, and shared power.

POLITICAL ETHIC

In *Mourning Becomes the Law* Rose invoked a different tradition to theorize the intersection of questions of power, ethics, and politics. Noble politics, she called it.[25] This tradition, however, offers a richer conceptual and historical trajectory than what Rose's formulation suggests. For instance, in addition to power and ethics, figures in this tradition, especially Machiavelli, placed strong emphasis on the need to "re-cognize" the scenes of power where a would-be political actor acts: to be precise, re-cognition of the continuities and discontinuities, occasions and accidents, sediments and moments of rupture constitutive of the situation to which she responds and the imperative it imposes. Political virtue precisely consists in re-cognizing such a context and acting in it with a constant reference to the political integrity of the actor and the entity or identity at stake, its binding principles and institutions, and the consequences of political actions. "Noble politics" may be a bit of a misnomer, too. This perspective is better characterized as a tradition of "political ethic," and its overarching concern can be defined as an attempt to re-cognize and dialectically conceptualize the modern diremption of ethical and political imperatives in political action.

The term *political ethic* is thus *speculative*, as it dialectically renders not only how the two terms are irreducible to one another but how they mutually mediate their concrete intersections: it at once rejects dampening the political element of collective life and abstractly eschewing ethical considerations from the realm of the political.[26] If ethics is the domain of individual life in which an ensemble of practices and values are devised to define, describe, and comprehend the way in which one relates to others qua individuals, politics is the domain in which public authorities and the uses of political power are enacted, sanctioned, and reproduced. A political ethic, accordingly, deals with the ethical moment of collective life as a field with its own internal problems, codes, and principles, and its object is to conceptualize how to order political life, the principles constituting the proper relationship between *rulers* and *ruled*, *governors* and *governed*, and the forms of actions, fidelity, and collective agencies needed to sustain collective life in its desired political forms. It thus refuses to reduce ethics—the domain of individual conduct and action qua individual, in situation, and thus similarly mediated by institutions, intersubjective and social relations—to politics, as much as it refuses to impose ethical categories and moralizing discourse in political life.

One category that is central to both ethics and politics, properly understood, is the primacy of the situation. This primacy, in each case, forces a reckoning with the intersections between the individual's practices and her relations with others both in nonpolitical domains and political life as such. Stated differently, whereas the initial locus of both ethical and political practices is individual action and conduct, the aims and goals for each differ, as do the content of each domain of action, its imperatives and principles, which is why the irreducibility of one to the other is frequently experienced as either antinomian or tragic.[27] One central tenet of this tradition of political ethic is to precisely focus on the situation itself, as historically constituted and politically legitimated, and to think of action in terms of the imperatives internal to a historically constituted and politically legitimated situation and the need to redress it. Weber's reflections are emblematic of some of the components that are central for a political ethic: when he identifies passion, a sense of responsibility, and a sense of proportion in the figure of the politician who has a vocation for politics, he lays bare the triad that constitutes his political ethic.[28] One can interpret his insistence on the need to have a combination of the two ethics he famously articulated—the ethic of conviction and the ethic of responsibility—in light of this triad: what is preserved of the ethics of conviction is the element of fidelity to a cause, a calling, and the passion that guides it, while the possible excesses that may spring from it are curbed by proportion and responsibility. Regardless of Weber's counterrevolutionary motives for conjuring this formulation, he lays out the significance of the elements of fidelity and sobriety in a political ethic of responsibility.

Fredric Jameson has offered an incisive formulation that bears on the foregoing question: "Politics is not ethics: a proposition that does not mean that it is amoral and nonethical (rather, it is collective and beyond matters of individual ethics), but is, on the contrary, designed to explain why political extremism can so often be found to be motivated by categories of ethical purity."[29] Jameson's formulation draws attention to the contrast between an ethical politics and a genuinely political ethic, an ethics of collective life. Contemporary ethical politics, like those discussed in previous chapters, ultimately revert not just to moralizations of political life, but to forms of individualized responsibilization, which are part and parcel of strategies of disaffiliation characteristic of the political rationalities sustaining the current neoliberal regime of capitalist accumulation. Disaffiliations, which in turn enable the abstractions that artificially homogenize and dedifferentiate predicaments of powers and the differentiations and degrees of responsibility constituting them. Indeed, the political and conceptual reductions characterizing ethical politics more than echo a long-standing conservative strategy of depoliticization that Pierre Bourdieu has memorably described as a drive "to reduce the public to the private, the social to the personal, the political to the ethical, and the economic to the psychological. In short, it tends to effect a depoliticization that returns to the domain of the most irreducibly singular 'actual experience' all the experiences that politicization aims on the contrary to detach from the 'person' in his or her singularity in order to make them appear to be common to a class."[30] In contrast to ethical politics, a political ethic resists moralization and the false imperative to derive normative moral principles that antecede predicaments of power but nevertheless claim to bind the subjects navigating them. Rather than zoning in on questions of character and ethos, subjective intentions and dispositions, a political ethic raises questions about the historically constituted situation in which the political actor finds herself, about how it came into being and how the actor in question came to be situated in it, along with the material processes, practices, and discourses mediating her situated actions.

Conversely, proponents of a political ethic have demanded the recognition of the role of violence in political life, its nature, uses, and representations.[31] Its central premise is that the realm of politics imposes a different set of imperatives on the political actor, especially in relation to acts of political creation, e.g., revolutionary acts in which a new order is oftentimes the offspring of the shattering of the old, or the reforming of political institutions and mechanisms where the use of power and force are intrinsic. In instances of political creation, the taxing political problem is not merely to create something new, but to reckon with those who insist on the preservation of "the old," that is, of old normative values and fixed structures of power. Such an insistence is frequently carried on through a combination of preemptive as well as reactive strategies of violence, counterviolence, and fear. Indeed, experiences of creation have historically unleashed cycles of violence and counterviolence, which in the twentieth century became known as the battles between the forces of progress and the forces of reaction. For some, experiences of creation are laudable exercises of political judgment; for others, they are experiences of destruction, loss, and catastrophe.[32]

In political theories prior to Machiavelli's, the centrality of power—and the violence that resides at its core—was often the subject of a variety of euphemisms that sought to disguise power's coercive nature while lessening its impact via representations that, for instance, assured members of the polity of an objective common good at work behind it.[33] Machiavelli, however, laid bare the violent aspects of political power and some of the modalities of violence binding collective life. The political actor has to negotiate between the demands of private virtue and the pressures of politics, between what the preservation of an established order, or the inauguration of a new one, requires and the reticence of private morality. This realization led Machiavelli to confront the diremption of a private and political ethic and the limitations of the former for a political actor. It demonstrated the need for a political ethic that requires a different conception of responsibility, one suited to the demands of political action. More important, the dividing line between these two sets of commitments has a direct bearing on Machiavelli's economy of violence.[34] But what serves as a controlling end for the use of violence? Machiavelli defines the controlling end in terms of acts of political creativity vis-à-vis acts of destruction. In the formulations found in his *Discourses*, the principal point of reference is the preservation of the city as a political entity, a commitment to the preservation of a republican order and its political form.

Sure enough, Machiavelli's political ethic was embedded in the crux of processes and crises that defined the political landscape of Europe at the onset of the sixteenth century; likewise, in *The Prince*, his account of political action was conceived and remains trapped in the figure of the individualized political actor, the conquering prince, who can descend anywhere across the Italian peninsula, even beyond it. This, in such a way that the content of his political thought proved incapable of adequately conceptualizing the new reality of the emergent absolutist state.[35] But the formal aspects of his account of political action, his thought forms, and his conceptualization of the primacy of the situation in any properly political account of the intersections between ethics and politics—that is, the need of a political actor to inhabit predicaments of power at once constrained and fractured, mediated by necessity and accidents, in whose interstices, or, to be more precise, from within whose interstices a mediated novum can emerge—remains one of the most powerful articulations of the demands of political action yet offered. While sedimentations of their context of emergence undoubtedly remain, as well as of the actual content Machiavelli furnished to his formulations, these constrain, but hardly fetter, the critical and political import of Machiavelli's political-theoretical forms.

The first aspect of the Florentine's thought forms relevant to understanding his political ethic is a proper appreciation of the way in which his political theory stages the relative autonomy of political life from ethics, an autonomy often misunderstood, and much maligned. This autonomy is best understood along the lines explored in Charles S. Singleton's still unsurpassed essay, "The Perspective of Art," where he argues that the autonomy of politics is best cast in terms of granting political life and its rules its own proper domain of action, reflection, and criteria for critical justification. It is not that the political field is immoral or bereft of ethical principles, but, rather, it is morally indifferent—or, more precisely, "extra moral"—in the way that art and literary works are.[36] The quality of a modernist artwork or literary text, for instance, is not judged on the basis of whether or not it posits the right political or ethical stance, or if it conforms to the moral codes and ethical sensibilities ruling individual conduct, or ethics, but in terms of criteria immanent to its field. Singleton connects this insight with the idea of action, as *doing* in opposition to *making*, and quotes Aquinas to drive the point across: "Art does not require of the craftsman that his act be a good act, but that his work be good."[37] One of Carl Schmitt's formulations also captures what is genuinely at stake in invoking this moral indifference, "The literary naturalness [of *The Prince*] is only an expression of an unconcealed interest in the subject with which this man sees political things politically without moralistic but also without immoralistic pathos."[38] In contrast, Machiavelli's political thought encompasses human capacities of "freedom and the imagination, interpretation and deliberation" in order to re-cognize the effective truths (*verità effettuale*) of political life and how to navigate politically constituted predicaments of power.[39]

But this autonomy entails a set of principles and limits internal to it, governing political action, that is called a political ethic. This political ethic has at least two dimensions running across Machiavelli's principal political writings: first, it prescribes how to understand the relations between rulers and ruled; second, how to conceptualize political change, the creation of new orders.[40] The latter is in reference to obdurate realities, which often resist the impress of new forms; yet realities not devoid of fissures and accidents, both of which create occasions for a virtuous political actor to seize and capitalize upon. Formally speaking, Machiavelli is the master thinker of the primacy of the situation and the need to respond to it. Conjunctures emerge in predicaments of power, which demand what could be conceptualized as a complex, nonarbitrary dialectic of rules and exceptions. That this is so is already clear in Machiavelli's *Ghiribizzi al Soderino* (1506), with his invocation of the need for the political actor to properly re-cognize the situation and adapt to different circumstances, changing times, and patterns of events (*tempi e l'ordini delle cose*) in order to respond to them.[41] Indeed, it is as a corollary to this conceptualization of the primacy of the situation in political action—and its structures and patterns— that the basic contours of the dialectic of rules and exceptions constituting Machiavelli's political ethic more clearly appear. The thinker of accidents and equivocations, possibilities and occasions went to great lengths to conceptualize rules on how to reckon with the predicaments of power in which these opportunities may be recognized, grasped, and seized.[42] Especially but not exclusively in *The Prince*, Machiavelli's reflections focus on the interplay between rules and exceptions, in their intersections, and skillfully seek to stage how a virtuous political actor navigates the tensions between the two, while responding to the politically and historically constituted situation he confronts.[43]

It is in the tension between the rules and the exceptions, which he always makes explicit, where the lineaments of his casuistic political ethic emerges, and for which he ultimately forges it, along with his idea of an economy of violence.[44] Rules and exceptions are first forged by recourse to the historically particular, and then to the general maxim action. Exceptions, by extension, are invoked in light of Machiavelli's thematization of contingencies and changing circumstances in the political situation, but are in turn theorized as governed by rules. Hence the need to provide nonarbitrary criteria to conceptualize this dialectical interaction between rules and exceptions: not only are there rules inductively arrived at, or at least presented as such by recourse to historical experience, but there are rules for the exceptions, too. Or, stated differently, exceptions have rules and cannot be invoked arbitrarily. It is in the interstices of the political negotiation of rules and exceptions in violent predicaments of power, also defined by class strife and uneven relations of ruling, the relation between means and ends, and the question of limits, where Machiavelli's political ethic of responsibility crystallizes.

The subsequent tradition of *raison d'état* has famously claimed Machiavelli as a theoretical parent. In doing so, it has subsumed the political ethic of responsibility within its immanent logic. In its subsequent developments, reason of state became increasingly associated with absolutist rule and the primacy of statecraft over private ethics, although it also signified a depersonalization of authority that allowed for the emergence of an autonomous political space, the constitution of a properly public domain.[45] Even so, within this tradition, the imperatives of statecraft eventually took on nationalist and imperial overtones from the nineteenth century on. Meanwhile, the concern for political identity and form, which in Machiavelli's *Discourses* takes on a popular dimension, along with the conception of responsibility were increasingly confined to ruling elites. As a result, in the tradition of *raison d'état*, statist considerations have increasingly overshadowed the concern with political identity. In its absolutist versions, reason of state dictates the ways in which governing elites act according to the imperatives of expansion and power; in its constitutional version, the imperatives of reason of state arise when the preservation and survival of the constitutional order entail actions that violate the primacy of the rule of law.

MARXIST HERETICS

In the twentieth century Marxist thinkers powerfully inherited this tradition of political ethic. Building on the legacy of Marx and Engels, thinkers ranging from Trotsky and Lukács, Brecht and Gramsci, and subsequent heirs such as Isaac Deutscher and Raymond Williams, or José Carlos Mariátegui and León Rozitchner, all the way to Perry Anderson and Terry Eagleton, have soberly reckoned with different aspects of the intersections of ethics and politics beyond the limitations of ethical socialism (say, that of Karl Kautsky and Edward Bernstein or William Morris and E. P. Thompson).[46] Roughly speaking, one can identify two levels of inquiry here: first, one finds dialectical accounts of this intersection historicizing ethics, but also showing the nonsynchronicity of ethical and moral language in any social formation—namely, how atavistic or aristocratic ethical codes from an early era could stubbornly persist, say, atavistic or aristocratic codes pervading liberal-democratic orders; second, the primacy of the political over the ethical in dealing with political questions, and the corollary need for a political ethic that, while avowing the relative autonomy of the political in capitalist social formations, also encompasses the ethical dimension immanent to it: ethical practices and dispositions outside ethics, but defined by fidelity to genuinely democratic and socialist principles.

Out of this political tradition, Brecht and Gramsci most forcefully articulated these dimensions amidst the wars, revolutions, and counterrevolutions conforming the catastrophic era of the European civil war. In Brecht's case, these found expression as part of his trenchant critique of the ruses of ethics, a critique he staged not only in his plays and poems but also in his prose.[47] Simply put, Brecht's political ethic consists of a relentless materialist critique of ethics, uncovering the ruses of ethical maxims dirempted from the material conditions in which ordinary people live, as well as the individualist conceits on which these revolve. To that end, Brecht brought to bear not only his considerable literary talent but also his remarkable ability to break down social and political relations to their fundamental relations of power. This ability was frequently characterized as Brecht's *plumpes denken*, or crude thinking, which is how political reasoning finds expression in his works as "the ultimate situationality of thought."[48] Brecht's works enact a form of "complex seeing," to borrow Raymond Williams's formulation, that stages the manner in which humans are always engaged "in the process of producing themselves and their situation," and they thus focus on *what* individuals are doing in a situation and "what is this doing to them."[49]

Entries culled from his *Arbeitsjournal* neatly sum up the gist of Brecht's position. There, while recalling a conversation with a proponent of ethical Marxism, he notices how "the ethical needs of these social strata need not be satisfied ethically. The satisfaction of their material needs is ethical enough," which is precisely what the ethical standpoint subtly disavows: or, as he more precisely articulates the thought, "In social terms things look like this; without satisfaction of material needs, no ethics, and that is acceptable. But: ethics for the satisfaction of these needs is not acceptable. Material needs as ethical, ethical ones as material, this is not grasped."[50] Echoing his critique of the lofty ethics imposed on the lower orders, or expected from them, memorably staged in *St. Joan of the Stockyards*, Brecht self-effacingly writes: "poets like to entrust the worker with a lofty mission. This fills him with justified suspicion, since he has no desire to serve as cannon-fodder on ethical missions. His goal is not morality even if it is moral. He need promise no one anything except himself."[51] Brecht thus juxtaposed ethics or morality with genuinely ethical or moral practices, something that he also expressed apropos of *Mother Courage*: "Its point of view is not a moral one: that is to say, it is ethical, but without being derived from the currently prevailing morality."[52] In this way, Brecht debunks the conceits of Ethics, especially how it disavows the historical processes constituting and sanctioning the situations in which individuals act ethically and politically. Still, this debunking is articulated in the name of a new ethic: a collective, more robustly political and socialist ethic. But an ethic that, while informing political action, does not abstractly subsume it.

Plays like *St. Joan of the Stockyards, The Good Person of Szechwan, The Caucasian Chalk Circle, The Life of Galileo,* and *The Days of the Commune* stage the primacy of the situation in any locus of action and how it entails an economy of violence in order to do good beyond the conceits of subjective goodness, in predicaments of power in which the ethical categories become nothing short of swindles. Respectively: the consequences of unreflective goodness in which subjective dispositions are radically at odds with an objectively unjust condition; the harmful, even fatal consequences of bourgeois ethics for the poor classes living under bourgeois orders and the necessary split of the self that surviving these predicaments demand; the vexatious relations between property, justice, and injustice, along with the possibility of a new communist ethic of activity; and the clashes and complexities in the intersections between science, ethics, and social orders, which also includes a mordant critique of the idea of heroism deepened in his *Dialogues of Refugees.*[53] In the last, Brecht articulates a caustic critique of superhuman sacrifices demanded in the name of heroic virtues for inhuman ends.[54] Or the demand of heroic sacrifices for lofty causes and hypostatized words: heretically, to the workers Brecht recommends promising nothing to anyone, for they are responsible only to themselves. This is all part of Brecht's critique of moralizing discourse and the intellectual posturing that mostly defines it. For no one is as exploited as the poor whose living conditions rigorously instruct in the ethical virtues—diligence, obedience, endurance, gratitude—from early on, which, however, serve the presiding political and social order. Or, as Brecht sardonically asserts, "Even their virtues are extorted."[55]

Correspondingly, in the face of the depoliticizing ploys of ethical invocation, honesty is paramount, something succinctly articulated in his "Five Difficulties in Writing the Truth" (1934–35). One of his most sober lessons stands out: "To say that the good were defeated not because they were good, but because they were weak, requires courage."[56] This is the courage of a sober re-cognizing of defeat, its causes and aftermaths, without reverting to moralizing consolations. A corollary to the re-cognition of defeat is the need for a political realism for the masses of ordinary people. This is lucidly illustrated in *The Downfall of the Egoist Johann Fatzer* and "Socrates Wounded." Interpreting the first text, Walter Benjamin perceptively noted Brecht's insistence on getting "to the bottom of things," which includes re-cognizing both victory and defeat: "The victor must not allow the defeated the experience of defeat. He must snatch this, too; he must share defeat with the defeated. Then he will become master of the situation."[57] Similarly, in "Socrates Wounded" Brecht trenchantly articulates his dialectical understanding of victory and defeat and the ruses of pacifism and war.[58] That these lessons are didactically articulated with the goal of a popular realism is clear in *The Downfall of the Egoist Johann Fatzer* where the participatory commitments informing this political realism are articulated: "You are finished, statesman / The State is not finished. / Allow us to change it / According to the circumstances / Allow us, statesman, to be statesmen / Beneath your laws stands your name. / Forget the name / Observe your laws, legislator. / Submit to order, man of order / The State no longer needs you / Hand it over to us."[59]

These claims make good on the primacy Brecht grants to the collective situation over individualist morality; his recasting of honesty is situational and thus devoid of Kantian pieties about "lying," and more truthful for all that. *The Life of Galileo* gives memorable expression to Brecht's sobering realism:

ANDREA: You were hiding the truth. From the enemy. Even in matters of ethics you were centuries ahead of us.

. . .

Like the man in the street we said "He'll die, but he'll never recant." You came back: "I've recanted, but I'm going to live."— "Your hands are stained," we said. You're saying: "Better stained than empty."

GALILEO: Better stained than empty. Sounds realistic. Sounds like me. New science, new ethics.[60]

"Better stained than empty": a fitting motto for a political ethic that avows the political literacy necessary to navigate deceitful and violent predicaments.[61] Or, in the more overtly political formulation found in *The Days of the Commune*, "GENEVIÉVE: But we weren't we anxious not to stain our hands with blood? / LANGEVIN: We were. But in this struggle the hands not bloodstained are the hands chopped off."[62] *The Days of the Commune* has been described as "a conscientious exercise in thinking beyond defeat"; in Brecht's own words it conveys both "the errors of the commune and its greatness."[63] Consonant with the political literacy invoked in *Galileo*, here Brecht reflects on the perplexities of formulating an economy of violence in revolutionary situations that involves a popular rule and the imperatives the enemy imposes upon those who want to inaugurate a new and more humane order. While the people genuinely claim that "the Commune rejects civil war" and "socialism marches without bayonets," they have to face the reality that "bayonets confront it."[64] Yet Brecht is far from hypostatizing violence or the pristine innocence of the people. Rather, he stages the conflict that the individuals in the situation at once produce and are subject to in its complexity; or, stated differently, he lends voice to the dilemmas involved as part of his commitment to re-cognize the question of violence:

> CRY: Citizens . . . we have decided that we do not wish to do
>   what the enemies of humanity are doing. They are monsters,
>   we are not.
> *Applause.*
>   . . .
> CRIES: . . . All they that take the sword shall perish with the sword.
> VARLIN *very loud*: And they that don't take the sword?
> *Brief silence.*
> CRY: The Commune's generosity will bear fruit. Let it be said of the
>   Commune: they burned the guillotine.
>   . . .
> RIGAULT: . . . Widows belong to no party. The Republic has bread for
>   all who are in misery and kisses all who are orphaned. And that is
>   right. But where is there action against murder, which I call the
>   active side of generosity? Don't say to me "Equal rights for those
>   who fight in their camp and in ours." The people do not fight as
>   wrestlers or traders fight. . . . And still all that I am asking for is
>   terror against terror, even though we alone have the right to terror.
> CRY: That is a blasphemy? Do you deny that the use of violence
>   debases the man who uses it?
> RIGAULT: No, I do not deny it.[65]

There is, in short, a constitutive moment of the tragedy of revolution, which, as Raymond Williams's memorably put it, "is not at all insurrection or the use of force against its enemies . . . The real tragedy occurs at those dreadful moments when the revolutionary impetus is so nearly lost, or so heavily threatened, that the revolutionary movement has to impose the harshest discipline on itself and over relatively innocent people in order not to be broken or defeated."[66] Impositions that put pressure on the political actor, whose political ethic is committed to the amelioration of superfluous suffering.[67]

Echoes of these formulations conform to a corollary of Brecht's political ethic: the strain that ethics places not only on those living in violent predicaments of power but, more pressingly so, on those who want to change this and inaugurate a new order. It is perhaps nowhere best expressed than in "To Those Born Later":

> Anger, even against injustice
> Makes the voice hoarse. Oh we
> Who wanted to prepare the ground for friendliness
> Could not ourselves be friendly.[68]

But there is another side to it: the impossible, and ultimately unethical, demands that ethics places on those called upon to elevate themselves to lofty moral standards or the lack of the necessary enabling social conditions that could concretely actualize ethical practices. *St Joan of the Stockyards* famously staged a mordant critique of this ethical swindle. A passage from "Life Story of the Boxer Samson-Körner" bluntly encapsulates Brecht's critique: "What I say about immorality is this: if only one didn't freeze when it gets cold and didn't stop feeling hungry when one has had a slice of bread, moral standards would be a lot higher."[69]

Ultimately, what Brecht called "crude thinking" bears a strong realist disposition that is not incompatible with conceptual precision. On the contrary, it finds expression in the carefully conceptual interventions defining Brecht's literary works. Ineluctable in the political field, crude thinking ultimately entails simplifying a situation, breaking it down to the fundamental political relations—Lenin's "who, whom" is apposite here—as part of the literacy constitutive of a political ethic. Such literacy, which is central for any politically robust and enabling account of a situation and the responses it requires and affords, in turn demands subtle thinking at the level of the cognitive categories that enable the crystallization of crude thinking. It is actually the opposite of dumbing down; rather, it requires that once the highest standards of reflection enter fields of action and power, these yield concrete knowledge or let it be interrogated by obdurate realities. It is thus possible to interpret the political realism and literacy of Brecht's *plumpes denken* in dialectical terms evocative of Machiavelli's dedication to *The Prince*: for a rigorous critical theory to be politically effective, it has not only to comprehend but articulate elevated reflection in politically meaningful terms; conversely, reflecting upon political life—both its most consistently ordinary phenomena and its occasional extraordinary moments—in the most refined, rigorous, conceptual terms demands theoretical forms whose autonomy consists of *distanced nearness* from its object and loci of reflection.

Gramsci, a contemporary of Brecht and an active member of the Italian Communist Party, explicitly reckoned with analogous dilemmas in terms of what he called the *etico-politico* and its role in Marxism, the philosophy of praxis, and formulated hitherto understated aspects of a socialist political ethic.[70] While primarily concerned with the future of socialist strategy in the West after the crushing defeats of revolutionary movements in western Europe—where defeat coincided with the rise and consolidation of European fascism and Hitlerism—he reflected deeply on the role of a political ethic in securing a socialist order and in sustaining a future socialist democracy.[71] Gramsci's political ethic could thus be best described in terms of his recasting of communism as an "ethics of the collective," to borrow Fernández Buey's formulation. Consistent with the tradition of political ethic as a whole, no treatise on ethics is found in Gramsci's writings. Instead, one finds situational and localized formulations, frequently worked through in terms of engagement with Croce, or sometimes in direct reference to the philosophy of praxis, and in his jottings on Kant. Succinctly put, Gramsci's political ethic pivots on three fundamental themes: his passionate, yet realist, defense of truth in political life; the relationships and intersections between Marxism, the philosophy of praxis, and Machiavelli to recast the idea of the autonomy of the political and the corollary idea of the primacy of the situation; and the already mentioned critique of Kantian ethics among ethical socialists.[72] But in Gramsci the political-ethical takes a historicist connotation that not only historicizes ethical practices, along with ethics, but also relates them to the concreteness of political practice.[73] Similarly, he offered critical commentaries about Kant's formulation of the categorical imperative to offer a historicized rendering of Kant's idea and to critically dissect its sociological and cultural presuppositions, something that he elsewhere carried on apropos of hypostatized ideas of "creativity."[74] On the whole, he aimed to forge a Marxist political ethic—to think through the ethical-political (*etico-politico*) dimension of collective life from a Marxist perspective.[75]

An important aspect of Gramsci's political ethic is the defense of truthfulness. He argued for politically enabling forms of re-cognition, and reworked the classic Socratic motto "Know thy self." But, like Brecht, the emphasis on honesty and self-knowledge is irreducible to conceits about individual character. Once politically cast, self-knowledge is collective and consists of re-cognizing equality and knowing that ordinary people can only usher in a self-governing political order through their own efforts, discipline, and responsibility.[76] Truthfulness thus stems from a sober realism that separates the spheres of ethical and political life and argues for the centrality of honesty and sobriety in political life as part of a political ethic of responsibility bound by fidelity to political-ethical principles of equality and freedom, fraternity and emancipation.[77] Fidelity to these principles and ends must be unflinching, even if there is a casuistic logic in the choice of means and the actualization of these ends and their actual concrete content. Yet here is the critical, binding proviso: these means must never overwhelm the prescribed ends.[78] Here Gramsci independently expresses an insight famously articulated by Trotsky about the dialectical interdependence of means and ends, their historical immanence. As Raymond Geuss has lucidly explained, "Appeal to such a dialectic [of means and ends] . . . is one way to try to save the deepest intuition behind Marxism, which is that humanity should be capable of collectively self-organizing activity, which instantiates appropriate self-control, self-direction, and even, when necessary, self-limitation, without needing to appeal to any external principle."[79]

The foregoing hinges upon Gramsci's defense of the autonomy of the political, which stems from one of his noblest impulses: the primacy of politics in his ethic of collective life responds to the genuinely democratic and socialist convictions that, in a new political order, honest individuals would actively share power as part of a collective life that could be genuinely understood as shared fate. Moreover, it goes beyond the elitist conceit built into Weber's heroic politician by emphasizing the need for mass political education, with corollary emphases on realism and political literacy. By and large, this moves in tandem with an original account of the interplay of force and consent in the advent and preservation of political orders, all of which Gramsci conceived in terms of his reworking of Machiavelli's intellectual legacy from the perspective of Marxism. In Gramsci's remarkable formulation, if Machiavelli proposed educating the people on how only a *realist* politics could achieve genuinely political ends, Gramsci contends that Machiavelli's position is, in a sense, close to the theory and practice of Marxism: "the philosophy of praxis has tried to create and disseminate a mass, popular 'realism'"; and this popular realism, a realism of the people, would be "consonant with different times."[80] In these times, the predicaments of power demanding action would require a different economy of violence and a stronger sense of shared power and responsibility. For the Florentine understood the centrality of enmity lines in political life, not in the hypostatized sense usually attributed to Schmitt, but in the changing configurations of political ruling, rulers, and ruled.[81]

Yet, for all their acuity, Brecht and Gramsci did not emphasize the spatial conditions for the actualization of their formulations of a political ethic or the formal contours of its corollary practice of political responsibility. It is Max Weber and Simone Weil, two contrasting exponents of political ethic during the age of catastrophes, who more explicitly articulated these notions. Weber offers a commanding formal account of an ethic of responsibility that is central for a political ethic forged along the lines pursued by Gramsci and Brecht, and Weil's emphasis on the city lends expression to the need for such bounded space to concretize political responsibility. That would be the socialist-democratic idea of a community of fate bound by a political ethic of collective life with a sense of fidelity toward the principles of equality, freedom, and solidarity and the political forms and institutions actualizing them.

RESPONSIBILITY AND SHARED FATE

It is hardly surprising that the dilemmas of political ethic reverberate in Weber's formulation of political responsibility. In his celebrated essay "Politics as a Vocation"—originally a speech given in 1919, in the anxious context of the immediate aftermath of the Great War and the Bolshevik triumph, as well as in the midst of the German revolution from the top—he lays bare the intersection between political responsibility, violence, and power in its complexity. Out of his distinction between the ethic of conviction (*Gesinnungsethik*) and the ethic of responsibility (*Verantwortung*), Weber formulates an account of the centrality of an ethic of responsibility for any conception of political ethic that accounts for the role of violence in political life.[82] By placing violence as one of the "specific means peculiar" to the modern state, Weber acknowledged its role in the constitution and maintenance of state power, without reducing the state's functions to the management of regularized conflict and pasteurized struggle.

While Weber perceptively theorized the unprecedented and daunting nature of "modern power" and the obstacles for meaningful political action in "modernity," he also sought a way to reclaim the vocation of politics within this predicament. His answer oscillated between differing balances of political education and political leadership, with varying degrees of emphasis placed on each choice at different times.[83] In "Politics as a Vocation" the tension between these two choices appears with blistering force: while he was still clinging to his professed hope of 1895, of "a colossal programme of *political* education" for the nation, this hope was largely overshadowed by an epic longing for a kind of political hero.[84] Even though his goal of political education might require an ethos of responsibility for the members of the nation, Weber's lecture suggests that political action is laid out in reference to an ideal-typical form of a leader, a charismatic hero whose actions will bestow meaning to an otherwise disenchanted world. This is a political actor who steadfastly confronts the daunting task of facing up to the rationalization process of modern power. In so doing, he "contracts with violent means" and "is exposed to its specific consequences."[85] In other words, this is a political actor that heroically responds to the calling of politics, notwithstanding the conglomeration of imperatives—capitalist, scientific, organizational, managerial, and bureaucratic—that the rationalization of life enacts.[86] The charismatic hero, as political actor, relies on the masses, especially on mass-oriented institutions such as parliaments. The masses, however, are hardly constitutive of political action. The masses are not actors, but instruments of action.[87] Political action is thus cast in terms of demotic leadership. What is the fate of political responsibility in this situation? Weber claims that in this predicament the leader is endowed with a new sense of responsibility. But the responsibility of the leader cannot be simply understood in terms of accountability or as an imperative to give an account of his positions and actions, with action, in "Science as a Vocation," cast as a nonpolitical "sense of responsibility" and one of the contributions that educators, not politicians, make to the "'ethical' forces."[88] Echoing Nietzschean themes Weber argues that political responsibility resides, instead, in the need to soberly recognize, and without self-deception respond to, a certain predicament, face the burdens of political action, and assume the obligations involved in being the leader of a collectivity.[89]

Expounding on the concerns of political ethic in nationalist terms, Weber further suggests that even if the ethic of responsibility is more appropriate for the demands of politics, it is a combination of both ethics that constitutes the temper of a "man who *can* have the 'calling for politics.'"[90] Yet principled conviction is not what sets the limits to an ethic of responsibility, even though considerations of "ultimate ends" are important here. For Weber, it is the well-being of the nation that constitutes the binding end achieved by violent means. It is an end that is infused with meaning, when the actor, driven by his vocation, fuses the two ethics in the moment of action: "By the same token, I find it incommensurably moving when a *mature* human being . . . who feels the responsibility he bears for the consequences of his own actions with his entire soul and who acts in harmony with an ethics of responsibility reaches the point where he says, 'Here I stand, I can do no other.'"[91] In this passage the moment of conviction brings about a sense of necessity, of fidelity, to political acts that is bound by the ethic of responsibility, a fidelity to the ideal animating the act, which in turn constitutes its legitimating end. This imperative of fidelity to a cause is yet another element that enhances the tragic quality of political action, of the unfolding of acts in a reality that is constituted by freedom, but whose exercise acquires an element of necessity.[92] However, the ethic of responsibility does not resolve in advance the dilemma involved in justifying certain *means* to reach an *end*. Political ethic is contextual. And in a context of loss and defeat, as will be clear momentarily, especially when loss is experienced as defeat, this question emerges with particular urgency.

Although somewhat troubled by a combination of pessimistic and nationalist feelings at the beginning of the Great War, a war he nevertheless embraced, Weber never envisioned the nature and extent of Germany's defeat. He experienced its aftermath as a catastrophe for Germany, an experience so disturbing it even shook Weber's sense of his own vocation.[93] The war shattered the illusion that by the "'natural' process of class ascension" a political class would emerge with the necessary maturity to rise to the task of leading the interest of the nation.[94] Weber's tone was severe: "By its reaction the German nation will then demonstrate whether it has attained political maturity."[95] But the years immediately following Germany's defeat and the Armistice were pregnant with uncertainty and provided the sternest test for both the masses and the bourgeoisie. The latter had been historically afraid of the "emotional radicalism" of the former. And the prospects for a new, stable regime of power depended on the fragile relationship between these two. Weber, however, was not content with leaving the outcome of this latent conflict to chance. Instead, he openly endorsed counterrevolutionary violence, as he had earlier supported a national imperialism, for the sake of stability. Violence provided the *means* for the *end* of national renewal. Reason of state, therefore, emerges as an important corollary of his political ethic. This time, however, it is part of an attempt to find a compromise that would include the masses, albeit in *tamed* form, and retrieve the vocation of politics as the sole prerogative of a ruling elite bound by the imperatives of national renewal. Ultimately, Weber's political ethic remains entangled with the imperatives of reason of state and never-recanted ideas about Germany's *"responsibility before history"* as a master people.[96] But his plea for a political actor with a vocation for politics could be read as an attempt to repersonalize it, to add that element of personality that was available to Machiavelli but no longer in place in an increasingly rationalized world. Even so, his reflections had the effect of candidly laying bare something about which many fellow liberals have been historically disingenuous: the centrality of violence for the construction and preservation of a liberal-democratic order, the state's monopoly not only of its legitimate uses but also of its representations, the centrality of strategies of preemptive counterviolence to assure such monopoly, and the restriction of the ethic of responsibility to governing elites.

Still, if one juxtaposes Weber's formalist account of political responsibility with one of his most imaginative, if sometimes vilified, notions, that of a "community of fate" (*Schicksalsgemeinschaft*), an unexpected constellation emerges. Out of it, aspects of Weber's formulations could be reclaimed without committing oneself to his use of them, let alone carrying the sediments accumulated in his thought forms. For even if often interpreted as unavoidably nationalist, Weber deploys "community of fate" in terms of non-nationalist communities. In *Economy and Society*, for instance, he relates it to prenational communities, as part of his account of the nature and origin of patriarchal domination.[97] But one need not explore all of Weber's usages to grasp its formal contours. Formally speaking, the concept highlights not only the mutual dependence between the members of a common household, or the bonds, "external and spiritual," formed between them. Bonds that are, sure enough, forged by demarcations, boundaries between interior and exterior, and enmity lines on the basis of threats, existential or otherwise, all of which bears on a more political interpretation of this notion. Once understood politically, however, this notion also embodies the idea of a bounded space in which the political actor—the bearer of political responsibility—acts. What is more, it tacitly asserts a central aspect of political accountability: how in a binding political order both rulers and ruled are bound in a determinate space, their fates thus deeply intertwined. And if the political order in question accommodates a modicum of popular sovereignty, the consequences of the actions of the ruler on the ruled would, in turn, be felt by ruling elites. The latter would have yet another reason to embrace a political ethic of responsibility beyond any nationalist conceits.

VIOLENCE AND THE CITY

In 1915 Weber praised the fortitude of civilized man and was confident in his ability "to rise to the horrors of war" without compromising his humanity. "People who live in a civilized milieu," he proclaimed, "and are nevertheless able to rise to the horrors of war (no achievement for a black man from Senegal!) and to return as honorably as most of our people do—that is real humanity."[98] But by 1918 he had adopted a more cautious stance: "Whosoever contracts with violent means for whatever ends—and every politician does—is exposed to its specific consequences."[99] The catastrophe of the Great War was the watershed. In its aftermath, some things transpired much more clearly: one can compromise with violence only so much without being swayed by its destructive logic. Weil delivered the most famous version of this warning. In her formulations, however, she set the stage for a democratically conceived ethic of responsibility that, while still situated within the tradition of political ethic, sought to resist the imperatives of *raison d'état*. If the experience of the Great War and the Bolshevik threat left an imprint in Weber's theoretical reflections, for Weil it was living in the aftermath of these events, coupled with the subsequent brutality of the Spanish Civil War and World War II, that led her to a vigorous reckoning with catastrophic violence.

Weil's powerful reflections on these themes are synthesized in her rather inscrutable, and often neglected, essay "The Iliad or the Poem of Force."[100] Out of an extraordinary interpretation of Homer's *Iliad*, Weil offers sobering reflections on the intersection between violence and action. She proclaims not Achilles as the hero of the epic poem but *force*, to which is attributed a capacity to enslave those that come in contact with it, "force before which man's flesh shrinks away."[101] Force is also capable of converting a human being into a *thing*.[102] In this succinct rendering, Weil makes a strong critique of the dehumanizing effect of the imperatives of violence. These imperatives effectively blur the realm of action and responsibility, as violence increasingly claims sovereignty over life and death. It is "force that kills" and converts those whom it holds under its sway into things, corpses. "Violence obliterates anybody who feels its touch," and in so doing it is represented "as external to its employer as to its victim."[103] In this way, Weil portrays a mystification of its uses, which oftentimes finds expression under the guise of *necessity* in times of war.[104] Or, as she puts it in a stark formulation found in her *Gravity and Grace*, "Evil when we are in its power is not felt as evil but as a necessity, or even a duty."[105] And such mystifications are intrinsic to the forms of violence that characterize times of war. But all parties involved in the cycle of violence suffer a mutual fate: dehumanization. Both perpetrator and victim, oftentimes shifting roles, are equally degraded in a violent cycle of warfare. Weil thus couples the violence of action with the no less violent reaction and locates that violence within the same logic of war. Even so, she is hardly arguing for a categorical or principled rejection of the use of violence and force.[106] In an essay originally published in 1933, "Reflections of War," she unequivocally writes: "This fascism, which is spreading in all directions, can only be crushed by force."[107] Likewise, as part of her political practice, Weil herself joined the Republican side during the Spanish Civil War, acknowledged the inevitability of fighting Hitler, and until her death was an active member of the French Resistance in London.[108]

In the essay on the *Iliad* Weil suggests a way out of this seemingly paradoxical scenario. "A moderate use of force," she argues, "which alone would enable man to escape being enmeshed in its machinery, would require superhuman virtue, which is as rare as dignity in weakness."[109] For all its inherent dynamics of dehumanization, violence's hold over individuals is not total. Between the impulse to act and the action itself, there is what Weil calls "the tiny interval that shelters reflection."[110] That, accordingly, is where the possibility for justice and responsibility resides, which is why Weil, in her writings, sought to spatially institutionalize this rather temporal moment—an "interval"—to break with the idolatry fostered by the modern state. But when force and power become ends in themselves, what is an already constrained space of reflection is further shrunken. In this predicament, something akin to Machiavelli's economy of violence based on a reflective response is called for. Yet Weil is not ready to endorse either the politics of deception that accompanies Machiavelli's practice of politics or his protoconsequentialist ethics and willingness to endorse commissarial dictators or Weber's ethic of responsibility, for that matter. These formulations remain too entangled with the constitutive principles of doctrines including reason of state, which represent the quintessential form of power as an end in itself, for Weil to endorse. Against this, Weil invokes the rather elusive idea of "superhuman virtue."

Although by invoking "superhuman" virtue Weil seems to rehearse the early modern view of the necessity of a virtuous or prudent individual to responsibly exercise power, in her case this superhuman virtue actually consists of a plea for a generalized ethos that is anchored in a fierce passion and commitment to justice. Much like "impersonality" and the capacity for grace—which, like reflexivity, are also constitutive of her idea of justice—this type of virtue is superhuman because it is one of those rare things that requires attention and re-cognition for an ensuing reflection to be achieved.[111] Although this type of virtue may not curb the indifference that accompanies violence, it might allow for the *tiny* space of reflection that is needed to resist its dominion.[112] It also anchors a strong sense of political responsibility.

Subsequently, in *The Needs for Roots*, Weil casts political responsibility as a need of the soul. "For this need to be satisfied it is necessary that a man should often have to take decisions in matters great or small affecting interests that are distinct from his own, but in regards to which he feels a personal concern. . . . Finally, he requires to be able to encompass in thought the entire range of activity of the social organism to which he belongs."[113] Enlarged thinking and shared power are thus constitutive of a sense of political responsibility. Indeed, shared power is defining of a political ethic of responsibility and of its immediate locus, "the city"—here understood as polity, as the political entity that provides the locus of action, the space in which these commitments are rooted and actualized. And both the enlarged thinking and the sense of fidelity that shared power brings with it have important implications for the question of violence and the possibility of moderately contracting with it. The latter can become an excruciating imperative in order to defend the space of the political, the spatial dimension of responsibility that mediates its temporal dimension, which is what Weil refers to as the moment of reflection before a response.

Weil sorts out the implications of this economy of violence ("a moderate use of force") in an insightful formulation: "moderation itself is not without perils, since prestige, from which force derives at least three-quarters of its strength, rests principally upon that marvelous indifference that the strong feel for the weak, an indifference so contagious that it infects the very people who are the objects of it."[114] Once a cycle of violence is unleashed, and a spiral of violent acts follows, violence's effects become less and less shocking. What emerges are forms of violence that perpetuate the cycle of vengeance and reaction, forms of violence that are often cushioned both *aesthetically* and *anesthetically* so as to normalize and routinize their pervasiveness.[115] Indifference, then, becomes the order of the day, especially toward those subjected to the crudest forms of violence in *distant* zones of exception that are constitutive aspects of reason of state's *lebensraum* and toward those who are victims of the violence of market imperatives.[116] Stated differently, the moderate use of force is a difficult aspiration, one that demands breaking the yoke of indifference to superfluous suffering and the immanent logic of war.

Weil learned this important political-ethical lesson primarily from the experience of the Spanish Civil War. In this particular case, as she observed, "the necessities and the atmosphere of civil war are sweeping away the aspirations that we are seeking to defend by means of civil war."[117] The imperatives of war constrain and structure the choices of those who partake in it, hence Weil's avowal of the necessity for a different kind of virtue to resist them. Still, the Spanish Civil War taught her the possibility of something even more vexatious: "In the agony of civil war, every common measure between principles and realities is lost, every sort of criterion by which one could judge acts and institutions disappears, and the transformation of society is given over to chance."[118] Ironically, the necessities of war lead to a paradoxical predicament: while war constrains one's actions and increasingly compromises one's principles, it also instills a strong sense of the contingent and boundless element of action, thus impairing foresight. If this logic is to be avoided, a sober and reflective response must be a precondition to any reaction to war and catastrophe, loss and defeat. Thus the tiny space for reflection resides *before* an escalating reaction is initiated. Once the logic of violence that defines war is in place, a process of defactualization stems from it and thus blurs the possibility of separating contingencies from necessities. When the war is treated as a force with its own autonomous will, it equally instills a sense of powerlessness. Apropos of the Spanish Civil War, the very same war that provided a formative experience for Weil, George Orwell offered a vivid formulation that acutely encompasses some of the foregoing concerns: "Everyone was rushing around and trying to buy food. And on every side you heard the same anxious questions: 'Do you think it's stopped? Do you think it's going to start again?' 'It'—the fighting—was now thought of as some kind of natural calamity, like a hurricane or an earthquake, which was happening to us all alike and which we had no power of stopping."[119]

This logic, however, is better understood in a larger context: the emergence of a distinctively modern notion of power. Weil's analysis of modern power was deeply concerned with the effects that the spread of technology and bureaucracy was having on social relations. Both developments led to a new kind of oppression that was exercised under the guise of *management* and was irreducible to the political regime presuming to contain it.[120] These sentiments are echoed in her *Reflections Concerning the Causes of Liberty and Social Oppression*. She writes: "The whole of our civilization is founded on specialization, which implies the enslavement of those who execute to those who co-ordinate; and on such a basis one can only organize perfect oppression, not lighten it. Far from capitalist society having developed within itself the material conditions for a régime of liberty and equality, the establishment of such a regime presupposes a previous transformation in the realm of production and that of culture."[121] But Weil's concern was as much about this form of modern oppression as it was about its legitimizing mystifications. Against the naive conceptions of pacifisms and power that her writings are often assimilated to, Weil asserts power's ubiquitous nature. "The necessity of power is obvious, because life cannot be lived without order," she writes.[122] Its "allocation," however, "is arbitrary because all men are alike, or very nearly."[123] In other words, it is in the hierarchical and unequal distribution of power, under the aegis of administration and managerial conceptions of politics, that equality is undermined: hence the centrality of a cognitive shift in relation to some of our basic concepts and categories, even of the term *hierarchy,* a concept that along with many others—such as respect, responsibility, and order—is purposely transmogrified in *The Need for Roots*.

Weil also recognizes that power relies on representations for its legitimacy, on the prestige it bestows to its holders. The latter is the "very essence of power." In a formulation reminiscent of Weber's analysis of power and prestige she further suggests: "All power is based, in fact, upon the interrelation of human activities; but in order to be stable it must appear as something absolute and sacrosanct, both to those who wield and those who submit to it and also to other external powers."[124] Power thus relies on the mystifications that come out of its ability to disguise the arbitrary nature of its allocations. Here, to be sure, Weil is struggling with a question that has plagued Western political thought since Machiavelli: "The fundamental principle of power and any political activity is that there should never be any appearance of weakness. A force makes itself not only feared but also at the same time a little loved even by those whom it disgusts with violence. . . . This force whose empire extends into people's minds is in large part imaginary."[125] Critical reflection needs to dispel some of these appearances, re-cognize the situation, and respond, not merely react, to it politically. The latter entails an economy of violence where force is always a *means* that is uncompromisingly subjected to a democratic (qua regime of liberty and equality) city. Fidelity to this political identity of the collectivity and a commitment to humane principles of equality and solidarity serve as controlling *ends*.

Perhaps the most crucial element in Weil's critique of modern power is what she sees as its inversion of means and ends, an inversion that leads to positing its own perpetuation as the ultimate end. Such an inversion is constitutive of the blindness of force. Accordingly, one of the primary tasks of Weil's reworked conception of political ethic is a restitution of this relationship. In *Oppression and Liberty* she refers to the *Iliad* in ways that illuminate this point: "in this ancient and wonderful poem there *already appears the essential evil besetting humanity, the substitution of means for ends*."[126] Power, and the forms of violence that are its surrogates, are means that have increasingly become ends in themselves, especially the forms of power crystallized in the capitalist nation-state. In this formulation Weil captures a distinctive aspect of a distinctively modern conception of power whose master theoreticians are Bacon, Hobbes, Descartes, and Leibniz.[127] Once rationalized, this form of power disguises itself as objective, as something that is above the fray of interests and politics; it becomes its own justificatory myth. It thus becomes its own end. Modern power thus dehistoricizes: it relies on abstraction and calculation, and its despotic element is better characterized as one that erases meaningful differences and translates them into diversities. Weil further explored these attributes of modern power in her somber consideration of the catastrophes that it has brought about. "Power, by definition, is only a means; or to put it better, to possess power is simply to possess means of action which exceed the very limited force that a single individual has at his disposal. But power-seeking, owing to its essential incapacity to seize hold of its object, rules out all consideration of an end, and finally comes, through an inevitable reversal, to take the place of all ends."[128] Modern power is driven by its own monopolistic imperatives; consequently, "for abolishing oppression itself, that would first mean abolishing the sources of it, abolishing all the monopolies."[129] Hence, she makes a tacit plea for decentralized forms of power that are publicly accountable.

Once cast in this light, modern power emerges as an offspring of instrumental reason. Its correlate is an intellectualization of violence within the context of what Sheldon S. Wolin has referred to as the modern "culture of despotism": a simplified political culture composed of mostly privatized citizens whose politicalness resides in their obedience to "rational" laws in a highly legalistic culture. Power not only operates unhindered in such a culture, but it appears decentralized, and acquires legitimacy by means of the mantle of legality bestowed by liberal-democratic institutions.[130] And yet, the claim to decentralization notwithstanding, modern forms of power cling to the monotheistic ambitions of the theism that the abstract language of scientific rationality came to replace. It is thus ubiquitous, and its violence is legitimized and routinized under the rubric of technological precision, scientific advancement, and market rationality. Its political correlates, however, are found in the ideal of dynamically stable liberal institutions that legitimize state violence as well as the violence that market imperatives inflict.

Yet the epitome of her critique of modern power is found in Weil's reflections in the essay "The Power of Words." Here she alludes to the senselessness of war by once again using the example of Helen of Troy. Besides Paris, she writes, no one "cared two straws about her": she was just an excuse to unleash the violence and hubris of conquest. Helen's equivalent in Weil's present is "the role . . . played by words with capital letters." Words that acquire meaning only by being impregnated by war: "If we grasp one of these words, all swollen with blood and tears, and squeeze it, we find it is empty." Here Weil indicts the incidence of abstractions in our received political language (say, *nation, national interest, democracy, capitalism, communism, freedom, fascism, reason of state*). For Weil, however, the problem is not the words themselves but their *abstract* use as means to justify the self-perpetuating practices of power. As soon as these words are defined concretely, they can help "us to grasp some concrete reality, or concrete objective, or method of activity"; once concretely rendered, these words "might be a way of saving human lives."[131] However, a more concrete rendering calls for a reckoning with the historical continuities and discontinuities in the uses of these terms, as well as with their role in instilling a certain conception of political identity. It also requires, as already discussed, a re-cognition of the dual meanings of these terms and calls for the resignification of terms at the service of emancipatory ideals of justice, love, and equality. In this vein one can see her critique of democracy as a word in the essay "Human Personality," where she places it in the region of "ordinary institutions."[132] But such critique is tempered by the democratic import of her reflections and the ideals of justice that animate it.

On the whole, force is not something that can be expunged from the human condition, but its configurations and purposes are changeable. As Weil puts it, "Force is not a machine for automatically creating justice. It is a blind mechanism which produces indiscriminately and impartially just and unjust results, but, by all laws of probability unjust ones."[133] Herein lies the centrality of her discussion of the distinction between "means" and "ends," and its inversion in modern conceptions of power, to understanding her critique of violence: force is constitutive of the human condition, and it can be organized on a humane and just basis if the right ends are kept in place and if it is kept in check as a last resort. The problem, then, is not force as such but those forms and modalities of force that enslave, from factory work to the brutality of war. Force needs to be re-cognized in its uses and abuses and reined in by a legitimate end. Its arbitrary nature might end up sabotaging one's political identity and the ideals it stands for. That is the warning of the sober and tragic sensibility that Weil brings to bear in her reflections.

There is yet another important aspect to the modality of re-cognition at work in Weil's political thought: "The strong are, as a matter of fact, never absolutely strong, nor are the weak absolutely weak, but neither is aware of this."[134] This is an awareness that may break with the reifying pieties of the language of "loss," as well as with the temptations of consolation found in "defeat." The logic of force conceals this simple truth from its victims as it also disables the possibility for both parties to acknowledge a shared *humanity*—an insight that only sober reflection can yield. The violence of war ravages human lives and reduces human bodies to a momentary shared vulnerability, although the frailty of the body is nevertheless culturally and politically mediated.[135] These moments of shared vulnerability hint at a

shared humanity whose pain hardly elicits an abstract ethical commandment, but demands an addressing of the political conditions
and actions that brought it into being. This is the element of tragedy
mediating Weil's political thought: it allows for these moments to be
re-cognized in the temporal and spatial determinations that constitute their politicalness. "In the catastrophe of our time," Weil severely
writes, "the executioners and their victims are, both together, before
anything else, the involuntary bearers of a testimony against the
appalling wretchedness in which we wallow."[136] Correspondingly, the
blindness of force is manifested as an incapacity for reflection. This
is particularly evident when, in a cycle of violence, the subject impli-
cated in the use of force eventually becomes its object. Weil neatly
captures this feature in one of her most memorable formulations:
"These men, wielding power, have no suspicion of the fact that the
consequences of their deeds will at length come home to them—they
too will bow the neck in their turn."[137] Largely due to the blindness of
violence in war, those who are in power sometimes fail to consider
this possibility, the possibility that in the contemporary world has
been fittingly called *blowback*.[138]

Weil thus sums up the *hubris* often found in unyielding Homeric
figures and brings it to bear on her meditations in the aftermath of
catastrophe. Cruel acts that are the offspring of power often unleash
cycles of violence whose implications the actors cannot fully control.
In its blindness, violence neglects unintended effects and defactual-
izes. This neglect is neatly captured in the ephemeral moments of
invincibility that characterize the victors of the different battles; in
such instances, the victorious party "forgets to treat victory as a transi-
tory thing."[139] Caught up in the euphoria of victory, the victorious—in
ways that are analogous to their refusal of a shared humanity with the
defeated—are incapable of conceiving the possibility of self-destruction, let alone the possibility that the cycle of violence is not over yet
and that the defeated, like dormant furies, sometimes patiently await a
future moment of reckoning that will perpetuate the cycle to no end.[140]
Homer's *Iliad* is thus not just a poem about force that speaks to its
dynamics and its impact on the human condition. It is also a deeply
political work, not only because of its considerations of collectively
shared force but perhaps more so because it deals with "the destruction of a city," which for Weil is "the greatest calamity the human

race can experience."[141] A city offers the space for political participation and for being rooted in a milieu of shared power, which instills a strong sense of political responsibility. Hence the poem's political and critical import, which also resides in its capacity to instill a sense of "regret that men are capable of being so transformed" by violence and hubris.[142] Weil's reading also instills another very important lesson: in her predicament, as in ours, violence is not something that one either embraces or condemns *tout court*. Rather, it is something to be re-cognized in its multifarious forms, in its self-perpetuating mystifications, in order to open up an interval of reflection leading to a politically bounded response rather than to an equally violent reaction. Stated differently, the pervasiveness of violence in political life demands a sober re-cognition of its uses and representations.

At this point, however, an obvious question emerges: what is the binding political mechanism that restrains the use of violence? As Weil's interpretation of the *Iliad* illustrates, it is first the refusal to compromise one's political identity—the identity embodied in the city, in the hands of the hubris of power—and second an awareness of a shared humanity that serves as a controlling *end*. Implicit in her reflections is a strong concern with defending a specific political identity to avoid compromising it. The latter is a concern when a collectivity is at war. In one of her later texts, "Reflections on War," she states this point rather clearly: "And, no matter what name it bears—fascism, democracy, dictatorship of the proletariat—the principal enemy remains the administrative, police, and military apparatus; not the apparatus across the border from us . . . but one that calls itself our defender and makes us its slaves."[143] That is, the imperatives of reason of state, of national security, which are consonant with the logic of violence—as described in the essay on the *Iliad*—threaten to eclipse the substantive democratic values the state claims to defend by effectively subordinating them to the imperatives of warfare.

In *The Need for Roots* this concern is elaborated on in relation to imperialism. In this text Weil offers a severe critique of French imperialism from the perspective of its betrayal of the principles of justice that inform French political identity. "Every other nation," she argues, "might possibly have had the right to carve out an empire for itself, but not France. . . . When one takes upon oneself, as France did in 1789, the function of thinking on behalf of the world, of defining justice for the world, one may not become an owner of human flesh and blood."[144] It has been argued that, precisely in this messianic gesture of universalizing justice, France was already embarking on an imperial path.[145] But the political import of this passage, in light of Weil's concern with preserving a democratic political identity—its corollary form and politically constituted space—as allegorized in her references to "the city," suggests a different interpretation. In its imperial venture, France was compromising itself, both in the particular and the universal moment, by its proclamation of ideals of justice. But this compromise of the ideal of justice was already present in the way the revolution was anchored in the idea of the nation as a homogeneous entity constituting the source of political sovereignty. Weil is certainly aware of this paradox, as it can be inferred from her alternative constitution for postwar France, a document she drafted as part of the Resistance in London. In it she sought to replace "nation" with "consenting people" as the source of political power and legitimacy, thus instituting a binding identity that was both political—as opposed to national— and democratic, as an unyielding *end*. In so doing, she sought to give institutional form to the moments of reflection that her reading of the *Iliad* calls for, and she also proposed a referendum every twenty years to institutionalize a space for reflection on and discussion about public life.[146]

Experiences of defeat, first in the Spanish Civil War and subsequently in World War II, led Weil to ponder the question of violence in its ethical and political dimensions. Her distinctive perspective offers a plethora of insights on our own predicament, one in which the dreams and catastrophes that were then nascent have already unfolded. Among these insights are the constitutive nature of violence in the capitalist modern nation-state, the blindness of violence in its military modality, and a conception of political action based on a sense of political responsibility within a broad tradition of political ethic. One of Hannah Arendt's most compelling formulations of what is at stake in thinking about political responsibility is apposite here: "*political* responsibility . . . exists quite apart from what the individual member of the group has done and therefore can neither be judged in moral terms nor be brought before a criminal court."[147] Rather, it is collective and, more importantly, inscribed in a historical sense and identification with the political principles binding the collectivity in question and fidelity to a political project that however internationalist always has a particular, concrete point of departure. What makes it political, though, is not just its collective connotation, however important that dimension is. Political responsibility, as the foregoing discussion has sought to delineate, entails fidelity to a political identity as well as identification with the historical travails of the unfolding political principles and forms binding collective life, from which no politicizing political project seeking a horizon beyond liberal-democratic capitalism is exempted. Inaugurating a new political order, reproducing and sustaining it, demands an even more complex, pressing, and ineluctable practice of political responsibility. Fidelity to forms of shared power that are coextensive with the collectivity in question becomes the binding controlling end that is constitutive of the concrete dialectic of means and ends that is the sine qua non of the tradition of political ethic.

Yet to reclaim the tradition of political ethic is not enough. In order to bring out the critical import of this tradition, it is necessary to recast it in genuinely democratic ways, anchored on a political commitment to a socialist project of shared power. And an attempt at a democratic, reflective response needs to pit the two preeminent legacies of political ethic—reason of state and an ethic of responsibility—against one another. Weil's rejection of the logic of reason of state is crucial in this effort, as she formulated an approach to thinking politically about power without binding it to the logic of reason of state. Even if, at some points, Weil was inclined toward pessimistic assessments of the prospects of action—e.g., "Present-day society is like an immense machine that continually snatches up and devours men and that no one knows how to control"—she never relinquished the possibility of meaningful collective action, let alone reified powerlessness.[148] Instead, she sought to re-cognize it. Correspondingly, in one of her last pieces she issued a warning: "But one could still not say that the atmosphere in our country is really impregnated and charged with the ideal in whose name we are fighting. In order to fight well it is not enough to defend an absence of tyranny. We must be rooted in a milieu in which every activity is really oriented in the opposite direction of tyranny. Our domestic propaganda cannot be made of words; to be effective, it must consist of dazzling realities."[149] To actualize these "realities," it is necessary to become politically responsible and *rooted* in a democratic collectivity that effectively enacts democratic values of participation and shared power, freedom and equality.

If in the opposition between knowledge and action resides Weber's ethic of political responsibility—the true bearer of the vocation for politics has a blend of the two—it is in Weil's emphasis on reflection and her concern for the materiality of what she refers to as the "needs of the soul" that the possibility to recast political responsibility democratically is found. From this perspective, and contra Nietzsche, there is a third moment, which is missing in the binary reaction/reflection: neither just reaction, nor just reflection, but a sober response. Political responsibility thus rests on a response based on a fidelity to a political identity, its enabling institutions and forms; in this case, the preservation of a democratic-socialist identity is what becomes a controlling *end*. By way of her concern with political identity, as embodied in the city, Weil sought to subdue the imperatives of reason of state and set the basis upon which one can democratize the conception of responsibility this notion has carried historically. This may well be the only way to responsibly mobilize for action without compromising one's fidelity to political ethical principles and the political forms actualizing them. In Weil's times, the challenge was that of waging a war against fascism without compromising one's ideals in the process; in our times the challenge seems to be that of reconceiving and reclaiming political responsibility from its already compromised form. To do so entails, among other things, displacing questions of leadership and envisioning responsibility in terms of the struggle for political orders in which the *demos* participates in power and publicly reflects on the actions done in its name from the perspective of a substantive democratic identity outside liberal-democratic capitalism and its regimes of accumulation. In other words, Weil's reflections open up the possibility of a consideration of the question of responsibility politically, from the perspective of a democratic public ethic that demands the active participation of citizens in sharing political power and seeks meaningful public accountability for the representations of violence and the ends it legitimizes, by means of action and fidelity to an idea of democratic justice, not fidelity to the liberal-capitalist imperatives or the imperatives of its state form and practices of idolatry.

But such a conception of democracy seems out of sync in the age of depoliticized politics. For it to be possible, the zealous present-day emphasis on the politics of difference and particularity has to be recast to make it serve as one pole of a politics that also involves the language of universalism, solidarity, and collectivity. The universalism, solidarity, and sense of a democratic political identity that claims on behalf of difference and particularity often presuppose, but never theorize, need to be avowed. These are two irreducible dialectical poles that democratic politics needs to re-cognize and speculatively render without an abstract mending; in an Adornian rendering these are two poles constituting integral moments of justice and freedom that never add up. Any politics worthy of the name has to have a place for both as much as it has to dialectically conjoin moments of radical attack with a defensive politics.

POLITICAL LITERACY

Enacting a political ethic and its corollary sense of political responsibility requires a politicizing critical discourse and practice. More precisely: a pressing question is how to, once again, learn to think politically. Such learning, however, requires, even demands, at the very least a modicum of shared power. Shared power brings a sense of proximity without any illusions of immediacy—shared power is thoroughly mediated—that fosters a different sense of responsibility. Political responsibility could thus be conceived as a practice of immanent transcendence that consists of ordinary people actively sharing power and gaining hard-earned political knowledge and the responsibilities that come with it. Reclaiming political literacy, a political return in the ways we think about the intersection between ethics and politics in struggles of power, requires redrawing enmity lines from the perspective of fidelity to socialist principles and their actualizing in robustly democratic political forms.[150] It also means retrieving the category of the citizen and the necessary spatial conditions that make the category politically meaningful.[151] If today, as in one of Wolin's acerbic formulations, "the citizen has become marginal and democracy more manageable," it is the idea of citizenship that needs to be reclaimed, as it entails assuming "responsibility for taking care of political and social arrangements, not only operating institutions but 'cultivating' them, caring for them, improving them, and, ultimately, defending them."[152]

Political responsibility is the responsibility of citizens. And to think politically means to think about the politics of the active citizen, not the theoretical subject, as well as to think about citizenship in current political orders and new possibilities of citizenship in future political orders that, at the very least, need to be more democratic and humane. Herein resides the centrality for critical theory to re-cognize democratic practices and political forms, avow a sober realism and an acute sense of political literacy as constitutive of citizenship, and re-cognize the political nature of lines of enmity. The latter point moves in tandem with the first two: enmity lines demand the re-cognition of the predicaments of power we navigate and the roles of elites, yesterdays, and todays in impairing access to a politics of shared power and commonality. In these predicaments it is imperative to think politically, namely, to think about the concrete dialectical mediations of power, structural imperatives, interests, and agents.

One step in the avowal of political literacy consists in resisting the prevailing logic where, under the mantle of terror and terrorism, everything is folded, to the point that distinctions between an act of sabotage and an act of terror are blurred. A politically literate political ethic refuses to surrender to the temptation of finding a pristine ethical anchoring for politics that antecedes the scenes of power one navigates and thus bypasses the need to contextually reckon with predicaments of power that defy any apodictic ethics or pristine ethical disposition.[153] This is nowhere more evident than in the current representations of violence. Subsuming violence as such, with no reference to content or context, let alone to the violent constitution of the predicaments of power and agents to what and to whom a violent response emerges, further compromises the political literacy necessary for thinking politically about the present. In his memoirs Régis Debray has retrieved a political distinction from a more robustly political age: the difference between revolutionary violence, or political radicalism, and terrorism.[154] Even when it is a strain to endorse his French republicanism and virtual collusion with neoimperial ventures in Haiti, one finds this veteran of Latin American guerrilla warfare, and former minister under Mitterrand, making the distinction sharply:

> The *lucha armada* had its own rules of etiquette. Rob a bank to get
> money to buy weapons: fine. Deliberately kill civilians in the street:

certainly not. "Execute" a . . . torturer: yes. Coldly liquidate a prisoner: never. . . . I can best define what distinguished revolutionary violence from repressive violence by pointing out that at that time the torture of a prisoner was unthinkable among adepts of the revolution, and routine among adepts of repression. Anyone reflecting on this detail will see that it defines a very important difference.[155]

That there needs to be a strict economy of violence in any political situation ought to be clear enough, as should the futility of adventurism in moments of epochal or political closure. But it is precisely this *important difference* Debray adduces that gets obliterated in our current depoliticized age. Re-cognizing this difference, however, cannot demand disavowing the moment of shared responsibility in a violent predicament. Rather, as Daniel Bensaïd has forcefully argued, it points to how in situations of "savage hyper-violence," which necessarily includes the "hyper-violence of armed globalization," "the dialectic of violence involves (at least) two parties, and that the relationship is as asymmetrical as that kind of warfare."[156] Even so, no political ethic, no matter how asymmetrical the conflict is, can dispense with the economy of violence—or "restrained violence," as Bensaïd called it—without undoing itself.

Of course, not every instantiation of a political ethic is formulated in the violent contexts out of which Debray draws these crucial distinctions. In an altogether different context, say, one in which the interplay of violence and civility is to the advantage of the latter, one needs to avow a sense of political literacy that entails re-cognition and critical mapping of these *situations* and the imperatives produced and reproduced by one's actions and inactions.[157] In civic times, that is, a staunch realist disposition entails assuming responsibility and democratic citizenship in addition to drawing critical mappings and enmity lines in one's collectivity and the forms of power it generates. These are the means: an unrelenting, if sober, fidelity to democratic political forms serves as the controlling end. Obviously, there is a humanism tacitly assumed in these formulations, a *minima humana*, as it were, but there is also an equally tacit avowal of the quest for political forms that can house it and make it concrete. And the dialectical mediation between the two is constitutive of a political ethic along the lines herein defended. For a political ethic that hinges on how a dialectical critical theory maps out the predicaments of power citizens navigate in the intersections between economic, cultural, and political fields of power, a sober sense of political realism and literacy is paramount.

There are, accordingly, two senses of political responsibility in the tradition of political ethic the foregoing discussion invokes: that of ruling, and thus sustaining an existing political order, and that of bringing about a new political order. Yet there is a third connotation of political responsibility, one that closely relates to the idea of responsible critical thinking formulated by Adorno and to the responsibilities of educators and intellectuals in the realm of representation, which becomes a preferred locus of action in epochs of political closure. This links to the idea of offering sober representations that attest to the foregoing sense of fidelity not only by contributing to enhance the political literacy of fellow citizens but also by forging the necessary mappings that would be conducive to political action, while instilling the sobriety and realism that is necessary for responsible political action. Ernst Bloch offered a keen formulation of the dialectic of realism and utopia, sobriety and enthusiasm that is constitutive of the political literacy intrinsic to a political ethic:

> And even if hope merely rises above the horizon, whereas only knowledge of the Real shifts it in solid fashion by means of practice, it is still hope alone which allows us to gain the inspiring and consoling understanding of the world to which it leads, both as the most solid, the most tendency-based and concrete understanding. . . . But the anticipatory of course must blossom, it still has its function, especially when this takes place in *sobriety* instead of in effusiveness and clouds. Likewise, enthusiasm assists sobriety, so that it does not abstractly-immediately foreshorten the *perspective* instead of keeping it on the globe of the concrete possibility. Enthusiasm is imagination in action, and the acid of sobriety must here become the most precious rather than the generally cheapest ingredient. . . . Therefore, it is equally alien and unwise . . . to reach under reality with nothing but sobriety, as it is to overreach it with nothing but enthusiasm; the Real, precisely as that of tendency, is attained only by the constant oscillation of both aspects, united in *trained perspective*.[158]

This dialectic is indispensable for responsible political action in all its modalities, as is dialectical critical theory for achieving a "trained perspective." *Responsible* need not mean tamed, let alone subdued, modalities of critical criticism, forms of moralizing inaction, or acquiescence with depoliticized politics. Rather, in this context it means instilling a sober and realistic sense of collective identity and action, which refuses to compromise the ends, but soberly reckons with a realist political disposition as one of its means. This dialectical articulation of means and ends—similarly that of realism and utopia, sobriety and enthusiasm—is central for a political ethic and, by extension, for any genuinely political sense of responsibility that is necessarily limited and thus a genuinely particular articulation of a universal.[159]

What exactly does the appeal to sober realism involve? Within the tradition of political ethic, realism is the antipode of wishful thinking and ideological conceits, not of utopia.[160] At least since Machiavelli, realism entails imagination not in order to idealize the present or abstractly posit an ideal situation but to rationally inquire why things are what they are and how they could be otherwise.[161] It consists of an uncompromising reckoning with political realities that requires not only dispensing with pieties and euphemisms when taking sober measure of a political situation, but the need to cognitively map it and accurately discern the realities of power the situation imposes in the name of the ideal that animates the need to rectify it. At its most uncompromising, political realism is concerned with limits, including pain and suffering. It is similarly concerned with history as a way of understanding the historicity of the present, how it came into being and what, if any, lines of flight can be conceived from it. Precisely because it refuses to relinquish utopia, it resists any accommodation to the ruling powers, as it relentlessly debunks the quest for silver linings. Instead, it highlights power differentials and dispenses with consolations about them. Of course, in the absence of meaningful alternatives, struggles that improve the lot of the many are never to be discounted, however inconsequential these are ultimately in altering the structures that perpetuate their predicaments. A sober and uncompromising realism thereby re-cognizes predicaments of power: how political power is exercised, produced, and reproduced in a given situation. Realism and political literacy are thus essential for a political ethic of responsibility.

Correspondingly, a political ethic of responsibility requires parsing out degrees of responsibility, which largely depend on the actor's location in the structured political situation in question. Unsurprisingly, the tropes of tragedy have provided a way to understand constrained choices and the dialectical structuring of situations to which a political actor—from the citizen to the ruler—responds and are differentially responsible for. This is a point emphasized in narratives of revolution, from C. L. R James's *Black Jacobins* to Isaac Deutscher's Trotsky trilogy, where social forces beyond the actor's control are presented and re-cognized without exonerating the political responsibilities incurred within such constraints. The sober realism of these works largely stems from this fundamental insight: responsibility is related to historical causality, without negating the constitutive gap between intention and effect. Precisely because this is not negated, one can think of responsibility as mediated, sometimes mitigated, lessened or enhanced, in reference to the structuring of the political situation in question. Deutscher's Trotsky and James's Toussaint are historical actors thoroughly mediated by larger historical forces: products of history, as it were, who were subjected to a wide range of social and political forces structuring the political situation they responded to—a structuring that their responses contributed to constituting, either by sanctioning, resisting, or modifying it, with their actions sometimes expressing, articulating, or refusing these forces.

It is in the intersections and mediations of historical causality and political agency within predicaments of power that a political ethic of responsibility is actualized, an actualization that entails a sense of political literacy consisting of clear-eyed mappings of the situation in question that resist idealizations and fantasies in the name of a realism that remains thoroughly mediated by the utopian moment of imagining an alternative order beyond the intractable density of the status quo and its continuous petrification. On this reckoning, one of today's most pressing political questions consists of siting where the most effective locus of political responsibility—where *rulers* and *ruled* confront and politically engage—resides. But one thing is clear: there is no genuine sense of political responsibility without common power and shared fate.

NOTES

PREFACE

1. Broadly speaking, depoliticized politics consists of the neutralization of any form of collective agency that could threaten the mainstay of the political order (say, liberal-democratic capitalism in the United States and its forms of managed democracy). The crystallization of forms of depoliticized politics, accordingly, conforms to a phenomenon in which the grip of capitalism is so firmly in place—no matter how abated by crises, it ideologically and structurally debars any political alternative that calls into question its mainstay—that *politicized* identity has displaced *political* identity and politics is increasingly played out in relation to local questions of status related to particularized identity (religious, ethnic, racial, gendered) within the collectivity in question. That is one crucial reason why in the U.S. political spectrum alternative ways of organizing political and economic life are never at stake, let alone parties contending the hierarchies of status and privilege that are asymmetrically distributed in this liberal-democratic capitalist regime. The ethical politics of religion and culture constitute notorious instances of depoliticized politics. It is this pacified political space that then makes possible, even promotes, "managed democracy," along with the politics of "small margins," ideological "gridlock," and the corporatization and marketization of governing processes that have come to define its rule. The political field is effectively pacified, and politics become so depoliticized that the demands and obduracies of genuinely political action, its predicaments and imperatives, becomes unthinkable. Accordingly, imperial citizens call for ethical responsibility, without political responsibility, while intellectual "bids" are theoretically scrutinized with no desire to embrace forms of collective agency

that could successfully vie for political power, much less acknowledge the imperatives of ruling, let alone entertain the inauguration of a different political order. For the original articulation of the idea of "depoliticized politics," see Wang Hui, *The End of the Revolution* (London: Verso, 2008), 3–18; and Theodore Huters, ed., *The Politics of Imagining Asia* (Cambridge: Harvard University Press, 2011), 34–36, 41; on managed democracy, see Sheldon S. Wolin, *Democracy Incorporated* (Princeton: Princeton University Press, 2008), 131ff. For alternative accounts emphasizing the present as postpolitical or postdemocratic, see, inter alia, Josep Ramoneda, *Después de la pasión política* (Madrid: Taurus, 1999), passim; Sheldon S. Wolin, "Political Theory: From Vocation to Invocation," in Jason A. Frank and John Tambornino, eds., *Vocations of Political Theory* (Minneapolis: University of Minnesota Press, 2000), especially 11–21, and *Tocqueville Between Two Worlds* (Princeton: Princeton University Press, 2001), 561ff.; Chantal Mouffe, *On the Political* (London: Verso, 2005), 1–34, 64–89; and Kenneth Surin, *Freedom Not Yet* (Durham: Duke University Press, 2009), 1–17, 28–33, 65–93, 242, 290ff.

2. Cf. Paul Ricoeur, *Reflections on the Just*, trans. David Pellauer (Chicago: University of Chicago Press, 2007), 254.

3. See, respectively, Robert Meister, *After Evil* (New York: Columbia University Press, 2011), passim; and Stephen L. Esquith, *The Political Responsibilities of Everyday Bystanders* (College Park: Penn State University Press, 2010), passim. Cf. Hannah Arendt, *Responsibility and Judgment*, ed. Jerome Kohn (New York: Schocken, 2005), 17–48.

4. Fredric Jameson, *The Ideologies of Theory* (London: Verso, 2008), 7.

5. Fredric Jameson, *Marxism and Form* (Princeton: Princeton University Press, 1971), 341.

6. A word about the term *diremption:* this rather archaic word will be deployed throughout this book for specific conceptual reasons. Herein it would be used in the sense specified by Gillian Rose: "'diremption' . . . implies 'torn halves of an integral freedom to which, however, they do not add up'—it formally implies the third . . . implicit in any opposition, qua sundered unity, without positing any substantial pre-existing 'unity,' original or final, neither finitely past or future, nor absolutely, as transcendent. 'Diremption' draws attention to the trauma of separation of that which was, however, as in marriage, not originally united"; see Gillian Rose, *The Broken Middle* (Oxford: Blackwell, 1992), 236.

7. Here *speculative* is deployed in the Hegelian sense of the term. For the best English-language discussion, see Gillian Rose, *Hegel Contra Sociology* (London: Athlone, 1981), passim. Sergio Valverde's ongoing research decidedly establishes its critical and political import.

8. Two other dimensions of a political ethic worth mentioning: on the one hand, this ethic of collective life is concerned with political forms and the institutions and practices sustaining it and, by extension, sustained by it; on the other hand, it draws attention to political aspect of questions ranging

from climate change, hunger, and war to the political dimension of traditional ethical questions—abortion, euthanasia, cloning—and what role, if any, the state or other forms of collective power have in dealing with them. Once politically conceived, these ethical questions become collective concerns and their valences and significance need to be recast. Even if these questions enjoy relative autonomy from political forms, or are indifferent to them, their concrete actualization is thoroughly mediated by the mainstay of collective life and how it is politically constituted and sanctioned. Cf. Francisco Fernández Buey, *Ética y filosofía política* (Barcelona: Bellaterra, 2000), passim.

9. See Manuel Cruz, "On Pain, the Suffering of Wrong, and Other Grievances," in María Pía Lara, ed., *Rethinking* (Berkeley: University of California Press, 2001), 198–209, *Hacerse cargo* (Barcelona: Paidós, 1999), passim, and *Las malas pasadas del pasado* (Barcelona: Anagrama, 2005), 89–144.

10. See Joan C. Tronto, "Revisiting Tragedy and Cultivating the Good," paper delivered at the Meeting of the American Philosophical Association, Central Division, Minneapolis, March, 30–April, 2, 2011.

11. See Joan C. Tronto, *Democratic Care* (New York: New York University Press, 2013), 46ff.

12. Cf. Paul Ricoeur, *The Just*, trans. David Pellauer (Chicago: University of Chicago Press, 2000), 11–35.

13. Sheldon S. Wolin, *Politics and Vision* (Princeton: Princeton University Press, 2004), 598, and cf. *The Presence of the Past* (Baltimore: Johns Hopkins University Press, 1989), 82–99.

14. See José Luis L. Aranguren, *Ética y política* (Madrid: Guadarrama, 1968), 61, 90.

15. See Wendy Brown, *States of Injury* (Princeton: Princeton University Press, 1995), 52–76.

16. John Dewey, *Freedom and Culture* (Amherst, NY: Prometheus, 1989), 100.

INTRODUCTION

1. Alfred Cobban, *In Search of Humanity* (New York: De Capo, 1960), 240.

2. Pierre Mesnard, *L'Essor de la philosophie politique au XVI siècle* (Paris: Vrin, 1951 [1936]), 3–4.

3. Williams's formulation is found in Bernard Williams, *In the Beginning Was the Deed* (Princeton: Princeton University Press, 2005), 2. See Charles Larmore, "What Is Political Philosophy?" *Journal of Moral Philosophy* 10 (2013): 305.

4. Larmore, "What Is Political Philosophy?," 305–6; cf. Charles Larmore's "The Moral Basis of Political Liberalism," *Journal of Philosophy* 96 (December 1999): 599–625. Larmore's essay offers a critique of Williams's "realism," but Raymond Geuss's work is secluded to a wearily discrete footnote.

5. Reviewing Michael Sandel's book "on the moral limits of markets," titled *What Money Can't Buy* (2013), Wendy Brown points out how it "offers a compelling expose [sic] of our current condition but frames what it exposes as a matter of values, decisions and inadvertent 'drift' rather than historical forces, social powers, a governing rationality or an economy whose life principle is growth and new markets. Consequently, he understates the dimensions and depth of the problem and places the burden of fixing it before the feet of a people interpellated by the condition he indicts and who cannot easily deliver us from the problem by deliberating about it," whose net effect "is to abstract markets from capitalism itself." See Book Reviews, *Political Theory* 42 (June 2014): 358.

6. Larmore, "What Is Political Philosophy?," 296.

7. E. P. Thompson, "The Long Revolution (Part I)," *New Left Review* 9 (May-June 1961): 25.

8. Cf. Stephen Eric Bronner, "Constructing a Critical Political Theory," *New Politics* 12 (Summer 2009): 72–83.

9. See Roberto Schwarz's parody of methodological protocols, *O pai de família e outros estudos* (São Paulo: Companhia das Letras, 2008), 112–14.

10. Cf. J. G. A. Pocock, "Historiography as a Form of Political Thought," *History of European Ideas* 37 (March 2011): 1–6.

11. See Fredric Jameson, *The Political Unconscious* (Ithaca: Cornell University Press, 1981), 75ff., and *The Ideologies of Theory* (London: Verso, 2008), 5–76.

12. Anthony Grafton, *Defenders of the Text* (Cambridge: Harvard University Press, 1991), 17. Accordingly, a good deal rides on how contexts are construed. One of the limitations of Quentin Skinner's important work is its overreliance on linguistic and rhetorical contexts, in and of itself an upshot of the so-called linguistic turn. Even if this turn has yielded richer, more encompassing historical accounts of texts, they nevertheless remain a sophisticated modality of textualism that is rather innocent to social and economic history and how these two bear on political forms and institutional developments. See, inter alia, James Tully, ed., *Meaning and Context* (Princeton: Princeton University Press, 1989); and Quentin Skinner, *Visions of Politics*, 3 vols. (Cambridge: Cambridge University Press, 2002), 1:passim. On the kinship between theory and the Cambridge School, see Anthony Grafton, *Worlds Made by Words* (Cambridge: Harvard University Press, 2009), 209; and Martin Jay, "Intention and Irony," *History and Theory* 52 (February 2013): 32–48. Important critiques of Skinner can be found in Nancy S. Struever, *Theory as Practice* (Chicago: University of Chicago Press, 1992), x–xii; Ellen Meiksins Wood, "Why It Matters," *London Review of Books*, 25 September 2008, 3–6, *Citizens to Lords* (London: Verso, 2008) 7–10, and *Liberty and Property* (London: Verso, 2012), 9ff., 224ff.; Lucien Jaume, "El pensamiento en acción," *Ayer* 53 (2004): 109–30; Enzo Traverso, *L'histoire comme champ de bataille* (Paris: La Découverte, 2012), 14–23.

13. See Jaume, "El pensamiento en acción," especially 110–20. A brilliant example of a historical account of a philosophical problematic whose focus could afford to bracket out political and social history is found in Eckart Förster,

The Twenty-Five Years of Philosophy, trans. Brady Bowman (Cambridge: Harvard University Press, 2012). Needless to say, a history of the *political* ideas and problematics of the very same thinkers Förster engages would demand a more historically robust account of their political and economic, cultural and social, contexts of emergence, as well as of the political ideas and choices of their proponents. Concepts and categories of "theoretical reason" lack the sociohistorical, spatial, and institutional presuppositions and content that ideas of, say, autonomy, state and civil society, equality and freedom possess. Similarly, a historicization of the idea of "the subject" looks very different than that of, say, the citizen. On the subject, see Vincent Descombes, *Le complément de sujet* (Paris: Gallimard, 2004), passim, and *Le parler de soi* (Paris: Gallimard, 2014),13–181. Cf. Étienne Balibar, *Citoyen sujet et autres essais d'anthropologie philosophique* (Paris: Presses Universitaires de France, 2011), 67–118.

14. Bindingness (*Verbindlichkeit*) is a central term in Adorno's negative dialectic that connotes the binding and obliging nature of genuinely philosophical insight. The bindingness of negative dialectics, as Robert Hullot-Kentor has lucidly formulated it, resides in it being devoid of the drive of subjective domination—it is at once noncompulsory and utterly obliging. Personal communication with the author, 13 August 2011.

15. Theodor W. Adorno, *Notes to Literature*, trans. Shierry Weber Nicholsen, 2 vols. (New York: Columbia University Press, 1992), 2:103.

16. Pierre Bourdieu, *Pascalian Meditations*, trans. Richard Nice (Stanford: Stanford University Press, 1997), 126–27.

17. Ibid., 121.

18. Adorno, *Notes to Literature*, 2:112.

19. Theodor W. Adorno, *Philosophie und Soziologie* (Berlin: Suhrkamp, 2011), 141.

20. Ibid., 142.

21. On autonomy, see inter alia, Theodor W. Adorno, *Aesthetic Theory*, trans. Robert Hullot-Kentor (Minneapolis: University of Minnesota Press, 1997), 1–15ff, and *Ästhetik (1958/59)*, ed. Eberhard Ortland (Frankfurt: Suhrkamp, 2009), 216–28, 244.

22. On the dialectic of displacement, see Roberto Schwarz, *Misplaced Ideas*, trans. John Gledson (London: Verso, 1992), 19–32; on "emergence," see Keya Ganguly, *Cinema, Emergence, and the Films of Satyajit Ray* (Berkeley: University of California Press, 2010), especially 36–39, 179ff.

23. See Carlo Ginzburg, "Our Words, and Theirs," *Historical Knowledge*, ed. Susanna Fellman and Marjatta Rahikainen (New Castle: Cambridge Scholars, 2012), 97–98.

24. Adorno acknowledges the first concern in his great essay "Parataxis"—see *Notes to Literature*, 2:119.

25. See Marc Bloch, "Pour une historie compare des sociétés européenes," in *Mélanges Historiques* (Paris: CNR, 2011), 16–40.

26. See ibid., 28.

27. Critical statements about the uses of anachronism are found in Margaret Leslie, "In Defense of Anachronism," *Political Studies* 18 (December 1970): 433–47; Nicole Loraux, "Éloge de l'anachronisme," *La genre humain* 27 (1993): 23–39; and Ginzburg, "Our Words, and Theirs," 97–119. Ginzburg explicitly objects to Loraux's characterization and pleads for a clear distinction of the anachronism involved in formulating research questions and the need to purge any trace of it from the answers given to them (108).

28. See Lucien Jaume, *Tocqueville*, trans. Arthur Goldhammer (Princeton: Princeton University Press, 2013), 6.

29. Christopher Hill, *The Experience of Defeat* (New York: Viking, 1984), 26.

30. Roger Crisp, "Homeric Ethics," in Roger Crisp, ed., *The Oxford Handbook of the History of Ethics* (Oxford: Oxford University Press, 2012), 11. Alasdair MacIntyre has observed something analogous about ideas of "duty" and "obligation"; see *A Short History of Ethics*, 2d ed. (Notre Dame: University of Notre Dame Press, 1998), 124–25. See also his discussion on the relationship between philosophy and history in *After Virtue* (Notre Dame: University of Notre Dame Press, 1981), 265–72. Early on in the book, he suggested that a moral philosophy "characteristically presupposes a sociology" (230).

31. See, for instance, the discussion of "subjective" and "objective" rights in Raymond Geuss, *Philosophy and Real Politics* (Princeton: Princeton University Press, 2008), 60–66.

32. Max Horkheimer, *Between Philosophy and Social Science*, trans. C. Fredrick Hunter, Matthew S. Kramer, and John Torpey (Cambridge: MIT Press, 1993), 17.

33. See Theodor W. Adorno, "Thesen über die Sprachen des Philosophen," in *Gesammelte Schriften*, ed. Rolf Tiedemann with Gretel Adorno, Susan Buck-Morss, and Klaus Schultz, 20 vols. (Frankfurt: Suhrkamp, 2003), 1:368. Hereafter referred to as *GS* followed by volume and page number. Unless otherwise indicated all translations are my own.

34. *GS* 1:368–69.

35. Ibid., 367.

36. See Theodor W. Adorno, *Philosophische Terminologie*, 2 vols., ed. Rudolf Zur Lippe (Frankfurt: Suhrkamp, 1973–75), 1:36.

37. Ibid., 2:10–11.

38. Ibid., 2:71.

39. Cf. Theodor W. Adorno, *Einführung in die Dialektik*, ed. Christoph Ziermann (Berlin: Suhrkamp, 2010), 187.

40. See Adorno, *Philosophische Terminologie*, 1:14–16.

41. See *GS* 20.1:318–26.

42. Michael Hofmann, *Where Have You Been?* (New York: Farrar, Straus and Giroux, 2014), 6.

43. Fredric Jameson, *The Modernist Papers* (London: Verso, 2007), xi.

44. The most collective connotations of this concept were already adumbrated in the early writings. See Simone de Beauvoir, *Philosophical Writings*, ed. Margaret A. Simmons (Urbana: University of Illinois Press, 2004), 90–149,

177–93, 245–60, 289–305; and Jean-Paul Sartre, *Notebooks for an Ethics*, trans. David Pellauer (Chicago: University of Chicago Press, 1992), especially 57–58, 78, 79, 142.

45. Jameson, *The Modernist Papers*, xi, xvii; see also, Jameson, *The Ideologies of Theory*, 150.

46. Sartre, *Notebooks for an Ethics*, 78, 79.

47. Beauvoir, *Philosophical Writings*, 187.

48. Sartre, *Notebooks for an Ethics*, 83.

49. Roberto Schwarz, "National Adequation and Critical Originality," *Cultural Critique* 49 (Fall 2001): 37.

50. See Adorno, *Notes to Literature*, 1:252.

51. For excellent discussions of these concepts, see Henri Lefebvre, *Critique of Everyday Life*, 3 vols., trans. John Moore (London: Verso, 2002), 2:31–97, 118–41, 356ff; and Jameson, *The Political Unconscious*, 27–50, 140–50.

52. See Fredric Jameson, *Sartre* (New York: Columbia University Press, 1984), 222ff.

53. See Fredric Jameson, *Marxism and Form* (Princeton: Princeton University Press, 1971), 378–79, 406–7.

54. Jameson, *Sartre*, 222–23.

55. Adorno, *Aesthetic Theory*, 33–34. Even the most austere and solipsistic individualism is situated in a predicament of power to which the individual responds. For a remarkable literary exploration of the antinomies of solipsistic effacing, see Enrique Vila-Matas, *Doctor Pasavento* (Barcelona: Anagrama, 2005).

56. Cf. Theodor W. Adorno, *Negative Dialectics*, trans. E. B. Ashton (New York: Continuum, 1973), 33–34, 144–46, 170–72, 183–86.

57. Cf. Terry Eagleton, *Sweet Violence* (Oxford: Blackwell, 2003), xii–xvi.

58. See Beauvoir, *Philosophical Writings*, 182.

59. Cf. Gillian Rose, *Love's Work* (New York: Schocken, 1995), 129.

60. For instance, Jameson's contribution to the dialectical legacy receives comprehensive and perforce more critical treatment in a book to appear, tentatively titled "Wayward Dialectics."

61. Cf. Wallace Stevens, *Collected Poetry and Prose* (New York: Library of America, 1997), 878.

1. HISTORICIZING THE ETHICAL TURN

1. See Peter Dews, "Uncategorical Imperatives," *Radical Philosophy* 111 (January/February 2002): 33–37. See also Marjorie B. Garber, Beatrice Hanssen, and Rebecca L. Walkowitz, eds., *The Turn to Ethics* (New York: Routledge, 2000).

2. Think of, say, James Tully's formidable ethical politics; see *Public Philosophy in a New Key*, 2 vols. (Cambridge: Cambridge University Press, 2008). I have

written about Tully in "At the Edges of Civic Freedom," in Robert Nichols and Jakeet Singh, eds., *Freedom and Democracy in an Imperial Context* (Oxon: Routledge, 2014), 48–70; for Tully's forceful response, see pp. 233–48. That there has been such a turn, however, is undeniable. Witness the proliferation of titles such as *The Ethics of . . . / Ethics and . . .* which then go on to encompass reading, writing, immigration, democracy, nationalism, business, corporations, and so on.

3. Alain Badiou, *Ethics*, trans. Peter Hallward (London: Verso, 2001), 90.

4. See Ella Myers, *Worldly Ethics* (Durham: Duke University Press, 2013), 1.

5. See, inter alia, Raymond Geuss, *Outside Ethics* (Princeton: Princeton University Press, 2005), 40–66.

6. Ibid., 9.

7. Raymond Geuss, *A World Without Why* (Princeton: Princeton University Press, 2014), 175–76.

8. Ibid., 175.

9. Christoph Henning, *Philosophie nach Marx* (Bielefeld: Transcript, 2005), 18, 556–57.

10. See Fredric Jameson, *Fables of Aggression* (London: Verso, 2008 [1979]), 56; cf. Jameson, *The Ideologies of Theory* (London: Verso, 2008), 189–93.

11. See Fredric Jameson, "Exit Sartre," *London Review of Books*, 7 July 1994, 12–14.

12. See Fredric Jameson, *Valences of the Dialectic* (London: Verso, 2009), 406, and *The Antinomies of Realism* (London: Verso, 2013), 115ff.

13. See Régis Debray, *I.F. suite et fin* (Paris: Gallimard, 2000), 95–106.

14. Ibid., 101.

15. See Daniel Bensaïd, *Le nouvel internationalisme* (Paris: Textuel, 2003), 47–54, 123ff.; and Paulo Eduardo Arantes, *Extinção* (São Paulo: Boitempo, 2007), 31–98.

16. Chantal Mouffe, "Which Ethics for Democracy?" in Garber, *The Turn to Ethics*, 86; see also Mouffe, *On the Political* (London: Verso, 2005), 72–76. Mouffe's statement only makes sense if it is taken as a tacit reference to such absence on the left.

17. Wendy Brown, *Politics Out of History* (Princeton: Princeton University Press, 2001), 29. Cf. Stuart Hall, *The Hard Road to Renewal* (London: Verso, 1988), 273.

18. On the idea of "metacommentary," see Jameson, *The Ideologies of Theory*, 5–76.

19. See Samuel Moyn, *The Last Utopia* (Cambridge: Harvard University Press, 2010), passim. For a critique, see Robin Blackburn, "Reclaiming Human Rights," *New Left Review* 69 (May-June 2011): 126–38. See also Moyn's "The Continuing Perplexities of Human Rights," *Qui Parle* 22 (Fall/Winter 2013): 95–115. With the onset of the cold war, there was another equally anti-Marxist ethical turn, which is relevant for an understanding of Levinas's ethics of the Other. See chapter 4, this volume.

20. Moyn, *The Last Utopia*, 220ff.

21. Even so, the logic of their historical eventuation as part of the same political constellation has yet to be unraveled. It is thought that Moyn is currently at work on it.

22. Moyn, *The Last Utopia*, 221.

23. See, respectively, Régis Debray, *Le moment fraternité* (Paris: Gallimard, 2009), 165; and Enzo Traverso, *El final de la modernidad judía*, trans. Gustau Muñoz (Buenos Aires: Fondo de Cultural Económica, 2014), 201ff.

24. For a discussion, see Antonio Y. Vázquez-Arroyo, "How Not to Learn from Catastrophe," *Political Theory* 41 (October 2013): 738–65 (especially 743–48).

25. Étienne Balibar, "Toward a Diasporic Citizen?," *The Creolization of Theory*, ed. Françoise Lionnet and Shu-mei Shih (Durham: Duke University Press, 2011), 212.

26. See, for instances, Etienne Balibar, "On the Politics of Human Rights," *Constellations* 20 (March 2013): 18–26; James D. Ingram, *Radical Cosmopolitics* (New York: Columbia University Press, 2013), 226ff.; and Robin Blackburn, *The American Crucible* (London: Verso, 2011), 477ff.

27. See Perry Anderson, "Imperium," *New Left Review* 83 (September-October 2013): 5–111; and Josep Fontana, *Por el bien del imperio* (Barcelona: Pasado & Presente, 2011), passim. Fontana offers a remarkable global history of the rise of American imperial hegemony after 1945 and provides a wealth of detail that independently confirms the main tenets of Anderson's essay.

28. See Mahmood Mamdani, *Saviors and Survivors* (New York: Pantheon, 2009), passim.

29. Robert Meister, "Human Rights and the Politics of Victimhood," *Ethics and International Affairs* 16 (September 2002): 91.

30. For a caustic critique of "the consecration of human rights" and its healing role as the civil religion of the North Atlantic West, see Debray, *Le moment fraternité*, 113–234. Cf. Marcel Gauchet, "Le droits de l'homme ne son pas une politique," *Le Débat* 3 (July-August 1980): 3–21. However much resonance could at first glance be perceived between Debray's scathing account of "the religion of human rights," and its disavowals of political responsibility in the name of ethical responsibility, with Gauchet's critique of the depoliticizing drive of human rights, the political impulses animating the two thinkers are drastically opposed, as are the terms upon which their respective critiques are couched. The distance between the two is best seen in their views of "totalitarianism": while Gauchet's reliance on the totalitarian/democracy dyad is notorious, Debray's trenchant critique of it during its heyday, when figures like Gauchet were riding the tide of "the antitotalitarian moment" of the late seventies, is no less so. Debray's mordant formulation, "In the arsenal of our 'political science' *totalitarianism* has roughly played the same role as *fanaticism* in the Enlightenment, and *totemism* in primitive anthropology: an alibi for misrecognition and a ritual of conjuration"; see Régis Debray, *Critique de la raison politique* (Paris: Gallimard, 1981), 22.

31. See Robert Meister, *After Evil* (New York: Columbia University Press, 2011), 316.
32. Ibid., 301.
33. See Theodor W. Adorno, *Guilt and Defense*, ed. Jeffrey K. Olick and Andrew J. Perrin (Cambridge: Harvard University Press, 2010), passim.
34. Meister, *After Evil*, 303.
35. For an overview of this history, see Jan Eckel and Samuel Moyn, eds., *The Breakthrough* (Philadelphia: University of Pennsylvania Press, 2014), 87–124. As Patrick William Kelly accurately writes, "the turn to human rights represented a significant scaling back of the parameters of social change, especially for Latin Americans who once longed for revolution and the enactment of a socialist state" (89). Even at its most robust, this discourse has been defensive and never systematically questioned the liberal-capitalist mainstay structuring postdictatorial orders.
36. Explaining what he calls a "rebirth of politics in the spirit of morality," Jan Eckel has suggested the advent of human rights in the seventies represented "a profoundly moral yet multifaceted way of revitalizing politics"—see Eckel and Moyn, *The Breakthrough*, 252. Yet the word "multifaceted" is misleading, as every significant instance of revitalized politics adduced consists of either the neutralization or pacification of the political field amidst, or the restoration of, a liberal-capitalist order.
37. Meister, *After Evil*, 47, 48.
38. Esther Benbassa, *Suffering as Identity*, trans. G. M. Goshgarian (London: Verso, 2010), 2–3.
39. See Mahmood Mamdani, "The Politics of Naming," *London Review of Books*, 8 March 2007, 5–8. Also relevant: Enzo Traverso, *L'histoire comme champ de bataille* (Paris: La Découverte, 2012), 59–183 and Étienne Balibar, *Violence et civilité* (Paris: Galilée, 2010), 9–142, 251–321. On "structural violence," see *New Political Science* 34 (June 2012): 191–227.
40. Jacques Rancière, "The Ethical Turn of Aesthetics and Politics," *Critical Horizons* 7 (2006): 1–20.
41. On autonomy and fields, see inter alia, Pierre Bourdieu, *Pascalian Meditations*, trans. Richard Nice (Stanford: Stanford University Press, 1997), passim.
42. Rancière, "The Ethical Turn of Aesthetics and Politics," 2 (emphasis added).
43. Ibid.
44. See Fredric Jameson, *Postmodernism, or, the Cultural Logic of Late Capitalism* (Durham: Duke University Press, 1991); and *The Cultural Turn* (London: Verso, 1998). Still the best critical discussion is found in Perry Anderson, *The Origins of Postmodernity* (London: Verso, 1998).
45. Rancière, "The Ethical Turn of Aesthetics and Politics," 3. Cf. Theodor W. Adorno, *Problems of Moral Philosophy*, trans. Rodney Livingstone (Stanford: Stanford University Press, 2000), 142–43.
46. León Rozitchner, *Moral burguesa y revolución* (Buenos Aires: Procyon, 1963), passim. On Rozitchner's intellectual itinerary, see Bruno Bosteels, *Marx and Freud in Latin America* (London: Verso, 2007), 97–157, cf. 304–10.

47. Rancière, "The Ethical Turn of Aesthetics and Politics," 9, see also 18–19.

48. For further discussion, see Vázquez-Arroyo, "How Not to Learn from Catastrophe."

49. Rancière, "The Ethical Turn of Aesthetics and Politics," 18.

50. Gillian Rose, *The Broken Middle* (Oxford: Blackwell, 1992), xi.

51. Gillian Rose, *Judaism and Modernity* (Oxford: Blackwell, 1993), 6.

52. Rose, *The Broken Middle*, xii.

53. Gillian Rose, *Mourning Becomes the Law* (Cambridge: Cambridge University Press, 1995), 3, 4.

54. Gillian Rose, *Paradiso* (London: Menard, 1999), 42–43.

55. Rose, *The Broken Middle*, 267; cf. G. W. F. Hegel, *Phenomenology of Spirit*, trans. A. V. Miller (Oxford: Oxford University Press, 1977), 228–37.

56. An aspect of this political ethic she allegorized by way of her beautiful retelling of the story of King Arthur—see Rose, *Love's Work*, 121ff.

57. For a meticulous historical account of the turn to ethics in French thought, see Julian Bourg, *From Revolution to Ethics* (Montreal: McGill-Queen's University Press, 2007). Bourg's book is best read alongside Michael Scott Christofferson's excellent book, *French Intellectuals Against the Left* (Oxford: Berghahn, 2004). These books provide accounts of the French intellectual and political scenes after 1968 that should put paid to the moralism, willful misreading, and liberal pieties marring the influential work of Tony Judt. For searching assessments of Judt's writings, see Dylan Riley, "Tony Judt," *New Left Review* 71 (September-October 2011): 31–63; and Julian Bourg, "Blame It on Paris," *French Historical Studies* 35 (Winter 2012): 181–97.

58. Bourg, *From Revolution to Ethics*, 5.

59. A prominent figure in the Anglo-American scene, whose recent work has taken an ethicist cast, is the Italian political thinker Antonio Negri. As influential as the political experience of the Italian '68 has been, it was his encounter with Gilles Deleuze in the early 1980s that proved most crucial, or, as Negri himself has put it, "I can truly say that I went to wash my clothes in the Seine!" See Cesare Casarino and Antonio Negri, *In Praise of the Common* (Minneapolis: University of Minnesota Press, 2008), 57ff. and 136. A fine historical account of the Italian '68 is found in Paul Ginsborg, *A History of Contemporary Italy* (Harmondsworth: Penguin, 1990), 298–347. See also Perry Anderson, *The New Old World* (London: Verso, 2009), 326–51; Rossana Rossanda, *The Comrade from Milan*, trans. Romy Clark Giuliani (London: Verso, 2010), 287ff.; and Lucio Magri, *The Tailor of Ulm*, trans. Patrick Camiller (London: Verso, 2011), 195–243. Of interest is Mario Tronti, "Our Operaismo," *New Left Review* 73 (January-February 2012): 119–39.

60. See Anderson, *The New Old World*, 221–22.

61. On the Green Party, see Werner Hülsberg, *The German Greens*, trans. Greg Fagan (London: Verso, 1988), 64–139; on the Red Army Faction, see Stefan Aust, *The Baader-Meinhof Complex*, trans. Anthea Bell (Oxford: Oxford University Press, 2009). See also Uli Edel's film *The Baader-Meinhof Complex*

(MPI Media Group, 2009), itself an adaption of Aust's book. Unlike the book, which is marred by many a colorful psychologizing and moralizing statement, the film captures the different layers of complexity and nuance in the actions of the RAF and the predicaments of power, as well as the generational differences.

62. See Hans Kundnani, *Utopia or Auschwitz* (New York: Columbia University Press, 2009), 1–28. He writes: "'1968' in Germany was therefore a moral movement before it was a political one" (11).

63. See Theodor W. Adorno, *Negative Dialectics*, trans. E. B. Ashton (New York: Continuum, 1973), 365. In his 1965 lectures, Adorno elaborated on its meanings by connecting Auschwitz to Vietnam; see Theodor W. Adorno, *Metaphysics*, trans. Edmund Jephcott (Stanford: Stanford University Press, 2000), 101.

64. For the significance of 1945 and 1968 for Habermas, see Martin Beck Matuštík's intellectual portrait, *Jürgen Habermas* (Lanham: Rowman and Littlefield, 2001), passim.

65. See Kristin Ross, *May '68 and Its Afterlives* (Chicago: University of Chicago Press, 2002), passim. This is a fine study of the historical roots of May 1968, offering a compelling periodization, which extends before (the Algerian War) and after (the counterculture of the 1970s) May of that momentous year.

66. A "fetishism of the event," which, as Daniel Bensaïd once eloquently suggested, misrecognizes "a strategic concept" and recasts it "as the deus ex machina of a history lacking any compass," rather than as part of a profane philosophy of history in which "awakening," and recommencement, "tie the necessity of historical determinations to the contingency of the event, making it possible to grasp on the wing the opportunity of a conjuncture"—see Daniel Bensaïd, *An Impatient Life: A Political Memoir,* trans. David Fernbach (London: Verso, 2013), 88, 204, 290–91.

67. See Christofferson, *French Intellectuals Against the Left*, 174–75, 270–74.

68. See Kundnani, *Utopia or Auschwitz*, 8–9.

69. On Mexico's '68, see Jorge Volpi, *La imaginación y el poder* (Mexico, DF: Era, 1998); and Bruno Bosteels, "Travesías del fantasma," *Metapolítica* 3 (1999): 733–68. On its own ethical content, see Adolfo Sánchez Vázquez, *Ética* (Barcelona: Crítica, 1999), 7–8.

70. See Ross, *May '68 and Its Afterlives*, 65–79. Cf. Christofferson, *French Intellectuals Against the Left*, 49–56. On role of workers and class struggles during the French sixties, see Michael Seidman, *The Imaginary Revolution* (Oxford: Berghahn, 2004), especially chapters 2–3.

71. See Anderson, *The New Old World*, 140–54; and Bensaïd, *An Impatient Life*, 75.

72. But not everyone on the French left saw it that way: see Régis Debray, "A Modest Contribution to the Rites and Ceremonies of the Tenth Anniversary," *New Left Review* 115 (May-June 1979): 45–65. For a spirited if not entirely persuasive critique, see Ross, *May '68 and Its Afterlives*, 182–95.

73. Debray, *Le moment fraternité*, 178.

74. Christofferson, *Intellectuals Against the Left,*, 90.
75. See Claude Lefort, *Le temps présent* (Paris: Belin, 2007), 301–8. For critical discussions, see Christofferson, *Intellectuals Against the Left,* 4–18, 68–74, 184–228; Bourg, *From Revolution to Ethics,* 237–46; and Peter Dews, "The *Nouvelle Philosophie* and Foucault," *Economy and Society* 8 (May 1978): 127–71. Lefort, of course, partook in the assault on the left. For a discussion of Lefort and the politics of his two most prominent heirs—Marcel Gauchet and Miguel Abensour—see James D. Ingram, "The Politics of Claude Lefort," *Thesis Eleven* 87 (November 2006): 33–50. For the best survey of the historical debates around totalitarianism, see Enzo Traverso, *Le totalitarisme* (Paris: Seuil, 2001), 9–110.
76. Christofferson, *Intellectuals Against the Left,* 229–66; and Anderson, *The New Old World,* 154–59, 164–68. Cf. Marcel Gauchet, *La condición histórica,* trans. Esteban Molina (Madrid: Trotta, 2007), 120–25. See also Michael Scott Christofferson, "François Furet Between History and Journalism, 1958–1965," *French History* 15 (December 2001): 421–47. On the actual substance of Furet's contribution, see the Michael Scott Christofferson, "An Anti-Totalitarian History of the French Revolution," *French Historical Studies* 22 (Autumn 1999): 557–611.
77. See, for instance, Pierre Rosanvallon, *La démocratie inachevée* (Paris: Gallimard, 2000), 390ff. Reconstructions of the intellectual itineraries of Gauchet and Rosanvallon are found in Samuel Moyn, "Savage and Modern Liberty," *European Journal of Political Theory* 4 (April 2005): 164–87; and Andrew Jainchill and Samuel Moyn, "French Democracy Between Totalitarianism and Solidarity," *Journal of Modern History* 76 (March 2004): 107–54. These essays present scrupulous historical analyses that nevertheless invite a more searching critique than what these authors provide. For refreshing contrasts, see Anderson, *The New Old World,* 154–69, 202–9; and Jacob Collins, "A Metaphysics of Democracy," *New Left Review* 74 (March-April 2012): 145–53.
78. The expression is Bernard Henri-Levy's, as cited by Samuel Moyn, *Origins of the Other* (Ithaca: Cornell University Press, 2005), 236.
79. See, respectively, Bensaïd, *An Impatient Life,* 197; and Perry Anderson, *In the Tracks of Historical Materialism* (London: Verso, 1983), 32.
80. Bourg, *From Revolution to Ethics,* 5.
81. Ibid, 33–42; see also Ross, *May '68 and Its Afterlives,* 190–95.
82. According to Bourg, *Anti-Oedipus* represents a "certain peak," which is perhaps best characterized as a plateau—see *From Revolution to Ethics,* 171.
83. On *Tel Quel,* see Christofferson, *French Intellectuals Against the Left,* 206. For a discussion of the circle around *Le Débat,* see Gérard Noiriel, *Le fils maudits de la République* (Paris: Fayard, 2005), 103–99; and Enzo Traverso, *Ou sont passes les intellectuels?* (Paris: Textuel, 2013), 52ff.
84. See Fredric Jameson, "Après the Avant Garde," *London Review of Books,* 12 December 1996, 5–7. See also Riley, "Tony Judt," 35–38; and Jameson, "Exit Sartre."

85. For an eloquent representative, see David Bromwich, *Moral Imagination* (Princeton: Princeton University Press, 2014), 3–179. Intellectually lucid and elegantly written, these essays constitute an exhibit of the assortments of heroes—obviously Lincoln, alongside Whitman and Martin Luther King Jr.—and commonplaces that define the American tradition of ethical politics mediating the advent of the turn to ethics.

86. For a powerful sociological dissection of these trends, see Robert Castel, *El ascenso de las incertidumbres*, trans. Víctor Goldstein (Buenos Aires: Fondo de Cultura Económica, 2010), passim.

87. Cf. Kristin Ross, "Historicizing Unseemliness," in Gabriel Rockhill and Philip Watts, eds., *Jacques Rancière* (Durham: Duke University Press, 2009), 17. Gauchet has candidly spoken about his Atlanticist disposition—see his *La condición histórica*, 35.

88. Bourg, *From Revolution to Ethics*, 303. This is not to say that the ethical turn exhausts the French intellectual scene of the late seventies and eighties. In addition to the aforementioned revival of political theory—even if, in the case of Aron, it betrays a moralizing tone in the form of occasional pleas for political responsibility or *responsible* exercise of political power, which actually amounts to a liberal anticommunist stance—a series of thinkers have built on the anthropological legacies of French thought to formulate impressive bodies of work that represent an original "attempt to rethink autonomous political collectivities along an anthropological axis." See Jacob Collins, "An Anthropological Turn?" *New Left Review* 78 (November-December 2012): 31–60. Curiously, Collins leaves out any consideration of Louis Dumont in this context; likewise, Georges Balandier is only cursorily mentioned as an influence on Debray.

89. See Vladimir Jankélévitch, *Le paradoxe de la morale* (Paris: Seuil, 1981), 7.

90. Ibid.

91. See Pierre Nora, "Mémoire et identité juives dans la France contemporain," *Le Débat* 131 (September-October 2004): 28.

92. León Rozitchner has emphasized these other determinants along with the loss of political illusions and the counterrevolutionary terror of right-wing dictatorships—see *Levinas o la filosofía de la consolación* (Buenos Aires: Biblioteca Nacional, 2013), 32, 27. In contrast, Enrique Dussel's work offers an ambitious attempt to recast Levinas's ethics in terms of a radical political theory and long predates the Lithuanian's ascendance in the North Atlantic world—see *Ética de la liberación en la edad de la globalización y la exclusión* (Madrid: Trotta, 1998), 359ff. The political and historical context out of which Dussel's philosophy emerged is reconstructed in Horacio Cerutti Guldberg, *Filosofía de la liberación latinoamericana* (Mexico, DF: Fondo de Cultura Económica, 2005).

93. See Jacques Derrida, *Writing and Difference*, trans. Alan Bass (Chicago: University of Chicago Press, 1978), 79–153. The essay was originally published in 1964. It was Paul Ricouer who introduced Derrida to *Totality and Infinity* in

the early sixties, which became a pivotal text in Derrida's own "religiously minded phenomenology." For a subtle discussion, see Edward Baring, *The Young Derrida and French Philosophy, 1945–1968* (Cambridge: Cambridge University Press, 2011), 267–73. On Ricouer's complex relationships with Derrida and Levinas, see François Dosse, *Paul Ricoeur*, trans. Pablo Corona (Buenos Aires: Fondo de Cultura Económica, 2013), especially 255–68, 391–96, 404–5, 676–97.

94. Derrida's protestations are found in Jacques Derrida, *Rouges*, trans. Pascale-Anne Brault and Michael Nass (Stanford: Stanford University Press, 2005), 39. For a careful discussion of Derrida's undeniable turn to ethical politics, see Jacob Rogozinski, *Faire part* (Paris: Lignes & Manifestes, 2005), 133–72.

95. Just how central structuralism was in the reformulation of Derrida's thought is carefully documented in Baring, *The Young Derrida and French Philosophy*, 190–220.

96. See Nancy Fraser, "The French Derrideans," *New German Critique* 33 (Autumn 1984): 127–54.

97. See Benoît Peeters, *Derrida* (Cambridge: Polity, 2013), 379–401.

98. Early on, to be sure, Derrida articulated a typical liberal response to the Algerian war—see Edward Baring, "Liberalism and Algeria," *Critical Inquiry* 36 (Winter 2010): 239–61.

99. Jonathan Culler, "Afterword," *South Atlantic Quarterly* (Winter 2011): 223–30.

100. For an account of periodization that bears directly on this question, see Jameson, *The Ideologies of Theory*, 483–515.

101. On the historicity of Theory, see: François Cusset, *French Theory*, trans. Jeff Fort (Minneapolis: University of Minnesota Press, 2008); Fredric Jameson, "Symptoms of Theory or Symptoms for Theory," *Critical Inquiry* 30 (Winter 2004): 403–8, and "How Not to Historicize Theory," *Critical Inquiry* 34 (Spring 2008): 563–82; Ian Hunter, "The History of Theory," *Critical Inquiry* 33 (Autumn 2006): 78–112; "Scenes from the History of Postructuralism," *New Literary History* 41 (Summer 2010): 491–516; Kenneth Surin, "Comparative Literature in America: Attempt at a Genealogy," in Ali Behdad and Dominic Thomas, eds., *A Companion to Comparative Literature* (Oxford: Blackwell, 2011): 65–72; Warren Breckman, "Times of Theory," *Journal of the History of Ideas* 71 (July 2010): 339–61, and "Theory Now," *The South Atlantic Quarterly* 110 (Winter 2011).

102. See Timothy Brennan, *Wars of Position* (New York: Columbia University Press, 2006), 9ff.; and Daniel T. Rodgers, *Age of Fracture* (Cambridge: Harvard University Press, 2011), 1–76.

103. Sheldon S. Wolin, "The Politics of the Study of Revolutions," *Comparative Politics* 5 (April 1973): 356.

104. See Sheldon S. Wolin, "The Destructive Sixties and Postmodern Conservatism," in Stephen Macedo, ed., *Reassessing the Sixties* (New York: Norton, 1997), 129–56, "A Look Back at the Ideas That Led to the Events, *New York Times*, 26 July 1998, *Politics and Vision* (Princeton: Princeton University Press,

2004), xv–xxi, 581ff., and *Democracy Incorporated* (Princeton: Princeton University Press, 2008), 95–107, 211–21.

105. See Fontana, *Por el bien del imperio*, 377–78.

106. See Herbert Marcuse, *Eros and Civilization* (Boston: Beacon, 1954), chapter 10, and *One-Dimensional Man* (Boston: Beacon, 1964), 72–83.

107. For an account, see Rodgers, *Age of Fractures*, 155–79.

108. Geoffrey Galt Harpham, *Shadows of Ethics* (Durham: Duke University Press, 1999), 18–37.

109. Ibid., 65.

110. See Sheldon S. Wolin, "The American Pluralist Conception of Politics," in Arthur L. Caplan and Daniel Callahan, eds., *Ethics in Hard Times* (New York: Plenum, 1981), 228ff. Notice how in 1981 Wolin recorded the intrusion of "ethicists" as part of elite-level attempts to manufacture consensus, a development he referred to as "a recent innovation in the practice of pluralism" (223). Yet it merely presaged a larger concatenation that would define the next two decades in which ethical language has come to colonize political life; see Wendy Brown, *Regulating Aversion* (Princeton: Princeton University Press, 2006), 1–24, 48–77.

111. See Barbara J. Keys, *Reclaiming American Virtue* (Cambridge: Harvard University Press, 2014), passim. Keys carefully documents Carter's belated embrace of human rights, along with the relative political fluidity of other devotees.

112. In contrast to the French embracing of human rights, in the U.S., anticommunism ran in tandem with a selective, slanted, and truncated rhetorical critique of Latin American dictatorships. On the larger crystallization of a human rights discourse in the overall international context of the seventies, with attention to the United States, see Eckel and Moyn, *The Breakthrough*, 1–48, 88–106, 226–59.

113. Cf. Bourg, *From Revolution to Ethics*, 336–40.

2. RESPONSIBILITY *IN* HISTORY

1. See Manuel Cruz, *Las malas pasadas del pasado* (Barcelona: Anagrama, 2005), 53–54; and Carol Gluck, "*Sekinin*/Responsibility in Modern Japan," in Carol Gluck and Anna Lowenhaupt Tsing, eds., *Words in Motion* (Durham: Duke University Press, 2009), 83–106.

2. The foregoing discussion is indebted to Lucien Lévy-Bruhl, *L'Idée de responsabilité* (Paris: Hachette, 1884); José Ferrater Mora, "Responsabilidad," in *Diccionario de filosofía*, 2 vols. (Buenos Aires: Sudamericana, 1951); Nicola Abbagnano, "Responsabilità," in *Dizionario di filosofia* (Turin: Utet, 1971); Michel Villey, "Esquisse historique sur le mot responsable," *Archives de philosophie du droit* 22 (1977): 45–58; and Manuel Cruz, *Hacerse cargo* (Barcelona: Paidós, 1999).

3. On the history of occidental ethics, see Alasdair MacIntyre, *A Short History of Ethics*, 2d ed. (Notre Dame: University of Notre Dame Press, 1998); and

Victoria Camps, *Breve historia de la ética* (Barcelona: RBA, 2013). See also Roger Crisp, ed., *The Oxford Handbook of the History of Ethics* (Oxford: Oxford University Press, 2012); and Terence Erwin, *The Development of Ethics*, 3 vols. (Oxford: Oxford University Press, 2011).

4. See, inter alia, J. Peter Euben, John Wallach, Josiah Ober, ed., *Athenian Political Thought and the Reconstruction of American Democracy* (Ithaca: Cornell University Press, 1994); Josiah Ober and Charles Hendrick, ed., *Demokratia* (Princeton: Princeton University Press, 1996); Kurt Raaflaub, Josiah Ober, Robert Wallace, ed., *Origins of Democracy in Ancient Greece* (Berkeley: University of California Press, 2007). On mediating antecedents, see Michael Mann, *The Sources of Social Power,* 4 vols. (Cambridge: Cambridge University Press, 1986–2012), 1:73–230. For a corrective of the unreflective Hellenocentrism, see Enrique Dussel, *Política de la liberación: historia mundial y crítica* (Madrid: Trotta, 2007), 11–66; but some of Dussel's historical claims are occasionally weak, and the less said about his etymological conceits the better. For succinct depiction of Athenian democracy, see G. E. M. de Ste. Croix, *The Class Struggle in the Ancient Greek World* (Ithaca: Cornell University Press, 1981), 283–85. An extended portrait is found in Luciano Canfora, *El mundo de Atenas*, trans. Edgardo Dobry (Barcelona: Anagrama, 2014), 13–170—see also *La guerra civile ateniese* (Milan: Rizzoli, 2013), passim.

5. See Ellen Meiksins Wood, *Citizens to Lords* (London: Verso, 2008), 28–50, and *Peasant-Citizen and Slave* (London: Verso, 1997), passim. Cf. Ste. Croix, *The Class Struggle in the Ancient Greek World*, 140–47.

6. Say, in Genesis 25, Exodus 9 and 20, or in Jeremiah 31:30 and Ezekiel 18. For an argument about the presence of an ethical politics, and a practice of responsibility, in the Hebrew Bible, see Michael Walzer, *In God's Shadow* (New Haven: Yale University Press, 2012), 111–25, 152, 199ff.

7. Cf. Roger Crisp, "Homeric Ethics," in *The Oxford Handbook of the History of Ethics*, 1–20. For a memorable discussion of fate and character in Homer, see Erich Auerbach, *Dante: Poet of the Secular World*, trans. Ralph Manheim (New York: NYRB, 2007), 1–3.

8. See Canfora, *El mundo de Atenas*, 74, cf. 100ff. But it is Thucydides who delivered the most trenchant account of political responsibility in violent predicaments of power defined by the Athenian empire and its wars, along with the demise of democracy and the monetary surge of an oligarchic order, in book 8 of his *History of the Peloponnesian War*.

9. For a fine overview, see Paula Gottlieb, "Aristotle's Ethics," in *The Oxford Handbook of the History of Ethics*, 44–72. See also Jill Frank, *A Democracy of Distinction* (Chicago: University of Chicago Press, 2005), chapter 1.

10. See Aristotle, *Nicomachean Ethics*, 1110b–11a24, 1179a35–79b5; and *Physics*, 194b17–195a15.

11. See Aristotle, *Nicomachean Ethics*, 1094a18–22 and 1112b10–15. See chapter 6, this volume.

12. For an account of prudence in Aristotle, see Pierre Aubenque, *La prudence chez Aristote* (Paris: Presses Universitaires de France, 1963), 64ff.; especially instructive is Aubenque's discussion of the centrality of limits in his conception of deliberation, responsibility, and judgment.

13. See Sheldon S. Wolin, *Politics and Vision* (Princeton: Princeton University Press, 2004), 83. On the Roman Empire as the first "true territorial empire," see Mann, *The Sources of Social Power*, 1:250–300.

14. Wolin, *Politics and Vision*, 85. Other accounts that I have found instructive are Carlo Galli, *Spazi politici* (Bologna: Il Mulino, 2001), 19–26; and Wood, *Citizens to Lords*, 99–163.

15. Wolin, *Politics and Vision*, 63. For a suggestive discussion of Aristotle that bears on questions of political space, see Mary G. Dietz, "Between Polis and Empire," *American Political Science Review* 106 (May 2012): 275–93.

16. Albeit these were not entirely secondary for Wolin—see *Politics and Vision*, 70.

17. Ibid., 69.

18. In Ellen Meiksins Wood's rendering, "The Roman Republic, and the Roman law, encouraged a perception of a clearly defined public sphere and a conception of the state as a formal entity apart from the citizens who comprised it, even distinct from the particular persons who governed them at any given moment"; see Wood, *Citizens to Lords*, 140.

19. Wolin, *Politics and Vision*, 83. It is important not to conflate Wolin's argument with any nostalgic lament or polis envy; see Wolin's "History and Theory," in John S. Nelson, ed., *Tradition, Interpretation, and Science* (Albany: State University of New York Press, 1986), 43–68.

20. Cf. Villey, "Esquisse historique sur le mot responsable," 46–52.

21. See *Oxford Latin Dictionary*, 2d ed., s.v. "respondeo" and "spondeo."

22. But this contrast between the visual and the abstract need not suggest that a visual politics is always participatory and decentralized. See Lauro Martines, *Power and Imagination* (Baltimore: Johns Hopkins University Press, 1988), 55.

23. For a fine overview of Cicero's political thought, see E. M. Atkins, "Cicero," *The Cambridge History of Greek and Roman Political Thought*, ed. Christopher Rowe and Malcolm Schofield (Cambridge: Cambridge University Press, 2005), 477–516. Atkins argues that the centrality accorded to patriotism in Cicero "constitutes an original development in political thought" (514).

24. Giorgio Agamben, *Opus Dei*, trans. Adam Kotsko (Stanford: Stanford University Press, 2013), 67. Characteristically, Agamben offers shrewd local insights among unconvincing and misguided broad claims.

25. Needless to say, Cicero was hardly oblivious to violence and sought to establish some fetters on cruelty from the perspective of the ruling power (see *On Duties*, I.23, 82, II.29–30, 63). For a trenchant account of Cicero, see Ronald Syme, *The Roman Revolution* (Oxford: Oxford University Press, 2002), 135–48.

26. The phrase is Goldschmidt's, who pairs it with *devoirs d'état*, and shows how both require adjusting to circumstances; see Victor Goldschmidt, *Le système stoïcien et l'idée de temps* (Paris: Vrin, 1989), 155–56.

27. See Syme, *The Roman Revolution*, 145. Brown characterizes the period as one "of mounting crisis"; see Peter Brown, *Through the Eye of a Needle* (Princeton: Princeton University Press, 2012), 129.
28. See Cicero, *On Duties*, trans. Walter Miller (Cambridge: Loeb Classical Library, 1913), 60.
29. In Erich Auerbach's formulation, "Vergil was *the* poet of the Roman Empire. It was he who replaced the ancient Roman national (*sic*) sense of identity . . . with the new ideology of Rome's global vision"; see James I. Porter, ed., *Time, History, and Literature*, trans. Jane O. Newman (Princeton: Princeton University Press, 2014), 125. For penetrating discussions, see Syme, *The Roman Revolution*, 440–75; and David Quint, *Epic and Empire* (Princeton: Princeton University Press, 1993), 50–96. For an instructive treatment of the visual culture of the Augustan imperial order, and the republican imagery it replaced, see Paul Zanker, *The Power of Images in the Age of Augustus*, trans. Alan Shapiro (Ann Arbor: University of Michigan Press, 1990), passim; a consistently interesting treatment of Augustus's "first march to Rome" is found in Luciano Canfora, *Augusto figlio di Dio* (Bari: Laterza, 2015), 3–7, 292ff.
30. See Nicholas Xenos, "A Patria to Die For" (unpublished MS), 16.
31. This dialectic unfolded down to the late Middle Ages where political thought hibernated, as it were, in the context of theology without becoming entirely effaced; for a discussion, see Wolin, *Politics and Vision*, 118–26. For an excellent account of the earthliness of Christianity at the time, which appropriately contrasts it with Epicurean and Stoic tendencies "to remain at least inwardly free from earthly ties," see Auerbach, *Dante*, 14ff.
32. On the intermediary classes between the very rich few and the extremely poor, see Brown, *Through the Eye of a Needle*, 23ff.
33. Ibid., 48. In an earlier work Brown called this process "aristocratization"; see Peter Brown, *The World of Late Antiquity* (New York: Norton, 1989), 32. On the continuities and discontinuities of aristocratic power structures down to the early Middle Ages, see Chris Wickham, *Framing the Early Middle Ages* (Oxford: Oxford University Press, 2005), 153–238.
34. See Brown, *Through the Eye of a Needle*, 73–79, 81–83. Brown offers a pertinent warning about overemphasizing the continuities in these transitions. Even so, the overall picture of a transition in which the Church emerges as at once substitute and locus for civic life holds.
35. See Peter Brown, *The Rise of Western Christendom*, 2d ed. (Oxford: Blackwell, 2003), 53–58.
36. See Brown, *The World of Late Antiquity*, 108.
37. For a discussion, see Brown, *Through the Eye of a Needle*, 126–47.
38. On *officium*, see Agamben, *Opus Dei*, 69–76ff.
39. See Brown, *The Rise of Western Christendom*, 102–03; and *The World of Late Antiquity*, 135. Cf. Perry Anderson, *Passages from Antiquity to Feudalism* (London: Verso, 1974), 73.

40. On the use of "public" in this context see Chris Wickham,' "The 'Feudal Revolution,'" *Past and Present* 155 (May 1997): 202. Of course, the lords in question resorted to violence and domination outside the purview of public authority: in Wickham's caustic formulation, "Aristocrats were brutal in all periods; it was one of the signs of aristocracy" (197), a violence that became more recrudescent with the demise of Carolingian public power. On lordship violence, see Thomas Bisson, *The Crisis of the Twelfth Century* (Princeton: Princeton University Press, 2009), passim.

41. See Anderson, *Passages from Antiquity to Feudalism*, 148ff. See also Wood, *Citizens to Lords*, 171ff., and *Liberty and Property* (London: Verso, 2012), 6–7.

42. See Perry Anderson, *Lineages of the Absolutist State* (London: Verso, 1979), 36–37.

43. See Giovanni Tabacco, *The Struggle for Power in Medieval Italy*, trans. Rosalind Brown Jensen (Cambridge: Cambridge University Press, 1989), 37–72, 144–208, 321ff.; Chris Wickham, "The 'Feudal Revolution' and the Origins of the Italian City-Communes," *Transactions of the Royal Historical Society* 24 (December 2014): 29–55, and *Sleepwalking Into a New World* (Princeton: Princeton University Press, 2015), passim.

44. Their significance, however, is vastly overstated in accounts that portray these communes as "desirous of liberty" or the unmistakable point of departure of the early modern republican ideal of liberty. Cf. Quentin Skinner, *The Foundations of Modern Political Thought*, 2 vols. (Cambridge: Cambridge University Press, 1978), 1:3.

45. See Wickham, *Sleepwalking Into a New World*, 194ff.

46. See ibid., 6. Wickham observes that the debate among recent historians is about "the nature of the elites," not their dominance, as the elites presiding over the early communes were economically heterogeneous and their configuration varied across cities—see 11, 156–60.

47. Discussions of this office are found in Martines, *Power and Imagination*, 42–44; Jones, *The Italian City-State*, 405ff.; and Mario Ascheri, *La Città-Stato* (Bologna: Il Mulino, 2006), 101ff.

48. The *popolo* cannot be conflated with the Athenian *demos*, or with the Anglo-Saxon *people*, let alone the Latin American *pueblo*. And yet the presence of nobles and a large merchant class within it cannot erase the differences between its vindications and the onset of seigniorial rule that followed its demise. For a balanced account of the *popolo*, see Martines, *Power and Imagination*, 62ff.; cf. John M. Najemy, *A History of Florence, 1200–1575* (Oxford: Wiley-Blackwell, 2006), 35–62.

49. See Jones, *The Italian City-State*, 403–6; and Martines, *Power and Imagination*, 51–61. Indeed, the podestá often amounted to the substitution of consular elites in ruling these cities.

50. See Skinner, *The Foundations of Modern Political Thought*, 1:4; and Wood, *Liberty and Property*, 42; *Citizens to Lords*, 219ff.

51. For a discussion see Martines, *Power and Imagination*, 34–71.

52. See Bisson, *The Crisis of the Twelfth Century*, 368, 429, 497, 577.

53. See Philip Jones, *The Italian City-State* (Oxford: Oxford University Press, 1997), 55.

54. See Max Weber, *Economy and Society*, ed. Guenther Roth and Claus Wittich (Berkeley: University of California Press, 1978), 2:1339–72; and Anderson, *Lineages of the Absolutist State*, 148ff.

55. See Martines, *Power and Imagination*, 7–21; and Jones, *The Italian City-State*, 333–47.

56. See Nancy S. Struever, *Theory as Practice* (Chicago: University of Chicago Press, 1992); and Francis Goyet, *Les Audaces de la prudence* (Paris: Garnier, 2009). On the continuities and discontinuities in "the political use of the city," see Manfredo Tafuri, *Interpreting the Renaissance*, trans. Daniel Sherer (New Haven: Yale University Press, 2006), esp. 59–97.

57. See Niccolò Machiavelli, *Opere*, ed. Corrado Vivanti, 3 vols. (Torino: Einaudi-Gallimard, 1997–2005), 1:197.

58. For a thoughtful discussion, see Alasdair MacIntyre, *After Virtue* (Notre Dame: University of Notre Dame Press, 1981), 39–61.

59. Cf. Georg Simmel, *The Sociology of Georg Simmel*, ed. and trans. Kurt H. Wolff (New York: Free Press, 1950), 64–84, and *On Individuality and Social Forms*, ed. Donald N. Levine (Chicago: University of Chicago Press, 1971), 217–26.

60. See Galli, *Spazi politici*, 27–28.

61. See Wolin, *Politics and Vision*, 166–70.

62. See Blaise Pascal, *The Provincial Letters*, trans. A. J. Krailsheimer (Harmondsworth: Penguin, 1967), 135, *Les Provinciales*, ed. Michel Le Guern (Paris: Gallimard, 1987), 145.

63. For a stimulating discussion of "diachronic identity," see Vincent Descombes, *The Institutions of Meaning*, trans. Stephen Adam Schwartz (Cambridge: Harvard University Press, 2014), 149–54.

64. Cf. ibid., 137. Elsewhere, Descombes accurately argues that by attributing a diachronic identity to a group the historical changes supervening it, which in the case of political collectivities include changes in its political form, are more adequately grasped; see Vincent Descombes, *Les embarras de l'identité* (Paris: Gallimard, 2013), 249.

65. On the latter, see chapter 3, this volume; on Hobbes's conception of "obligation," see Raymond Polin, *Hobbes, Dieu et les hommes* (Paris: Presses Universitaires de France, 1981), 153–75. For the discursive context, see Quentin Skinner, *Visions of Politics*, 3 vols. (Cambridge: Cambridge University Press, 2002), 3:264–86.

66. Thomas Hobbes, *Leviathan*, ed. Richard Tuck (Cambridge: Cambridge University Press, 1996), 254.

67. See Polin, *Hobbes, Dieu et les hommes*, 207–33. For contrasting accounts of the exact relationship between ethics and politics in Hobbes, see, inter alia, Leo Strauss, *The Political Philosophy of Hobbes*, trans. Elsa M. Sinclair (Chicago: University of Chicago Press, 1963), 6–29, 108–28; C. B. Macpherson, *The Political Theory of Possessive Individualism* (Oxford: Oxford University Press, 1964),

78–81; and Richard Tuck, *Hobbes* (Oxford: Oxford University Press, 1989), 51–64.

68. Hobbes, *Leviathan*, 90.

69. See J. G. A. Pocock, *The Machiavellian Moment* (Princeton: Princeton University Press, 1975), 518. Cf. Polin, *Hobbes, Dieu et les hommes*, 107. Still highly instructive on Hobbes and representation is Raymond Polin, *Politique et philosophie chez Thomas Hobbes* (Paris: Presses Universitaires de France, 1953), 221–50; and Hanna Fenichel Pitkin, *The Concept of Representation* (Berkeley: University of California Press, 1967), 14ff. See also José María Hernández, *El retrato de un dios mortal* (Barcelona: Anthropos, 2002), 125–203.

70. Skinner records the novelty of this insight; see *Visions of Politics*, 2:368–404, 3:177–208.

71. Hobbes, *Leviathan*, 111.

72. Ibid., 112.

73. Ibid.

74. Ibid, 121.

75. How Hobbes tends to collapse the two is clearly seen in chapter 17; see ibid., 120.

76. This term is nowadays associated with Foucault-inspired discussions of neoliberalism to denote "the process whereby subjects are rendered individually responsible for a task which previously would have been the duty of another—usually a state agency—or would not have been recognized as a responsibility at all." See Pat O'Malley, s.v. "Responsibilization," in *The Sage Dictionary of Policing*. I herein invoke the term to highlight this early instantiation of the mechanism involved—namely, holding someone responsible in ways hitherto unavailable and without any shared power in determining one's fate—which in this context it is necessarily devoid of its neoliberal connotations. Also, my usage echoes verb-forms found in Romance languages: *responsabilisation* (French), *responsabilizar* (Spanish), *responsabilizzare* (Italian).

77. Hobbes, of course, is hardly the only early modern thinker theorizing a form of neutralization. A humanist writer like Alberico Gentili sought to analogously theorize and enact political neutralization, albeit through different means; see Carlo Galli, *Contingenza e necessità nella ragione politica moderna* (Bari: Laterza, 2009), 72–92. Cf. Richard Tuck, *The Rights of War and Peace* (Oxford: Oxford University Press, 1999), 109.

78. See Victoria Kahn, *Wayward Contracts* (Princeton: Princeton University Press, 2004), 57–79.

79. Hobbes, *Leviathan*, 112.

80. Ibid., 117. For this securitization and protection a "common power to keep them all in awe" is paramount (118; the need to keep subjects in "awe" is repeated throughout). For an insightful discussion of "the conversion of violence" in Hobbes, see Étienne Balibar, *Violence et civilité* (Paris: Galilée, 2010), 50–58; 349–60. "Conversion," as Balibar specifies it, consists of "a

sublimation or spiritualization, but also the transformation of violence into (historically) productive *force*, the annihilation of violence as a destructive force and its re-creation as an energy or power internal to institutions" (60). In the case of Hobbes this conversion is part of larger theoretical strategy of reducing political complexity and dehistoricizing space as part of a preemptive counterrevolutionary order seeking to theoretically conceive subjects that are calculable and predictable. For instructive discussions, see Sheldon S. Wolin, "Hobbes and the Culture of Despotism," in Mary G. Dietz, ed., *Thomas Hobbes and Political Theory* (Lawrence: University Press of Kansas, 1990), 9–36; and Khan, *Wayward Contracts*, 147–51. On the political uses of force in Hobbes, see Polin, *Politique et philosophie chez Thomas Hobbes*, 53ff.

81. See Sheldon S. Wolin, "Postmodern Politics and the Absence of Myth," *Social Research* 52 (Summer 1985): 235. Here it is worth reclaiming Kahn's aforementioned discussion of the anxiety about contracts and the sense of fragility lurking in even colossal constructions like Hobbes's.

82. Hobbes, *Leviathan*, 112–13.

83. On reason as a passion for order, see Remo Bodei, *Geometría de las pasiones*, trans. Isidro Rosas (Mexico, DF: Fondo de Cultura Económica, 1995), 84.

84. Hobbes, *Leviathan*, 114; see also 112–13.

85. Ibid., 114.

86. Ibid.

87. Cf. Pitkin, *The Concept of Representation*, 19–28.

88. This account of personation constitutes a departure from *De Cive* (1642), where the transfer of power to the sovereign takes place once and for all. In contrast, in *Leviathan* personation implies at once responsibility and limits. On the variations between the two books, see Noel Malcolm, "Editorial Introduction," in Thomas Hobbes, *Leviathan*, ed. Noel Malcolm, 3 vols. (Oxford: Oxford University Press, 2012), 1:12–24.

89. See Pitkin, *The Concept of Representation*, 20.

90. See Hobbes, *Leviathan* (ed. Malcolm), 2:388.

91. See Wood, *Liberty and Property*, passim.

92. In Wolin's formulation, "[Hobbes's] world is a bare place of abstract space and time, and his man is a de-historicized bit of matter in motion"; see "Hobbes and the Culture of Despotism," 25. Political space is thus pacified and neutralized. For a complementary discussion of the spatiality of *Leviathan*, see Galli, *Spazi politici*, 40–49, 51–72. See also Galli, *Contingenza e necessità nella ragione politica moderna*, 38–71. It is well known how Hobbes's formidable theoretical edifice sought to displace, among other things, the egalitarian sense of freedom associated with the Levellers. Less discussed, however, is how it also challenged the corollary sense of responsibility. For, built into the Leveller idea of democracy, there was a different sense of responsibility: the many "good laws" formulated after the Agreement of the People of 1647 included "responsibility of ministers to parliament." An idea not only at odds with his logic of sovereignty and personation but that also

required historically constituted spatial differentiations running against the smoothness of Hobbes's rather undifferentiated conception of space. See Christopher Hill, *The Experience of Defeat* (New York: Viking, 1984), 30. Not that these positions exhaust the range of invocations for responsibility. See, for instance, Richard Tuck, *Philosophy and Government, 1572–1651* (Cambridge: Cambridge University Press, 1993), 229–30. For a sobering assessment of seventeenth-century English republicanism, see Wood, *Liberty and Property*, 228–31.

93. See Paul Hazard, *The Crisis of the European Mind*, trans. J. Lewis May (New York: NYRB, 2013), 284ff.

94. See ibid., 330–31.

95. Rousseau's *Emile* (1762) articulates this transition. Also relevant are his musings on duty and obligation in the Sixth Walk of *Reveries of the Solitary Walker* (1782). On Rousseau's contribution, see Marshall Berman, *The Politics of Authenticity* (London: Verso 2009), 57ff.

96. See Benedict Anderson, *Imagined Communities* (London: Verso, 1991), 37–65; and D. A. Brading, *The First Americans* (Cambridge: Cambridge University Press, 1991), passim. On the centrality of space, its artificial production, and regularization, see Jürgen Osterhammel, *The Transformation of the World*, trans. Patrick Camiller (Princeton: Princeton University Press, 2014), 105.

97. See James Madison's contribution to *The Federalist Papers* (1787–88). Constant's views are explicitly set out in two works: his *Responsabilité des ministres* (1815) and in *Principes du politique* (1815). For the latter, see Benjamin Constant, *Political Writings*, ed. and trans. Biancamaria Fontana (Cambridge: Cambridge University Press, 1988), 227–50.

98. See Simón Bolívar, *Obras completas*, 3 vols. (Caracas: Librería Piñango, 1982), 3:674–97. On Bolívar, and Constant's influence on his thought, see Carolina Guerrero, *Liberalismo y republicanismo en el pensamiento de Bolívar* (Caracas: Universidad Central de Venezuela, 2005), passim.

99. See Alexander Hamilton, John Jay, and James Madison, *The Federalist*, ed. Jacob E. Cooke (Middletown: Wesleyan University Press, 1961), 195.

100. See Hamilton, Jay, and Madison, *The Federalist*, 193; on means/ends, see also Hamilton's comments in no. 23 (147). Wolin has acutely observed how Hamilton's "maxims turn out to be exclusively about power, and they promote a grandiose conception of it which foreshadows virtually all of Hamilton's later arguments"; see Wolin, *The Presence of the Past* (Baltimore: Johns Hopkins University Press, 1989), 97; on the conception of reason and rationality underpropping these maxims, see 100–19.

101. See Hamilton, Jay, and Madison, *The Federalist*, 194.

102. Ibid., 195–96.

103. Ibid., 256. Later on Madison writes about how certain powers constitute "necessary means of attaining a necessary end" and how "in every political institution, a power to advance the public happiness, involves a discretion which may be misapplied and abused" (no. 41); ibid., 268–69.

104. See Harvey C. Mansfield Jr., *Taming the Prince* (New York: Free Press, 1989), 247ff.

105. Hamilton, Jay, and Madison, *The Federalist*, 424.

106. Mansfield, *Taming the Prince*, 271.

107. Hamilton, Jay, and Madison, *The Federalist*, 423.

108. See, for instances, ibid., 140, 248–49 (nos. 22, 38). A not insignificant aspect of Madison's preference for republicanism over democracy is its susceptibility to expansion; see p. 63.

109. See Jason Frank, *Publius and Political Imagination* (Lanham: Rowman and Littlefield, 2014), 125ff.

110. For a discussion see Wolin, "The American Pluralist Conception of Politics," 241–56.

111. See Hamilton, Jay, and Madison, *The Federalist*, 62–65. That protection of property was the central concern, even when others are adduced, is clear by how much emphasis Madison places on it (58–59).

112. Ibid., 64 (emphasis added).

113. Ibid., 59.

114. Contemporary advocates of neo-Roman theories of liberty have similarly contributed to this trend. The moniker "neo-Roman" is Skinner's; see Quentin Skinner, *Liberty Before Liberalism* (Cambridge: Cambridge University Press, 1998). On the centrality of responsibility, see Maurizio Viroli, *Republicanism*, trans. Antony Shugaar (New York: Hill and Wang, 2002); and Philip Pettit, *A Theory of Freedom* (Oxford: Oxford University Press, 2001), 11ff., 105–24; and "Responsibility Incorporated," *Ethics* 117 (January 2007): 171–201. Pettit's republicanism advocates a modicum of depoliticization that acquiesces with the forms of depoliticized politics that have come to define the present – see "Depoliticizing Democracy," *Ratio Juris* 17 (March 2004): 52–65.

115. See Jules Michelet, *Historie de la Révolution français*, 2 vols. (Paris: Gallimard, 1952), 1:406; see also 21ff. Cf. Edgar Quinet, *La Révolution* (Paris: Belin, 1987), 149–90.

116. See Arno J. Mayer, *The Furies* (Princeton: Princeton University Press, 1999), 148–50, 533ff.; and Eric J. Hobsbawm, *The Age of Revolution* (New York: Vintage, 1996), 77–98.

117. This is not to deny the constitutive tensions between the spatial logics of capitalism and the territorial nation-states necessary for the stable reproduction of capitalist social relations. See Perry Anderson, *English Questions* (London: Verso, 1992), 112; and Robert Brenner, "What Is, and What Is Not, Imperialism," *Historical Materialism* 14 (2006): 79–105; cf. Pierre Rosanvallon, *Le capitalisme utopique* (Paris: Seuil, 1979), 89–112, 229ff.

118. At the outset of *Responsabilité des ministres,* Constant writes: "La responsabilité des Ministres est la condition indispensable de toute monarchie constitutionnelle."

119. Instructive treatments of Constant's political thought are found in Lucien Jaume, *L'individu effacé* (Paris: Fayard, 1997), 63–117, 185–92; Andreas Kalyvas

and Ira Katznelson, *Liberal Beginnings* (Cambridge: Cambridge University Press, 2008), 146–75; and Marcel Gauchet's essays in Benjamin Constant, *Écrits politiques* (Paris: Gallimard, 1997), 11–110, and *La condition politique* (Paris: Gallimard, 2005), 277–304.

120. On the 1798, see Aurelian Craiutu, *A Virtue for Courageous Minds* (Princeton: Princeton University Press, 2012), 214; the 1819 speech is found in Constant, *Political Writings*, 309–28.

121. See Constant, *Political Writings*, 239. On Constant's views of political responsibility, see Mary S. Hartman, "Benjamin Constant and the Question of Ministerial Responsibility in France, 1814–1815," *Journal of European Studies* 6 (1976): 248–61; and Lucien Jaume, "Le concept de 'responsabilité des ministres' chez Benjamin Constant," *Revue française de Droit constitutionnel* 42 (2000): 227–43.

122. Constant, *Political Writings*, 239. For his views on arbitrary power, see also *Des réactions politiques* (1797), in Benjamin Constant, *De la force du gouvernement actuel de la France et de la nécessité de s'y rallier—Des réactions politiques—Des effets de la Terreur*, ed. Philippe Raynaud (Paris: Flammarion, 1998), 141–52.

123. Cf. Jaume, "Le concept de 'responsabilité des ministres' chez Benjamin Constant," 235–36. Here, as elsewhere, Constant struggled with a contradiction stemming from liberalism's colonization of democracy: it presupposes a politicalness (and its corollary sense of political responsibility), which it actively undermines. For a discussion see Antonio Y. Vázquez-Arroyo, "Liberal Democracy and Neoliberalism," *New Political Science* 30 (June 2008): 141–45.

124. Alexis de Tocqueville, *Democracy in America*, trans. Arthur Goldhammer (New York: Library of America, 2004), 44, 103, *Œuvres*, ed. André Jardin, 2 vols. (Paris: Gallimard, 1992), 2:43, 101. Subsequent references will be given to the English edition followed by French original (i.e., 44/43, 103/101).

125. For instance, when he speaks of "the sole responsibility for the laws," the connotation of responsibility is that of *chargés*; or elsewhere that of *se charge*. See ibid., 240/238, 278/278, and 422/424.

126. Ibid., 155/153, 235/233. Apropos of this question in relation to executive power, see 174/173.

127. For all his notorious admiration of New England localism, the category of the citizen is truncated in the theoretical armature of Tocqueville's reflections. On Tocqueville's "social" concept of democracy, see Jack Lively, *The Social and Political Thought of Alexis de Tocqueville* (Oxford: Oxford University Press, 1962), 71–126; see also Lucien Jaume, *Tocqueville*, trans. Arthur Goldhammer (Princeton: Princeton University Press, 2013), 15–93.

128. Giuseppe Mazzini, *The Duties of Man and Other Essays* (London: Everyman's Library, n.d.), 28–39, 39–40.

129. By just glancing at Mazzini's account of responsibility, one can better grasp what Nietzsche was trying to debunk. For this defender of "historical sense"

knew exactly what was happening in European politics and sought to subvert it by, among other things, recasting responsibility in ways that dirempted it from the social matrix avowed by the likes of Mazzini. See, for instance, Friedrich Nietzsche, *The Gay Science*, trans. Walter Kaufmann (New York: Vintage, 1974), 80. For a discussion, see Domenico Losurdo, *Nietzsche, il ribelle aristocratico* (Turin: Bollati Boringhieri, 2002), 295, 370–73; on his "robust sense of history," see 386–87.

130. See Anderson, *English Questions*, 118.

131. Fernando Ortiz, *Contrapunteo Cubano del tabaco y del azúcar* (Madrid: Cátedra, 2002), 213.

132. At the very least, as Wolin once observed, "political responsibility has traditionally connoted a form of responsibility owed to a general constituency," and that is precisely what ideas of responsible corporate management increasingly undermined, as their locus of responsibility was not the political collectivity, but groups within it. And even then it threatened to become tenuous; see Wolin, *Politics and Vision*, 388.

133. See John Stuart Mill's *A System of Logic* (1843), in *Collected Works of John Stuart Mill*, ed. J. M. Robson (Indianapolis: Liberty Fund, 2006), 8:861–74. On "the idea of character," see Stefan Collini, *Public Moralists* (Oxford: Oxford University Press, 1991), 91–118. The actual sociological content of these theorizations, and the moralization of poverty these often reverted to, is sharply described in Gareth Stedman Jones, *Outcast London* (New York: New Press, 1984), 262ff.

134. See Enrica Villari, "Il dovere," in *Il Romanzo*, ed. Franco Moretti, 4 vols. (Torino: Einaudi, 2003), 1:449.

135. See, inter alia, Alain Supiot, "Grandeur and Misery of the Social State," *New Left Review* 82 (July-August 2013): 99–113, *The Spirit of Philadelphia*, trans. Saskia Brown (London: Verso, 2012), 117–28, and *La gouvernance par les nombres* (Paris: Fayard, 2015), 388ff.; and François Ewald, *L'état providence* (Paris: Grasset, 1986), esp. 9–140, 225ff. Heir of Foucault and de facto executor of his intellectual estate, Ewald subsequently became a staple in the French corporate world, "the house intellectual of the French insurance industry"; see Michael C. Behrent, "Accidents Happen," *Journal of Modern History* 82 (September 2010): 585–624.

136. Ewald refers to the 1898 piece of legislation enacting this change as a "philosophical event" (*évènement philosophique*); see Ewald, *L'état providence*, 9; 143–91 (on risk).

137. See ibid., 191, 283–87, 349–51, 600.

138. In Supiot's succinct formulation: "Whoever experiences the benefits bears the burdens, and is therefore liable"; see Supiot, *The Spirit of Philadelphia*, 122.

139. See Karl Marx and Friedrich Engels, *The Communist Manifesto* (London: Verso, 1998), 51–62. The idea of interpreting Marx's proletariat as an attempt "to revive the dormant ideal of a politically active demos" is Wolin's; see his *Politics and Vision*, xix.

140. See Arno J. Mayer, "Internal Crises and War Since 1870," in Charles L. Bertrand, ed., *Revolutionary Situations in Europe* (Montréal: Centre Universitaires, 1977), 201–32.

141. See, inter alia, Arno J. Mayer, *The Persistence of the Old Regime* (New York: Pantheon, 1981), ix–15, 129–87, 275–329; Eric Hobsbawm, *The Age of Empire* (London: Abacus, 1994), 302–27; Perry Anderson, "Internationalism," *New Left Review* 14 (March-April 2002): 11–14. For a remarkable explanation of the origins of the Great War, see Paul W. Schroeder, *Systems, Stability, and Statecraft* (New York: Palgrave, 2004), chapters 7–8; on the recent scholarship, see Thomas Lacquer, "Some Damn Foolish Thing," *London Review of Books*, 5 December 2013, 11–16.

142. See Michael Mann, *Fascists* (Cambridge: Cambridge University Press, 2004), 31–91; and Enzo Traverso, *À feu et à sang* (Paris: Stock, 2007), passim.

143. Anderson, "Internationalism,"14.

144. Simmel, *The Sociology of Georg Simmel*, 33. Weber is discussed in chapter 6, this volume.

145. Ibid., 36.

146. The most infamous formulation is found in Gustave Le Bon's *The Crowd* (1895). For an excellent account of this ideology, see Stefan Jonsson, *Crowds and Democracy* (New York: Columbia University Press, 2013), passim. Jonsson offers acute observations on Simmel (54–61), who emerges as a pivotal figure in the arrival of "mass" as a pseudo-concept by reworking insights from French and Italian sources into a different sociological context peppered by Nietzschean motifs, thus turning "mass" into a respectable sociological category. Early on, Simmel reviewed Le Bon's book in 1895, as well as the German translation of Scipio Sighele's *La folla delinquente* (1895); the latter, the more substantial contribution, from an Italian *grande* who notoriously reflected on the power of "suggestion" as part of mass action—see *La folla delinquente* (Torino: Fratelli Bocca, 1895), 118ff. Alongside many a colorful reference to cannibalism and the unstoppable sanguinary instinct of the masses, there is the following description of the masses during the French Revolution: "Allora il popolo era una belva, insaziabile nella sua sete di rapine e di sangue" (86); in English: "The people was a beast, insatiable in its thirst for rapine and blood." For the significance of this ideology in the initial forging of "democratic theory," see Richard Bellamy, "The Advent of the Masses and the Making of the Modern Theory of Democracy," in Terrance Ball and Richard Bellamy, eds., *The Cambridge History of Twentieth Century Political Thought* (Cambridge: Cambridge University Press, 2003), 70–103. In *La rebelión de las masas* Ortega y Gasset, reflecting on intellectual responsibility and the irresponsibility of demagogues, argues that, historically, the nobility is characterized by is acute sense of responsibility and writes about how "it is only the illusion of empire and the discipline of responsibility which it inspires that can keep Western souls in tension"; see José Ortega y Gasset, *La rebelión de las masas* (Madrid: Espasa, 2010), 191.

147. Jonsson, *Crowds and Democracy*, 53.

148. Simmel, *The Sociology of Georg Simmel*, 133–34.

149. Ibid., 103, 111.

150. Cf. Wendy Brown, *Undoing the Demos* (New York: Zone, 2015), 17–45, 131–34.

151. Friedrich Hayek, *The Constitution of Liberty* (Chicago: University of Chicago Press, 2011), 133ff.

152. For a contrast between Rawls and Hayek along these lines, see Vázquez-Arroyo, "Liberal Democracy and Neoliberalism," 149–54. While the deepening of neoliberalism exhibits attributes of the world-capitalist economy—its imperatives and relations of reproduction—unforeseen by, say, Hayek, these inflections constitute a deepening, not a departure, of earlier visions.

153. See Robert Castel, *El ascenso de las incertidumbres*, trans. Víctor Goldstein (Buenos Aires: Fondo de Cultura Económica, 2010), 15–58, 227ff.

3. AUTONOMY, ETHICS, *INTRA*SUBJECTIVITY

1. For a lucid discussion see Adolfo Sánchez Vázquez, *Ética* (Barcelona: Crítica, 1999), 17–60.

2. See Immanuel Kant, *Critique of Pure Reason*, trans. Norman Kemp Smith (New York: St Martin's, 1965), 41 (B1).

3. On the British moralists, see Terry Eagleton, *Trouble with Strangers* (Oxford: Blackwell, 2009), chapter 2. See also Istvan Hont and Michael Ignatieff, eds., *Wealth and Virtue* (Cambridge: Cambridge University Press, 1983), 13–26, 179–202; and Joan C. Tronto, *Moral Boundaries* (New York: Routledge, 1993), chapter 2.

4. Still instructive discussion is Robert Paul Wolff, *Kant's Theory of Mental Activity* (Cambridge: Harvard University Press, 1963). See also Karl Ameriks, *Kant and the Fate of Autonomy* (Cambridge: Cambridge University Press, 2000), and *Interpreting Kant's Critiques* (Oxford: Oxford University Press, 2003), part 1; and Robert B. Brandom, *Reason in Philosophy* (Cambridge: Harvard University Press, 2009), 32–66.

5. Kant's aesthetics and moral theory could be interpreted as attempts to address the antinomies generated by the concept of freedom in which Kant, in the *Critique of Pure Reason*, anchors his transcendental idealism. Cf. Eckart Förster, *The Twenty-Five Years of Philosophy*, trans. Brady Bowman (Cambridge: Harvard University Press, 2012), 125–52.

6. Kant, *Critique of Pure Reason*, 120ff. (B 116–22).

7. For a discussion, see Dieter Henrich, *The Unity of Reason*, ed. Richard L. Velkley (Cambridge: Harvard University Press, 1994), chapters 1, 4.

8. On Kant's moral philosophy, see Andrew Reath, "Kant's Moral Philosophy" and Otfried Höffe, "Kantian Ethics," both in Roger Crisp, ed., *The Oxford Handbook of the History of Ethics* (Oxford: Oxford University Press, 2012), 444–82.

Of interest is Reath's *Agency and Autonomy in Kant's Moral Theory* (Oxford: Oxford University Press, 2006), passim.

9. See Immanuel Kant, *Practical Philosophy*, trans. Mary J. Gregor (Cambridge: Cambridge University Press, 1996), 47, 513.

10. See Brandom, *Reason in Philosophy*, 34ff.

11. Brandom acknowledges this and suggests that Hegel historicizes the Kantian insight about the normativity of mental activity; see ibid., 66. This is, of course, something argued in more politically robust terms by Taylor, who recasts Hegel's inheritance of the idea of mental life as conceptual activity in terms of a form of self-understanding that is historical and thus predicated on shared institutions and practices; see Charles Taylor, *Human Agency and Language* (Cambridge: Cambridge University Press, 1985), 77–96. Moreover, for all the acuity of Brandom's formulations, his account of Hegel's idea of *geistig* is ultimately reductionist. By unfortunately reducing it to a "normative order," the sociological and historical mediations of his dialectical formulations freedom, ethical, and political life are significantly distorted with the effect of decreasing its critical and political import. Cf. Robert Pippin, *Interanimations* (Chicago: University of Chicago Press, 2015), 39–61, 117–38.

12. Brandom also suggests that becoming "epistemically responsible" entails "a commitment to justify many, if not most, of her beliefs, under suitable circumstances," even if the social dimension of responsibility is only perfunctorily avowed; see Robert B. Brandom, *From Empiricism to Expressivism* (Cambridge: Harvard University Press, 2015), 165, 113.

13. As Schopenhauer pointed out, in Kant's moral philosophy the actual reasons for acting morally are ultimately unfathomable; see Arthur Schopenhauer, *On the Basis of Morality*, trans. E. F. J. Payne (Indiana: Hackett, 1995), passim.

14. See Étienne Balibar, *Citoyen sujet et autres essais d'anthropologie philosophique* (Paris: Presses Universitaires de France, 2011), 15.

15. Kant, *Practical Philosophy*, 512, 525.

16. The phrase is from Robert B. Brandom, *Making It Explicit* (Cambridge: Harvard University Press, 1994), 11.

17. On the post-Kantian philosophical milieu, see Robert B. Pippin, *The Persistence of Subjectivity* (Cambridge: Cambridge University Press, 2005), 1–53; Terry Pinkard, "Virtues, Morality, and *Sittlichkeit*," *European Journal of Philosophy* 7 (1999): 217–38, and *German Philosophy, 1760–1860* (Cambridge: Cambridge University Press, 2002), 1–16; and Raymond Geuss, "Post-Kantianism," in Crisp, *The Oxford Handbook for the History of Ethics*, 483–84. Indispensable guides on the philosophical trajectory of German idealism are Dieter Henrich, *Between Kant and Hegel*, ed. David S. Pacini (Cambridge: Harvard University Press, 2003); and Förster, *The Twenty-Five Years of Philosophy*.

18. See Pippin, *The Persistence of Subjectivity*, 10, 11.

19. Eagleton, *Trouble with Strangers*, 126. Cf. Vincent Descombes, *The Institutions of Meaning*, trans. Stephen Adam Schwartz (Cambridge: Harvard University

Press, 2014), 295–313; and Robert B. Pippin, *Hegel's Practical Philosophy* (Cambridge: Cambridge University Press, 2008), chapter 9.

20. Brandom, *Reason in Philosophy*, 67–68.

21. See Gillian Rose, *Hegel Contra Sociology* (London: Athlone, 1981), especially 84–97. See also Domenico Losurdo, *Hegel and the Freedom of Moderns*, trans. Marella and Jon Morris (Durham: Duke University Press, 2004), 260–63; and Robert B. Pippin, "Hegel on Political Philosophy and Political Actuality," *Inquiry* 53 (October 2010): 410–16.

22. For a compelling account of Hegel's understanding of the externalization of action, see Fredric Jameson, *The Hegel Variations* (London: Verso, 2010), 59, 66–68, 75–115.

23. See G. W. F. Hegel, *Phenomenology of Spirit*, trans. A. V. Miller (Oxford: Oxford University Press, 1977), 233–34.

24. For an excellent discussion, see Carla Cordua, *El mundo ético* (Barcelona: Anthropos, 1989), passim.

25. See Eliseo Cruz Vergara, *La concepción del conocimiento histórico en Hegel* (Río Piedras: Editorial de la Universidad de Puerto Rico, 1997), 1–244, and "Filosofía y espiritualidad," *Diálogos* 81 (2003): 131–60.

26. See G. W. F. Hegel, *Elements of the Philosophy of Right*, trans. H. B. Nisbet (Cambridge: Cambridge University Press, 1991), 238.

27. Also relevant is Hegel's account of externalization, purpose, and responsibility in his *Encyclopedia*, §504ff., see *Hegel's Philosophy of Mind*, trans. William Wallace and A. V. Miller (Oxford: Oxford University Press,), 249ff.

28. Hegel, *Elements of the Philosophy of Right*, 145.

29. See Carla Cordua, "Hegel y la participación política," *Ideas y Valores* 100 (April 1996): 19–36.

30. See Max Horkheimer, *Between Philosophy and Social Science*, trans. C. Fredrick Hunter, Matthew S. Kramer, and John Torpey (Cambridge: MIT Press, 1993), 29.

31. For a fine discussion, see Pinkard, "Virtues, Morality, and *Sittlichkeit*," especially 226ff. and 234–35*n*37.

32. See Karl Marx, *Critique of Hegel's "Philosophy of Right*," ed. Joseph O'Malley (Cambridge: Cambridge University Press, 1977), 24. Cf. Balibar, *Citoyen sujet et autres essais d'anthropologie philosophique*, 77–78. Jacobin ideas of citizenship were never far from Marx's vision of political action—see Jonathan Sperber, *Karl Marx* (New York: Liverlight, 2013), 535.

33. For overly formalist discussions of Nietzsche's grand politics, see Mark Warren, *Nietzsche and Political Thought* (Cambridge: MIT Press, 1988), 206–26; and Keith Ansell-Pearson, *An Introduction to Nietzsche as a Political Thinker* (Cambridge: Cambridge University Press, 1994), 147–62.

34. Walter Kaufmann offered the seminal interpretation that turned this mordant and irreverent thinker, one of the nineteenth century's foremost philosophers of power, into an apolitical ironist, "a charming and inoffensive *salonfähig* existentialist"; see Jennifer Ratner-Rosenhagen, *American Nietzsche* (Chicago: University of Chicago Press, 2012), 224.

35. Variations of this theme can be found in Christa Davis Acampora, "On Sovereignty and Overhumanity," in Christa Davis Acampora, ed., *Nietzsche's On the Genealogy of Morals* (Lanham: Rowman and Littlefield, 2006), 147–62; Vanessa Lemm, *Nietzsche's Animal Philosophy* (New York: Fordham University Press, 2009); and Raymond Geuss, *Morality, Culture, and History* (Cambridge: Cambridge University Press, 1999), chapters 1, 7.

36. Malcolm Bull, "Where is the Anti-Nietzsche?" *New Left Review* 3 (May-June 2000): 121–45.

37. Robert B. Pippin, *Nietzsche, Psychology and First Philosophy* (Chicago: University of Chicago Press, 2010), 9, 68, 80n15; Bonnie Honig, *Political Theory and the Displacement of Politics* (Ithaca: Cornell University Press, 1993), 52, 64; Vanessa Lemm, "Memory and Promise in Arendt and Nietzsche," *Revista de Ciencia Política* 26 (2006): 161–73 (167, 168); see also her *Nietzsche's Animal Philosophy*, 36–47; David Owen, "Equality, Democracy and Self-Respect," *Journal of Nietzsche Studies* 24 (Fall 2002): 113–31 (118); Christian Emden, *Friedrich Nietzsche and the Politics of History* (Cambridge: Cambridge University Press, 2008), 166, 298, 224, 298; Robert Gooding-Williams, *Zarathustra's Dionysian Modernism* (Stanford: Stanford University Press, 2002), 143; and Paul Franco, *Nietzsche's Enlightenment* (Chicago: University of Chicago Press, 2011), 84, 178, 132 (see also 128, 135).

38. *Quasi* insofar as defenses of hierarchical order are sometimes qualified by the word *hitherto* (*bisher*), something that constitutes a tacit avowal of historicity, which is precisely what a transcendental structure of argumentation explicitly disavows. These invocations of *hitherto*, however, at once connote obduracy and plausible deniability. For contrasting interpretations, see the essays by Peter Dews and Raymond Geuss, respectively: "Nietzsche for Losers?" and "Systems, Value, and Egalitarianism," *New Left Review* 86 (April-March 2014): 95–120.

39. For instance, see Ananda Abeysekara, *The Politics of Postsecular Religion* (New York: Columbia University Press, 2008), 84–127, 194–226.

40. See Wendy Brown, *States of Injury* (Princeton: Princeton University Press, 1995), chapter 3; and Geuss, "Systems, Value, and Egalitarianism."

41. Nietzsche's reflections on power are mostly silent about the role of institutional—market and Statist—imperatives. His explicit account mostly operates at the level of culture and for the sake of a radical, albeit individualist, and often aristocratic, ethos of action, even if there is an institutional mainstay implicit in it. This ethos is well captured by Jacques Derrida, *Politics of Friendship*, trans. George Collins (London: Verso, 1997), chapters 2–3.

42. For a discussion of Nietzsche's "ecology of value," cf. Malcolm Bull, *The Anti-Nietzsche* (London: Verso, 2011), chapters 2–3.

43. Dews, "Nietzsche for Losers?," 99.

44. See Domenico Losurdo, *Nietzsche, il ribelle aristocratico* (Turin: Bollati Boringhieri, 2002), especially 5–103, 195–401, 555–90, 767–896. That any contextualization is quickly reduced to a caricature of Georg Lukács's position in *The*

Destruction of Reason, or as a reductionism, can be seen in the defensive posture or silence vis-à-vis this study. For instance, in *Nietzsche's Animal Philosophy* Lemm quickly mentions Losurdo and hastily dispatches his arguments as an iteration of the casting of Nietzsche "as a precursor of authoritarian and totalitarian politics" (168n1). But Lemm scuffles away from any direct reckoning with the evidence Losurdo presents of the political and theoretical obduracy of aristocratic categories in Nietzsche's political thought either by abjuring some of the textual evidence that fits awkwardly with her constructions or by dehistoricizing Nietzsche and interpreting his radical assertions in terms of broader and altogether looser categories: say, euphemisms about civilization or "aristocratic culture." *Noyer le poisson*, the French call it. For Lemm's most recent revamping of Nietzsche's aristocratic posture, and the idea of an "order of rank," see *Nietzsche y el pensamiento político contemporáneo* (Santiago: Fondo de Cultura Económica, 2013), 65–91.

45. See Losurdo, *Nietzsche*, 1007–29.

46. Ibid., 893; see also 1077ff.

47. See Arno J. Mayer, *The Persistence of the Old Regime* (New York: Pantheon, 1981), 275ff.; and Perry Anderson, "Internationalism," *New Left Review* 14 (March-April 2002): 11–16.

48. Losurdo, *Nietzsche,* 935. One can state things slightly differently by invoking a series of passages from Adorno that articulate a dialectical interpretative principle analogous to Losurdo's ideas of "theoretical excess:" "I believe that Max Weber's thought, like any other intellectual formation of considerable magnitude, can only be understood by understanding at which points such a formation goes beyond that which it understands itself to be, and which it purports to be." To be precise, by immanently discerning those moments of nonidentity between intention and effect in the architecture of a theory, one can see how it exceeds itself in ways that it could be productively recast. But such recasting has to scrupulously consider how "even if one operates with concepts defined in a purely instrumental manner, the structured character of the subject matter asserts itself in such a way that something of the objective structure imprints itself on these . . . concepts through their own structural determinateness." See Theodor W. Adorno, *Introduction to Sociology*, trans. Edmund Jephcott (Stanford: Stanford University Press, 2000), 121, 123.

49. Cf. Friedrich Nietzsche, *Human All Too Human*, trans. R. J. Hollingdale (Cambridge: Cambridge University Press, 1996), 57–59.

50. Multiple references and characterizations of the new philosopher are found in Friedrich Nietzsche, *Beyond Good and Evil*, trans. R. J. Hollingdale (London: Penguin, 1973), passim. See also Nietzsche's *Human All Too Human*, 5–11, and *On the Genealogy of Morals and Ecce Homo*, trans. Walter Kaufmann (New York: Vintage, 1967), 218; cf. *The Gay Science*, trans. Walter Kaufmann (New York: Vintage, 1974), 228–29.

51. Nietzsche, *On the Genealogy of Morals and Ecce Homo*, 58ff.

52. Cf. Jorge Luis Borges, "Funes El Memorioso," in *Obras completas,* 4 vols. (Mallorca: Emecé, 1996), 1:490; and "El hilo de la fábula," ibid., 3:477.
53. Nietzsche, *Beyond Good and Evil,* 86, 142–43. See also Friedrich Nietzsche, *Thus Spoke Zarathustra,* trans. Walter Kaufmann (London: Penguin, 1978), 196ff.
54. See Nietzsche, *Beyond Good and Evil,* 72, 192; and Friedrich Nietzsche, *Twilight of the Idols and The Antichrist,* trans. R. J. Hollingdale (London: Penguin, 1990), 100–3, 112–13.
55. Roberto Alejandro, *Nietzsche and the Drama of Historiobiography* (Notre Dame: University of Notre Dame Press, 2011), 81.
56. Ibid., 80–90.
57. Friedrich Nietzsche, *On the Genealogy of Morality,* trans. Carole Diethe (Cambridge: Cambridge University Press, 1997), 36–37.
58. See Nietzsche, *Beyond Good and Evil,* 14, 37; and *On the Genealogy of Morality,* 26.
59. Cf. Robert C. Salomon, "Nietzsche *ad hominen,*" in Bernd Magnus and Kathleen Higggins, eds., *The Cambridge Companion to Nietzsche* (Cambridge: Cambridge University Press, 1996), 180–222; and Alejandro, *Nietzsche and the Drama of Historiobiography,* 43–44, 308–9n17.
60. See Nietzsche, *Twilight of the Idols and The Antichrist,* 103.
61. Ibid., 103–4.
62. Ibid., 104. For a thoughtful interpretation Nietzsche's idea of overcoming, even if mostly evasive about its political presuppositions, see Robert B. Pippin, "How to Overcome Oneself," in Ken Gemes and Simon May, eds., *Nietzsche on Freedom and Autonomy* (Oxford: Oxford University Press, 2009), 69–87, cf. *Nietzsche, Psychology, and First Philosophy* (Chicago: University of Chicago Press, 2010), 105ff.
63. Nietzsche, *Twilight of the Idols and the Anti-Christ,* 190–191.
64. Nietzsche, *On the Genealogy of Morals and Ecce Homo,* 274.
65. In 1872, as part of his lectures in Basel "On the Future of our Educational Institutions," he asserted, "not the education of the masses can be our goal but the education of individually selected people, armed for great and permanent achievements." As a leading historian of Germany explains, Nietzsche then "went on to charge that those who argued for a further extension of *Volksbildung* were seeking to destroy 'the natural order of rank in the kingdom of the intellect'"; see Gordon A. Craig, *Germany, 1866–1945* (Oxford: Oxford University Press, 1978), 187–88.
66. See Friedrich Nietzsche, *Writings from the Late Notebooks,* ed. Rüdiger Bittner (Cambridge: Cambridge University Press, 2003), 32.
67. See Mayer, *The Persistence of the Old Regime,* 285–90; Losurdo, *Nietzsche,* 370–98, 767ff.; and Corey Robin, *The Reactionary Mind* (Oxford: Oxford University Press, 2011), 2–60.
68. Of course, at stake is not just political rule but rather the self-cultivation of a cultural elite: a race "whose task is not limited to governing; but a race with *its own sphere of life*"; see Nietzsche, *Writings from the Late Notebooks,* 166.

69. Ibid., 232; see also 251.

70. See Ellen Frankel Paul et al., eds., *Responsibility* (Cambridge: Cambridge University Press, 1999), passim.

71. See, for instance, Alexander Brown, *Personal Responsibility* (London: Continuum, 2009), 1, 177–80.

72. Thomas M. Scanlon, *What We Owe to Each Other* (Cambridge: Harvard University Press, 1998), 5–6.

73. Ibid., 254, 256.

74. See Thomas M. Scanlon, *Moral Dimensions* (Cambridge: Harvard University Press, 2008), 4ff.

75. Scanlon, *What We Owe to Each Other*, 9, 247–94.

76. Ibid., 290. On blame, see Scanlon, *Moral Dimensions*, chapter 4.

77. See Scanlon, *What We Owe to Each Other*, 263ff.

78. See Hannah Arendt, "Organized Guilt and Universal Responsibility," in Jerome Kohn, ed., *Essays in Understanding* (New York: Harcourt Brace, 1994), 125.

79. See Scanlon, *Moral Dimensions*, 202.

80. Ibid., 207–8.

81. See also Bernard Williams, "Moral Responsibility and Political Freedom," *The Cambridge Law Journal* 56 (March 1997): 96–102. For earlier accounts, see Bernard Williams, *Moral Luck* (Cambridge: Cambridge University Press, 1981), 20–39, 54–70, 114–23, *Ethics and the Limits of Philosophy* (Cambridge: Harvard University Press, 1985), 1–21, 174ff., and *Making Sense of Humanity and Other Philosophical Papers, 1982–1993* (Cambridge: Cambridge University Press, 1995), 22–34, 241–47. Williams is unconventionally analytical, especially in the way he draws from classical works and literary texts, refuses to take ethical questions in isolation, frequently adducing, albeit abstractly, sociological and historical contexts. And yet, Williams's critique of ethics is expressed in a thoroughly analytical structure of argumentation. In 1976, for instance, he confidently asserted the superiority of "the methods and standards of analytical philosophy," which he contrasted to the "more archaic philosophical forms" in which the claims of "neo-Marxists and neo-Hegelian critics of our society" were couched. A claim that, despite lukewarm expressions about "so-called analytical tradition," was never explicitly disavowed; see Bernard Williams, *Essays and Reviews: 1959–2002* (Princeton: Princeton University Press, 2014), 124, cf. 405. For subtle discussions of Williams, see Raymond Geuss, *Outside Ethics* (Princeton: Princeton University Press, 2005), 219–33, and *A World Without Why* (Princeton: Princeton University Press, 2014), 175–222.

82. See Bernard Williams, *Shame and Necessity* (Berkeley: University of California Press, 1993), 55. For an original and highly suggestive elaboration of his idea of responsibility, see Farid Abdel-Nour, "National Responsibility," *Political Theory* 31 (October 2003): 693–719, and "Responsibility and National Memory," *International Journal of Politics, Culture and Society* 17 (Spring 2004): 339–63.

83. Williams, *Shame and Necessity*, 56.

84. See Williams, "Moral Responsibility and Political Freedom," 97.

85. Williams, *Shame and Necessity*, 57.

86. Ibid., 187*n*12.

87. Although Williams is routinely credited with a realist disposition and an acute sense of history, his invocations of realism and history are rather labile and severely dehistoricized—see, inter alia, Bernard Williams, *Truth and Truthfulness* (Princeton: Princeton University Press, 2002), 20–40, 149–71, and *Essays and Reviews*, 119–24, 405–12.

88. See Geuss, *A World Without Why*, 184.

89. See Talal Asad, *Formations of the Secular* (Stanford: Stanford University Press, 2003), 96.

90. Cf. Brandom, *Reason in Philosophy*, 71ff.

91. See Iris Marion Young, *Responsibility for Justice* (Oxford: Oxford University Press, 2011), 3–41.

92. See Manuel Cruz, "On Pain, the Suffering of Wrong, and Other Grievances," in María Pía Lara, ed., *Rethinking* (Berkeley: University of California Press, 2001), 199.

93. This is, of course, part of what Jonas emphasizes: a need to be more responsive to the vulnerability of nature and the forms of power that largely unaccountable technological achievements have inaugurated; see Hans Jonas, *The Imperative of Responsibility*, trans. Hans Jonas in collaboration with David Herr (Chicago: University of Chicago Press, 1984), passim.

94. Descombes, *The Institutions of Meaning*, 9. Also relevant is Vincent Descombes, *Le complément de sujet* (Paris: Gallimard, 2004), 7–44, 457ff.

95. Full elucidation of dialectical materialism goes beyond the scope of the present work. Suffice it for now to establish that it is not an "ontological standpoint," nor a mere opposition to idealism, but, rather, a critique of both idealism and existing reality, which nevertheless does not reject the moment of critique embedded in reflection. See Theodor W. Adorno, *Negative Dialectics*, trans. E. B. Ashton (New York: Continuum, 1973), 178–98; the German text is found in *Gesammelte Schriften*, 20 vols., ed. Rolf Tiedemann with Gretel Adorno, Susan Buck-Morss, and Klaus Schultz (Frankfurt: Suhrkamp, 2003), 6:382. For an illuminating account of the dialectic of materialism and idealism, see Eliseo Cruz Vergara, "Idealismo y materialismo," *Diálogos* 32 (1997): 53–108.

96. Cf. Taylor, *Human Agency and Language*, 39–44.

4. ETHICAL REDUCTIONS

1. See François Raffoul, *The Origins of Responsibility* (Bloomington: Indiana University Press, 2010), 163, 164. Cf. Vincent Descombes, *Le parler de soi* (Paris: Gallimard, 2014), 52ff.

2. See Judith Butler, *Parting Ways* (New York: Columbia University Press, 2012), 27.

3. See Jacques Derrida, *Adieu to Emmanuel Levinas*, trans. Pascale-Anne Brault and Michael Naas (Stanford: Stanford University Press, 1999), 17.

4. See, for instance, Emmanuel Levinas, *Difficult Freedom*, trans. Seán Hand (Baltimore: Johns Hopkins University Press, 1990), 291ff.

5. See "Responsabilité," in Sylvie Mesure and Patrick Savidan, ed., *Le dictionnaire des sciences humaines* (Paris: Presses Universitaires de France, 2006), 1001.

6. See Samuel Moyn, *Origins of the Other* (Ithaca: Cornell University Press, 2005), 196.

7. See Carlo Galli, *Spazi politici* (Bologna: Il Mulino, 2001), 114.

8. See Peter Galison, *Einstein Clocks, Poncairé's Maps* (New York: Norton, 2003). *Empires of Time* is the book's apt subtitle.

9. On neo-Kantianism see Gillian Rose, *Hegel Contra Sociology* (London: Athlone, 1981), 1–47. For a helpful overview, see Peter E. Gordon, *Continental Divide* (Cambridge: Harvard University Press, 2010), 52–86. On Heidegger's dismantling of tradition and his ontologization of history, see Martin Heidegger, *Being and Time*, trans. Joan Stambaugh (Albany: SUNY Press, 1996), 17ff., and *Ontology—The Hermeneutics of Facticity*, trans. John van Buren (Bloomington: Indiana University Press, 1999), 58–60.

10. See Heidegger, *Ontology*, 5. Heidegger even temporalized the notion of "concept," thus disavowing how concepts acquire their formal determinations, the contents of conceptual forms, and their historicity; see ibid., 12–13.

11. On Heidegger's "originary ethics" of responsibility, see Raffoul, *The Origins of Responsibility*, 220–81.

12. On Barth's influence, see Moyn, *Origins of the Other*, 116, 134–41, 229–37, 250ff. For a lucid overview of this intellectual milieu, see Peter E. Gordon, "Weimar Theology," in Peter E. Gordon and John P. McCormick, eds., *Weimar Thought* (Princeton: Princeton University Press, 2013), 150–78.

13. Phenomenological reductions, as one of Husserl's best commentators has explained, entail "a radical shift in attention from factuality and particularity to essential and universal qualities," namely, a turn to transcendental subjectivity. See Maurice Natanson, *Edmund Husserl* (Evanston: Northwestern University Press, 1973), 65.

14. See Edmund Husserl, *Ideas*, trans. W. R. Boyce Gibson (Oxon: Routledge, 2002), 96.

15. See Heidegger, *Being and Time*, 36.

16. For sound criticism of this strategy, see Theodor W. Adorno, *Against Epistemology*, trans. Willis Domingo (Oxford: Blackwell, 1982), 188. See also Gunther Anders, "On the Pseudo-Concreteness of Heidegger's Philosophy," *Philosophy and Phenomenological Research* 8 (March 1948): 337–71.

17. If in Heidegger there is a pseudoconcreteness accompanied by invocations of historicity without history, in Levinas a similar pseudoconcreteness is at work, even if the appeal to the history of the twentieth century is more concrete and historical than anything found in Heidegger. But the narrative of the twentieth century on which his account pivots is thoroughly

294 4. ETHICAL REDUCTIONS

dehistoricized; the century is primarily cast as representing an ethical failure; see Emmanuel Levinas, *Entre Nous*, trans. Michael B. Smith and Barbara Harshav (New York: Columbia University Press, 1998), 97.

18. See Moyn, *Origins of the Other*, 87ff.

19. Ibid., 195ff.

20. Ibid., 214–19.

21. On the U.S.'s vision of postwar order in the aforementioned nations, see Gabriel Kolko, *The Politics of War* (New York: Pantheon, 1990), 1–98, 131–38, 172–93, and 428–56.

22. Moyn, *Origins of the Other*, 226–27.

23. Ibid, 227. But a defensive politics never precluding the offensive politics of Zionism and their casting as "a kind of politics beyond polity." On his ethical politics, their continuities and innovations, which gained different accents depending on the occasion, see Howard Caygill, *Levinas and the Political* (London: Routledge, 2002).

24. See Emmanuel Levinas, *Totality and Infinity*, trans. Alphonso Lingis (Pittsburgh: Duquesne University Press, 1969), 21.

25. Indeed, consideration of what Simone de Beauvoir shrewdly characterized as "the antinomies of action" is preemptively (and peremptorily) debarred in Levinas's ethics; see Simone de Beauvoir, *Pour une morale de l'ambiguïté* (Paris: Gallimard, 1947), 120–43.

26. Peter Dews, *The Idea of Evil* (Oxford: Blackwell, 2008), 162; later on, Dews observes how, by shifting the burden of responsibility onto inwardness, Levinas's ethical responsibility "threatens to drain of all meaning the very ethical demand whose unconditional pressure it seeks to disclose" (182).

27. See Levinas, *Difficult Freedom*, 291. But see Moyn, *Origins of the Other*, 195ff.

28. See Dews, *The Idea of Evil*, 166; Terry Eagleton, *Trouble with Strangers* (Oxford: Blackwell, 2009), 234; and Ella Myers, *Worldly Ethics* (Durham: Duke University Press, 2013), 57.

29. See Bertolt Brecht, *Prosa* (Frankfurt: Suhrkamp, 2013), 926.

30. Cf. Eagleton, *Trouble with Strangers*, 227. Even if Eagleton's overall argument is marred by his version of Marxist ethical politics in lieu of a properly political ethic, he never conflates the two domains—see pp. 306ff.

31. Ibid., 234.

32. Cf. Eckart Förster, *The Twenty-Five Years of Philosophy*, trans. Brady Bowman (Cambridge: Harvard University Press, 2012), 373ff.

33. Adorno, for instance, immanently criticized and discerned the truth content of this tradition. For him, consciousness is historically situated and embodied, but, crucially, never at one with itself. Mediating consciousness is both the obduracy of its own objectivity and the constitutive block that is nonidentity. For a suggestive contrast of the primacy of the other (Levinas) with the primacy of the object (Adorno), see Jeffrey M. Jackson, "Persecution and Social Histories," *Philosophy and Social Criticism* 36 (2010): 719–33.

34. See chapter 2, this volume.

35. Maurice Blanchot, *The Writing of the Disaster*, trans. Ann Smock (Lincoln: University of Nebraska Press, 1995), 25.

36. Ibid., 22.

37. Ibid. 22, 24.

38. See chapter 1, this volume. Another version of this inheritance is found in Simon Critchley, *Infinitely Demanding* (London: Verso, 2007). For contrasting critiques, see Myers, *Worldly Ethics*, 68–75; and Slavoj Žižek, *In Defense of Lost Causes* (London: Verso, 2008), 339–50. That Critchley's ethical politics today stands for a radical political ethic is symptomatic of the degree of political illiteracy and disorientation in the North Atlantic left. So politically labile and intellectually negligible is his treatment of ethics and politics that the book could be more aptly titled *Infinitely Undemanding*.

39. For sympathetic elucidations, see Gayatri Chakravorty Spivak, *A Critique of Postcolonial Reason* (Cambridge: Harvard University Press, 1999), 426–28; Rodolphe Gasché, *Inventions of Difference* (Cambridge: Harvard University Press, 1994), 227–50; and Ananda Abeysekara, *The Politics of Postsecular Religion* (New York: Columbia University Press, 2008), 84–127.

40. See Jacques Derrida, *Politics of Friendship*, trans. George Collins (London: Verso, 1997), 250ff.

41. On the transcendental and the quasi-transcendental, see Jacques Derrida, *Paper Machine*, trans. Rachel Bowlby (Stanford: Stanford University Press, 2005), 83.

42. Jacques Derrida, *Psyche*, 2 vols. (Stanford: Stanford University Press, 2007), 1:15; see also Derrida, *Paper Machine*, 81.

43. Cf. Simon Lumsden, "Dialectic and Différance," *Philosophy and Social Criticism* 33 (December 2007): 667–90.

44. See Fredric Jameson, *Archaeologies of the Future* (London: Verso, 2005), 10–21, 107–18, 210–33, 281–95, and 412–16. Modernist techniques of the "middle voice" and "effacement" pervade Derrida's work, and so does the conceit of unmediated innovation.

45. Derrida, *Psyche*, 23.

46. With the exception of his first work, Derrida consistently disavows the dialectic—see Jacques Derrida, *The Problem of Genesis in Husserl's Phenomenology*, trans. Marian Hobson (Chicago: University of Chicago Press, 2003), passim.

47. See Jacques Derrida, *The Gift of Death*, trans. David Willis (Chicago: University of Chicago Press, 1995), 5.

48. See Jacques Derrida, *Acts of Religion*, ed. Gil Anidjar (New York: Routledge, 2002), 56.

49. As cited by Simon Critchley, "Remarks on Derrida and Habermas," *Constellations* 7 (December 2000): 458.

50. Emmanuel Levinas, *Otherwise Than Being and Beyond Essence*, trans. Alphonso Lingis (Pittsburg: Duquesne University Press, 1998), 14. Cf. Derrida, *Adieu to Emmanuel Levinas*, 55.

51. For a critical discussion, see Peter Dews, *Logics of Disintegration* (London: Verso, 1987), chapter 1, and *The Limits of Disenchantment* (London: Verso, 1995), chapters 1, 4.

52. The year 1964 is a crucial moment here—see Edward Baring, *The Young Derrida and French Philosophy, 1945–1968* (Cambridge: Cambridge University Press, 2011), 277ff.

53. Derrida's statements are found in John D. Caputo, Mark Dooley, and Michael J. Scanlon , eds., *Questioning God* (Bloomington: Indiana University Press, 2001), 66. For discussions of the "impossible," see Derrida, *Paper Machine*, chapters 8, 12.

54. Jacques Derrida, *Speech and Phenomena and Other Essays on Husserl's Theory of the Signs*, trans. David B. Allison (Evanston: Northwestern University Press, 1973), 70–87, 129ff.; see also his *Margins of Philosophy*, trans. Alan Bass (Chicago: University of Chicago Press, 1982), 3–27.

55. Derrida, *Speech and Phenomena*, 103.

56. Ibid. 86–87. Cf. Adorno, *Against Epistemology*, 1–40, 124–85.

57. Dews, *Logics of Disintegration*, 19; see also Dews, *The Limits of Disenchantment*, 31–33, and "Déconstruction et dialectique négative," in Patrice Maniglier, ed., *Le moment philosophique des années 1960 en France* (Paris: Presses Universitaires de France, 2011), 409–27.

58. Derrida, *The Politics of Friendship*, 69.

59. Even if in both cases the boundless nature of action, or Event, is vastly overstated. Cf. Žižek, *The Ticklish Subject* (London: Verso, 1999), 135–41. For a thoughtful formulation of the relative boundlessness of action, see Patchen Markell, *Bound by Recognition* (Princeton: Princeton University Press, 2003), chapter 3.

60. Spivak, *A Critique of Postcolonial Reason*, 427.

61. Jacques Derrida, *Specters of Marx*, trans. Peggy Kamuf (New York: Routledge, 1994), 92.

62. Ibid., 91.

63. Ibid., 91–92.

64. Ibid., 93.

65. See José María Ripalda, *Los límites de la dialéctica* (Madrid: Trotta, 2005), 225.

66. See Derrida, *Politics of Friendship*, 39. Cf. Friedrich Nietzsche, *Beyond Good and Evil*, trans. R. J. Hollingdale (London: Penguin, 1973), 56–57, 210, 214.

67. Derrida, *The Gift of Death*, 6.

68. Ibid. 71.

69. Eagleton, *Trouble with Strangers*, 258.

70. On the "responsibility to protect," see Anne Orford, *International Authority and Responsibility to Protect* (Cambridge: Cambridge University Press, 2011), and "Moral Internationalism and the Responsibility to Protect," *European Journal of International Law* 24 (February 2013): 83–108. In the contemporary "nomos of the earth," the ethical politics of infinite responsibility for the Other bears an elective affinity with the catechism of "Responsibility to

Protect." For a gullible articulation of their affinity, see Alain Toumayan, "The Responsibility to the Other and the Responsibility to Protect," *Philosophy and Social Criticism* 40 (2014): 269–88.

71. Cf. Eagleton, *Trouble with Strangers*, 235.

72. Judith Butler, *Giving an Account of Oneself* (New York: Fordham University Press, 2005), 86.

73. A lucid formulation of the distinction between an intersubjective and a social relation is found in Descombes, *Le parler de soi*, 225–30.

74. At times Butler shows awareness of the need for this epistemological dimension, but not of the challenge that her refusal to theorize it presents to her project. But the political and the epistemological aspect of critique emerges as belated "add-ons" to a theoretical architecture that otherwise disowns it. See, for instance, Butler's *Giving an Account of Oneself*, 96, 99, 107.

75. For a rigorous elucidation of the ethical and political significance of *parrhesia*, see Nancy Luxon, *Crisis of Authority* (Cambridge: Cambridge University Press, 2013), passim. For a critique of conceiving democratic relations in terms of it, see James Tully, *Public Philosophy in a New Key*, 2 vols. (Cambridge: Cambridge University Press, 2008), 2:291.

76. As cited in Butler, *Giving an Account of Oneself*, 130.

77. Judith Butler, *Precarious Life* (London: Verso, 2004), 20, 22.

78. Ibid., xii.

79. Ibid., 33.

80. Ibid., 31, 42–43.

81. For a different materialist tradition that takes the vulnerability of the body as the point of departure for a radical politics, see Sebastiano Timpanaro, *On Materialism* (London: Verso, 1980); Raymond Williams, "Problems of Materialism," *New Left Review* 109 (May-June 1978), 3–17; and Terry Eagleton, *Sweet Violence* (Oxford: Blackwell, 2003), ix–xvii.

82. Occasionally Butler has veered from vulnerability to subordination; see Amy Allen, *The Politics of Ourselves* (New York: Columbia University Press, 2007), 81ff.

83. See Butler, *Giving an Account of Oneself*, 100–1.

84. Butler, *Precarious Life*, 21, see also 139–40, and *Giving an Account of Oneself*, 83ff.

85. See Judith Butler, "Ethical Ambivalence," in Marjorie B. Garber, Beatrice Hanssen, and Rebecca L. Walkowitz, eds., *The Turn to Ethics* (New York: Routledge, 2000), 25.

86. See Drew Gilpin Faust, *This Republic of Suffering* (New York: Knopf, 2008), passim.

87. At one point Butler reverts to the language of "national melancholy" and of national—as opposed to political—identity; see Butler, *Precarious Life*, 41.

88. Cf. Judith Butler, "Finishing, Starting," in Pheng Cheah and Suzanne Guerlac, eds., *Derrida and the Time of the Political* (Durham, NC: Duke University Press, 2009), 295–300.

89. See Judith Butler, *Frames of War* (London: Verso, 2009), 1–62. The differentiations that the concept of precarity is meant to thematize are not formulated as such in earlier works. Furthermore, this distinction does not always hold up in Butler's formulations; elsewhere, precarity is virtually conflated with precariousness—see Butler, *Parting Ways*, 174; cf. Myers, *Worldly Ethics*, 77–81, 175n134.

90. Butler, *Parting Ways*, 27.

91. Ibid., 56.

92. See Theodor W. Adorno, *Ontologie und Dialektik*, ed. Rolf Tiedemann (Frankfurt: Suhrkamp, 2008), 305.

93. Ibid., 336; see also Theodor W. Adorno, *Negative Dialektik* (Frankfurt: Suhrkamp, 1997), 173. Unfortunately, Ashton's English translation completely goes astray in this crucial section.

94. See Theodor W. Adorno, *Negative Dialectics*, trans. E. B. Ashton (New York: Continuum, 1973), 384–90, and *Kant's Critique of Pure Reason*, trans. Rodney Livingstone (Stanford: Stanford University Press, 2001), 138–79.

95. See Adorno, *Ontologie und Dialektik*, 325.

96. Cf. Theodor W. Adorno, *Hegel: Three Studies* (Cambridge: MIT Press, 1993), 53–88.

97. Adorno, *Against Epistemology*, 23, *Gesammelte Schriften*, 20 vols., ed. Rolf Tiedemann with Gretel Adorno, Susan Buck-Morss, and Klaus Schultz (Frankfurt: Suhrkamp, 2003), 5:30.

98. See Butler, *Parting Ways*, 205ff. Not incidentally, the concluding essay of *Parting Ways* is virtually lacking Levinasian motifs. It accordingly provides a rare example of what a political ethic could look like along the lines of Butler's ethical politics.

99. Ibid. 12, 44.

100. On Jewish modernity, see Enzo Traverso, *El final de la modernidad judía*, trans. Gustau Muñoz (Buenos Aires: Fondo de Cultural Económica, 2014), 9–40, 67–108.

101. See Judith Butler, "Judith Butler Responds to Attack: I Affirm a Judaism That Is Not Associated with State Violence," mondoweiss.net, 27 August 2012, http://mondoweiss.net/2012/08/judith-butler-responds-to-attack-i-affirm-a-judaism-that-is-not-associated-with-state-violence (last accessed 17 December 2015).

102. Butler, *Parting Ways*, 99.

103. The year 1948 is when "the imperial baton" was officially passed to the U.S.; see Perry Anderson, "Scurrying Towards Bethlehem," *New Left Review* 10 (July-August 2001): 5–30.

104. Butler, *Parting Ways*, 93.

105. Walter Benjamin, *Selected Writings*, ed. Marcus Bullock and Michael W. Jennings, 4 vols. (Cambridge: Harvard University Press, 1996–2003), 1:250, *Gesammelte Schriften*, ed. Rolf Tiedemann and Hermann Schweppenhäuser, 14 vols. (Frankfurt: Suhrkamp, 1991), 2.1:200–1.

106. See León Rozitchner, *Ser judío y otros ensayos afines* (Buenos Aires: Losada, 2011), passim.

107. See León Rozitchner, *Persona y comunidad* (Buenos Aires: Biblioteca Nacional, 2013), 181–94, 270, 289ff, and *Levinas o la filosofía de la consolación*, 10ff.

108. León Rozitchner, *Acerca de la derrota y de los vencidos* (Buenos Aires: Quadrata, 2011), 45ff.

109. León Rozitchner, *El terror y la gracia* (Buenos Aires: Norma, 2003), 256–62.

110. Cf. Isaac Deutscher, *Marxism, Wars, and Revolutions* (London: Verso, 1984), 256–62.

111. Cf. Étienne Balibar, *Violence et civilité* (Paris: Galilée, 2010), 390ff.

112. Eagleton, *Trouble with Strangers*, 241.

113. See, inter alia, Jürgen Habermas and Jacques Derrida, "February 15, or What Binds Europeans Together," *Constellations* 10 (September 2003): 291–97; and Jacques Derrida, *Negotiations: Interventions and Interviews, 1971–2001* (Stanford: Stanford University Press, 2002), 117–214, 371ff. While not partaking in the "antitotalitarian" moment in French thought, in 1961 Derrida tacitly subsumed the FLN and the PCF "under the banner of totalitarianism"; see Edward Baring, "Liberalism and Algeria," *Critical Inquiry* 36 (Winter 2010): 256. An aversion to revolutionary forms of collective agency never recanted.

114. See Roland Barthes, *Mythologies*, trans. Richard Howard and Annette Lavers (New York: Hill and Wang, 2012), 161.

115. Ibid., 162.

116. On "the beautiful soul" as ethical equivocation, see Gillian Rose, *The Broken Middle* (Oxford: Blackwell, 1992), 153–246.

117. Cf. Soraya Tlati, "Algeria as an Archive," in Cheah and Guerlac, *Derrida and the Time of the Political*, 177–95. Derrida's neither/nor stance is invoked and tacitly vindicated as a political stance vis-à-vis French Algeria in Baring's "Liberalism and Algeria," 258. Obviously, in this particular situation, Derrida's "neither/norism" is ultimately the perspective of the colonist, not the colonized.

118. See Jacques Rancière, "Ethics and Politics in Derrida," in Cheah and Guerlac, *Derrida and the Time of the Political*, 278–80.

119. Wendy Brown, "Sovereign Hesitations," in Cheah and Guerlac, *Derrida and the Time of the Political*, 25.

5. ADORNO AND THE DIALECTIC OF RESPONSIBILITY

1. Theodor W. Adorno, *Prisms*, trans. Samuel Weber and Shierry Weber (Cambridge: MIT Press, 1981), 245.

2. See Fabio Akcelrud Durão, "Adorno Thrice Engaged," *Cultural Critique* 60 (Spring 2005): 261.

3. See Lambert Zuidervaart, *Social Philosophy After Adorno* (Cambridge: Cambridge University Press, 2007), 155–81.

4. See, respectively, J. M. Bernstein, *Adorno* (Cambridge: Cambridge University Press, 2001), passim; Drucilla Cornell, *The Philosophy of the Limit*

(London: Routledge, 1992), 13–38; and Romand Coles, *Rethinking Generosity* (Ithaca, NY: Cornell University Press, 1997), chapter 2. For a cogent discussion of efforts to reconstruct the argument of the book on ethics that Adorno never wrote, and an important contribution in its own right, see Marta Tafalla, *Theodor W. Adorno* (Barcelona: Herder, 2003), 44–66. See also the special issue and the dossier on the subject of Adorno and ethics published by two preeminent journals: "Adorno and Ethics," *New German Critique* 33 (Winter 2006); "Adorno: Critique, Ethics, Knowledge," *Constellations* 12 (March 2005): 3–82. For other recent accounts, see James Gordon Finlayson, "Adorno on the Ethical and the Ineffable," *European Journal of Philosophy* 10 (April 2002): 1–25; and Fabian Freyenhagen, "Moral Philosophy," in Deborah Cook, ed., *Theodor Adorno* (Stocksfield: Acumen, 2008), 99–114.

5. Elsewhere, Bernstein has readily grasped this aspect of Adorno: see his essay, "Negative Dialectics as Fate," in Tom Huhn, ed., *The Cambridge Companion to Adorno* (Cambridge: Cambridge University Press, 2004), 19–50. Still, the imperative to make Adorno speak "analytic" abides. On Bernstein, see Durão, "Adorno Thrice Engaged," 262–68; and Deborah Cook, "From the Actual to the Possible," *Constellations* 12 (March 2005): 21–35.

6. Martin Seel, "Adorno's Contemplative Ethics," *Critical Horizons* 5 (2004): 259–60ff.

7. See Hent de Vries, *Minimal Theologies*, trans. Geoffrey Hale (Baltimore: Johns Hopkins University Press, 2005), 7.

8. On the intellectual matrixes of Adorno's critical theory, see Susan Buck-Morss, *The Origin of Negative Dialectics* (New York: Free Press, 1979); and Gillian Rose, *The Melancholy Science* (New York: Columbia University Press, 1979). Other thoughtful introductions to Adorno are Simon Jarvis, *Adorno* (Cambridge: Polity, 1998); Gerhard Schweppenhäuser, *Theodor W. Adorno*, trans. James Rolleston (Durham: Duke University Press, 2009); and Brian O'Connor, *Adorno* (Oxon: Routledge, 2013).

9. For an illuminating discussion, see Robert Hullot-Kentor, *Things Beyond Resemblance* (New York: Columbia University Press, 2006), 15.

10. For a discussion, see my essay "Minima Humana," *Telos* 149 (Winter 2009): 105–25.

11. "The celebrated quest for genuine foundations, for some external source of authority rather than one derived from rigorous reflection, already harbors a reactionary dimension, and the intellectuals like to call this 'ontology'"; see Theodor W. Adorno and Thomas Mann, *Correspondence, 1943–1955*, trans. Nicholas Walker (Cambridge: Polity, 2006), 35.

12. See Detlev Claussen, "Malentendu?," *Telos* 155 (Summer 2011): 7–20, and, "Intellectual Transfer," *New German Critique* 33 (Winter 2006): 5–14.

13. On the political, cultural, and intellectual ambience of this period, see Eric D. Weitz, *Weimar Germany* (Princeton: Princeton University Press, 2007), passim. On the early history of the Frankfurt School, see Martin Jay, *The*

Dialectical Imagination (Berkeley: University of California Press, 1996). Instructive, if quite slanted by its barely concealed hostility to Adorno, is Rolf Wiggershaus, *The Frankfurt School*, trans. Michael Robertson (Cambridge: MIT Press, 1995). Adorno's life and intellectual itinerary are well documented in Stefan Müller-Doohm, *En tierra de nadie*, trans. Roberto H. Bernet and Raúl Gabás (Barcelona: Herder, 2003); and Detlev Claussen, *Theodor W. Adorno*, trans. Rodney Livingston (Cambridge: Harvard University Press, 2008).

14. This felicitous formulation is Schwarz's, who employs it apropos of the Brazilian poet Francisco Alvim; see Roberto Schwarz, *Two Girls and Other Essays* (London: Verso, 2012), 191–222.

15. See Adorno's "Trying to Understand Endgame," his best statement of the historicity and critical import of minimalism, in Theodor W. Adorno, *Can One Live After Auschwitz?* ed. Rolf Tiedemann (Stanford: Stanford University Press, 2003), 259–94.

16. I have elaborated on this question in "Minima Humana."

17. On the meanings of Catastrophe and catastrophes, see my essays "The Antinomies of Violence and Catastrophe," *New Political Science* 34 (June 2012): 211–21, and "How Not to Learn from Catastrophe," *Political Theory* 41 (October 2013): 738–65.

18. See Jan-Werner Müller, *Contesting Democracy* (New Haven: Yale University Press, 2011), 125–70; "Beyond Militant Democracy?" *New Left Review* 73 (January-February 2012): 39–47.

19. See Claussen, "Intellectual Transfer." On the actual historical details of postwar Germany's rather tortuous reckoning with the Nazi past, see Jeffrey K. Olick, *In the House of the Hangman* (Chicago: University of Chicago Press, 2005); Norbert Frei, *Adenauer's Germany and the Nazi Past*, trans. Joel Glob (New York: Columbia University Press, 2002); and Robert G. Moeller, *War Stories* (Berkeley: University of California Press, 2001). These works are best read alongside Adam Tooze, "Reassessing the Moral Economy of Post-War Reconstruction," *Past and Present* 210 (2011): 47–70.

20. Theodor W. Adorno, *Negative Dialectics*, trans. E. B. Ashton (New York: Continuum, 1973), 17.

21. Theodor W. Adorno, *Philosophische Terminologie*, 2 vols. (Frankfurt: Suhrkamp, 1973–75), 1:83.

22. Adorno, *Negative Dialectics*, 202.

23. Ibid., 203–04.

24. Cf. Michael Marder, "Minima Patientia, *New German Critique* 97 (Winter 2006): 53–72.

25. Adorno, *Can One Live After Auschwitz?*, 435.

26. See Rolf Tiedemann, "Not the First Philosophy but a Last One," ibid., xx.

27. Dews has persuasively argued that in Adorno's critical theory "evil is primarily a category of the social, and only in a secondarily sense applicable to human beings and their actions"; see Peter Dews, *The Idea of Evil* (Oxford: Blackwell, 2008), 198.

28. Theodor W. Adorno, *Lectures on Negative Dialectics*, trans. Rodney Livingstone (Cambridge: Polity, 2008), 19. See also Theodor W. Adorno, *Metaphysics*, trans. Edmund Jephcott (Stanford: Stanford University Press, 2000), 101, 103–28.

29. Dews accurately captures this aspect of Adorno's thinking when he writes, "Evil is not the equivalent of a historical fate. . . . It is something for which human beings are responsible, collectively, if not individually." Indeed, "the social world *obliges* people to be evil, in the interest of survival." A social world mediated by the catastrophic nature of history as domination. See *The Idea of Evil*, 199, 201.

30. Theodor W. Adorno, *Critical Models: Interventions and Catchwords,* trans. Henry W. Pickford (New York: Columbia University Press, 2005), 192. Of course, here Adorno's essay "The Meaning of Working Through the Past" is also central, as is his controversial assertion about fascism living on, as well as his collaborative studies on group psychology. For an excellent discussion and translations of key texts, see Theodor W. Adorno, *Guilt and Defense*, ed. Jeffrey K. Olick and Andrew J. Perrin (Cambridge: Harvard University Press, 2010).

31. Cf. Adorno, *Critical Models*, 289–93.

32. See ibid., 195, 201; and 281–88.

33. Ibid., 203.

34. See Adorno, *Can One Live After Auschwitz?*, 96.

35. See Adorno, *Critical Models*, 281.

36. For an alternative formulation of this intersection, see Raymond Geuss, *Outside Ethics* (Princeton: Princeton University Press, 2005), 111–30.

37. Adorno, *Negative Dialectics*, 365; for the original, see Theodor W. Adorno, *Negative Dialektik* (Frankfurt: Suhrkamp, 1997), 358. All references hereafter will be to the English translation followed by the original: i.e., *ND* 365/358. For contrasting interpretations of this "imperative," see Bernstein, *Adorno*, 371–96; and Tafalla, *Theodor W. Adorno*, especially 49–66. Tafalla offers an arresting interpretation of the "materialism" of this new imperative.

38. *ND* 361/354.

39. Cf. Dews, *The Idea of Evil*, 205.

40. On the "primacy of the object," see, inter alia, *ND* 183–89/184–90; Adorno, *Critical Models*, 129, 245–58, 265, *Lectures on Negative Dialectics*, 154–56, 200; and *Ontologie und Dialektik*, ed. Rolf Tiedemann (Frankfurt: Suhrkamp, 2008), 333–36.

41. Cf. Geuss, *Outside Ethics*, 126–30.

42. See *ND* 192/193.

43. Ibid., 242/240.

44. G. W. F. Hegel, *Outlines of the Philosophy of Right*, ed. Stephen Houlgate, trans. T. M. Knox (Oxford: Oxford University Press, 2008), 131. Cf. G. W. F. Hegel, *Phenomenology of Spirit*, trans. A. V. Miller (Oxford: Oxford University Press, 1977), 365ff.

45. Cf. Freyenhagen, "Moral Philosophy." Of interest is the glossing of Hegel's passage, and the ultimate ineffectiveness of Kantian responses to Hegel's critique, found in Fabian Freyenhagen, "Empty, Useless, and Dangerous?," *Bulletin of the Hegel Society of Great Britain* 63 (2011): 95–118.

46. *ND* 242/240–41 (translation modified and emphases added).

47. Ibid., 242–43/241 (translation modified). NB: *ingenuim* is Latin for natural disposition, capacity, or innate quality. See *Oxford Latin Dictionary*, 2d ed., s. v. "ingenium."

48. An excellent discussion of this aspect of Adorno's critical theory is found in José Antonio Zamora, *Theodor W. Adorno* (Madrid: Trotta, 2004), 262ff.

49. For a concise elucidation of "model" and its role in his negative dialectic, see Theodor W. Adorno, *History and Freedom*, trans. Rodney Livingstone (Cambridge: Polity, 2006), 184–85.

50. See *ND* 274–76/271–72.

51. See Theodor W. Adorno, *Problems of Moral Philosophy*, trans. Rodney Livingstone (Stanford: Stanford University Press, 2000), 149.

52. Ibid., 162.

53. See *ND* 211–99, especially 281–85/211–94, especially 277–81.

54. Schweppenhäuser, *Theodor W. Adorno*, 71–72.

55. For a sensitive discussion of this aspect of Adorno's reflections on responsibility, see Fabian Freyenhagen, *Adorno's Practical Philosophy* (Cambridge: Cambridge University Press, 2013), 95–100. This subtle study came too late to my attention; hence I cannot engage with it here, nor fully encompass its findings.

56. Adorno, *History and Freedom*, 203.

57. Adorno, *Problems of Moral Philosophy*, 146.

58. Adorno, *History and Freedom*, 190–200.

59. *ND* 285/281.

60. See ibid., 299/294 (translation modified). One of Roberto Bolaño's most unsettling short stories, "El policía de las ratas," comes to mind here, as it at once lends expression to an analogous insight and complicates it. See Roberto Bolaño, *El gaucho insufrible* (Barcelona: Anagrama, 2003), 53–86.

61. See Bertolt Brecht, *Prosa* (Frankfurt: Suhrkamp, 2013), 778–917. The broad outlines of Brecht's political ethic are discussed in chapter 6, this volume.

62. Adorno, *Problems of Moral Philosophy*, 167.

63. See Bertolt Brecht, *Collected Plays*, ed. John Willett and Ralph Manheim, 8 vols. (London: Methuen, 1998), 3:305–6.

64. Adorno, *Problems of Moral Philosophy*, 142, 143. Needless to say, references to Brecht are more positive in these lectures than in "Commitment"; see Adorno, *Can One Live After Auschwitz?*, 246–47.

65. Adorno, *Problems of Moral Philosophy*, 143.

66. Ibid., 165, cf. 143–45.

67. Elsewhere, Adorno acknowledges the power of Hegel's critique of the contradictions of bourgeois civil society, but mischaracterizes his account of the state; see Theodor W. Adorno, *Einführung in die Dialektik* (Berlin: Suhrkamp, 2010), 118.

68. This poignant phrase is from Gillian Rose, *Judaism and Modernity* (Oxford: Blackwell, 1992), 54.

69. Theodor W. Adorno, "Marginalia to Theory and Praxis," in Critical Models, 264.

70. Ibid.

71. See *ND* 173–74/174–75.

72. Adorno, "Marginalia to Theory and Praxis," 264, in *Gesammelte Schriften,* ed. Rolf Tiedemann with Gretel Adorno, Susan Buck-Morss, and Klaus Schultz, 20 vols. (Frankfurt: Suhrkamp, 2003), 10:765; hereafter referred to as *GS* followed by volume and page number.

73. Ibid.

74. Adorno alludes to the political closure of the Federal Republic in a 1949 letter to Thomas Mann: "We are discussing extremely obscure questions at the very limits of logic and metaphysics, but precisely as if they were political issues—perhaps because there is in truth no longer politics"; he adds, "Germany has ceased to be a political subject at all, and politics is now simply role play"; see Adorno and Mann, *Correspondence,* 34, 35. But acknowledging the lucidity of Adorno's registration of epochal closure need not justify every single political judgment on his part. His 1969 correspondence with Marcuse shows yet another instance of how philosophical rigor and political literacy rarely move on a par: in this case, Marcuse, the lesser philosopher, proved to be the superior political observer; see Herbert Marcuse, "Correspondence on the German Student Movement," *New Left Review* 223 (January-February 1999): 123–36.

75. Jameson, *The Seeds of Time,* 70–71.

76. See Fredric Jameson, "The End of Temporality," *Critical Inquiry* 29 (Summer 2003): 695–718.

77. Adorno, "Marginalia to Theory and Praxis," 266. Adorno pedagogically expanded on the dialectic of the totality, system and antisystem, tendencies and trends with implications to the question of spontaneity, in Theodor W. Adorno, *Philosophische Elemente einer Theorie der Gesellschaft,* ed. Tobias ten Brink and Marc Philip Nogueira (Fankfurt: Suhrkamp, 2008), 37–49, 191ff.

78. Ibid., 264.

79. Adorno: "To a real fascism, one can only react with violence. I am anything but rigid on this point"; see Theodor W. Adorno, "Who's Afraid of the Ivory Tower?," *Monatshefte* 94 (Spring 2002): 18. For excellent commentary on the dialectic of violence in Adorno's engagement with the aesthetic realm, see Hullot-Kentor, *Things Beyond Resemblance,* 207.

80. Elsewhere, Adorno and Horkheimer pose the quintessential political question: "One must ask, who speaks of peace, on whose behalf and in function of what"; see *GS* 20:391.

81. Adorno, "Marginalia to Theory and Praxis," 268.

82. See *GS* 20:399.

83. Adorno, "Marginalia to Theory and Praxis," 272ff.

84. See Deborah Cook, *Adorno, Habermas, and the Search for a Rational Society* (New York: Routledge, 2004), 1–38, 130ff., and "Staying Alive," *Rethinking Marxism* 18 (July 2006): 433–47.

85. See Adorno, *Problems of Moral Philosophy*, 144–45.

86. Ibid., 145.

87. Cf. ibid., 165, 162.

88. Adorno, *Critical Models*, 292–93 (emphasis added).

89. Terry Eagleton, *The Ideology of the Aesthetic* (London: Blackwell, 1990), 360.

90. For a discussion, see Schweppenhäuser, *Theodor W. Adorno*, 91ff.

91. See Theodor W. Adorno, *Minima Moralia*, trans. E. F. N. Jephcott (London: Verso, 1978), 150.

92. See Hullot-Kentor, *Things Beyond Resemblance*, 1–22. The concluding paragraphs build upon my "Minima Humana," 125.

93. At least since *Dialectic of Enlightenment*, Adorno had been preoccupied with the logic of fungibility, which bears on his critiques of superfluity and abstract identity, not least in his account of torture and its reduction of the tortured body to a specimen—a logic of power that in his lectures on metaphysics he suggests remains "untouched even by political forms of rule." See Adorno, *Metaphysics*, 109.

94. See Adorno, *History and Freedom*, 213–18, and "Marginalia to Theory and Praxis," 266.

95. Cf. Theodor W. Adorno, *Notes to Literature*, trans. Shierry Weber Nicholsen, 2 vols. (New York: Columbia University Press, 1992), 1:80–85.

6. POLITICAL ETHIC, VIOLENCE, AND DEFEAT

1. See Cathy Caruth, "Unclaimed Experience," *Yale French Studies* 79 (1991): 182.

2. See David L. Eng and David Kazanjian, eds., *Loss* (Berkeley: University of California Press, 2002), 6. See also Peter Gray and Kendrick Oliver, eds., *The Memory of Catastrophe* (Manchester: Manchester University Press, 2004), 1–14; and Alessia Ricciardi, *The Ends of Mourning* (Stanford: Stanford University Press, 2003), 1–68. Cf. Sumathi Ramaswamy, *The Lost Land of Lemuria* (Berkeley: University of California Press, 2004), passim.

3. See Susan Buck-Morss, *Dreamworld and Catastrophe* (Cambridge: MIT Press, 2000), 68; and Fredric Jameson, *The Ideologies of Theory* (London: Verso, 2008), 649–52.

4. For a scathing critique of the superimposition of "pathological" psychoanalytic categories on collective life, see Kristin Ross, *May '68 and Its Afterlives* (Chicago: University of Chicago Press, 2002), 1–3.

5. For political statements on "loss" within political theory, see Sheldon S. Wolin, "Political Theory: From Vocation to Invocation," in Jason A. Frank and John Tambornino, eds., *Vocations of Political Theory* (Minneapolis: University of Minnesota Press, 2000), 5ff.; Wendy Brown, *Politics Out of History*

(Princeton: Princeton University Press, 2001), passim, and *Edgework* (Princeton: Princeton University Press, 2005), chapter 6. Unsurprisingly, in an essay where Wolin meditates about loss and defeat, Adorno and Gramsci constitute important signposts. For a philosophically sophisticated account of loss that does not eschew its political dimensions, see Adi Ophir, *The Order of Evils*, trans. Rela Mazali and Havi Carel (New York: Zone, 2005). passim.

6. Eng and Kazanjian, *Loss*, 5.

7. See Sheldon S. Wolin, *The Presence of the Past* (Baltimore: Johns Hopkins University Press, 1989), 4. For an earlier account of political losses see Hannah Arendt, *The Origins of Totalitarianism* (New York: Schocken, 2004), 372–79.

8. Carl Schmitt notoriously gave expression to this aspect of political life, even if his formulation tended to hypostatize it by placing this constitutive aspect at the center of "the political," as its defining attribute. Yet this hypostatization is itself historically symptomatic of the period of hyperpoliticization he lived through, which is a historical sediment of his formal definition. For a thoughtful discussion of Schmitt, see Gopal Balakrishnan, *The Enemy* (London: Verso, 2000), 1–9, 101–37, 260ff.

9. Wolin, *The Presence of the Past*, 4.

10. León Rozitchner, *Acerca de la derrota y de los vencidos* (Buenos Aires: Quadrata, 2011), 25ff.

11. On defeat, see: María Zambrano, "Sentido de la derrota," in José Luis Argos, ed., *Islas* (Madrid: Verbum, 2007), 164–68; Carl Schmitt, *Ex captivitate salus*, trans. Anima Schmitt de Otero (Madrid: Trotta, 2010), 37–42; Reinhart Koselleck, *The Practice of Conceptual History*, trans. Todd Samuel Presner (Stanford: Stanford University Press, 2002), chapter 4; Eric Hobsbawn, *On History* (New York: Free Press, 1997), chapter 18; Christopher Hill, *The Experience of Defeat* (New York: Viking, 1984), 17ff; Perry Anderson, *Spectrum* (London: Verso, 2005), chapter 13, especially pp. 315–20; Wolfgang Schivelbusch, *The Culture of Defeat* (New York: Metropolitan, 2003), 1–35; David Quint, *Epic and Empire* (Princeton: Princeton University Press, 1993), 3–209; and Ana María Amar Sánchez, *Instrucciones para la derrota* (Barcelona: Anthropos, 2010), 9–124.

12. Amar Sánchez, *Instrucciones para la derrota*, 12.

13. For a discussion, see José Luis L. Aranguren, *Ética y política* (Madrid: Guadarrama, 1968), 1–28, 93–111.

14. See the highly suggestive account of defeat and the figure of the vanquished found in Amar Sánchez, *Instrucciones para la derrota*, 77ff.

15. See Perry Anderson, "The Antinomies of Antonio Gramsci," *New Left Review* 100 (November-December 1976): 5–78. Decried by many a Gramsci scholar, this essay remains one of the most intelligent interpretations of this opposition, and Gramsci's concept of "hegemony," available in English. For a critique, see Peter D. Thomas, *The Gramscian Moment* (Leiden: Brill, 2009), 47–83ff. While Thomas offers a thoughtful philological approach to Gramsci,

and a critique of Anderson's, his critique is marred by a fundamental misunderstanding of Anderson's interpretative strategy and the conflation of historical judgments with political commitments, say, the difference between accurately registering the noncapitalist nature of the czarist state overthrown by the Russian Revolution and endorsing "a Menshevik analysis." Ibid., 75n111.

16. See Zambrano, "Sentido de la derrota," 167.

17. Adolph Reed Jr., "Nothing Left," *Harper's Magazine* (March 2014): 34–35.

18. On this question in relation to neoliberalism, see Antonio Y. Vázquez-Arroyo, "Liberal Democracy and Neoliberalism," *New Political Science* 30 (June 2008): 156ff.

19. See Sheldon S. Wolin, "Democracy, Difference, and Re-cognition," *Political Theory* 21 (August 1993): 480ff.," and *Democracy Incorporated* (Princeton: Princeton University Press, 2008), 212ff.

20. Here my argument is indebted to but does not follow Badiou's theorization of fidelity. Cf. Alain Badiou, *Ethics*, trans. Peter Hallward (London: Verso, 2001), 40–48.

21. Buck-Morss, *Dreamworld and Catastrophe*, 68.

22. Gillian Rose, *Mourning Becomes the Law* (Cambridge: Cambridge University Press, 1995), 5.

23. See Gillian Rose, *The Broken Middle* (Oxford: Blackwell, 1992), 310; and *Mourning Becomes the Law*, 13.

24. See Rose *Mourning Becomes the Law*, 13–14, 121–22.

25. Ibid., 141–46. Cf. Bonnie Honig, *Political Theory and the Displacement of Politics* (Ithaca: Cornell University Press, 1993), 42–75.

26. The best treatment of the centrality of political ethic in twentieth-century European political thought—Arendt, Benjamin, Brecht, Krauss, Lukács, Levi, Weil—is found Francisco Fernández Buey, *Poliética* (Madrid: Losada, 2003), passim. On his own original contribution, see Manuel S. Almeida Rodriguez, "La política como ética de lo colectivo," in Artemis Torres and Márcia Cristina Machado Pasuch, eds., *Encontros com Paco Buey* (Cuiabá-MT: Editora da Universidade Federal Mato Grosso, 2013), 55–63.

27. See Aranguren, *Ética y política*, 29–34; and Raymond Polin, *Éthique et politique* (Paris: Sirey, 1968), 101–40.

28. See Max Weber, "Politics as a Vocation," in David Owen and Tracy Strong, eds., *The Vocation Lectures* (Indianapolis: Hackett, 2004), 72.

29. See Fredric Jameson, "The Dialectics of Disaster," *South Atlantic Quarterly* 101 (Spring 2002): 303.

30. Pierre Bourdieu, *The State Nobility*, trans. Lauretta C. Clough (Cambridge: Polity, 1996), 282. Or, in Jameson's formulation, "Ethical maxims and categories only work within a situation of homogenous class belonging; when operative from one class to another, they absorb the signals of class struggle and tension itself and begin to function in a very different, socio-political way"—see Fredric Jameson, *The Antinomies of Realism* (London: Verso, 2013), 212.

31. The classic treatment of this question is found in Sheldon S. Wolin, *Politics and Vision* (Princeton: Princeton University Press, 2004), 175–213. See also Nancy S. Struever, *Theory as Practice* (Chicago: University of Chicago Press, 1992), 147–81.

32. For an instructive discussion, see Arno J. Mayer, *The Furies* (Princeton: Princeton University Press, 1999), chapters 1–6. See also Étienne Balibar, *We, The People of Europe?*, trans. James Swenson (Princeton: Princeton University Press, 2004), 116–17. Cf. Jean Starobinski, *Action and Reaction*, trans. Sophie Hawkes (New York: Zone, 2003), chapter 7. On liberal democracy's furtive forces of reaction and counterrevolution, see Greg Grandin and Gilbert M. Joseph, eds., *A Century of Revolution* (Durham: Duke University Press, 2010).

33. See Sheldon S. Wolin, "Violence and the Western Political Tradition," *American Journal of Orthopsychiatry* 33 (January 1963): 15–28.

34. The *locus classicus* on this question (and the phrase "economy of violence") is Wolin's *Politics and Vision*, 197–200. For a stimulating treatment of the centrality of violence in the foundation of political orders, see Thomas Burns, *Violence de la loi a la renaissance* (Paris: Kimé, 2000), 9–218. Yet the instrumental nature of violence is not exhaustive of Machiavelli's thematization of violence. For a vivid account of another dimension, see Yves Winter, "Plebeian Politics," *Political Theory* 40 (December 2012): 736–66. For a fascinating earlier interpretation of Machiavelli's account of the Ciompi revolt, see Simone Weil's 1934 essay, "Un soulèvement prolétarien a Florence au XIV siècle," in *Œuvres complètes*, 8 vols. (Paris: Gallimard, 1988): 2.1:334–50.

35. See Perry Anderson, *Lineages of the Absolutist State* (London: Verso, 1979), 163–69. For a depiction of Florentine realities, see John M. Najemy, *A History of Florence, 1200–1575* (Oxford: Wiley-Blackwell, 2006), 374ff.

36. See Charles S. Singleton, "The Perspective of Art," *Kenyon Review* 15 (Spring 1953): 169–89.

37. Ibid., 173.

38. As cited in Balakrishnan, *The Enemy*, 105. On Schmitt and Machiavelli, see Carlo Galli, *La mirada de Jano*, trans. María Julia de Ruschi (Buenos Aires: Fondo de Cultura Económica, 2008), 97–124.

39. See Victoria Khan, *The Future of Illusion* (Chicago: University of Chicago Press, 2014), 92. Khan productively engages with Singleton and offers a terrific interpretation of Machiavelli's "poetics" of political autonomy with emphasis on his account of religion.

40. For a compelling account of the centrality of political accountability for Machiavelli's understanding of ruling, which also has the virtue of accurately registering the centrality of institutions in his political thought, see John P. McCormick, *Machiavellian Democracy* (Cambridge: Cambridge University Press, 2011), passim.

41. See Niccolò Machiavelli, *Opere*, ed. Corrado Vivanti, 3 vols. (Torino: Einaudi-Gallimard, 1997–2005), 2:137; cf. *The Prince*, chapter 25; and *Discourses on*

Livy, 3.9, ibid., 1:186–89, 448–50. On the *Ghiribizzi al Soderino,* see Gennaro S. Sasso, *Machiavelli e gli antichi e altri saggi,* 3 vols. (Milano-Napoli: Ricciardi, 1987–88), 2:3–56; and Carlo Ginzburg, "Diventare Machiavelli," *Quaderni Storici* 121 (April 2006): 151–64.

42. Chapter 6 of *The Prince* deftly encapsulates this aspect of his political thought. Here Machiavelli soberly emphasizes that "one must consider how there is nothing more difficult to handle, dubious to succeed and danger-ous to manage, than to be in charge of introducing new political orders," and along these lines brings into sharp relief the cognitive dimension of his political action. This is something that Machiavelli had already stressed in "Del modo di trattare i popoli della Valdichiana ribellati" (1502): "che siano conoscitor della occasione et che la sappiano usare benissimo"; see *Opere,* 1:132, 26. On the centrality of occasions, accidents, and ruptures in Machia-velli's thought, see Giorgio Inglese, *Per Machiavelli* (Rome: Carocci, 2013), 104–7; and Gopal Balakrishnan, *Antagonistics* (London: Verso, 2009), 265–79.

43. For an excellent discussion, see Carlo Ginzburg, "Machiavelli, l'eccezione e la regola," *Quaderni Storici* 112 (April 2003): 195–213.

44. On Machiavelli's "casuistry," see ibid.; and Bernard Guillemain, *Machiavel* (Genève: Droz, 1977), 347ff. Cf. Luigi Russo, *Machiavelli* (Bari: Laterza, 1949), 123–24. As Carlo Ginzburg has shown, this logic is exhibited not only in the content of Machiavelli's political thought but also at the level of the sen-tence: Machiavelli's penchant for conjunctive adverbs such as *nevertheless* (*nondimeno*) and *nonetheless* (*nondimanco*); see ibid, 199–202.

45. On this tradition, which has both an absolutist and a constitutional variant, see Friedrich Mienecke, *Machiavellism,* trans. Douglas Scott (New Brunswick, NJ: Transaction, 1998), 429ff. See also C. J. Friedrich, *Constitutional Reason of State* (Providence, RI: Brown University Press, 1957), passim; Wolin, *The Pres-ence of the Past,* 151–79; Maurizio Viroli, "The Revolution in the Concept of Politics," *Political Theory* 20 (August 1992): 473–95; Pierre Bourdieu, "From the King's House to the Reason of State," *Constellations* 11 (March 2004): 16–36; and Victoria Khan, "Machiavelli's Reputation to the Eighteenth Century," John M. Najemy, ed., *The Cambridge Companion to Machiavelli* (Cambridge: Cambridge University Press, 2010), 247–50.

46. See, for instance, Marx's scathing essay "Moralizing Criticism and the Cri-tique of Morality," in Karl Marx, *Collected Works,* 50 vols. (New York: Interna-tional, 1975–2004), 6:312–40.

47. See, for instances, Bertolt Brecht, *Prosa* (Frankfurt: Suhrkamp, 2013), 778–1030. Instructive discussions about Brecht's critique of ethical categories and the primacy he accords to collective situations are found in Fernán-dez Buey, *Poliética,* 157–96; and Jameson, *Brecht and Method* (London: Verso, 1998), passim.

48. See Jameson, *Brecht and Method,* 158.

49. Raymond Williams, *Drama from Ibsen to Brecht* (New York: Oxford University Press, 1971), 277–90.

50. See *Bertolt Brecht Journals*, trans. Hugh Rorrison (New York: Routledge, 1996), 30.

51. Ibid., 124.

52. Ibid., 145.

53. See *Bertolt Brecht Letters*, ed. John Willett, trans. Ralph Manheim (New York: Routledge, 1990), 408–9, 412–13.

54. See Brecht, *Prosa*, 1008–9.

55. Ibid., 942. Here one might think of how Shen Teh is violently torn asunder by the demands of goodness in *The Good Person of Szechwan* or of Frau Hausmann's tragic predicament in the short story "The Job." Through these characters, Brecht recasts Machiavelli's dictum on the need to "learn how not to be good" in order to survive their predicaments, a demand that places a strain on the political actor that he poetically captures in "The Mask of Evil."

56. See Bertolt Brecht, *Ausgewählte Werke in sechs Bänden* (Frankfurt: Suhrkamp, 2005), 6:172.

57. Walter Benjamin, *Understanding Brecht*, trans. Anna Bostock (London: Verso, 1998), 30, 29.

58. See Bertolt Brecht, *Collected Short Stories*, ed. John Willett and Ralph Manheim (London: Methuen, 1984), 150.

59. Bertolt Brecht, *Der Untergang der Egoisten Johann Fatzer* (Frankfurt: Suhrkamp, 1994), 118. See also Bertolt Brecht, *Poems*, ed. John Willett and Ralph Manheim (London: Methuen, 2000), 286–89.

60. Bertolt Brecht, *The Life of Galileo*, scene 14, in *Collected Plays*, ed. John Willett and Ralph Manheim, 8 vols. (London: Methuen, 1998), 5:98.

61. Brecht's invocation of a new ethics, and a new science, not only evokes Machiavelli's own new science of politics, but it similarly emphasizes the need to allocate terminology to its proper domain of inquiry and valuation. This is readily articulated in Brecht's short story "The Experiment:" "There were . . . some words that it was better not to use since, strictly speaking, they meant nothing: words like 'good,' 'bad,' 'beautiful,' and so on. The boy soon realized that there was no sense in calling a beetle 'ugly'"; see Brecht, *Collected Short Stories*, 154.

62. Brecht, *The Days of the Commune*, in *Collected Plays*, 8:111.

63. See, respectively, ibid., xviii; and *Bertolt Brecht Letters*, 486.

64. Brecht, *The Days of the Commune*, 8:103.

65. Brecht, scene 11b, ibid., 115.

66. Raymond Williams, *Politics and Letters* (London: NLB, 1979), 395.

67. Or as Brecht put it apropos of epic theater: "The sufferings of this man appall me, because they are unnecessary"; see *Brecht on Theater*, ed. and trans. John Willet (New York: Hill and Wang, 1964), 71.

68. Brecht, *Poems*, 318–20; see also 450.

69. Brecht, *Collected Short Stories*, 211. In "The Experiment" the proper use of "good" is specified along materialist lines: "'Now here you may safely use

the word 'good,' said the old man, 'for bread is for people to eat and can be good or bad for them.'" Ibid., 154.

70. For the best overall discussion of Gramsci's political ethic, one that I am deeply indebted to, see Francisco Fernández Buey, *Leyendo a Gramsci* (Barcelona: El Viejo Topo, 2001), 83–128. Other highly suggestive treatments are found in Aldo Tortorella, "Il fondamento etico della politica in Gramsci," *Critica marxista* 2/3 (March-June 1997): 62–71; and Domenico Jervolino, "Etica e politica in Gramsci," in Giorgio Baratta and Guido Liguori, eds., *Gramsci da un secolo all'altro* (Roma: Riuniti, 1999), 199–210.

71. See Antonio Gramsci, *Quaderni del carcere*, ed. Valentino Gerratana (Torino: Einaudi, 2007), 2103; hereafter referred to as *QC* followed by page number.

72. *QC* 1599. For a discussion, see Fernández Buey, *Leyendo a Gramsci*, 119ff. Cf. Benedetto Croce, *Etica e politica* (Bari: Laterza, 1956), 255–61.

73. Gramsci's polemic against Kant mostly stemmed from a historicist account of humanity; see *QC* 1598–99; and on the Kantian turn in Marxism, see *QC* 1855. For a thoughtful discussion, see Tortorella, "Il fondamento etico della politica in Gramsci," 65–67.

74. *QC* 1486.

75. On the centrality of the *etico-politico* in the philosophy of praxis, see *QC* 1224, 1244.

76. See Antonio Gramsci, *Antología*, ed. Manuel Sacristán (Madrid: Akal, 2013), 21–23, 29.

77. *QC* 699–700, 749–50.

78. Despite the different usages of *Jesuit*—ranging from substantive to adverbial and adjectival forms, often with a derogatory content—Gramsci considered the Jesuits Machiavelli's best disciples in practice (*in pratica i migliori discepoli*)—see ibid., 1857. That they notoriously perfected casuistic ethics, and inaugurated new orders, might not be far from Gramsci's mind here.

79. Raymond Geuss, *A World Without Why* (Princeton: Princeton University Press, 2014), 66.

80. *QC* 1691.

81. For a compelling discussion of this dialectic and how it constitutes the interpretative key to interpret Gramsci's political thought, see Manuel S. Almeida Rodríguez, *Dirigentes y dirigidos* (Bogotá: Envión, 2010), passim.

82. See Max Weber, "Politics as a Vocation," in *From Max Weber*, ed. and trans. H. H. Gerth and C. Wright Mills (New York: Oxford University Press, 1946), 77–78.

83. See Max Weber, "Economic Policy and National Interest in Imperial Germany," in W. G. Runciman, ed., *Max Weber* (Cambridge: Cambridge University Press, 1978), 267. See also Max Weber, *Economy and Society*, ed. Guenther Roth and Claus Wittich (Berkeley: University of California Press, 1978), 2:1392; Max Weber, "Science as a Vocation," in Runciman, *From Max Weber*, 152; and Wolfgang Mommsen, *Max Weber and German Politics, 1890–1920*, trans. Michael S. Steinberg (Chicago: University of Chicago Press, 1984), 286.

84. Weber, "Economic Policy and National Interest in Imperial Germany,"267–68; see also "Politics as a Vocation" (Gerth and Mills, eds.) 79–80, 128. Weber was not only responding to the crises of bourgeois life in Germany, but to the decline of the aristocratic class, the political class par excellence in European imagery. For a discussion, see Harvey Goldman, *Politics, Death, and the Devil* (Berkeley: University of California Press, 1992), 5, 163–64.

85. Weber, "Politics as a Vocation" (Gerth and Mills, eds.), 124.

86. Passion, perspective, the boldness to reach out for the impossible, sober heroism, unwillingness to crumble or seek refuge when the world does not conform to one's ideals—these are the attributes of Weber's political hero, the possessor of a true vocation for politics; see Weber, "Politics as a Vocation" (Gerth and Mills, eds.), 78, 128.

87. On this last point, see Sheldon S. Wolin, "Agitated Times," *Parallax* 11 (2005): 5–7. Cf. David Owen and Tracy B. Strong, "Introduction," in Owen and Strong, *The Vocation Lectures*, ix–lxii.

88. Max Weber, "Science as a Vocation," in Owen and Strong, *The Vocation Lectures*, 26–27. Cf. Charles Thorpe, "Violence and the Scientific Vocation," *Theory, Culture and Society* 21 (June 2004): 59–84.

89. Here one finds an embryonic version of the distinction between accountability and responsibility subsequently formulated by Arendt. Cf. Hannah Arendt, "Organized Guilt and Universal Responsibility," in Jerome Kohn, ed., *Essays in Understanding* (New York: Harcourt Brace, 1994), 121–39, and *Eichmann in Jerusalem* (New York: Penguin, 1994), 297–98.

90. Weber, "Politics as a Vocation" (Gerth and Mills, eds.), 127.

91. Ibid. (Owen and Strong ed.), 92.

92. Ibid., 78. On freedom and necessity in tragedy, as a genre, see Terry Eagleton, *Sweet Violence* (Oxford: Blackwell, 2003), chapter 5.

93. "My inward 'calling' is scholarly work and scholarly teaching. And the nation does not need that now. So I shall have to try to reorient myself. But how? To what? I still do not know." Weber in a letter dated 10 October 1918, as cited by Mommsen, *Max Weber and German Politics*, 286.

94. See Goldman, *Politics, Death, and the Devil*, 166.

95. Weber, "Parliament and Government," in *Economy and Society*, 1461. In this formulation, there is a tension between the concern for leadership and the concern with the political sophistication of the nation. But as will become clearer in his reflections on parliamentary government, it is leadership, a new aristocracy of spirit, that ultimately concerns Weber. See ibid., 1414, 1447ff., 1449ff.

96. See Max Weber, *Gesammelte Politische Schriften*, ed. Johannes Winckelmann (Stuttgart: UTB, 1988), 176, 442–43. Statements that are, of course, consistent with his rendering of how in the Nation there is a "responsibility towards succeeding generations;" one that is related to the great power structures and the "responsibility of their own for the way in which power and prestige are distributed between their own and foreign polities"; see Weber, *Economy and Society*, 921–22.

97. See Weber, *Economy and Society*, 1007.

98. As cited in Mommsen, *Max Weber and German Politics*, 191.

99. Weber, "Politics as a Vocation" (Owen and Strong ed.), 124.

100. On Weil's political thought, see Emilia Bea Pérez, *Simone Weil* (Madrid: Trotta, 1993); David McLellan, *Utopian Pessimist* (New York: Poseidon, 1990); and Mary G. Dietz, *Between the Human and the Divine* (Totowa, NJ: Rowman and Littlefield, 1988).

101. Simone Weil, "The Iliad or the Poem of Force," in *Simone Weil*, ed. Siân Miles (New York: Grove, 1986), 163.

102. Ibid., 163, 184–85.

103. Ibid., 179.

104. Ibid.

105. See Simone Weil, *Gravity and Grace*, trans. Emma Crawford and Mario von der Ruhr (London: Routledge, 2002), 71.

106. Force is a concept that many interpreters of Weil's thought have found enigmatic. This is not the place to elucidate its multifarious meanings. Suffice it to say here that force cannot always be equated with violence, as Weil makes abundantly clear in other places; in the context of the essay on the *Iliad*, however, it refers to the violent forms that force takes in a predicament of war.

107. See Simone Weil, *Formative Writings, 1929–1941*, ed. and trans. Dorothy Tuck McFarland and Wilhelmina Van Ness (Amherst: University of Massachusetts Press, 1987), 240; and the meditations on action, reaction, and limits found in Weil's *Cuadernos*, trans. Carlos Ortega (Madrid: Trotta, 2001), especially 217–20.

108. For details, see Bea Pérez, *Simone Weil*, 115–32. See also Raymond Aron, *Memorias*, trans. Amanda Forns de Gioia (Barcelona: RBA, 2013), 144–45.

109. Weil, "The Iliad or the Poem of Force," 179.

110. Ibid., 163, translation modified; see Simone Weil, *Œuvres*, ed. Florence de Lussy (Paris: Gallimard 1999), 537.

111. Weil, *Simone Weil*, 56ff. Weil's formulations, especially her treatments of "reflection," "attention," and "virtue," imply a cognitive shift that is well captured by the term *re-cognition*. On the re-cognitive dimension of "attention," see Sharon Cameron, "The Practice of Attention," *Critical Inquiry* 29 (Winter 2003): 216–52. Cf. Dietz, *Between the Human and the Divine*, 96–103; and Alexander Irwin, *Saints of the Impossible* (Minneapolis: University of Minnesota Press, 2002), 59–63. Of interest is Françoise Meltzer, "The Hands of Simone Weil," *Critical Inquiry* 27 (Summer 2001): 611–28.

112. The logic of opposition operative in the terms *force* and *reflection* can be understood as the political equivalent of that of *gravity* and *grace* in Weil's reflections—see Carmen Revilla, *Simone Weil* (Madrid: Trotta, 2003), 162ff.

113. Simone Weil, *The Need for Roots*, trans. A. F. Willis (London: Routledge, 1996), 15.

114. Weil, "The Iliad or the Poem of Force," 179.

115. For elucidation of these terms, see Susan Buck-Morss, "Aesthetics and An-aesthetics," in *October*, ed. Rosalind E. Krauss (Cambridge: MIT Press, 1998), 375–413.

116. On distance and indifference, see Carlo Ginzburg, *Wooden Eyes*, trans. Martin Ryle and Kate Soper (New York: Columbia University Press, 2001), 157–72.

117. See Weil, *Formative Writings*, 255.

118. Ibid.

119. George Orwell, *Homage to Catalonia* (New York: Harcourt, Brace, 1952), 139.

120. See McLellan, *Utopian Pessimist*, 84–85.

121. See Simone Weil, *Oppression and Liberty*, trans. Arthur Willis and John Petrie (Amherst: University of Massachusetts Press, 1973), 41 (translation slightly modified); see Weil, *Œuvres*, 279.

122. Simone Weil, *Selected Essays*, trans. Richard Rees (Oxford: Oxford University Press, 1962), 168.

123. Ibid.

124. Weil, *Simone Weil*, 235. Cf. Weber, *From Max Weber*, 160–61.

125. Weil as cited by McLellan, *Utopian Pessimist*, 133.

126. See Weil, *Oppression and Liberty*, 68 (emphasis added). Elsewhere, Weil offers insightful remarks on the ways in which capitalism and centralization contribute to an increasing powerlessness and to an inversion of ends and means. She then defines oppression as a relation in which "man is treated as a means." See Simone Weil, *Lectures on Philosophy*, trans. Hugh Price (Cambridge: Cambridge University Press, 1978), 136, 148–51.

127. See Sheldon S. Wolin, "Constitutional Order, Revolutionary Violence and Modern Power," the First York Lecture in Political Science, Department of Political Science, York University (1990), *Politics and Vision*, 393–405, and *Tocqueville Between Two Worlds* (Princeton: Princeton University Press, 2001), 13–33.

128. Weil, *Oppression and Liberty*, 66.

129. Ibid., 69–70.

130. See Sheldon S. Wolin, "Hobbes and the Culture of Despotism," in Mary G. Dietz, ed., *Thomas Hobbes and Political Theory* (Lawrence: University Press of Kansas, 1990).

131. For the foregoing passages, see Weil, *Simone Weil*, 220–22. She also refers to the power of words in terms of "their power of illusion and error." Ibid., 76.

132. Ibid., 77.

133. Weil, *The Need for Roots*, 232.

134. Weil, "The Poem of Force," 173.

135. The strong materialist import of Weil's thought can be discerned in her account of "needs of the soul," which include equality, security, order, and the like—see *The Need for Roots*, 3–38.

136. Ibid., 230.

137. Weil, "The Iliad or the Poem of Force," 174.

138. See Chalmers Johnson, *Blowback* (New York: Owl, 2004), passim.

139. Weil, "The Iliad or the Poem of Force," 175.

140. Ibid., 174.

141. Ibid., 189. On the centrality of the city in Weil's late political thought, see Juan Carlos González Pont, "De lo 'social' a 'la cité,'" *Revista Anthropos* 211 (April-June 2006): 83–96.

142. Weil, "The Iliad or the Poem of Force," 190–91, 193.

143. Weil, *Formative Writings*, 248.

144. Weil, *The Need for Roots*, 161. See also *Simone Weil on Colonialism*, ed. J. P. Little (Lanham: Rowman and Littlefield: 2003), especially 63–119.

145. See, inter alia, Nicholas Xenos, "The Two Lives of the French Revolution," *Grand Street* 8 (Summer 1989): 201–8 and "The State, Rights, and the Homogeneous Nation," *History of European Ideas* 15 (1992): 77–82.

146. Simone Weil, *Escritos de Londres y últimas cartas*, trans. Maite Larrauri (Madrid: Trotta, 2000), 76, 80. Even so, as *The Need for Roots* makes clear, while offering a powerful critique of the idolatry of the nation-state, Weil always remained ambivalent about the nation, as a form, and sought ways to conceive of it on a different basis. She was not impervious to the temptation to recast patriotism, either—see Dietz, *Between the Human and the Divine*, chapters 7–8.

147. Arendt, *Eichmann in Jerusalem*, 298.

148. Weil, *Formative Writings*, 247–48.

149. Ibid., 278.

150. On fidelity, universalism, and enmity lines, see Kenneth Surin, "Can a 'Chosen' People Have a 'True' Politics?" *Angelaki* 12 (April 2007): 145–50.

151. Yes: to think politically means *descending* from theoretical subjectivity to conceptualizing citizenship. And no other contemporary political thinker has contributed more to the critical retrieval of citizenship as a politically meaningful category than Balibar. Cf. Étienne Balibar, *Equaliberty*, trans. James Ingram (Durham: Duke University Press, 2014), 1–131, 145–64, 231ff., and *Citoyen sujet et autres essais d'anthropologie philosophique* (Paris: Presses Universitaires de France, 2011), 1–66ff.

152. Wolin, *Democracy Incorporated*, 131, 138.

153. For an early critique of these pleas, see Simone de Beauvoir, *Philosophical Writings*, ed. Margaret A. Simmons (Urbana: University of Illinois Press, 2004), 113ff.

154. Cf. Sheldon S. Wolin, "Separating Terrorism from Radicalism," *New York Times*, 3 November 1981, A19. That this piece found a berth in the *New York Times*, which would be unthinkable today, is in and of itself a marker of the political regression of the last thirty years.

155. Régis Debray, *Praised Be Our Lords*, trans. John Howe (London: Verso, 2007), 72–73.

156. Daniel Bensaïd, *An Impatient Life: A Political Memoir*, trans. David Fernbach (London: Verso, 2013), 164–65. Cf. Claudio Pavone, *A Civil War*, trans. Peter Levy (London: Verso, 2013), 495–613.

157. Cf. Étienne Balibar, *Violence et civilité* (Paris: Galilée, 2010), 9–199.
158. Ernst Bloch, *The Principle of Hope*, trans. Neville Plaice, Stephen Plaice, and Paul Knight (Cambridge: MIT Press, 1986), 1367–68.
159. To this list of dialectically mediated oppositions, one could also add that of hope and despair. Suggestive reflections on despair are found in Andrew J. Douglas, *In the Spirit of Critique* (Albany: SUNY Press, 2013), passim. The most sustained defense of its critical and political import is found in Robyn Marasco, *The Highway of Despair* (New York: Columbia University Press, 2015), passim.
160. On the dialectic of realism and utopia, see Raymond Geuss, "Realismus, Wunschdenken, Utopie," *Deutsche Zeitschrift für Philosophie* 58 (2010): 419–29. For an excellent conspectus of realism, see Pier Paulo Portinaro, *El realismo político*, trans. Heber Cardoso (Buenos Aires: Nueva Visión, 2007), passim.
161. On Machiavelli's realism, which is constitutive of his inauguration of a modern tradition of political ethic, see Pierre Mesnard, *L'Essor de la philosophie politique au XVI siècle* (Paris: Vrin, 1951), 77–85, 674–77; and Maurizio Viroli, "Machiavelli's Realism," *Constellations* 14 (December 2007): 466–82.

INDEX

NEW DIRECTIONS IN CRITICAL THEORY

Amy Allen, General Editor

Narrating Evil: A Postmetaphysical Theory of Reflective Judgment,
María Pía Lara
*The Politics of Our Selves: Power, Autonomy, and Gender in Contemporary
Critical Theory,* Amy Allen
Democracy and the Political Unconscious, Noëlle McAfee
The Force of the Example: Explorations in the Paradigm of Judgment,
Alessandro Ferrara
Horrorism: Naming Contemporary Violence, Adriana Cavarero
Scales of Justice: Reimagining Political Space in a Globalizing World,
Nancy Fraser
Pathologies of Reason: On the Legacy of Critical Theory, Axel Honneth
States Without Nations: Citizenship for Mortals, Jacqueline Stevens
The Racial Discourses of Life Philosophy: Négritude, Vitalism, and Modernity,
Donna V. Jones
Democracy in What State?, Giorgio Agamben, Alain Badiou,
Daniel Bensaïd, Wendy Brown, Jean-Luc Nancy,
Jacques Rancière, Kristin Ross, Slavoj Žižek
Politics of Culture and the Spirit of Critique: Dialogues, edited by Gabriel
Rockhill and Alfredo Gomez-Muller
Mute Speech: Literature, Critical Theory, and Politics, Jacques Rancière
The Right to Justification: Elements of Constructivist Theory of Justice,
Rainer Forst
The Scandal of Reason: A Critical Theory of Political Judgment,
Albena Azmanova
The Wrath of Capital: Neoliberalism and Climate Change Politics, Adrian Parr
Media of Reason: A Theory of Rationality, Matthias Vogel
Social Acceleration: The Transformation of Time in Modernity, Hartmut Rosa
The Disclosure of Politics: Struggles Over the Semantics of Secularization,
María Pía Lara
Radical Cosmopolitics: The Ethics and Politics of Democratic Universalism,
James Ingram
Freedom's Right: The Social Foundations of Democratic Life, Axel Honneth
Imaginal Politics: Images Beyond Imagination and the Imaginary,
Chiara Bottici
Alienation, Rahel Jaeggi
The Power of Tolerance: A Debate, Wendy Brown and Rainer Forst, edited by
Luca Di Blasi and Christoph F. E. Holzhey
Radical History and the Politics of Art, Gabriel Rockhill
The Highway of Despair: Critical Theory After Hegel, Robyn Marasco
A Political Economy of the Senses: Neoliberalism, Reification, Critique,
Anita Chari
The End of Progress: Decolonizing the Normative Foundations of Critical Theory,
Amy Allen